Dostoevsky's Incarnational Realism

10/2021

For David,
   With gratitude
for your nourishing
work — & for your
particular help with
note. 241!

          + Peace,
          Paul

Dostoevsky's Incarnational Realism

Finding Christ among the Karamazovs

PAUL J. CONTINO

Afterword by
CARYL EMERSON

CASCADE *Books* · Eugene, Oregon

DOSTOEVSKY'S INCARNATIONAL REALISM
Finding Christ among the Karamazovs

Cascade Books
An Imprint of Wipf and Stock Publishers
199 W. 8th Ave., Suite 3
Eugene, OR 97401

www.wipfandstock.com

PAPERBACK ISBN: 978-1-7252-5074-1
HARDCOVER ISBN: 978-1-7252-5075-8
EBOOK ISBN: 978-1-7252-5076-5

Cataloguing-in-Publication data:

Names: Contino, Paul J., author. | Emerson, Caryl, afterword writer.

Title: Dostoevsky's incarnational realism : finding Christ among the Karamazovs / Paul J. Contino.

Description: Eugene, OR: Cascade Books, 2020 | Includes bibliographical references and index.

Identifiers: ISBN 978-1-7252-5074-1 (paperback) | ISBN 978-1-7252-5075-8 (hardcover) | ISBN 978-1-7252-5076-5 (ebook)

Subjects: LCSH: Dostoyevsky, Fyodor, 1821–1881—Religion | Dostoyevsky, Fyodor, 1821–1881. Bratya Karamazovy. | Dostoyevsky, Fyodor, 1821–1881—Criticism and interpretation | Christianity and literature—History—19th century | Redemption in literature | Religion and literature—Russia

Classification: PG3328.Z7 C66 2020 (print) | PG3328.Z7 (ebook)

Manufactured in the U.S.A.   AUGUST 10, 2020

For Maire,
who has been very patient,

and for our daughters,
Mai Rose and Teresa Marie:
✝ Go with God

"Literary criticism should arise out of a debt of love. In a manner evident and yet mysterious, the poem or the drama or the novel seizes upon our imaginings. We are not the same when we put down the work as we were when we took it up."

—George Steiner, Tolstoy or Dostoevsky

"The only wisdom we can hope to acquire
Is the wisdom of humility: humility is endless. . . .
And what there is to conquer
By strength and submission, has already been discovered
Once or twice, or several times, by men whom one cannot hope
To emulate —but there is no competition—
There is only the fight to recover what has been lost
And found and lost again and again: and now, under conditions
That seem unpropitious. But perhaps neither gain nor loss.
For us, there is only the trying. The rest is not our business."

—T. S. Eliot, "East Coker," The Four Quartets

"The hint half guessed, the gift half understood, is Incarnation.
Here the impossible union
Of spheres of existence is actual,
Here the past and future
Are conquered, and reconciled . . ."

—T. S. Eliot, "The Dry Salvages," The Four Quartets

"No one teaches contemplation except God, Who gives it. The best you can do is write something or say something that will serve as an occasion for someone else to realize what God wants of [her] or him."

—Thomas Merton, New Seeds of Contemplation

"Nothing is absolutely dead: every meaning will have its homecoming festival."

—Mikhail Bakhtin, "Methodology in the Human Sciences"

"I believe that for all of us [Dostoevsky] is an author that we must read and reread due to his wisdom."

—Pope Francis[1]

Contents

Acknowledgements

I began work on this book over thirty years ago, when working on my dissertation and teaching a course on "The Novel" at the University of Notre Dame. I remain grateful to the professors who guided me at Notre Dame, especially Thomas Werge—whose class in Fall 1983, my first semester at Notre Dame, helped me to understand the novel more fully. The late James Walton was a consistent source of bracing realism. Jim Dougherty is a model of academic and personal integrity. Thanks too to Larry Cunningham, who sat in on my dissertation defense. I remember him asking about the apophatic dimension in Dostoevsky; I'm still thinking about his question, even as this book, with its emphasis upon Dostoevsky's analogical imagination, tends toward the cataphatic. While at Notre Dame, I encountered the work of two thinkers who continue to inform my understanding of reality: William F. Lynch, S.J. and Mikhail Mikhailovich Bakhtin. I remain grateful for their work.

I continued to write on and teach Dostoevsky during my twelve years teaching at Christ College, the honors college of Valparaiso University. My wonderful colleagues there—especially Dean Mark Schwehn, Mel Piehl, Bill Olmstead, Warren Rubel, David Morgan, John Ruff, Margaret Franson, and John Steven Paul—were always generous in their support, encouragement, and friendship. Valparaiso University granted me sabbaticals and University Professorships, and granted me time to work. My twelve years at Christ College were a blessing: the students were remarkable, and I remember many of their faces, names, and our conversations about Dostoevsky's novel.

In Fall 2002, I was blessed by an offer to teach in the Great Books Colloquium at Pepperdine University. I accepted, and have since been leading discussions of *The Brothers Karamazov* with excellent students (and faculty). In my writing I have been consistently supported by my Divisional Deans—Constance Fulmer, Maire Mullins (my ever-encouraging wife), Michael Ditmore, and Stella Erbes—and by the gifts of time and sabbatical renewal granted by Deans David Baird and Michael Feltner, and Associate Provost Lee Kats. Most recently, it's been an honor to direct two undergraduate research projects on Dostoevsky's novel with Callaghan McDonough and Raquel Grove. Jessica Hooten Wilson, a former student, has gone on to write very fine books on Dostoevsky's affinities with Flannery O'Connor and Walker Percy.

Here at Pepperdine, I am grateful to many friends and colleagues, past and present, who have supported my work over the course of eighteen years, among them Darryl Tippens, Richard Hughes, Bob Cochran, Ron Highfield, Chris Soper, Robert Williams, David Holmes, Cindy Colburn, Jason Blakely, Jeff Zalar, and colleagues with whom I discussed the novel in summer faculty seminars sponsored by Pepperdine's Center for Faith and Learning, as well as our Great Books faculty—Cyndia Clegg, Jacqueline Dillion, Michael Gose, Tuan Hoang, Don Marshall, Frank Novak, Victoria Myers, Jane Kelley Rodeheffer, Jeff Schultz, and Don Thompson—and our librarians.

I am grateful to the gifted cohort of Lilly Graduate Fellows that I mentored with my friend Susan Felch, with whom we discussed *Confessions*, *Commedia*, and the *Karamazovs* over the course of three enlivening years. In July 2017, the Sisters of St. Benedict provided kind hospitality, welcomed me to community worship, and gave me an office in which to work. And I am grateful to so many others who have sown seeds of inspiration and encouragement over the years: Monsignor John Sheridan, Edward Weisband, Louis Dupré, Robert Kiely, Mary Breiner, Karin Hart, Rich Mitchell, Hans Cristoffersen and many others whom I'm sure—and am sorry—to be forgetting.

And I am grateful to the brilliant and hospitable scholars of Slavic literature. In the late 1980s, I discovered the work of Mikhail Mikhailovich Bakhtin, and contacted a scholar whose studies of his thought I'd found especially illuminating: Caryl Emerson responded with generosity beyond what I could have imagined. In the years since then, I have been grateful for Caryl's friendship, good counsel, and for the careful reading she gave an earlier version of this manuscript. Caryl's suggestions have been invaluable in improving the quality of my book, the remaining faults of which remain my own. I am also very grateful for Caryl's willingness to write the luminous Afterword to this book.

Dostoevsky scholars are some of the most thoughtful and kind people a scholar could ever hope to meet. Some of the scholars with whom I conversed are now of blessed memory: Joseph Frank, Robert Belknap, Victor Terras, and Diane Oenning Thompson. Others remain vital contributors to the study of Dostoevsky: Carol Apollonio, Brian Armstrong, Robert Bird, Julian Connolly, Yuri Corrigan, Octavian Gabor, Robert Louis Jackson,

Deborah Martinsen, Greta Matzner-Gore, Susan McReynolds, Gary Saul Morson, Riley Ossorgin, Maxwell Parlin, Robin Feuer Miller, George Pattison, Randall Poole, Amy Ronner, Gary Rosenshield, Rowan Williams, Peter Winsky, Alina Wyman, Denis Zhernokleyev, and many others whom I am sorry to be forgetting. At one time or another, each has given their kind attention to my work. My focus upon Dostoevsky's Christian dimension follows decades of work by distinguished scholars, among them Boyce Gibson, Sven Linner, Robert Louis Jackson, Steven Cassedy, Malcolm Jones, Susan McReynolds, Rowan Williams, Wil Van Den Bercken, George Paniches, and P. H. Brazier, and many other international and Russian scholars, such as Vladimir Nikolaevich Zakharov.[2] Books focused solely upon *The Brothers Karamazov* and closely attuned to its spiritual dimension—especially those by Robin Feuer Miller, Diane Oenning Thompson, and Julian Connolly—have been consistent sources of insight. I have found the works of countless scholars to be helpful, and hope this small contribution may be heard in dialogue with theirs, and contribute to what continues to be a vital conversation, especially timely in our "secular age."

In the book's final stages, Hilary Yancey's expert typesetting and careful indexing proved to be indispensable. My gratitude, too, to the attentive team at Cascade Books / Wipf and Stock—especially Robin Parry, but also Matt Wimer, Ian Creeger, Zechariah Mickel, George Callihan, Adam McInturf, Savanah Landerholm, Jim Tedrick, and Joe Delahanty.

Finally, I am deeply thankful for the support of my family: to my parents, Salvatore and Kathryne, for their love and guidance during their earthly lives. My Mom passed on to me not only her love of reading, but also her love for our Catholic Christian faith and tradition. Many years ago, when I was vocationally at sea, my sister Kathy encouraged me to become a teacher: I'm very grateful she did. Nick Pellicciari was always interested, always kind. My wife's parents, Harriet and Peter Mullins, always thoughtfully granted me space to work while we visited. Above all, I am very grateful to my wife Maire Mullins, who for thirty years has been my companion, conversation partner, source of good humor, counselor, sometime-typist, perceptive reader, and daily support in writing, teaching, parenting, and living. I thank our beautiful daughters, Mai Rose and Teresa Marie, who learned to pronounce "Karamazov" earlier than any child should ever be asked to attempt. While I worked on this book, they excused my absence from some of the family fun. All their young lives, they have encouraged me by their kindness, good humor, insight, and grace.

I hope that whoever picks up this book—be it a teacher, student, pastoral counselor, therapist, general reader (and we all inhabit each of these roles at some time)—will be guided toward a recognition of the uniquely transformative and edifying potential of Dostoevsky's final novel. Readers —especially those exploring the novel for the first time—may wish to use the Norton Critical (Second) Edition of the novel as my analysis is keyed to that translation. First-time readers sometimes find Russian names to be a challenge, and will find assistance in Appendix II here. I've sometimes said that my vocation is simply to get people to read *The Brothers Karamazov*. If *this* book gets more people to read *that* book, I'll consider it a success.

***

In part, this book draws upon and revises work on Dostoevsky I have previously published. Below, I list these publications with gratitude to the publishers for any permissions that may be required. In this book I've integrated some of this past work, in different form, and employed words and ideas that first appeared there:

"Catholic Christianity." In *The Cambridge Companion to Literature and Religion*, edited by Susan M. Felch. Cambridge: Cambridge University Press, 2016.

"'Descend That You May Ascend': Augustine, Dostoevsky, and the Confessions of Ivan Karamazov." In *Augustine and Literature*, edited by Robert Kennedy, Kim Paffenroth, and John Doody. Lanham, MD: Lexington, 2006.

"Dostoevsky." Entry in *The New Catholic Encyclopedia*. Gale Research, 2011.

"Dostoevsky: *The Brothers Karamazov*." In *Finding a Common Thread: Reading Great Texts from Homer to O'Connor*, edited by Robert C. Roberts, Scott H. Moore, and Donald D. Schmeltekopf. Notre Dame, IN: St. Augustine's Press, 2011.

"Dostoevsky and the Ethical Relation to the Prisoner." *Renascence: Essays on Values in Literature* 48.4 (1996).

"Dostoevsky and the Prisoner." In *Literature and the Renewal of the Public Sphere*, edited by Susan VanZanten Gallagher and M. D. Walhout. New York: St. Martin's Press, 2000.

"Incarnational Realism and the Case for Casuistry: Dmitri Karamazov's Escape." In *"The Brothers Karamazov": Art, Creativity, and Spirituality*, edited by Pedrag Cicovacki and Maria Granik. Heidelberg: Universitätsverlag C. Winter, 2010.

"Merton and Milosz at the Metropolis: Two Poets Engage Dostoevsky, Suffering, and Human Responsibility." *Renascence: Essays on Values in Literature* 63.2 (2011).

"The Prudential Alyosha Karamazov: The Russian Realist from a Catholic Perspective." In "Dostoevsky and Christianity: Art, Faith, and Dialogue," a special volume of *Dostoevsky Monographs*, Volume VI, edited by Jordi Morillas. St. Petersburg: Dmitry Bulanin, 2015.

"Zosima, Mikhail, and Prosaic Confessional Dialogue in *The Brothers Karamazov*." *Studies in the Novel* 27.1 (1995).

Thank you to all.
Orthodox Christmas, January 7, 2020

Preface

The Brothers Karamazov as Transformational Classic

Near the end of his life, as Fyodor Mikhailovich Dostoevsky was completing *The Brothers Karamazov*, he was invited to Moscow to give a speech in honor of the poet Pushkin. Most people there had been reading the novel as it was published in serial form,[3] and Dostoevsky wrote a letter to his wife Anna, describing the way they greeted him: "crowds of men and women came backstage to shake my hand. As I walked across the hall during intermission, a host of people, youths and graybeards and ladies, rushed toward me exclaiming, 'You're our prophet. We've become better people since we read *The Karamazovs*.' (In brief, I realized how tremendously important *The Karamazovs* is.)" (*Selected Letters*, 504).[4] The author was, of course, delighted. He'd hoped his novel—which would be his last—would have such a positive impact on readers.

But can a work of literature really make one a "better" person? Early in the novel, the eldest brother, Dmitri Fyodorovich Karamazov, declares his doubt. He's read great poets like Schiller and Goethe—he quotes them by heart!—but confesses to his brother, Alyosha: "Has it reformed me? Never! . . ." (96).[5] A literary classic may move the reader by its aesthetic beauty, its integrity of form, its radiant representations of goodness. But, assuming the reader aspires to be good, can it move her or him further toward that goal—toward the "reformation" or transformation, for which Mitya yearns?

The premise of this book is that it can—and that *The Brothers Karamazov* has an especially powerful capacity to inspire its readers to be "better people." David Tracy notes that in a classic, we "find something valuable,

I

something 'important': *some disclosure of reality* in a moment that must be called one of 'recognition' which surprises, provokes, challenges, shocks, *and eventually transforms us*" (108, emphasis added).[6] Some scholars, such as Mikhail Epstein, observe that regnant critical practices, typically marked by suspicion toward the text, have weakened our capacity for such recognition: "the humanities are no longer focusing on human reflection and self-transformation" (*Transformative Humanities* 2). Recently, Rita Felski has suggested that "literary theory would do well to reflect on—rather than condescend to—the uses of literature in everyday life: uses we have barely begun to understand. Such a reorientation, with any luck, might inspire more capacious, and more publicly persuasive, rationales for why literature, and the study of literature, matter." She calls for "sustained attention to the sheer range and complexity of aesthetic experiences, including moments of recognition, enchantment, shock, and knowledge" (191). And, we might add, transformation.[7]

When I was nineteen, I was looking for a summer novel, and had heard of the classic called *The Brothers Karamazov*. I decided to read it during breaks from my summer job as a Manhattan messenger, and picked up a used copy at the Strand. Alas, I recall few shocks of recognition. I remember the used paperback's plain, black and white Modern Library 1950 cover. I was baffled by the unrelenting intensity of its characters, impressed by the words of the wise Russian monk, but remember little else. I'd have made better sense of it all if I'd read it in a class or reading group, conversing with peers, guided by a good teacher. Six years later, I found such a class in Professor Tom Werge's graduate seminar entitled "The Religious Imagination in Modern Literature." This time I felt more of the novel's deep "disclosure of reality." It's been part of my "equipment for living" ever since. For the past thirty years, I've been teaching the novel in "great books" curricula, and have re-read it so many times I've lost count.

The novel inspires me—as it has so many others—in its truth, beauty, and its portrayal of goodness in the face of evil. Its hero Alexei Fyodorovich Karamazov—from here on simply "Alyosha," as he's called in the novel—does not, at first, seem very heroic or "remarkable." The narrator himself admits this in his preface (7). The youngest of the Karamazov brothers, Alyosha is sent from the comforting shelter of the monastery by his mentor, the Elder Zosima, to practice "active love" (54) as "a monk in the world" (247). He attends lovingly, prudently to his drunken, lecherous father, his guilt-laden brothers and their lovers, a group of boys, and a troubled teenage girl. Active love is hard work, requiring habitual practice; it's "harsh and dreadful" compared to "love in dreams." His brother Ivan claims that "Christ-like love for men is a miracle impossible on earth" (205). But given Zosima's insistence that grace is ever-present, "the miraculous power of the Lord" (56) guides even our feeblest efforts. Receptive to this reality of grace, Alyosha emerges as a luminous image of active love. At first glance an "eccentric," he "carries within himself the very heart of the whole" (7). St. Paul says that "all things hold together" in Christ (Col 1:17). Analogously, in the world of this novel, all things hold together in Christ-like Alyosha Fyodorovich Karamazov.

Dostoevsky described his final novel as a "Hosannah," but admitted that his prayer of praise had passed through a "great *furnace of doubt*" ("From Dostoevsky's *Notebooks*" 667). The novel gives narrative form to the author's purgatorial passage. Dostoevsky knew suffering: the deaths of his mother and father when he was young; his youthful revolutionary exploits of behalf of the serfs and his subsequent arrest, mock execution, and years in Siberian prison; punishing debt, compulsive gambling, family turmoil, and the death of two of his little children. He knew that faith is buffeted by human experiences of finitude and pain. He gives "full latitude" to the rebellious voice of his character, Ivan Fyodorovich Karamazov (128), the intellectual middle brother.[8] But he also portrayed characters who mediate Christ's love in the midst of suffering, even as he anxiously wondered whether he'd offered "answer enough" to Ivan's rebellion. You can hear Dostoevsky's anxiety when he writes to his editor:

> If I can bring it off I will have accomplished something useful: *I will force them to admit* that a pure and ideal Christian is not an abstraction but a tangible, real possibility that can be contemplated with our own eyes and that it is in Christianity alone that the salvation of the Russian people lies. . . . It is for this theme that the entire novel is written, and I only hope that I will carry it off—that's what concerns me most now! (*Letters* 469–70)

Dostoevsky knew that he couldn't really "force" his readers to accept his Christian ideal. Throughout the novel, he respects his readers' interpretive freedom by portraying characters who resist the givenness of graced being—and who express potent reasons for doing so. Mikhail Mikhailovich Bakhtin, among the most influential commentators on Dostoevsky's work, highlights the novelist's "polyphony": the many, oft-clashing voices he represents in his novels. Bakhtin described the novelist's world as a "church" comprised "of unmerged souls, where sinners and righteous men come together" (*Problems* 26–27). Dostoevsky's characters are "unfinalizable": the reader can't quite "peg" them or ever reduce them to their worst actions. As artistic creator, Dostoevsky respects the freedom of his characters as *persons*, made free in the image of their Creator, and always capable of change. His personalism deepened the transformative potential of his final novel. He "carried it off."

Of course, he risked the possibility that some would find the rebellious voices more persuasive. James Wood offers only one example: "Dostoevsky's parable of the Grand Inquisitor, in *The Brothers Karamazov*, is for me, an unanswerable attack on the cruelty of God's hiddenness. In my early twenties, it proved decisive" (254). But there are many—I dare say more—who have found the novel to be a source of spiritual sustenance and hope.[9]

Hope is the indispensable virtue for pilgrims "on the way" and "bound for beatitude."[10] Hope rejects the Janus-faced temptations of presumption and despair, both forms of pride. But a pilgrim isn't immune from doubt; in its depiction of human anguish, the novel raises *reasons* to doubt. Alyosha tries to bring wholeness to his dysfunctional, disfigured family, but wonders if he—and even God—are failing: "My brothers are destroying themselves. My father too. And they are destroying others with them. It's 'the earthly force of the Karamazovs,' . . . a crude unbridled earthy force. Does the spirit of God move above that force?" (191). Dostoevsky asks Alyosha's very question: Is divine grace present in the midst of human violence, trauma, and deformation, and if so where can it be found? Dostoevsky suggests that grace remains ever present, often mediated by persons like Alyosha, who serve as analogies of divine love.

A word about the structure of the book that follows. Part I presents a Prelude: these two initial chapters outline the theological ideas comprising Dostoevsky's incarnational realism, and specific ways in which the novel embodies these ideas. Part II focuses upon the novel's fictional *persons*: in their decisions and actions, the characters give personified form to the theme of incarnational realism, over the course of quotidian time. Some, especially those reading the novel for the first time, may wish to begin here and later circle back to Part One. In Chapter 3, we trace the way in which Zosima's capacity as a confessor, his vision of responsibility "to all, for all," develops, especially in his youthful encounter with Mikhail, his "mysterious visitor" and with others in his capacity as Elder in the local monastery. In Chapter 4, we follow Alyosha as he takes up the mantle of his elder, develops as a "monk in the world," and, at the end of three days, ascends in his vision of Cana. In Chapter 5, we turn to Mitya's struggle to become a "new man," his torments, new life, and agonizing final decision, aided by Alyosha and Grushenka. In Chapter 6, we turn to Ivan's rebellion, his anguished groping toward responsibility, and confession in court. Finally, in Chapter 7, we join Kolya, Ilyusha, the boys, and Lise, trace Alyosha's generative role with the young people he encounters, and hear his final message of hope.

I

Prelude

Chapter 1

The Analogical Imagination
and Incarnational Realism

Dostoevsky sought to portray the "person in the person." His "higher realism," rooted in his Christian faith, sees visible, finite reality as bearing an *analogical* relationship to an invisible, infinite reality. An analogical imagination recognizes that human persons are creatures, both like and radically unlike their Creator. Created in God's image, persons are like God in their rationality, freedom, and capacity to create and love. But God is one and persons are many; God is unchanging and persons are mutable; God is infinite and persons are finite. Above all, persons are dependent as their existence is contingent upon God's. God is not simply another being, but Being itself, the One in Whom all persons live and move and have their particular beings.[11] Our existence as beings does not place us in the same ontological category as God. But the divine is not so utterly transcendent that our own rational conceptions of the good and true and beautiful bear no relation to God.[12] They bear an *analogical* relation.

Christian faith understands God not only as Being but as Love. God is a unity of three persons bound in infinite, inter-relational, self-giving love. God's love overflows to form creation and, in time, enters history and a particular place in the person of Christ. In Christ, the believer sees most clearly the image of God's beauty, goodness, and truth. The infinite Word takes on creaturely flesh and finitude. But Christ's descent into finitude and death brings forth resurrection, ascension, and the gifts of the Holy Spirit. As Trinity, God is *both* One *and* three differentiated persons; Christ is *both* God *and* man, "without confusion . . . without separation."[13] The

7

analogical imagination is built upon the two doctrinal beams that undergird the Christian faith: Trinity and Incarnation. Analogy recognizes the unity in our human plurality: for all our particularity and diversity, we are each persons, and, in analogy to God's trinitarian nature, created to be in integral relation to other persons. Analogy recognizes that human love is both *like* and—given our creaturely, fallen frailty—*unlike* the Creator's love.[14]

Both like *and* unlike: a "both/and" approach to reality recognizes both its complexity and wholeness. It resists the temptation to order that complexity with too-tidy "either/or" categorizations.[15] Dostoevsky's novel represents reality as *both* graced gift *and* arduous task; the world as *both* sacramentally charged *and* sinfully fallen; paradise as *both* here *and* yet to come; persons as *both* open in their freedom to change *and* closed given the realities of time, interpersonal commitment, consequences of past actions, and even genetic inheritance. Dostoevsky depicts the human desire for holiness as demanding *both* willing receptivity *and* a willed (but never will*ful*) effort of self-denial.[16]

A both/and vision should not be understood as resulting in static indecision. Rather, it fosters a prudential appreciation of particularity that, in time, *necessitates* decisive action. Taking one road precludes taking another. Thus, the novel's "both/and" vision recognizes that "either/or" moments are inevitable in human experience, and require the preparatory work of discernment. Having reached a clear apprehension of the truth of a particular situation, each character in the novel must decide and act. Rather than depleting personhood by foreclosing options, decisive action enhances it. Wholeness is found in the passage *through* the limited. Grace remains ever available in the place of fragmentation. As St. Thomas Aquinas emphasized, uncreated grace builds upon created nature;[17] infinite freedom fosters finite, creatural freedom. Freedom exercised in "active love" is grounded in the person's "precious mystic sense of our living bond with the other world" (276).

Active love itself has a both/and form: it integrates *both* human inclination, our attraction to the good and beautiful (*eros*) *and* sacrificial self-emptying on behalf of others (*agape*). Persons are called to participate in the divine self-emptying, the *kenosis* of "perfect self-forgetfulness in the love of [their] neighbor" (54), in acts of self-transcendence *not* of self-obliteration.[18] Dostoevsky distinguishes the relational *person* from the autonomous *self*: "For Dostoevsky, it is a bad thing to lose one's personality, but a good thing to lose one's self" (Corrigan 12). Paradoxically, he affirms that fullness of personhood—one's "true self"—emerges only through the gift of self. In this way, Dostoevsky's vision bears deep affinities to those of St. Augustine and Dante Alighieri—two other Christian "classics" to whom

I will sometimes refer in this study. For all three writers, *eros* and *agape* find a "hidden wholeness"[19] in the practice of *caritas*. "Except a corn of wheat falls into the ground and dies, it abideth alone: but if it die, it bringeth forth much fruit" (John 12:24). Jesus spoke these words as he entered Jerusalem, and into his passion, death, and resurrection. The words comprise the novel's epigraph and suggest its recurring theme. The epigraph presents a seminal image of both finitude and fruition. It suggests that self-giving love, in response to God's own, is the human person's deepest desire.[20]

To reiterate, a both/and vision *must include* the reality of a decisive "either/or."[21] "See, I have today set before you life and good, death and evil" (Deut 30:15). Moses presents here a stark either/or, and in its similarly high-stakes choice between life and death the novel is *both* "both/and" *and* "either/or." Paradoxically—and aptly—the cross becomes "the tree of life" "the roots" of which lie in the "other world" (276). The cross stands as the novel's symbol for that which "brings forth much fruit."[22] Its counter image is the gallows, chosen by the suicide. The night before the trial, Ivan vows to Alyosha: "Tomorrow the cross, but not the gallows" (549). This "either/or" is decisive. But even the tiniest of charitable deeds can re-direct and re-align a person to the form of Christ: the gift of a kiss, a pillow, or a "pound of nuts" that open an orphaned child's eyes to the hidden ground of Trinitarian love (567–68). A gratuitously offered "little onion" (307, 311) can be salvific.[23]

Given Dostoevsky's radically inclusive vision of salvation "for all," what of those who choose the gallows? Does Smerdyakov have *his* onion? Here too we find complexity: the novel complicates any quick condemnation of those who, like Smerdyakov (or Judas, his scriptural prototype), choose suicide. In the Gospel of Matthew, Judas "deeply regret[s] what he had done." He returns the thirty pieces of silver and confesses. Only after being rebuffed by the priests does he commit suicide (Matt 27:3–5).[24] Similarly, on the night before the trial, when Smerdyakov describes his murder to Ivan and hands him the blood money, the narrator admits that "It was impossible to tell if it was remorse he was feeling, or what" (529). Both tragic images complicate the reader's overly hasty judgment, as does Zosima's meditation which emphasizes both justice *and* mercy:

> But woe to those who have slain themselves on earth, woe to the suicides! I believe that there can be none more miserable than they. They tell us that it is a sin to pray to God for them and outwardly the Church, as it were, renounces them, but in my secret heart I believe that we may pray even for them. Love can never be an offense to Christ. For such as those I have prayed inwardly all my life, I confess it, fathers and teachers, and even now I pray for them every day. (279)

The reader, implicated, is called to "go and do likewise." In Zosima's vision, and that of the novel as a whole, God's love and the possibility of redemption extends even into hell, where God continues to call souls (279) and angels offer onions (303). "God wills everyone to be saved and to come to knowledge of the truth" (1 Tim 2:3–4); Zosima fulfills the Christian "obligation to hope for the salvation of all."[25]

Dostoevsky sees like both a fox *and* a hedgehog: he perceives diverse particulars, but also their participation in a deeper "living unity."[26] His analogical vision of reality fosters clear-eyed hope left unavailable by an imagination that is univocal or equivocal.[27] The univocal imagination forces unity where it doesn't exist. Recoiling from disorder, it imposes a totalizing and unblessed rage for order. Its political form is totalitarianism: the Grand Inquisitor annihilates human freedom in the name of "love [of] mankind" (223). In its interpersonal form, the univocal distorts reality by seeing the world in rigid, reified binaries: something or someone is either *wholly* good or *wholly* bad, either saved or damned. In a despotic insistence on sameness, the univocal rejects the mixed, messy, and imperfect. It elides the finite realities of time and place. It ignores the partial and particular by projecting a constructed ideal upon the real.[28] It's impervious to surprise. In the novel, the univocal takes various forms, inevitably absurd, such as Ferapont's hallucinatory asceticism, Katerina's lacerating "self-sacrifice," or Madame Khokhlakova's "love in dreams."

But here too complexity arises: even "love in dreams" can't be too simply opposed to "active love." It can't be reduced to a negative in a neat Manichean binary, demonically defended as an "indispensable minus" (545).[29] Madame Khokhlakova fantasizes about "becoming a sister of mercy," but Zosima cannily (and comically) detects a grain of good in her dreams: "'It is much, and well that your mind is full of such dreams and not others. Sometime, unawares, you might do a good deed in reality'" (54). Some fantasies *are* better than others; Ivan's wish for his father's death corrodes his capacity for commitment. Contemporary psychologists corroborate Zosima's insight: contemplating a change is the first step in the process of change.[30]

But finally, after prudentially reaching a decision, one *must* act. As Zosima makes clear, if an overweening desire for others' "approbation" takes precedence over integrally made decisions, one's "whole life will slip away like a phantom" (55).[31] The Grand Inquisitor reveals the destruction wrought by the univocal: his proclaimed "love of humankind" masks his contempt for persons, and his inclination to annihilate them. His demonic dehumanization foreshadows the totalitarian horrors of recent history. In Zosima's (and Dostoevsky's) imagination, hell is the refusal to love. In both this world and the next, hell has an exit, but as an existential condition remains a real option. Some *refuse* the way out, and for them "hell is voluntary" (279).[32] The univocal imagination can lead to such hell.

The equivocal imagination is similarly infernal. It distorts the real by seeing in it *nothing but* intractable difference. Rather than imposing a false unity, the equivocal imagination relishes the mess, with a perverse amalgam of willful *jouissance* and Sartrean *nausea*. It rejects the unity, wholeness, and harmony that are *given*, but that also emerge out of the slow work of active love. Ethically, equivocation rejects the ordinary bonds that comprise human personhood: responsibilities to family, friends, and the common good. In the novel, Ivan and the illegitimate, unacknowledged fourth brother, Smerdyakov, exemplify equivocation. Ivan articulates the nihilistic vision (65) and Smerdyakov enacts it (531): "if there is no immortality [i.e. heaven, *theosis*, the *telos* of communal beatitude], there is no immorality. *Everything is permitted*" (65; emphasis added). In the novel, the equivocal imagination produces a "love of disorder," motivated by willful, irrational self-assertion. Ivan and Smerdyakov, the younger Grushenka, Katerina, and Lisa melodramatically luxuriate in lacerating both themselves and others. They thus oppose the incarnational work of active love.

Janus-faced, the univocal and equivocal imaginations comprise a refusal of reality. By rejecting the ontological reality of the "hidden ground of love," both reject unity within diversity. In place of that ontology they assert an epistemology that projects upon and cuts "against the grain" (545) of the real.[33] The univocal compels order; the equivocal exacerbates disorder. Both reject reality as grounded in God's self-giving love. Both choose "the gallows": violence toward others and self.[34]

The "analogy of being" has been described as the "fundamental Catholic form" (Przywara 348). As a lifelong Catholic, I'm aware that my partiality to the novel's analogical dimension stems partly from my rootedness in that tradition.[35] The many forms of Catholicism—liturgical, doctrinal, cultural, intellectual—in-form my reading of Dostoevsky's novel. As Appendix I illustrates, a wide array of notable Catholic writers have deeply resonated with Dostoevsky's novels. Of course, the Russian novelist (and nationalist) wrote withering critiques of both Catholicism and Protestantism. Dostoevsky believed that through the truth of Orthodoxy "the star [would] arise in the East" (62) and save the world.[36] I approach Dostoevsky's classic with a degree of readerly "outsideness" and hermeneutic "prejudice." But as Bakhtin and Gadamer suggest, such a readerly position *can* be hermeneutically fruitful.[37] Furthermore, Catholicism and Orthodoxy share a sacramental tradition and an understanding that analogy entails both likeness *and* even greater unlikeness.[38] In both their cataphatic *and* apophatic forms,

Orthodoxy and Catholicism evince the incarnational *realism* I emphasize in my reading of the novel.

Incarnational Realism

"Realism" is a word with a complex literary, philosophical, and theological valence to which I cannot do justice here. Suffice it to say "incarnational realism" refers not only to the late-nineteenth-century literary genre in which Dostoevsky writes, but to his philosophical/theological belief that the human mind is capable of apprehending the world as it is ontologically, even with our epistemological limitations and inheritance of "social constructions." As literary scholar Susan Felch writes, the world outside of us "impinges upon us and sets limits to our ways of seeing, being, and acting in the world" (25). And we are ourselves limited by our particularity of perspectives; thus Susan's term, "*perspectival* realism." Realism must be "critical"; theologian N. T. Wright defines "critical realism" as: "a way of acknowledging the process of 'knowing' that *acknowledges the thing known as something other than the knower* (hence 'realism') while also fully acknowledging that the only access we have to this reality is through the spiraling path of *appropriate dialogue or conversation between the knower and the thing known* (hence 'critical')" (35). And, here, in part, is sociologist Christian Smith's description:

> Critical realism's central organizing thought is that much of reality exists independently of human consciousness of it; . . . that humans can acquire a truthful though fallible knowledge and understanding of reality through various forms of disciplined conceptualization, inquiry, and theoretical reflection . . . [and] that knowledge and understanding of the truths about reality position knowers to critically engage the world in normative, prescriptive, and even moral terms . . . and [to] intentionally try to shape the world for the better. (92–93)[39]

Ethically, realism entails the indispensable practice of prudence. Through prudence we become more discerning, more responsible. By degrees, we become better able to receptively apprehend and respond to the real.[40] In ordinary parlance, we aim to "be realistic." Aware of human limits, we set practical, attainable goals—and (when it's prudent to do so!) implore those whom we care about to "get real." Consider Zosima's practical advice to Fyodor: "If you can't close all [your taverns], *at least two or three*" (43; emphasis added). You have to start somewhere. And for Dostoevsky, God's grace, which sustains reality itself, gives us the strength to begin again, to apprehend and respond to divine love. Moments after counseling Fyodor, Zosima exhorts a woman in despair to have faith, to know "that God loves you as you cannot conceive, that He loves you with your sin, in your sin" (50).

Textual examples such as these help clarify Dostoevsky's vision of incarnational realism. In this chapter I'll present three passages from *The Brothers Karamazov* in the hope of providing a clearer sense of what Dostoevsky meant when he insisted "I am only a realist in a higher sense, i.e., I depict all the depths of the human soul."[41] Dostoevsky portrays the depths of human personhood, and envisions creation in the light of "incarnational realism."

The first passage is from Book 6, which records teachings of the Elder Zosima spoken in "a last effort of love" (248). Read in full, this passage offers "what is probably the master key to the philosophical interpretation, as well as to the structure, of *The Brothers Karamazov*" (Terras, *Companion* 259).[42] As a whole, Dostoevsky's novel gives narrative embodiment—word made flesh—to the vision articulated by Zosima.[43] Heard as a symphonic whole, the novel renders reality as "being as communion,"[44] "the coinherence of creation with God and of creatures with one another" (Barron 145). More simply, the novel offers a *practical* spirituality to anyone who senses this "coinherence,"[45] and desires to respond to it with the gritty work of active love. Here are Zosima's words:

> My friends, pray to God for gladness. Be glad as children, as the birds of heaven. And let not the sin of men confound you in your doings. Fear not that it will wear away your work and hinder its being accomplished. Do not say, "Sin is mighty, wickedness is mighty, evil environment is mighty, and we are lonely and helpless, and evil environment is wearing us away and hindering our good work from being done." Fly from that dejection, children! There is only one means of salvation, then take yourself and make yourself responsible *for all* men's sins, that is the truth, you know, friends, for as soon as you sincerely make yourself responsible *for all* men, you will see at once that it is really so, and that you are to blame for everyone and *for all* things. But throwing your own indolence and impotence on others you will end by sharing the pride of Satan and murmuring against God. Of the pride of Satan what I think is this: it is hard for us on earth to comprehend it, and therefore it is so easy to fall into error and to share it, even imagining that we are doing something grand and fine. Indeed many of the strongest feelings and movements of our nature we cannot comprehend

on earth. Let that not be a stumbling block, and think not that it may serve as a justification to you for anything. For the Eternal Judge asks of you what you can comprehend and not what you cannot. You will know yourself hereafter, for you will behold all things truly then and will not dispute them. *On earth, indeed, we are as it were astray, and if it were not for the precious image of Christ before us, we should be undone and altogether lost, as was the human race before the flood.* Much on earth is hidden from us, but to make up for that we have been given *a precious mystic sense of our living bond with the other world, with the higher heavenly world,* and the roots of our thoughts are not here but in other worlds. *That is why the philosophers say that we cannot apprehend the reality of things on earth.* God took seeds from different worlds and sowed them on this earth, and His garden grew up and everything came up that could come up, but what grows lives and is alive only through the feeling of its contact with other mysterious worlds. If that feeling grows weak or is destroyed in you, the heavenly growth will die away in you. Then you will be indifferent to life and even grow to hate it. That's what I think. (276; emphasis added)

While he acknowledges that "much is hidden," Zosima affirms that we *can* apprehend "the reality of things on earth" by sustaining "a precious mystic sense of our living bond with . . . the higher heavenly world," the seeds of which have been sown in creation. Christ's incarnation follows the creation: "The Word" (whom Ivan resists [203]) "became flesh and dwelt among us" (John 1:14). Thus "the precious image of Christ"[46] re-sacralizes reality and remains present in the church, the body of Christ—in its unlikely saints, and in the ecclesial forms of word, sacrament, and icon.

Some Orthodox critics, such as Sergei Hackel, have found the novel to be insufficiently ecclesial. Closer examination suggests otherwise. For example, Zosima recalls attending the Divine Liturgy at the age of eight. During Holy Week, he sees sunlight streaming through "the narrow little window," and "consciously received the seed of God's word in [his] heart" (255). Decades later and near death, Zosima longs for the sacraments: "he desired to confess and take communion at once" and then receives extreme unction (145). The church reflects and mediates the precious image of Christ, and Zosima recognizes Christ as the grain of wheat that has fallen to bring forth much fruit (John 12:24). Divine love sows (Matt 13:18–23) "seeds from other worlds" that sustain persons' participation in Christ's pattern of descent and ascent. In cooperative effort, through the work of love grounded in grace, they too bring forth much fruit (John 15:8).

Christ's "precious image" propels its beholder into active participation in what theologian Hans Urs von Balthasar calls the "theodrama" in which the Creator's infinite freedom fosters the finite freedom of God's beloved creatures. God's sustaining presence provides the warrant for persevering in the work of responsible active love. As Augustine emphasized, love builds on humility. It accepts epistemological and other limits, and rejects the defensive impulse to justify self, blame the world, and thus share the "pride of Satan." Through experience, a person learns to discern reality more clearly, to respond appropriately ("Know measure, know the proper time, study that" [279]),[47] and to do so decisively ("If you remember in the night as you go to sleep 'I have not done what I ought to have done,' rise up at once and do it" [277]). However one interprets the contours of reality at any particular time, the real remains founded upon what Thomas Merton called the "hidden ground of love."[48] Our "roots" lie here, in worlds Zosima describes as "heavenly," "higher," and "mysterious" (276).

Zosima's realism attends to both the limits and graces found in quotidian life. Finitude curbs the pilgrim's rough path to eternity. By accepting responsibility in our particular time, place, and community, we discern glimpses of transcendent beauty, of "paradise" (249), often unexpectedly. Zosima articulates a both/and eschatology: paradise is both *here* and *yet to arrive*. Faith in eternal beatitude incorporates a vision of life's goodness, here and now. Incarnational realism suspects the romantic, utopian, sentimental, and apocalyptic.[49] It not only "confesses the reality of the triune God revealed in Jesus Christ" (Moore 9), but sees all beings as participating in the integral realities of Trinity and Incarnation.

The second passage to which I will point occurs early in the novel, as the narrator introduces Alyosha as a "realist." Holding up the apostle Thomas, he suggests that Alyosha's realism not only accepts miracles, but that it's integrally related to his faith in Christ's resurrection:

> Alyosha was more of a realist than any one. Oh, no doubt, in the monastery he fully believed in miracles, but, to my thinking, miracles are never a stumbling-block to the realist. . . . Faith does not, in the realist, spring from the miracle, but the miracle from faith. If the realist once believes, then he is bound by his very realism to admit the miraculous also. The Apostle Thomas said that he would not believe until he saw, but when he did see he said, "My Lord and my God!" Was it the miracle forced him to believe? Most likely not, but he believed because he desired to believe and possibly he fully believed in his secret heart even when he said, "I shall not believe except I see." (28)

For Thomas, as for Alyosha, beholding Christ's risen image fosters an *already-present* faith in the Word made flesh.[50] Faith grounds incarnational realism: Thomas can see the physical and spiritual reality of the risen Christ *because* he believes. So too Alyosha who thus counters the "unbelieving realism" of Rakitin. Egotism blinds Rakitin to the genuine spiritual transformations, "resurrections" of others.[51] His materialism[52] reduces human freedom to the chemical reactions of nerve cells (497).[53] At the end of the catalytic "Onion" chapter, in which Alyosha and Grushenka image Christ for each other, Rakitin sneeringly calls their encounter a "miracle" (308). In fact, it is. Faith lends vision to believers like Zosima, Alyosha, Mitya, Grushenka and others, giving them the "ability to see what God chooses to show and which cannot be seen without faith" (von Balthasar, *Form* 175).

Of course, the life of faith is not free of doubt. Mikhail Bakhtin suggests that one of the most "pure and profound examples of confessional self-accounting . . . may be found" in the prayer of the father with the possessed child who "said with tears, Lord, I believe; help thou my unbelief" (Mark 9:24) (*Author* 145).[54] Given the crucible through which he passed, Dostoevsky understood this father's prayer. Most believers do. But as James P. Scanlan observes, while Dostoevsky doubted, he never actively disbelieved.[55] Like Thomas, Dostoevsky believed in his "secret heart." His faith enabled him to see the reality of human participation in the death and resurrection of Christ, which he invokes in the novel's final pages and elsewhere.[56]

In the narrator's "midrash" on John 20, Thomas's beholding of the risen Christ *fosters* Thomas's faith, but he sees *because* he believes. So too Alyosha: he discerns the spiritual dimension of reality in ways that the materialist Rakitin refuses. As do others in the novel, Alyosha speaks of having been "risen up," as when he declares to Grushenka, "You've raised my soul from the depths" (302). The imprisoned Mitya avows that "a new man has risen up in me" (499). Rakitin witnesses the "resurrections" of both Alyosha and Mitya, but disbelief blinds him to the miracle embodied in both. Rakitin is unwilling to open himself to any gracious surprise that may exist outside his egocentric consciousness. He is a rationalist, a "theoretician." Victor Terras elucidates: "A 'realist' according to Dostoevsky is a person who lives and thinks in terms of immediately, or intuitively, given reality. The opposite, then, is the 'theoretician' (*teoretik*), who seeks to create and to realize a subjective world of his own" (*Companion* 137).

In Thomist terms, the realist's attunement to "given reality" enables a capacity for *prudential* action. Josef Pieper writes: "Reality is the basis of the good, . . . to be good is to do justice to objective being" ("Reality" 112); prudence "is the proper disposition of the practical reason insofar as it knows what is to be done concretely in the matter of ways and means" (163).

Prudence attends to the context of "particular realities and circumstances which 'surround' every individual moral action" (166). Through experience, a prudent person learns to apprehend reality more clearly, and to respond more decisively.

Without prudence, a person cannot act virtuously, cannot flourish. Rather than egocentrically projecting a predetermined schema *upon* reality, prudence remains receptively open *to* reality. Aristotle's discussion of *phronesis* in *Nicomachean Ethics* is seminal: "prudence is a state grasping the truth, involving reason, concerned with action about things that are good or bad for a human being"; prudence "is concerned with particulars as well as universals, and particulars become known from experience, but a young person lacks experience, since some length of time is needed to produce it"; prudence entails "deliberation . . . that accords with what is beneficial, about the right thing, in the right way, and at the right time"; finally, prudence is "the eye of the soul, [and] requires virtue in order to reach its fully developed state; . . . full virtue cannot be acquired without prudence" (1140b–1144b). Pieper says that for St. Thomas, who reads Aristotle through the eyes of faith, "'reason' means . . . nothing other than 'regard for and openness to reality,' and 'acceptance of reality.' And 'truth' is to him nothing other than the unveiling and revelation of reality, of both natural and supernatural reality" (*Cardinal* 9). Pieper defines prudence as "the perfected ability to make decisions in accordance with reality [and] . . . the quintessence of ethical maturity" (*Cardinal* 31). Fellow Thomist Jacques Maritain, citing Claude Tresmontant, emphasizes the *realism* inherent in practical reason: "[I]f reason is not constituted *a priori*, if the principles belonging to reason are in fact *drawn from the real* itself through our knowledge of the real, then one need hardly be astonished if there is accord between reason and the real. . . . Rationality is not an order or a structure constituted *a priori*, but a *relation* between the human mind and the real . . ." (*Peasant* 109).[57]

Practical reason attends to "the rough ground,"[58] the gritty textures of everyday reality and the graces to be found there. Upon first impression, Dostoevsky's intensely emotional characters don't seem to be characterized by "reason." His great biographer Joseph Frank claims that during the time he wrote *The Brothers Karamazov*, Dostoevsky saw as "central" "the conflict between reason and faith—faith now being understood very sharply as the irrational core of the Christian commitment" (*Prophet* 570).[59] For Frank, Dostoevsky's understanding of Christian hope was "justified by nothing but what Kierkegaard called a 'leap of faith' in the radiant image of Christ the Godman" (*A Writer in His Time* 859). But for all the existential anguish of his characters, I see Dostoevsky's vision—and most fully so in his final novel—as bearing a deeper affinity to Thomas Aquinas's emphasis on practical wisdom forged in communal relations than to Kierkegaard's stress on absurdity and subjectivity. At least in *Fear and Trembling*, Kierkegaard praises an image of faith that suspends the ethical and remains incommunicable to others: when Abraham sets out to journey to Mount Moriah with Isaac, he cannot tell Sarah of his plans. Nor (Kierkegaard would argue) can he tell her what happened there when he returns home.[60] In contrast, *The Brothers Karamazov* emphasizes a grace-infused yet communicable ethic of active love. The practice of active love *itself* fosters faith, and those who extend it to each other experience mutual comprehension. Certainly the novel has its apophatic dimension: no orthodox understanding of Christian faith can lack it.[61] But the apophatic—which emphasizes God's transcendence by naming what God is *not*—is consistent with an understanding of analogy that affirms both similarity *and* dissimilarity between creature and Creator. As David Bentley Hart notes:

> [A]ll the major theistic traditions insist at some point that our language about God consists mostly in conceptual restrictions and fruitful negations. "Cataphatic" (or affirmative) theology must always be chastened and corrected by "apophatic" (or negative) theology. We cannot speak of God in his own nature directly but at best only analogously, and even then only in such a way that the conceptual content of our analogies consists largely in our knowledge of all the things God is not. (*Experience* 142)

Dostoevsky is always alert to the apophatic, as some of his best commentators have elucidated.[62] Yet *The Brothers Karamazov*'s cataphatic dimension consistently demonstrates the human capacity to discern God's will and to communicate it to others. Zosima's counsel to his fellow monks is consistently realistic and reasonable. Even when young, Dostoevsky insisted that he saw "nothing more *reasonable*" than Christ.[63] Consistently, he rejected rational*ism*—the "rational egoism" of his contemporary Chernyshevsky[64] and the positivism of Rakitin—as a de-formation of reason that dissolves the freedom of persons as images of God.[65] Freedom entails the practice of virtue, most prominently, active love, and, as A. Boyce Gibson understatedly noted almost fifty years ago, "the faith displayed in 'active love' is not so far from being 'reasonable'" (211).[66] *The Brothers Karamazov* presents active love as graced, reasonable, and possible.

Dostoevsky's conception of faith cannot be reduced to an act of emotional will, a voluntaristic "leap." Voluntarism exalts the human will, and in Dostoevsky's world the unfettered, irrational will leads to demonic violence and un-freedom. Aware of impinging limits, incarnational realism fosters freedom in its uniting of "reason and will, knowledge and love in the act of choice. This places the image of God in the power humans have to act on their own, in mastery and moral responsibility" (Pinckaers 137). Zosima and Alyosha gradually and *rationally* arrive at the maturity of prudence through their abiding faith in the "precious image of Christ." Their faith is animated by what Dostoevsky's contemporary St. John Henry Newman called "the illative sense." "The term first appears in *The Grammar of Assent* where Newman describes the illative sense as an intellectual analogue to *phronesis*. The 'illative sense' . . . describes the day-to-day ability of the mind to gather together many small pieces of evidence into a grand conclusion that is not strictly warranted by logical criteria" (Kaplan and Coolman 624). Aidan Nichols describes the illative sense as "the heaping together of tiny indications, none of which by itself is conclusive, [but which] produces certitude in ordinary human affairs" (Kaplan and Coolman 624).[67]

These "tiny indications," sown with "seeds from different worlds" (276), can be found in quotidian life. As Pieper observes, the saints are those who understand this most clearly: "We would . . . remind our readers how intensely the great saints loved the ordinary and commonplace, and how anxious they were lest they might have been deceived into regarding their own hidden craving for the 'extraordinary' as a 'counsel' of the Holy Spirit of God" (*Cardinal* 39). The ego-ridden ascetic Ferapont craves the extraordinary: his mushroom diet elicits hallucinatory distortions of reality. He condemns Zosima for enjoying cherry jam, and for prescribing a laxative when a brother monk sees devils. Saint Zosima provides a model of sensible, faithful prudence.

Prudence fosters hope in a transcendent *telos*, a pilgrim's vision of slow, quotidian progress toward union with Love in heaven. In the West, we may call this communal beatitude or the beatific vision;[68] in the East *theosis* or deification. Persons are called to sanctification in this life and "Godmanhood" in the next. "Man, according to St. Basil, is a creature who has received a commandment to become God. But this commandment is addressed to human freedom, and does not overrule it. As a personal being man can accept the will of God; he can also reject it" (Lossky 124). In *The Brothers Karamazov*, characters de-form themselves through laceration (*nadryv*) and assertion of autonomous "man-godhood." Ivan's youthful writing evokes Nietzsche's valorization of the *übermensch*:[69] "Man will be lifted up with a spirit of divine Titanic pride and the man-god will appear" (546). The assertion of man-godhood—with its consequent denial of the personhood of others—proves infernal. But "paradise" remains the alternative, and not only in its ultimate form of *theosis*, but in the analogical joys experienced here and now: "life is a paradise, and we are all in paradise, but we won't see it, if we would, we should have heaven on earth the next day"

(249). Here Zosima's dying brother Markel articulates his experience of joy, as do Mikhail (268), Alyosha (311), Mitya (429), and Kolya and the boys (646). But their taste of the infinite is preceded by an incarnational descent into finitude.

Descent and Ascent

In Dostoevsky's novel, paradisal joy emerges after a Christic passage *into* the suffering intrinsic to our free yet finite, creatural existence. The practice of active love is "harsh and dreadful" (55), and entails a Christic passage of descent and ascent. As William F. Lynch writes, "the great fact of Christology, that Christ moved down into all the realities of man to get to his Father" (*Christ and Apollo* 13). Lynch briefly traces this passage in Alyosha's experience after Zosima's death, but readers can discern its recurring pattern in the lives of each major character in the novel.

The descent/ascent pattern provides the form for two other great Christian narratives of conversion and confession: Saint Augustine's *Confessions* and Dante's *Commedia*.[70] In the Milan garden, Augustine tearfully falls to the ground and hears a child's sing-song voice repeat "Pick up and read." He reads the words of St. Paul, and rises up a new man. Dante, with the graced guidance of Virgil, descends into hell and a deeper awareness of his self-imprisoning sin. With Virgil's help, he climbs Mount Purgatory. At its apex, he meets his confessor, Beatrice, before whom, weeping, he takes responsibility for his sin. Washed clean, he is prepared for his ascent into the beatific vision of paradise.

In Dante's "poetics of conversion" "the need for another's guidance and for a descent into humility" are crucial; "Augustine's *Confessions* provides the model and supreme analogue" (Freccero xii). The *Confessions* enact both a confession of faith and confession of sin. Similarly, Dante the pilgrim's confession before Beatrice bears fruit in Dante the poet's concluding hymn of praise for "the Love that moves the sun and the other stars" (*Par.* 33). Dante's confession comprises the crux of his journey out of the dark wood. As von Balthasar observes, "The confession scene is not just an episode in the *Comedy*; it is the dynamic goal of the whole journey. And yet it is just as much the point of departure for Paradise" (*Glory III, Lay Styles* 61). The *Brothers Karamazov* presents a "*prosaics* of conversion" in which confession to Zosima or Alyosha prove crucial in character's incarnational passage of descent and ascent. Christ's incarnation is central to the imagination of all three writers. Like Augustine and Dante, Dostoevsky sees Christ as *both* human *and* divine, and as the incarnate model to which every human life is called to conform. Near the end of *A Secular Age*, Charles Taylor posits a potent imperative: "we have to struggle to recover a sense of what the Incarnation means" (754). Part of that project of recovery entails an awareness of those medieval sources in which Christ's incarnation is understood as pivotal. Dostoevsky's novel retrieves this "old Christian realism" (Auerbach, *Mimesis* 521).[71]

A pictorial analogue may be found in the quattrocento Italian art of Giotto, whose fresco series in Padua's Arena Chapel renders key moments in the life of Christ in homely, embodied form. A few years earlier, he had done much the same in Assisi's Basilica, depicting the Christ-like life of St. Francis, the *"Pater Seraphicus,"* whose title Ivan lends to Zosima (230).[72]

Influenced by Francis's incarnational spirit, his love of the natural world, Giotto marks the decisive break from the Byzantine tradition of iconic representation practiced for centuries in Italy—gold-laden backgrounds, stylized, transfigured flesh—and an entry into the naturalism of the Renaissance.[73]

In Giotto's imagination, the incarnation, death, and resurrection of Christ transforms *time* and affirms the value of *narrative* as that which necessarily transpires over time. Discussing Giotto's friend Dante, John Freccero elucidates a passage from St. Paul's Letter to the Ephesians in which "Christ is described as 'the fullness of time'" (267). All that precedes Christ's incarnation can be understood as figural anticipation of that decisive joining of divine and human. All that proceeds from that event can be understood as its recapitulation.[74] The human drama is one of conversion, confession, and virtuous effort, one of descent into humility, penitence and ascent into the practice of active love: the "theodrama" of descent and ascent recapitulates the life, death, and resurrection of Christ.

So too does the drama of saints like Zosima and Alyosha (or Sonia, in *Crime and Punishment*) who serve as confessors for others. In their encounters, each descends and empties himself in kenotic attention to the other. Thus the scriptural figural patterns in the novel observed by many of the novel's best commentators.[75] As Harriet Murav notes, "the basic proposition of Dostoevsky's novel [is] that human history can be touched by God, that we are not limited to the horizontal time frame. Our world and other worlds converge, to use the language of the novel" (134).

By locating his characters' stories within the context of the biblical narrative, Dostoevsky follows the "traditional realistic interpretation of the biblical stories" (Frei 1). Hans Frei contrasts realistic reading with two others. The first, "mythological reading," denies the concrete reality represented in narrative; the second, scientific/historical criticism, reduces Christ solely to his material, finite condition, and severs him from the spiritual, infinite realty also affirmed by the Gospel narratives. "[T]he traditional reading of Scripture" recognizes both spiritual reality and "referred to and described actual historical occurrences." Scripture thus forms "one cumulative story," and provides the warrant for interpreting "earlier biblical stories [as] figures or types of later stories and of their events and patterns of meaning."[76] The shape of *The Brothers Karamazov*, its characters and events, are likewise presented "as figures of [the scriptural] storied world." Its characters gradually discern its figurative pattern woven into reality, even as the reader—especially upon rereading—hears recurring rhymes and chimes within the world of the novel. Throughout, "the sublime or at least serious effect mingles inextricably with the quality of what is casual, random, ordinary, and everyday" (Frei 14).

Frei draws upon the work of Erich Auerbach, who sees "three historical high points in [realistic narrative's] development: the Bible, Dante's *Divine Comedy*, and the nineteenth-century novel" (16), specifically the Russian novel, and especially Dostoevsky's work:

> It seems that the Russians were naturally endowed with the pos-
> sibility of conceiving of everyday things in a serious vein; that
> a classicist aesthetics which excludes a literary category of "the
> low" from serious treatment could never gain a firm foothold
> in Russia. Then, too, as we think of Russian realism, remember-
> ing that it came into its own only during the nineteenth century
> and indeed only during the second half of it, we cannot escape
> the observation that it is . . . *fundamentally related . . . to the
> old-Christian than to modern occidental realism.* (*Mimesis* 521;
> emphasis added)

The Brothers Karamazov retrieves "old Christian realism" for our "secular age." The novel's perennial relevance provides one means of "recover[ing] a sense of what the incarnation might mean" (Taylor, *Secular* 754).

An illustration of this figural descent/ascent pattern can be found in the novel's first chapter, and comprises my third (long-promised) textual example. The narrator, an ordinary townsperson of Skotoprigonevsk, recalls events that occurred there thirteen years earlier (in about 1867). He introduces Fyodor Pavlovich as "an ill-natured buffoon and nothing more" (3). His tone is insistent and dismissive. But in the final paragraph, as he describes the old man's reaction to the death of his first wife, he relaxes his judgment:

> Fyodor Pavlovich was drunk when he first heard of his wife's
> death: they say that he ran out into the street and began shout-
> ing with joy, raising his hands to Heaven: "Lord, now lettest

Thou Thy servant depart in peace," but according to others he wept without restraint like a little child, so much so that it was pitiful to look at him, in spite of the repulsion he inspired. It is quite possible that both versions are true, that is, that he rejoiced at his release, and at the same time wept for her who released him—both at the same time. In most cases, people, even the wicked, are much more naive and simple-hearted than we suppose. And we ourselves are, too. (13)

By the end, the narrator releases his earlier "finalization" of Fyodor, and suggests, humbly, the limits of his omniscience:[77] Fyodor may have *both* buffoonishly travestied Scripture *and* wept like the child Christ counselled all to become (Matt 18:3). Humbly, the narrator lets this mystery be.

The humility of this narrative style—which alternates with a more conventionally omniscient one—bears an affinity to patristic Christian realism: the *sermo humilis* or low style exemplified by St. Augustine, especially his sermons. As Erich Auerbach explains, the low style employs "humble everyday things" ("*Sermo*" 37) and language to signify the most sublime subjects—God, grace, redemption—and were authorized in doing so by the event of the incarnation. "*Humilis* is related to *humus*, the soil, and literally means low, low lying, of small stature" ("*Sermo*" 39). The word "*humilis*" became the most important adjective characterizing [Christ's] Incarnation" (40). For the patristic and later monastic literary imagination, "the humility of the Incarnation derives its full force from the contrast with Christ's divine nature: man and God, lowly and sublime, *humilis et sublimis*; both the height and the depth are immeasurable and inconceivable . . ." (43). Such a paradoxical combination of sublime subject matter and humble style baffled its contemporary audience: "Most educated pagans regarded the early Christian writings as ludicrous, confused, and abhorrent . . ." (45). But to the Christian believer, Christ's refusal to clutch and hold on to his divinity—to live as a person of lowly station and die as a criminal—is the reason every knee should bend at the sound of his name (Phil 2:10–11). After his conversion, Augustine "recognized the 'lowliness' of the Biblical style, which . . . [given the incarnation] possessed a new and profound sublimity" (47).[78] The *sermo humilis* style bears affinities to Dostoevsky's Christian or incarnational realism, both in the narrator's relationship to characters like Fyodor, and in its deep valuing of ordinary life's capacity to point, analogically, to the divine.

The novel's narrator "descends to all men in loving-kindness" ("*Sermo*" 65) by pointing to the possibility of the two conflicting responses—both histrionic, buffoonish exultation *and* authentic, childlike grief. He thus humbly acknowledges Fyodor's possibilities and his own lack of omniscience. He

descends from a position above Fyodor, to a position alongside. He slows
down and gives Fyodor a more attentive look. The narrator's negative capability allows him to resist an all-too-neat explanation of Fyodor's apparently
contradictory behavior, and reveals a respect for his ineluctable personhood.
"But who knows[?]" the narrator muses earlier in the paragraph, comment-
ing on conflicting explanations of Fyodor's antics: the narrator—and Dostoevsky behind him—accepts a less-than-omniscient stance in relation to
the characters in his story. In the chapter's final sentence, he reminds us that
we ought to go and do likewise. After all, we too can be inconsistent. Thus,
in the very first chapter, the narrator-chronicler suggests that the book we
are about to read will make a claim upon us: by entering into its characters'
lives, we will recognize some of our own follies. But we may also recover the
child-like simple-heartedness that acknowledges our need for others, and
that grieves when we lose them to death. "Amen, I say to you, unless you
turn and become like children, you will not enter the kingdom of heaven"
(Matt 18:3).[79]

The narrator's "loving descent" from a finalizing position *above* Fyodor,
to an open position *beside* him is analogous to the *kenosis* or self-emptying
of Christ. In their pioneering biography of Mikhail Bakhtin, Katerina Clark
and Michael Holquist first suggested this analogy. If Flaubert situates himself in a controlling distance above his characters, Dostoevsky, "in the best
kenotic tradition, . . . gives up the privilege of a distinct and higher being
to descend into his text, to be among his creatures. Dostoevsky's distinctive
image of Christ results in the central role of polyphony in his fiction" (249).
Bakhtin's concept of "polyphony"—Dostoevsky's respect for the freedom of
his characters, and his willingness to let them speak in their many, diverse
voices—is thus integral to the aesthetic form of incarnational realism.[80]

Here form deeply reflects content: perhaps the key thematic affirmation of *The Brothers Karamazov* is that each created person is free and thus
has a sacred dignity. Dostoevsky's respect for his character's freedom is
analogous to divine respect for human freedom. Given the human person's
created reality as *imago Dei*, freedom is intrinsic to human identity. The
Grand Inquisitor rejects the "anguish" often occasioned in human freedom,
and he insists that Christ's "gift" has overwhelmed the ordinary person:
"Respecting him less, Thou wouldst have asked less of him. That would have
been more like love, for his burden would have been lighter" (223). In response, Christ offers no defense. He simply, silently attends, and leaves the
Inquisitor with a loving kiss. Christ evinces his respect for the Inquisitor's
personhood, who, after all, has insisted that Christ remain "silent" (217).[81]
Analogously, the active love exemplified by Zosima and Alyosha respects

the freedom of those who seek their counsel. Dostoevsky's polyphonic authorship respects the freedom and complexity of his characters.

Repetitions or recapitulations of this pattern—Christ's kenotic descent and ascent—create what Robin Feuer Miller calls "a novel of rhymes": "[T]he very rhyming or interconnectedness of the parts of *The Brothers Karamazov* becomes the reader's own thread through [its] labyrinth of events and ideas. . . . Characters, fragments of plot, fragments of time—all echo and reverberate in unexpected ways and places" (*Worlds* 13).[82] These rhymes lend the novel its formal beauty and recurring sense of mystery. In the next chapter I turn to Dostoevsky's understanding of beauty, and the way its iconic manifestations call the novel's characters to moral conversion and confession.

Chapter 2

Beauty and Re-formation

Early in the novel, Mitya confesses to Alyosha: "I always read [Schiller's] poem about Ceres and man. Has it reformed me? Never! . . ." (96). But if we look at the scene more closely, we *do* see signs of Mitya's reform. His confession—which next draws on Goethe—becomes a prayer, a bow to God: "Let me be vile and base, only let me kiss the hem of the veil in which my God is shrouded. Though I may be following the devil, I am Thy son, O Lord, and I love Thee, and I feel the joy without which the world cannot stand" (97). The beauty of poetry propels Mitya's desire for *metanoia*, and a recognition of his continuing capacity for joy. Robert Louis Jackson puts it well: "Precisely in his keenly felt sense of ignominy, . . . in [Mitya's] moral despair at what he discovers in himself and in man, lies the measure of the possibility for change" (*Form* 64). Mitya's encounter with poetic beauty— and the ideal to which it points—elicits his sense of sin and still-inchoate resolve to change. "An apparent enthusiasm for the beautiful is mere idle talk when divorced from the sense of a divine summons to change one's life" (Balthasar, "Revelation" 107). Mitya senses this summons. By the end of the novel he will give it moral and spiritual form as his "consciousness of a new man within himself is accompanied by an aesthetic awareness of himself as an 'image and likeness of God'" (Jackson, *Form* 65).

Mitya faces many challenges, and one of them can be found here, in the way he bifurcates beauty into two "ideals"—one divine, one demonic. He desires the human person to be less "broad" in his capacities, but in achieving that aim, would remove flesh from spirit, and thus cripple his apprehension of beauty's analogical potential. Specifically, he doesn't yet recognize the sanctifying potential in his desire for Grushenka:

> Beauty is a terrible and awful thing. . . . I can't endure the thought that a man of lofty mind and heart begins with the ideal of the Madonna and ends with the ideal of Sodom. What is still more awful is that a man with the ideal of Sodom in his soul does not renounce the ideal of the Madonna, and his heart may be on fire with that ideal, genuinely on fire, just as in his days of youth and innocence. (98)

Mitya rightly retains the ideal of Mary, the Madonna whose free consent made possible the incarnation. But his emphatic "either/or" severs the saintly receptivity modelled by Mary—"Let it be done to me according to your word" (Luke 1:38)—from human *eros*. He imagines an internal war in which spiritual beauty (represented by God) battles the beauty of fleshly form (represented by the devil): "The awful thing is that beauty is mysterious as well as terrible. God and the devil are fighting there and the battlefield is the heart of man" (98). For the gnostic or Manichaean, the battlefield presents armies equally matched. For the Christian realist, the Creator remains invulnerable to the wiles of demons, who are, after all, creatures. Out of love for creatures, the Creator enters bodily, created reality and thus hallows it. The person, made in the Creator's image and likeness, can exercise freedom, and draw upon the Creator's grace to do so fully. Christian realism is incarnational: body and soul are integrally related; desire can be well-directed or dis-ordered. Rightly, Mitya rejects the lust and violence captured in the image of "Sodom." But his desire for Grushenka—who is very much on his mind in this discourse with Alyosha—can't be reduced to "Sodom." Sodom surfaces when Mitya reduces and reifies her personhood to her "supple curve" (107). Misapprehending her personal reality, Mitya allows himself to be consumed by lust and the disordered rage he imposes on his father Fyodor and others: Snegiryov, Ilyusha, Grigory. Even after he becomes a "new man" and has "taken all [of Grushenka's) soul" into his own (501), he becomes jealous when she's kind to other men (477).

Mitya remains human, a work-in-progress. But through his difficult descent into finitude—still in process at the novel's close—he slowly learns to integrate *eros* and *agape*. Even in his marriage with Grushenka, he will find beauty's most "mysterious and terrible" (98) form in the "precious" (276), kenotic image of Christ.[83] His marriage will entail a cross of its own; he does not "run away from crucifixion" (502) in his commitment to the woman whom he passionately loves and will serve as a husband. "The humiliation of the servant only makes the concealed glory shine more resplendently, and the descent into the ordinary and commonplace brings out the uniqueness of him who so abased himself" (Balthasar, "Revelation" 114).[84] Mitya comes to accept his particular cross through a "descent into the ordinary and commonplace"—flight to America—as I will elucidate fully in Chapter 5.

Mitya provides one example of the way the novel imagines Christ as the novel's paragon of transformative beauty. In the 1854 letter mentioned in the previous chapter, Dostoevsky declared that he knew "nothing more beautiful" than Christ.[85] He then boasted: "if someone succeeded in proving to me that Christ was outside the truth, and if, *indeed*, the truth was outside Christ, I would sooner remain with Christ than with the truth." Twenty-five years later, as he wrote *The Brothers Karamazov*, he saw no need to pose such a hypothetical: here Christ, and all that he stands for, coincides with the truth. With full artistic freedom, Dostoevsky "powerful[ly]" challenges Christ's truth through Ivan and his Inquisitor ("Notebooks" 667).[86] But read as a whole, his final novel fully reflects his faith in the Word made flesh, in Christ who calls persons to conform to the beauty of his image.[87]

The Beauty of the Icon

The Christian tradition has long understood "beauty" to be one of the names of God.[88] Along with goodness and truth, beauty forms a trinity of "transcendentals" intrinsically related with each other and their source in "the hidden ground of love." As they developed the doctrine of Christ, the church fathers emphasized this interrelationship:

> Corresponding to that classical triad, though by no means identical with it, is the biblical triad of Jesus Christ as the Way, the Truth, and the Life, as he described as having identified himself in the Gospel of John (John 14:6). . . . As one ancient Christian writer [St. Gregory of Nyssa] had put it in an earlier century, "He who said 'I am the Way' . . . shapes us anew to his own image," expressed as another early author [Gregory of Nyssa] said, in "the quality of beauty"; Christ as the Truth came to be regarded as the fulfillment and the embodiment of all the True, "the true light that enlightens every man" (John 1:9); and Christ as the Life was "the source" for all authentic goodness [Augustine]. (Pelikan 7)

As von Balthasar insists, beauty can never be separated from "her sisters" goodness and truth without "an act of mysterious vengeance. We can be sure that whoever sneers at her name as if she were the ornament of a bourgeois past . . . can no longer pray and soon will no longer be able to love" (*Form* 18). Denigrated in modernity, Dostoevsky retrieves the beautiful in its integral relation to the good and the true. He depicts its radiance in the visage of those who *iconically* reflect the beauty of Christ.[89]

In the Orthodox tradition, the icon reminds the viewer of her participation in divine beauty by virtue of her creation as *imago Dei,* and the divine call to recover her divine likeness. Dostoevsky's earliest memory—akin to Alyosha's—was of reciting a prayer before the icon of the Mother of God (Kjetsaa 1). As an adult, Dostoevsky's Sunday worship was apparently irregular, although it may have become more consistent in later years, perhaps inspired by Anna's patient example. But from childhood, he would have known the entrance prayer of the *Divine Liturgy according to St. John Chrysostom*, in which the priest and deacon "go before the icon of Christ, and kissing it, say: 'We venerate Thy most pure image, O Good One, and ask forgiveness of our transgressions, O Christ, our God'" (5). An appreciation of the icon can help us better understand the role of beauty in the novel, and specifically Zosima's insistence that "On earth, indeed, we are as it were, astray and if it were not for the precious *image* of Christ before us, we should be altogether lost, as was the human race before the flood" (276; emphasis added).

The icon lends tangible, visible form to the trans-figured image of the human person. As theologian Leonid Ouspensky observes, the icon "forms a true spiritual guide for the Christian life and, in particular, for prayer" (180), for "holiness is a task assigned to all men . . ." (193).[90] Whether the prayerful setting be communal, liturgical prayer or solitary, devotional, the beauty of the icon calls its prayerful beholder to recover her own beauty, to restore her image—in Russian, her *obraz*, a word Dostoevsky employs often. The icon fixes the viewer's attention on that which the incarnation has made possible: Christ becomes flesh—lives, dies, rises, ascends, and sends the life-breath of the Spirit. Through Christ, persons recover their divine likeness. The icon affirms the goodness of the created world, but opens "a window" to the uncreated, infinite kingdom, in which human passions are purified and rightly ordered. The icon represents the beauty of the transfigured Christ and the saints who conform to his image.

In his eighth-century defense, St. John of Damascus emphasized that the incarnation provides the foundational warrant for venerating icons. Christ's embodiment sanctifies all physical reality. Thus, the icon's material substance of wood and paint can mediate the divine presence, and the image it represents be venerated, not worshipped: "I do not worship matter; I worship the Creator of matter, who became matter for me, taking up His abode in matter, and accomplishing my salvation through matter. 'And the Word became flesh and dwelt among us.' It is obvious to everyone that flesh is matter, and that it is created. I salute matter and I approach it with reverence, and I worship that through which my salvation has come. I honor it" (*Divine Images* 61). Analogous to the sacraments, the icon visibly, tangibly communicates an invisible, intangible grace. In an Orthodox church the iconostasis between nave and sanctuary represents the heavenly community of Christ and the saints. It charges the liminal space between the congregation and the priest who consecrates the bread and wine in the Anaphora or Eucharistic prayer. *The Brothers Karamazov* can itself be read as a "narrative icon" (Murav 135) as it points to the person's eternal *telos*, even as it recalls and sends her back into *this* life, with all its mundane responsibilities.

As novelistic creator, Dostoevsky is analogous to the divine Creator. He respects the freedom not only of his "creatures," his characters, but of his readers as well. Thus the many, varied interpretations of a novel in which those like Zosima and Alyosha, who represent their creator's values, are powerfully challenged by others, like Ivan. In a letter to his editor, Dostoevsky described the Elder Zosima as "a tangible real possibility that can be contemplated with our own eyes" (*Letters* 470). One approaches the icon contemplatively, receptively. Dostoevsky hoped the reader might be receptive not only to the "iconic" images of Zosima and Alyosha, but to the novel as a polyphonic whole, and that his final work of art would elicit a free response.[91]

The icon calls its viewer to conversion and renewal: turning, re-turning to God. It calls its viewer to sanctity, to serve as a living icon for others. In understanding this sanctifying process—and its both/and dynamism—I find the sixth-century Sinai icon of Christ Pantocrator (reproduced on the following page) to be uniquely illuminating. This icon was painted in the sixth century, not long after the Council of Chalcedon (451) had forged the definitive statement on the incarnation: Christ is both man and God, finite and infinite, "without separation or confusion." In it, Christ's face gazes upon the viewer's with both gift and summons. Please take a moment to view the icon attentively:

Christ Pantocrator, St. Catherine's Monastery on Mount Sinai
(used with permission)

Observe the asymmetry of Jesus' face. From the viewer's left, Jesus' face is open, receptive. His eyes gaze into the viewer's with tenderness, acceptance, and mercy. Here is the redemptive Christ whom Alyosha affirms, just after Ivan's insistence that no one dare forgive the torturer of an innocent child. Alyosha responds "suddenly, with flashing eyes": "there is a Being [who] can forgive everything, all *and for all*, because he gave his innocent blood for all and everything" (213; emphasis in original). But on the viewer's right side, Jesus' face seems different: his lip turns slightly down, and his eye seems to judge the viewer and find him wanting. On this side, *we* are responsible for the violence that blights our world; Jesus' eye interrogates: what have we done, and what have we left undone? "There is only one means of salvation, then take yourself and make yourself responsible *for all* men's sins . . ." (276; emphasis added): Zosima articulates this imperative just before he affirms the "precious"—and salvific—image of Christ. The viewer—and reader—feels a simultaneous release *from* and imposition *of* a burden.

We are each responsible to all and for all. Zosima's refrain, with its emphasis upon the phrase "for all," draws from the Eucharistic Prayer of the *Divine Liturgy*:

> Remembering this commandment of salvation,
> And all those things which for our sakes were brought to pass,
> The Cross, the Grave, the Resurrection on the third day,
> The Ascension into Heaven, the Sitting on the right hand,
> The Second and glorious Advent—
> Thine own of thine own we offer unto Thee,
> *In behalf of all and for all* . . . .
> (cited by Schmemann, 41; emphasis added)[92]

"For all": the phrase is crucial in understanding *how* the salvific image of Christ is represented in the novel. Alyosha's and Zosima's utterances link two complementary claims: first, Christ offers redemption *for all*; second, we must respond to Christ's work by working in active love *for all*.

Christ forgives *all* and yet we are responsible *for all*. How can the weight of redemption be removed and imposed at the same time? Zosima clarifies the paradox by pointing to the "precious image of Christ" which stands "before us" (276) as both sublime model and gracious ground. In his invective, Ivan refers to Christ as "the Word to Which the universe is striving" (203). His tone is bitter but his words are true: the Word creates, enters, and sustains the world in all its groaning and travail. Through grace, "in contact with other mysterious worlds" (276), our responsible example may challenge others to go and do likewise. Responsibility entails the work of active love, including the work for justice for the weak victimized by the strong. Grace fosters persevering through that work, and the suffering it often entails. Furthermore—and given Ivan's description of tortured innocents, this is crucial—suffering retains an integral meaning when understood as a *participation* in the salvific suffering of Christ (see Col 1:24).

Recall Charles Taylor's imperative: "We have to struggle to recover a sense of what the Incarnation means" (*Secular Age* 754). Earlier in his book, Taylor had suggested that a Christocentric understanding of suffering remains a live option, a "divine initiative" available even in our "secular age." Like Dostoevsky, he recognizes that the invitation can be willfully rejected or willingly accepted:

> God's initiative is to enter, in full vulnerability, the heart of [human] resistance to be among humans, offering *participation* in the divine life. The nature of the resistance is that this offer arouses even more violent opposition, . . . a counter-divine one.
>
> Now Christ's reaction to the resistance was to offer no counter-resistance, but to continue loving and offering. This love can go to the very heart of things, and open a road even for the resisters. . . . Through this loving submission, violence is turned around, and instead of breeding counter-violence in an endless spiral, can be transformed. A path is opened of non-power, limitless self-giving, full action, and infinite openness.
>
> On the basis of this initiative, the incomprehensible healing power of this suffering, it becomes possible for human suffering, even of the most meaningless type, to become associated with Christ's act, and to become a locus of renewed contact with God, an act that heals the world. *The suffering is given a transformative effect, by being offered to God.*
>
> A catastrophe thus can become part of a providential story, by being responded to in a certain way. . . . (*Secular Age* 654; emphasis added)

Unflinchingly, *The Brothers Karamazov* represents a world of "human suffering." But the Sinai icon illuminates the ways in which a "providential story" can be discerned in that world. Both ancient icon and modern novel suggest that the person who would conform to "the precious image of Christ" must nurture *both* trust in divine grace *and* the responsive work of love. To borrow terms from Bakhtin, the icon calls its viewer to respect the *unfinalizability* of the other person, to retain a hope in the other's capacity to change, to surprise (*Problems* 63). But it also insists that persons must embody intentions in concrete, responsible deeds (*Act* 51–52).

Given human fallibility, such deeds often commence in the action of confessing past faults to confessors. In their deep respect for the personhood of their confessants, both Elder and "monk in the world" are able to integrate the openness promised by mercy with the closure demanded by responsibility. In so doing they mediate "the precious image of Christ."

Dostoevsky's Theodrama: The Open and Closed Dimensions of Personhood

Dostoevsky depicts what von Balthasar calls the great "theo-drama" of salvation: gifted with finite freedom, persons are called to respond to God's infinitely free initiative with either receptivity or refusal, either cross or gallows. When characters resist, the door remains open: the beauty of another's Christ-like action may inspire a conversion that begins with the resolve to confess.[93] In *Problems of Dostoevsky's Poetics*, Bakhtin recognizes the "enormous importance in Dostoevsky [of] the confessional dialogue" (262), and observes the way the novelist's best confessors respect the freedom of those whom they counsel.[94] They resemble their author, who refuses to stand in a controlling position above his characters, but treats them as persons, descending and dwelling among them. Dostoevsky "affirms the independence, internal freedom, *unfinalizability*, and indeterminacy of the hero" (63). But he is not a relativist. He has his own voice (often channeled through his narrator) that "frequently interrupts, but . . . never drowns out the other's voice" (285). Dostoevsky's polyphony reflects his incarnational realism: like God, he respects the open freedom of his characters, his "creatures."

But he is also rigorously unsentimental in depicting the consequences wrought by his characters' decisions. Like his author, Alyosha respects the unfinalizability of persons,[95] but also insists that they must, finally, decide, and accept responsibility for that which they decide upon. Alyosha's mercy attracts others to him: "There was something about him which said and made one feel at once (and it was so all his life afterwards) that he did not want to be a judge of people, that he would never take judgment upon himself and would never condemn anyone for anything" (22). He takes up Zosima's mantle, and as a "monk in the world," serves as a confessor to many.

Alyosha is often compared with Prince Myshkin, hero of *The Idiot*, Dostoevsky's earlier attempt at creating a Christ-like character. I see the two characters in stark contrast. Myshkin's "stubborn reductive benevolence" sees *only* the open: the inner potentiality for good in others.[96] Myshkin refuses to decide between Nastasha and Aglaya and accept the closure of commitment. Myshkin lacks realism, and brings disaster upon himself and others. In contrast, Alyosha is "more of a realist than anyone" (28). He grows in discernment and decisiveness, and thus learns to better assist others who experience anguish in their "freedom of conscience" (221).[97] Through Zosima's example, and his own experiences of failure, Alyosha learns to practice "active love." He learns to see, accept, and act within the contours of reality. Active love can't simply be imagined or accomplished in a single, epiphanic moment, "some action quickly over" (270). Of course, at unexpected moments, Dostoevsky's characters do receive the gifts of sudden illumination and unbidden ecstasy. But active love prepares the ground for such moments—the slow, habitual grind over the rough ground. It tills the soil and sows seeds yet to sprout. Zosima stresses this reality when he counsels doubt-stricken Madame Khokhlakova:

> Strive to love your neighbor actively and indefatigably. Insofar as you advance in love you will grow surer of the reality of God and the immortality of your soul. . . . It is much, and well that your mind is full of such dreams and not others. Sometime, unawares, you may do a good deed in reality. . . . Love in action is a harsh and dreadful thing compared with love in dreams. Love in dreams is greedy for immediate action, rapidly performed, in the sight of all. . . . But active love is labor and fortitude, and for some people too, perhaps, a complete science. (54–55)

Active love is hard; it takes time. A person can't practice it while anticipating applause or obsessing over the fruits of his actions.[98] And active love is impossible without grace, as Zosima makes clear: "just when you see with horror that in spite of all your efforts you are getting further from your goal instead of nearer to it—at that very moment I predict that you will reach it and behold clearly the miraculous power of God who has been *all the time loving and mysteriously guiding you*" (55–56; emphasis added). Like Jesus' image in the Sinai icon, active love balances the open and closed: it attends to *this* particular moment with *this* person (the closed) and remains receptive to the infinite freedom of God's grace and to the possibility that a small act, in "great time,"[99] may eventually bear fruit (the open). The novel depicts this closed yet open reality of active love. As an artist, Dostoevsky represents the reality of "the open" in his polyphonic relation to his characters, and his portrayal of Zosima's and Alyosha's ethically exemplary treatment of other persons: persons are finite yet always free to receive the infinite freedom of divine grace. But Dostoevsky also represents the reality of "the closed" by portraying characters who turn potential into actuality through decision and action. Dostoevsky's balance of both "the open" and "the closed" is integral to his incarnational realism, and is especially embodied in the novel's dramatic scenes of confessional dialogue which, as we'll see, Bakhtin illuminates.

Bakhtin was a both/and thinker, with a keen sense of both the open and closed dimensions of human experience.[100] His early work, *Toward a Philosophy of the Act*, developed a philosophy of personal responsibility that emphasizes closure: To act ethically, one must refuse the realm of theoretical system and ideal, inner potential, and embody decisions in imperfect acts. Every day, people face ethical decisions—usually small, occasionally big. Universal principles may apply to such situations, but only with a concomitant sense of particular circumstance. Bakhtin's early philosophical work draws upon neo-Kantian and Schelerian ideas,[101] but his emphasis upon the *particular* aligns with the classical Christian conception of prudence or *phronesis*. As discussed earlier, prudence applies universals to the complex contours of specific situations. Bakhtin employs the helpful metaphor of "signature" in describing a person's responsibility to discern, act, and "sign"—not only for her actions, but also the particular and perhaps painful circumstances that she is simply *given*. By refusing to "sign," a person dwells in a static realm of empty potential, fantasizing any number of possibilities. Dwelling in an eternal realm of "maybe" allows nothing to "be": love in dreams must be embodied in actual deeds of active love. Signature-refusers are akin to Kierkegaard's aesthete, floating in an airy yet paradoxically suffocating realm, flying from commitment, ever-ready with an evasive, self-rationalizing "loophole." Such a life is "non-incarnated" (*Act* 43).

In contrast, when a person signs for her actions and situation, she becomes "visible," to use a helpful word that recurs in Rowan Williams's brilliant study (*Dostoevsky* 117, 119, 130).[102] Persons are unavoidably communal: when a person acts, it's likely that others will see the act and perhaps be affected by it. For the moment the viewer will "finalize" the person in the light of that act. But such "finalizing" can be liberating. In another early work, Bakhtin celebrated the boundaries that the viewer offers to the acting person. Such boundaries lend a person the form of "rhythm." As Bakhtin writes, "the unfreedom, the necessity of a life shaped by rhythm is not a *cruel* necessity, . . . rather, it is a necessity bestowed as a gift, bestowed with love: it is a beautiful necessity" (*Author* 119). For Sartre (and some contemporary theorists), "the look" the other casts upon me objectifies me, pins me down: thus "hell is other people." For Bakhtin, the other's apprehension of my personhood comes as a gift around which my sense of self takes form. Bakhtin is a personalist.[103] He recognizes that a person flourishes to the extent that he "signs" for his circumstances and deeds, and accepts the "rhythm" bestowed by others. In his Dostoevsky book, Bakhtin does not employ the specific terms he employed in his earlier philosophical work.

But these terms are helpful in observing the ways in which Dostoevsky's characters resist applying their "signature" or accepting the "rhythm" bestowed by others: the Underground Man in *Notes*, Raskolnikov until the end of *Crime and Punishment*, Prince Myshkin in *The Idiot*, Stavrogin in *Demons*. Recuperating these earlier terms serves a heuristic purpose by illuminating Dostoevsky's own personalist vision.

For Dostoevsky's robust realism points to the possibility of fully realized personhood. Recent studies seek to recover the concept of "person," and recognize the word's roots in the Christian tradition. "Person" stands in stark contrast to modernity's model of the autonomous, voluntaristic subject.[104] Philip A. Rolnick analyzes the ways a robust understanding of personhood has been dissolved in the acids of modernity, specifically in neo-Darwinian naturalism and the deconstructive denial of *logos* and transcendence. Rolnick recovers the patristic conception of the person as it developed in the early church's understanding of the Trinity, and the outpouring of trinitarian love in Christ's incarnation. Later, Thomas Aquinas roots his integration of reason and will in these trinitarian and christological sources. Created in the Trinity's image and likeness, each person is particular—she is unique, differentiated, irreplaceable. But, in her personhood, she is like all other persons in being rationally, lovingly oriented toward both God and neighbor.

For Dostoevsky, to assert solitary, autonomous subjectivity is to refuse personhood as a given, inherently interpersonal reality.[105] Like fellow personalist Jacques Maritain, both Dostoevsky and Bakhtin envision the *givenness* of an embodied person who "tends *by nature* to communion" (*Person* 47; emphasis added). By nature, the person is teleologically oriented toward both the common good and communion with God. Thus Bakhtin's description of Dostoevsky's ontology: "*To be* means *to communicate*." A person is "nonself-sufficient": "To be means to be for another, and through the other, for oneself. A person has no internal sovereign territory, he is always and wholly on the boundary; looking inside himself, he looks *into the eyes of another* or *with the eyes of another*" ("Reworking" 287). For Bakhtin, the words one speaks are necessarily shared, infused not only with the speaker's sense of his listener but by the chorus of speakers he's heard throughout his life. Persons change. And yet an essential, created "true self" remains real. When confessional dialogues succeed, they manifest what Bakhtin calls an encounter of the "*deepest I* with another and others" and reveal "the *pure I* from within oneself" ("Reworking" 294; emphasis added).

What is this "*deepest I*" or "true self"? I read Bakhtin here as elliptically signaling[106] Dostoevsky's Christian belief that a person remains grounded in the loving being of her Creator. Her "deepest I" reflects the divine image.

Her pilgrim hope is to recover her divine likeness.[107] The deep, "pure I" that Bakhtin discerns in Dostoevsky is not a Platonic form, divorced from material and social realities. It is not Descartes's "I am" asserted through solitary introspection. Rather, the "deepest I" signifies a person who accepts his ordinary life among others, both receptive and available to others, and who sustains a "*good taste of self*" and a "realistic imagination" (Lynch, *Faith* 133), capable of "spiritually relevant [and] morally productive communicative efforts" (Wyman 4). Such a person accepts the twin realities of freedom and necessity, and the "third," the ever-present reality of grace. Lynch writes that "some *good taste of the self*, as it is now, no matter how small the taste . . . will help bridge the gap between the actual and the promise" (*Faith* 130; emphasis added). The deepest, truest self is a graced gift, both actual *and* promised.

The Brothers Karamazov suggests that the patristic and monastic traditions offer indispensable practices that abet the recovery of one's "deepest I" or "true self." The novel's narrator describes the monastic means of "self abnegation" in order "to attain the end of perfect freedom." The narrator specifies that end: to find "their true selves" (30). Here too the work of Thomas Merton, well-known twentieth-century Cistercian monk (and lover of *The Brothers Karamazov*), can be illuminating—especially in an understanding of the novel's description of Alyosha as "a monk in the world" (247). Merton wrote for countless readers outside the monastery, and understood that the "true self" could be discovered only in a person's dying and rising and life in Christ. The person thus recovers the likeness into which he was created. Like Zosima—who, he admitted to Dorothy Day, "can always make me weep" (*Ground* 138)—Merton also believed that *all* are called to such self-abnegation, to be "monks in the world," "contemplatives in action." As he writes in *Contemplative Prayer*, "the Zosima type of monasticism can well flourish. . . even in the midst of the world" (28). Merton's description of the "true self," "the ascetic and contemplative recovery of the lost likeness," entails small spiritual victories that any person may seek in the goal of "overcoming of conflict, anxiety, ambivalence, compulsiveness and the radical, repressed psychological claim that every individual harbors to a kind of omnipotence, a tendency to absolutize oneself" (Carr 52).[108] I read the phrase that Bakhtin uses—"deepest I"—as congruent with Merton's conception of the "true self," and with "the person in the person"[109] that Dostoevsky sought to portray in his novels. The "deepest I" is recovered through the grace of the Godman, Christ, not in pursuit of "mangodhood." It is rooted in the kenotic Christ and participates in the self-giving life of the Trinity. Incarnational realism is grounded in and directed toward this embodied ideal: "the ideal," as Father

Paissy puts it, "given by Christ of old" (152), revealed in "the precious image of Christ" (276), whose face is mediated by icons like that from Sinai.[110] The saint reflects Christ's image and descends into the prosaic particulars of responsibility with a pilgrim hope of eventual ascent and homecoming. The scriptural saints—Abraham, Moses, Isaiah, Mary—hear God's call and answer "Here I am." Each responds not with an assertion of autonomous, imperial subjectivity (Descartes' "I think, therefore I am") but with an acceptance of finite, particular circumstances—"Here"—and a willingness to conform to the infinite Divine—the God whose name is "I am" (Exod 3:14), who became flesh and dwelt among us. The saint's "*hineni*," "Here I am," bespeaks the "deepest I," the "true self."

"On earth" (276) persons remain pilgrims—*viator*, "on the way." Fully recovering the "lost likeness" and "deepest I" transpires on a farther shore. But "bound for beatitude," persons are here granted analogies of "paradise" (259) in the "good taste of self" experienced in relationship with others and the Other, in the "joy" for which Mitya rightly claims we are compelled to give thanks (499–500). When a person's self-respect is secure,[111] the gazes and words he shares with others need not deteriorate into the "vicious circle" of "sideward glances" and self-justifying "loopholes" so often represented in Dostoevskian dialogue. He can speak without "cring[ing] anticipation" of the other's judgment (*Problems* 196). Lacking such security, a person seeks validation in the eyes of others, and can do so in excruciatingly self-defeating ways. Fearing the judgment he imagines in the other's eyes, he hates both himself for seeking it and the other for imposing it. The will of the "true self" is sufficiently grounded in a rational intellect and creaturely confidence in the love of his Creator, in whose image he is made. In contrast, the false-self reacts to the other person absurdly. He asserts his will perversely and hurts both himself and others. Like no previous or subsequent novelist, Dostoevsky depicted these capricious assertions of will, and exposes their compulsivity and falsity.

But, especially in his final novel, he also depicted the recovery of "the deepest I," the "true self." Dostoevsky believed that "the person in the person," in all his or her particularity, shares with "all" a common grounding in God's oceanic love. Zosima observes that "all is like an ocean" (299); sharing in common creatureliness, each person is sustained by the overflowing of trinitarian love, and called to participate in that love.

Confessional Dialogue and Kenotic Attentiveness

Given the reality of sin, a "good taste of self" can be difficult to achieve and sustain in ordinary life. Dostoevsky portrays characters who fail, and who experience the guilt and shame that separate them from others through projection, fear, and egotism. The novice reader of Dostoevsky can be baffled by the absurd contortions into which these characters disfigure themselves.[112] Confession offers an exit, but it "cuts both ways" and is a "two-edged sword" (31).[113] Dostoevsky sees the pathological turn confessional dialogue can take. But he also recognizes confession's crucial role in recovering health, the root meaning of "salvation" (Ford 1). He portrays the possibility of interpersonal—or *intercreatural*[114]—relations marked by enlivening mutuality.

Salvific confessions evince incarnational realism in their integration of openness and closure. The confessant experiences *openness* by exercising freedom, both in choosing to confess and in the *way* that he confesses. He articulates his fault without the pressure of inquisitorial coercion. He reveals himself with a clear sense of both his limits and potential. He can acknowledge and thus quell the anxiety that may arise in the "visualization of the self from the eyes of another" (Bakhtin, "Reworking" 294). If the other *seems* to be looking at him with judgment—and the good confessor strives not to—the confessant need not internally conform to that judgment. For example: imagine that I've done something cruel, confessed it to you, and then catch your eyes looking into mine. I think, "You're looking at me as if I *were* really cruel. I guess it must be true: I'm nothing *but* a cruel person." Apart from the projection that may be distorting my apprehension of the confessor, such a conclusion would be false in its univocal closure, its too-easy submission to the "form" imposed in your attention to me. As Morson and Emerson note: "I can be enriched by the other's 'rhythmicizing' of me because I know that a particular image of me does not define me completely. But I can only be impoverished if I try to live as if another could rhythmicize me completely; such an attempt would be another path to pretendership" (*Prosaics* 194)—that is, a flight from responsibility. I remain responsible for my cruel deed, but it doesn't utterly define me. To say that it does so is to utter "a false ultimate word" ("Reworking" 294).[115]

Another way of finalizing oneself, and ruining a confession, is by wearing a mask formed by "visualiz[ing] the self from the eyes of another" (294). The mask-wearer knows that his personhood can't be reduced to a single characteristic. But the mask proves hard to remove when he habitually wears it and plays the role others expect. The family's patriarch, Fyodor Pavolovich, exemplifies this habit. Even in Zosima's cell, Fyodor relishes center stage, playing the role of buffoon, and then "confessing" it to all. When Zosima "pierce[s]" Fyodor with his insight into the old man's motivation—"above all, do not be so ashamed of yourself, for that is the root of it all" (43)—Fyodor responds with a rare moment of truthfulness: "I always feel when I meet people that I am lower than all, and that they all take me for a buffoon. So I say, 'Let me really play the buffoon. I am not afraid of your opinion, for you are every one of you worse than I am'" (43).[116] Fyodor is smart—but he's also lazy and stubborn. He refuses to humbly resolve, "I've been a buffoon. I'll stop." He immediately reverts to his "deceitful posturing" (43) and, later, bursts into the Father Superior's dinner, smashes the mask to his face in wild revenge: "His eyes gleamed, and his lips even quivered. 'Well, since I have begun, I may as well go on,' he decided suddenly. His predominant sensation at that moment might be expressed in the following words, 'Well there is no rehabilitating myself now, so I'll spit all over them shamelessly. "I'm not ashamed of you," I'll show them and that's that!'" (79). Ivan differs from his father in many ways, but Smerdyakov cannily observes that in his shame, Ivan is "more like [Fyodor] than any of his children" (531). In court, Ivan will publicly confess—but then, in a defensive posture born of shame, falsely and publicly affix to himself the mask of full-fledged "murderer" (as we'll see in Chapter 6). Old habits are hard to break; new ones kick in only after arduous work. Fyodor has worn a mask for years; sustaining an honest confession may be beyond his capacity.[117] But with Ivan, as we'll see, there's hope.

In confessing, one must also accept *closure* by taking responsibility. Imagine a man confessing to his wife without evasion, using the active voice, "Two weeks ago I lied to you. I take responsibility for that lie, and I'm sorry." The husband enacts two "signings": the first for the lie he told, and the second for the present confessional utterance. In this sense confessional utterance is "performative": the words *do* something by enacting a person's taking public responsibility for a particular deed.[118] Consider Raskolnikov's public confession in *Crime and Punishment*: his words comprise an efficacious deed. They restore—or begin to restore—a communal bond his murders had severed.[119]

A true confession rejects "loopholes." But like so much else in *The Brothers Karamazov*, loopholes can "cut both ways." On the positive side, there's a loophole of personal growth, that which enables me to exercise my unfinalizability. If I've been a coward in the past, and others justly see me as a coward, I need not act cowardly now. "Forgetting" the way others view me, I can utilize the "loophole" of my freedom to act bravely and thus grow in a new and healthy direction.[120] But if I employ a loophole in order to evade responsibility, it corrodes my confession. Perceiving what I take to be judgment, I strain to pull *off* the mask of "coward." I begin my confession accurately: "I deserted my comrades in battle." The trouble starts when I catch your gaze from the corner of my own, and interpret it—accurately or not—as labelling me as a "coward," branding my very being. I feel shame and react. What began as a genuine attempt to sign for my failing deteriorates into a power struggle—my insistence upon personal unfinalizability versus your finalization. With a firmer sense of personhood and a better "taste of self," I wouldn't be so sensitive. Bereft of it, I grab a loophole: "I saw others running away. Some of them needed my help." Squirming to retain my unfinalizability—"I'm not *really* a coward!"—I deny the freedom I exercised when I chose to run. I erase my "signature" and lose the opportunity to bring closure to one part of my life. The more habitually I grab a loophole, the less free I become.

Dostoevsky depicts numerous such fractured confessions in his work. Although he offers no sustained analysis of *The Brothers Karamazov*, Bakhtin's close analysis of the narrator's confession from *Notes from Underground* offers a heuristic that can be applied to his final novel. Bakhtin observes that "from the very first the hero's speech has already begun to cringe and break under the influence of the anticipated words of another . . ." (*Problems* 228). He thus flees reality. He begins with a self-description, a pause, and a second self-description: "I am a sick man . . . I am a spiteful man." His first utterance is accurate: "I am a sick man." But in his pause, the reader can imagine the Underground Man casting a "sideward glance" at his listener, anticipating her forming an evaluation ("poor man, he needs help"). The Underground Man *does* seek pity from his listener. But simultaneously he *hates* his listener (to whom he has now become "visible") for the privileged position from which she offers her sympathy. He recoils, and tries to destroy his need for her by insisting that he alone can speak any final word about himself: "I am a spiteful man." But this is a "false ultimate word" for *again* the Underground Man looks at his listener, and cringes in anticipation: what if she should agree, and respond, "Yes, you really are spiteful." The Underground Man has his "noble loophole" (67) at hand as he asserts his capacity for his "lofty and beautiful dreams" (65).

The Underground Man refuses to simply acknowledge his deeds and resolve to change. He could say: "I've been spiteful in the past, but would like not to be in the future." "[S]uch a soberly prosaic definition [of himself] would presuppose a word without a sideward glance, a word without a loophole . . ." (*Problems* 232). By refusing to admit his ordinary human imperfection, the Underground Man refuses to live healthily with others. Perversely, he asserts his freedom by ranting that only *he himself* can have the final word about himself, even as he compulsively glares at the other from the corner of his eye. He is "caught up in the vicious circle of self-consciousness with a sideward glance . . . obtrusively peering into the other's eyes and demanding from the other a sincere refutation. . . . The loophole makes the hero ambiguous and elusive even for himself. In order to break through to his self the hero must travel *a very long road*" (*Problems* 234; emphasis added). The "very long road" to his "true self"—his "deepest I"—requires humility, the virtue that grounds love. Liza offers him love, and he rejects her cruelly. Willfully, he persists in scrawling his notes, which an outside editor cuts off arbitrarily.[121]

Other characters in Dostoevsky's fiction employ confession as a meretricious means toward self-justification, punishment, aggrandizement, or exhibition. Robin Feuer Miller analyzes these and uncovers Dostoevsky's implicit critique of Rousseau, whose *Confessions* stands in stark contrast to St. Augustine's: "In Dostoevsky's canon . . . the literary—bookish—written confession most often tends to be, to seem self-justification, or to aim at shocking the audience. But Dostoevsky does concede that the choice of an audience is important, and successful, genuine confessions do occur— witness Raskolnikov with Sonya, or 'the mysterious visitor' with the elder Zosima" ("Rousseau" 98). Julian Connolly highlights Dostoevsky's "characteristically multifaceted way [of showing] both the shining potential of an effective confession and the frustration and suffering that result from a perversion of the confessional impulse" ("Confession" 28). Fellow novelist J. M. Coetzee concludes that "Dostoevsky explores the impasses of secular confession, pointing finally to the sacrament of confession as the only road to self-truth" (230).

But Dostoevsky never *depicts* the actual sacrament of confession. In fact, Father Zosima is actually accused by "opponents" of "arbitrarily and frivolously degrad[ing]" the sacrament of confession by attending to the many who come to the monastery "to confess their doubts, their sins, and their sufferings, and [to] ask for counsel and admonition" (31), apart from the sacrament's traditional form. Nevertheless, Zosima's encounters with his visitors are portrayed as *sacramental*. They are penetrated by divine grace. Zosima and Alyosha help their confessants to step out of their vicious circles, to humbly accept their "visibility" before others, and to speak with clarity and resolve. To each, they bring a Christ-like authority.

Their authority lies both in their faith and in their profound capacity to be attentive to others. In stressing the "penetrative" quality of their authoritative words, Bakhtin draws from Ivanov's *Freedom and the Tragic Life*, which emphasizes "*proniknovenie*, which properly means 'intuitive seeing through' or 'spiritual penetration' . . . . It is a transcension of the subject. In this state of mind we recognize the Ego not as our object, but as another subject. . . . The spiritual penetration finds its expression in the unconditional acceptance with our full will and thought of the other-existence—in 'thou art'" (26–27). The confessor's attentiveness allows him to discern the "pure I from within" the confessant; his authoritative discourse penetrates and is received by the confessant as "internally persuasive" (*Discourse* 342).

Deep attention requires the relinquishment of distraction and self-absorption. In her seminal essay on "School Studies," Simone Weil stresses the *kenotic* dimension of attentiveness: "The soul *empties itself* of all its own contents in order to receive into itself the being it is looking at, just as he is, in all his truth. Only he who is capable of attention can do this" (115; emphasis added). Ivanov also employs the Greek word *kenosis*: "If this acceptance of the other existence is complete; if, with and in this acceptance, the whole substance of my own existence is rendered null and void (*exinanito*, κένωσις) then the other existence ceases to be an alien 'Thou'; instead, the 'Thou' becomes another description of my Ego" (27). But as Bakhtin would insist, and as Alina Wyman extensively demonstrates, kenotic, Christ-like love or "*active empathy*" does not entail self-obliteration: "Incarnation is seen as a model of an active existential approach to one's neighbor" (Wyman 6).

The concept of *kenosis* is, of course, central to the theological understanding of Christ's incarnation, and is especially pronounced in the Russian Orthodox tradition.[122] The *locus classicus* is the letter to the Philippians in which Paul commends Christ's "self-emptying" as exemplary:

> Let the same mind be in you that was in Christ Jesus,
> who, though he was in the form of God,
> did not regard equality with God
> as something to be exploited,
> but emptied himself,
> taking the form of a slave,
> being born in human likeness.
> And being found in human form,
> he humbled himself
> and became obedient to the point of death—
> even death on a cross.
> Therefore God also highly exalted him
> and gave him the name
> that is above every name,
> so that at the name of Jesus
> every knee should bend,
> in heaven and on earth and under the earth,
> and every tongue should confess
> that Jesus Christ is Lord,
> to the glory of God the Father. (Phil 2: 5–11)[123]

In *The Russian Religious Mind*, George P. Fedotov stresses the importance of kenotic spirituality in Russian Orthodoxy and traces its roots to
two eleventh-century sources: first, to the cult surrounding the politically
motivated murder of the Princes Boris and Gleb, who treated their murder-
ers with humility and "forgiving nonresistance" (101), and so were canon-
ized as saints; second, to the life of Saint Theodosius, who was born rich but
willingly wore poor clothes and worked in the fields with slaves. As a monk,
he opened up relations between the monastery and the lay world; he began the long tradition (of which Zosima is exemplary) of monks serving as
confessors for lay people.[124] Dostoevsky wrote, "'In childhood I heard these
narratives myself, before I even learned to read.' These stories of the lives
of the saints were no doubt steeped in the special spirit of Russian kenoticism—the glorification of passive, completely non-heroic and non-resisting
suffering, the suffering of the despised and humiliated Christ—which is so
remarkable a feature of the Russian religious tradition" (Frank, *Seeds* 48).

In their relinquishing of self, and willingness to enter into the suffering of others, Zosima and Alyosha reflect the "attitude that is also [theirs]
in Christ Jesus."[125] Thus, they elicit the conversion of others, helping them
move from willful assertion to willing receptivity. And thus the recurring
resonance of the novel's epigraph. Paradoxically the "deepest I" of the confessor who, through attention, "dies to himself" emerges as most fully himself and *authentically* authoritative. And for Christ's *kenosis* the Father gives
him "the name which is above all other names" (Phil 2:9). Analogously,
Dostoevsky's confessors emerge as truly authoritative by relinquishing the
power others may project when they plead, "Decide for me!" The confessor
never decides for the person struggling under the burden of conscience.
Instead, without manipulation or coercion, he or she guides.

The novel's counter-image to Christ, the Grand Inquisitor, *does* decide
for others: "we shall allow them even sin" (225). As Roger Cox observes, the
Inquisitor's authority is actually tyranny, his miracle sorcery, his mystery
mystification (Terras 235). The Inquisitor claims to love humanity but sees
persons only as "impotent rebels" (222, 223), "pitiful children" (225), and
"geese" (227). Zosima and Alyosha see persons, and help them to recover "a
good taste of self."

The authoritative words of Zosima and Alyosha reverberate with
divine inspiration. In the phrase "penetrated word" Caryl Emerson aptly
translates Bakhtin's *proniknovennoe slovo* by suggesting its two dimensions:
the word penetrates the one who hears it, but is itself "penetrated" and au-
thored by the authority of God. It is thus "capable of actively and confidently
interfering in the interior dialogue of the other person, helping the person to find his own voice" ("Tolstoy" 156). Bakhtin's illustration is Prince

Myshkin, who admonishes Nastasya after she taunts Rogozhin in Ganya's crowded apartment, provoking melodrama and violence. She is wearing a mask, "desperately playing out the role of 'fallen woman,'" and "Myshkin introduces an almost decisive tone into her interior monologue":

> "Aren't you ashamed? Surely you are not what you are pretending to be now? It isn't possible!" cried Myshkin suddenly with deep and heartfelt reproach.
>
> Nastasya Filippovna was surprised, and smiled, seeming to hide something under her smile. She looked at Ganya, rather confused, and walked out of the drawing-room. But before reaching the entry, she turned sharply, went quickly up to Nina Alexandrovna, took her hand and raised it to her lips.
>
> "I really am not like this, he is right," she said in a rapid eager whisper, flushing hotly; and turning around, she walked out so quickly that no one had time to realise what she had come back for. (*The Idiot*, Part One, ch. 10, cited in *Problems* 242)

For a moment Nastasya speaks clearly and resolutely, without a mask; she seems "to find her own voice."[126] But in the events that follow, Myshkin flies from the finitude of decision. He responds to others, especially Nastasya, with a kind of boundless pity and reveals a "deep and fundamental horror at speaking a decisive and ultimate word about another person" (*Problems* 242). In fact, in the scene cited above, his words are "almost decisive" in displaying both an appreciation of Nastasya's potential—"surely you are not what you are pretending to be now"—along with a judgment of actions for which she ought to take responsibility: "Aren't you ashamed?" he cries "with deep and heartfelt reproach" (242). But Myshkin grows increasingly indecisive, and his affect upon others proves violent and tragic. By the novel's end, he emerges as a Christ-manqué.

By contrast, Zosima and Alyosha do speak decisively and image Christ. Deeply attentive, they reject the univocal pity "which wipes out the need and the agony of all partial and analogical choices of the good" (Lynch, *Christ and Apollo* 172). Their utterances—sometimes "spoken" in the forms of bow, blessing, or kiss—accrue beyond their initially penetrative effect. They serve as healing presences for those tempted toward destruction and help them to sustain integral personhood.

With this conceptually laden prelude behind us, we turn to a close examination of the *persons* whom Dostoevsky creates—Zosima and Alyosha—and the persons to whom they lovingly attend.

II

Persons

Chapter 3

The Elder Zosima

To understand Alyosha, the hero of the novel, we must first attend to the story of his mentor, the Elder Zosima, whose life story Alyosha himself authors. Of Book 6, "The Russian Monk," Dostoevsky wrote to his editor N. A. Lyubimov: "It is not a sermon but rather a story, the tale of [Elder Zosima's] own life. If it succeeds I shall have done a good deed: *I shall compel them to recognize* that a pure, ideal Christian is not something abstract but is graphically real, possible, obviously present . . ." ("Selections from Dostoevsky's Letters" 660). Dostoevsky intended Zosima's life story to provide "the answer to that whole *negative side*," the apologia for atheism that Ivan presents in Book 5 (662). Dostoevsky wrote Book 6 "with a great deal of love," but upon its completion he worried: "I tremble for it in this sense: will it be answer enough? The more so as it is not a direct point for point answer to the propositions previously expressed (in the Grand Inquisitor and earlier) but an oblique one . . . in artistic form" (662). The "oblique artistic form" and language of Book 6 is inspired by the old Russian genre of "a saint's life (*zhitie*) . . . not a reliable factual biography, but a sort of dramatized sermon" (Rosen 727).[127] Written by Alyosha "from memory, some time after his elder's death" (247), the book relates Zosima's early life (when he was called "Zinovy") and later teachings. As a boy, Zosima recalls the conversion of his older brother, Markel. Markel experiences a mysterious and sudden conversion to faith, but despite this, his story bears many of the earmarks of incarnational realism, as do Zosima's other memories of childhood.

Zosima's Childhood and Youth

"In the end is my beginning":[128] As Zosima approaches death, he remembers his childhood. He confides to his six listeners that Alyosha reminds him of his elder brother, Markel, who died at seventeen. Markel's mysterious deathbed conversion stands for Zosima as "a guidance and a sign" (247), apart from which he "should never perhaps . . . have become a monk" (247). Now Zosima has "taken [Alyosha] for that young man come back to me at the end of my pilgrimage, as a reminder and an inspiration." The images of the two Christ-like young men converge, and grant Zosima a sense of wholeness: "I look at my whole life at this moment as though living through it again . . ." (247). Finding "incredible energy" in this "last effort of love" (248), Zosima tells his story.

Although some have critiqued the elder's Orthodox practice as thin,[129] Zosima's recollections are implicitly rooted in the incarnation, with its sacralization of time, space, and story, and the church as Christ's body. Markel's conversion transpires during Lent and Holy Week, and culminates in his death on the third week of Easter (250): his *metanoia* has a liturgical form. When he had first fallen ill, his mother had pleaded with him to visit the church, and he refused her. But on the Tuesday morning of Holy Week he goes, but only to "please and comfort" her. He "shows up"—and something happens: confessing, participating in the Divine Liturgy, and receiving Communion elicits a change in Markel. Confined to his sickbed, he continues to share the sacramental life of the church. Christ's resurrection is mirrored in Markel's spiritual renewal, "a wonderful transformation": his face becomes "bright and joyous." He not only exhorts the old nurse to light a lamp before the icon, but apologizes for his earlier rudeness, and prays *with* her: "So we are praying to the same God" (249).

Markel's *metanoia* call to mind two saints from the Catholic tradition: Francis of Assisi and Catherine of Siena. His humble discourse with the birds recalls thirteenth-century St. Francis and his sermon to the birds; we recall the name Ivan gives Zosima, "*Pater Seraphicus*," a traditional title of the poor man from Assisi.[130] Further, Markel's paradisal experience of the "for all" paradox—"I have sinned against everyone, yet all forgive me, too, and that's heaven"—recalls the oft-quoted teaching of the Dominican mystic St. Catherine of Siena: "all the way to heaven is heaven, because Jesus said, 'I am the way.'"[131] Markel's vision, adopted by Zosima (259), bears affinities to a both/and eschatology: the heavenly kingdom as both "realized" and still to come.[132]

As a child, Zosima is rooted in the sacramental life of the church, and these are among his most "precious" memories. His home is depicted as a "domestic church."[133] Zosima remembers the "slanting rays" that illuminate Markel's bedroom much as he recalls that a year earlier, on the "Monday before Easter," his mother had brought him to church where he watched the rising incense meeting the rays of "sunlight that streamed in at the narrow little window." During the readings of Scripture at the Divine Liturgy, he "consciously received the seed of God's word in [his] heart" (251). At home he had "eagerly" read his illustrated collection of Bible stories (which he keeps as a "precious relic"); in church he hears the story of Job. As he listens, the camels capture his imagination; like his brother, the elder Zosima praises the beauty of the created world, "every blade of grass, every insect, ant, and golden bee . . . bear[ing] witness to the mystery of God" (254). He sees "meekness in the faces" of horses, oxen, and bears "since the Word [Christ] is *for all*" (255; emphasis added).[134] From seeds sown in his childhood, mediated by family and church, young Zinovy comes to sense that in Christ "all things hold together" (Col 1:17).

But Zosima's receptivity to God's presence diminishes when he moves to St. Petersburg. In cadet school, he had "picked up so many new habits and opinions that [he] was transformed into a cruel, absurd, almost savage being" (255). Much like Mitya, he willfully constructs a drama of projected love, insult, and potential violence. He is attracted to a young woman but "put[s] off any decisive step"—any act of "signature" or commitment—because he is "loath to part with the allurements of [his] free and licentious bachelor life" (256). His sense of self depends on externals and his actions no longer reflect his *own* beliefs In his concern to maintain appearances in the eyes of others, he falls into "the vicious circle of self-consciousness with the sideways glance" (*Problems* 234), and allows the other's look to incite a reaction abhorrent to his deepest beliefs. When he discovers that the woman with whom he had flirted is now married, and had been long-betrothed, he is "mortified" and "filled with sudden irrepressible fury" both because "almost everybody had known all about it while I knew nothing," and "she must . . . have been laughing at me all the time" (256). Enslaved by shame and "the look" of others, he seeks vengeance: on the one hand, to punish those others upon whom his self is so dependent, and, on the other, to refurbish his image. He resists "visibility" before others. He dons a mask: he is an officer who will *not* be laughed at. And, as with mask-wearer Fyodor, his shame leads to lies: "my wrath and revengeful feelings were extremely oppressive and repugnant to my own nature, for being of an easy temper, I found it difficult to be angry with anyone for long, and so *I had to work myself up artificially and became at last revolting and absurd*" (256; emphasis added). Zosima seeks vengeance "on purpose":[135] he cuts "against the grain" of his own nature (to use Ivan's devil's potent phrase [545]). He insists upon the destructive drama of a duel.

As does each character in *The Brothers Karamazov*, Zosima recovers his own voice only after he has passed through a crucible of transgression, remorse, and—with the necessary mediation of another—confession and atonement. In a "laceration of falsity" (204), Zosima arrives home "in a savage and brutal humor . . . [he flies] into a rage with [his] orderly Afanasy. He "[gives] him two blows in the face with all [his] might so that it was covered with blood." After three hours of sleep, his "ferocious cruelty" haunts him: "It was as though a sharp dagger had pierced me right through. . . . I hid my face in my hands, fell on my bed and broke into a storm of tears. And then I remembered my brother Markel and what he said on his deathbed to his servants: 'My dear ones, why do you wait on me, why do you love me, am I worth your waiting on me?' Yes, am I worth it? flashed through my mind" (257). After twelve dormant years, the word-seeds Markel had sown now bear fruit: "we are each responsible to all, for all." Before riding to his duel, he finds a voice that reflects his "deepest I": "'Afanasy,' I said, 'I gave you two blows on the face yesterday, forgive me,' I said. He started as though he were frightened, and looked at me; and I saw that it was not enough, and on the spot, in my full officer's uniform, I dropped at his feet and bowed my head to the ground. 'Forgive me,' I said." (258)

Moving as the moment is, it resonates with a minor note of humor. Zosima is sincerely sorry but he's also exhilarated by the recovery of his true self. When he thinks his words "are not enough," he bows before the frightened Afanasy. Rather than clarifying matters, his imprudent bow scares Afanasy, and only intensifies the drama. One might observe that the Elder Zosima's bow before Dmitri does the same thing. But there's a difference: as an elder, Zosima has come to know "time and measure" (278); as a youth, he "flies" out of the room leaving Afanasy "completely aghast" (258). The humor here is gentle, not grotesque or satiric (as it can be in earlier works of Dostoevsky).[136] And though shot through with mystery and the intervention of grace, Zinovy's conversion seems lighthearted, not as apocalyptically solemn as Raskolnikov's. The scene of his duel—and many that precede and follow—suggests an important quality of *The Brothers Karamazov*, one that distinguishes it from his other novels: a smiling acceptance of human limitations and the comical incongruities of everyday life. Humor and humility share the etymological root of *humus*, earth. For all of its moments of ecstatic transport, the novel remains rooted, "down to earth." The last page of *The Brothers Karamazov* resounds with rapturous cries—and laughing boys trudging through the snow to eat pancakes.

Like those boys, Zosima is "in ecstasy, laughing" (258) when he rides with his second to the duel. The scene that follows sustains the droll tone. After taking his opponent's shot, and casting his own gun into the wood— "'That's the place for you,' I cried"—he again asks forgiveness from another, and again meets an incongruous response: all three men begin to shout at him at once. Zosima entreats them: "Gentlemen, is it really so wonderful in these days to find a man who can repent of his stupidity and publicly confess his wrongdoing?" "But not in a duel[!]" his second "cries." Incongruity deflates the gravitas of the male ritual, and points up its absurdity. Dismissing decorum, Zosima "own[s] [his] fault," signs for it publicly, and announces that he will become a monk. Zosima has "started on the road" (261), but he will need to take many small steps: when he claims his unworthiness, he clings too hard to his new-found humility by refusing his "rival's" offer to shake hands (259). When he returns home, he's "ashamed to look [Afanasy] in the face" and sends him back to the regiment (260). But the two will meet again, when Zosima is better able to receive the gift offered by the other person (272).

Zosima and Mikhail

On the verge of his monastic vocation—probably about Alyosha's age— young Zosima provides the richest example of successful confessional dialogue in the novel. He is visited by a "mysterious visitor" Mikhail, burdened with guilt for a murder he'd committed fourteen years earlier. Here Dostoevsky shows again the way confessional dialogue can deteriorate—but also the ways in which it can bear fruit. The story engages central themes in the novel: How can a scene of violence be transformed into one of reconciliation and peace? How can the confessor be at the same time authoritative *and* respectful of the freedom of the other? The Grand Inquisitor asserts that people embrace authority in order to escape the anguish of human freedom, and claims to "love mankind" (223) because he's willing to "save them from the great anxiety and terrible agony . . . in making free decisions for them" (225). What are the capacities and limits of human love when one stands before the anguish of another person? A close analysis of this encounter sheds light on the dynamics of other confessional dialogues in the novel.

When they begin their evenings of "stirring and fervent talk" (262), Zosima and Mikhail seem to share a friendship in which each sustains "a good taste of self." Each seems comfortable being "visible" before the other. Mikhail, articulates a "fervent" vision to which the novel as a whole gives form: anticipating and sustained by "the sign of the Son of Man" persons can draw others away from suicidal "terrible individualism" and toward "love" (262). Young Zosima does just this as he relates the details of his conversion, and the two men exchange looks of trust and clear-eyed admiration: "All the while he was speaking, I looked him straight in the face and I felt all at once a complete trust in him" (261); "I liked the way he looked at me as he listened" (261). At the end of their first meeting, Mikhail announces "I will come to see you again and again" (262) and his declaration suggests a healthy acceptance of temporality, that his growing resolve to confess—to Zosima and to the public—will take time, that there will be, in William Lynch's phrase, "intermediate steps" (*Hope* 180) to take before he is ready.

Mikhail's sense of self, however, is far from firm. He gradually reveals his self-division, torn between his "deepest I" (capable of wishing and acting on that wish), and an "unstable I" (dependent upon Zosima's response and the way the younger man may be "finalizing" him). Signs appear early, as when he declares, "Paradise lies hidden within all of us," yet stares at Zosima as if for corroboration: "he was . . . gazing mysteriously at me, as if he were questioning me" (261). When Zosima expresses "bitter" doubts that the kingdom of heaven will ever become a "living reality," Mikhail lashes back, as if to kick away the pedestal on which he's placed Zosima: "What then you don't believe it . . . . You preach it and don't believe it yourself" (261).

Unexpectedly, after a month or so, Mikhail stammers his confession to Zosima: "I . . . do you know . . . I murdered someone" (263). On the one hand, his confession to Zosima is a "first step" toward a self-determined, public signing of his deed: "Now I have said [the first word] I feel I've taken the first step and shall go on." But on the other, the utterance that follows reveals his sideward glance: "'You see,' he said with a pale smile, 'how much it has cost me to say the first word'" (263). He demands that Zosima *sees* him in a specific way: not as a murderer, but as self-sacrificing, noble, willing to pay the price.

Mikhail's confession contains a "loophole," and in the weeks that follow, its corrosive effects become clearer. He moves back and forth between a "determined" (266) resolve to confess, rooted in "the pure I from within," and an intensifying itch to know the way others are looking or will look at him, visualizing himself "through the eyes of another" (Bakhtin, "Reworking" 294). His decision to confess publicly, and his visits with Zosima, have been inspired by a healthy perception of the younger man's goodness: "Looking at you I have made up my mind." But his appreciation sours into envy, and his gaze grows jaundiced: "'Looking at you, I reproached myself and envied you,' he said to me almost sullenly" (265). On the night of his first visit, he reveals an especially pained consciousness of the way Zosima may be looking at him: "Every time I come to you, you look at me so inquisitively as though to say, 'He has still not proclaimed it!' Wait a bit, don't despise me too much. It's not such an easy thing to do as you would think" (266). Increasingly, Mikhail projects his own self-derision onto Zosima's gaze, to the point that Zosima is "afraid to look at him at all" (266). Like the Underground Man, Mikhail craves approval from the other, even as he hates himself and others for his hankering. His sideward glance sweeps the public: "will people recognize it, will they appreciate it, will they respect it?" Lynch observes aptly that "a man who is truly wishing does not need an audience . . ." (*Hope* 154). To truly *wish* is to practice *prudence*, as Denys Turner suggests in his explication of St. Thomas Aquinas: "the moral life consists in the first place in those practices that enable the discovery of what it is that we really want, the happy life, and the power of insight that leads to that discovery is what Thomas calls *prudentia*, skill in seeing the moral point of human situations, what true desires are to be met within them" (180). Craving the approval of others, Mikhail loses sight of what he truly desires. Thus, his internal capacity to wish, resolve, and act is enfeebled: "Perhaps I shall not do it at all." He baits Zosima by falsely accusing the younger man of planning to turn him in (266), projecting to avoid responsibility.

As Mikhail's "deepest I" grows more elusive, his intellect is clouded and capacity for free action is blinkered. He deeply wishes to confess, but evades applying his "signature" to an embodiment of that wish. He pleads with Zosima to consider his wife and children, "as though all [the decision] depended on [him]" (265). His sense of agency depleted, he pleads, "Decide my fate!" (266). He rejects his God-given freedom, and insists that Zosima, the "authority," decide *for* him—like the Grand Inquisitor.

Zosima refuses to do so. He counsels Mikhail, but will not decide *for* him. Consistently, Zosima balances the both/and realities of openness and closure. Authoritatively, he exhorts Mikhail to enact his deed through signature, and bring his resolution to closure: "Go and proclaim" (267). Moreover, he fosters Mikhail's desire to serve the truth through his confession: "if not at once, [all] will understand later; for you have served truth, the higher truth, not the earthly one" (266). In the novel, the earthly truth is perceived "through a glass darkly" even as it analogically reflects "the higher," divine truth. The "closed" dimension of Zosima's response, grounded in openness and respect, fosters the freedom Mikhail sought to flee when he demanded that Zosima determine his fate.

Throughout their encounter, Zosima respects Mikhail's freedom. He renounces any will toward omniscience or verbal "ambush." He refuses coercive inquisition, any "attack from behind" (*Problems* 299). He keeps a tactful silence when he senses Mikhail "brooding over some plan in his heart": "Perhaps he liked my not showing curiosity about his secret, not

seeking to discover it by direct question or by insinuation" (262). He re-
frains from looking at Mikhail when his visitor is at his most defensive: "far
from looking at him with indiscreet curiosity, I was afraid to look at him
at all" (266). And he prudently forbears from embracing him at a delicate
moment: "I wanted to take him in my arms and kiss him, but I did not
dare—his face was contorted and somber" (267). Zosima is deeply *attentive*
toward Mikhail in Simone Weil's sense of that word: "the soul empties itself
of all its own contents in order to receive into itself the being it is looking
at, in all his truth" (43). He empties himself of any egocentric distraction
or will to power over Mikhail. Letting the other be can be understood as a
dimension of kenotic attentiveness.[137]

To let the other be, however, does not mean detachment. Zosima enters
into Mikhail's agonizing situation such that his own "heart ache[s]" (266),
and his own soul is "full of tears" (266). Inwardly, he chastises Mikhail for
"thinking of other people's respect at such a moment," but then feels for
himself the horror of public confession: "I was aghast, realizing with my
heart as well as my mind, what such a resolution meant" (266).

Crucially, Zosima recognizes that Mikhail *himself* has resolved to confess. This recognition is of perennial relevance to pastoral and therapeutic
practice: Zosima not only enters into the pain of Mikhail, he enters into
his *resolve*. Zosima does not impose a decision from above, like the Grand
Inquisitor, whose "authority" is tyranny. Zosima recognizes and respects
Mikhail's "resolution" to confess (266); he supports that decision as Mikhail's
own. Zosima cannot wish *for* Mikhail; in his "active empathy,"[138] however,
he wishes *with* him. When Mikhail departs, with "contorted and somber"
face, Zosima "[falls] on [his] knees before the icon and wept for him before
the Holy Mother of God, our swift defender and helper" (267). He is "half
an hour praying in tears" for his friend, feeling the horror of what Mikhail
has "gone to face" and prayerfully supporting him in his wish to do so (267).

In Zosima's prayer we see his renewed "contact with other mysterious
worlds" (276), his vital openness to grace.[139] He utters his first authoritative
exhortation to Mikhail—"'Go!' said I, 'proclaim it to the world'" (266)—only
after he has "sat still and repeated a silent prayer" (265). His utterance, "Go
and proclaim" (267), comprises a "penetrated word" infused as it is by God's
response in both prayer and Scripture, of which Zosima states, "the Holy
Spirit" is the author. Zosima shows two passages from the New Testament to
Mikhail. The first, from John's Gospel, calls Mikhail to a Christ-like descent
and ascent to new life: "Verily, verily I say unto you, except a corn of wheat
fall into the ground and die, it abideth alone: but if it die, it bringeth forth
much fruit" (John 12:24). The second passage (Heb 10:31) reminds Mikhail
that he is not under the control of his confessor—Zosima holds no such

power—but in "the hands of the living God." Like the silent Christ—who kisses the Inquisitor when he discerns his longing for a response[140]—Zosima does not impose his word upon Mikhail from above, but utters it on "an equal level" (188), respectful of Mikhail's freedom to find it internally persuasive, if he chooses to do so. Zosima's authority is grounded in his attention to Mikhail; *kenosis* grounds his authentic authority.[141]

But Mikhail doesn't hear Zosima's words as authoritative. Although they accrue authority over time, Mikhail initially rejects them. On the night before he confesses, Mikhail has reached the nadir of a vicious circle. In his first visit, weeks earlier, he'd spoken with integral resolve. In the weeks that follow, he grows increasingly conscious of the way others—his family, the public—will view him if he confesses. Most perniciously, he obsessively imagines Zosima's judgement. He defers confessing, and his "deepest I"—capable of rational resolve and free action—disintegrates. The gift of freedom becomes an intolerable burden, which Mikhail desperately throws upon Zosima: "Decide my fate!" (266). Alyosha will face similarly desperate demands from Katerina (167), Grushenka (306), and Mitya (502).

Zosima's whispered exhortation to Mikhail—"Go and proclaim"—articulates a deep respect for Mikhail's freedom *as it wishes with the resolution Mikhail has already made.* But in his weakness Mikhail hears Zosima's words as a dominating imposition from above rather than a respectful echo of his own "deep I from within." He recalls the Underground Man who observes that persons will always resist authority imposed rationalistically from without. In reaction, they will assert their "autonomous" will: "What man needs is only his *independent* wishing, whatever that independence may cost, and wherever it may lead. And the devil knows what this wishing . . ." (28–29).[142] Tragically, the Underground Man refuses to see that his "independent wishing" is precisely *not* that. He rejects the communal reality of personhood, even as he habitually thumbs his nose at others, his sideward glance cringing in anticipation. Endlessly dependent upon others for his chimeric identity, he despairs. Incapable of authentically wishing, he viciously *wishes against.* His capacity for integral will crippled, he strikes back *willfully*—at others and at himself.

So too, at his lowest point, Mikhail. Wishing *against* Zosima, he profoundly distorts his confessor's authentic authority. Zosima humbly attributes authorship of the Scriptures to the Holy Spirit, and Mikhail lashes back, "almost with hatred": "It's easy for you to prate" (267). Mikhail refuses to see that Zosima wishes *with* him, and would strike him down as an opposing power. Zosima has renounced any impulse to finalize or control Mikhail. But in his midnight hour, Mikhail walks the dark streets and hates Zosima so much that he can "hardly bear it" (269). He imagines Zosima looking at him in condemnation—panoptical, ubiquitous, omniscient, and condemning: "I thought, 'How can I look him in the face if I don't proclaim my crime?' And if you had been at the other end of the earth, but alive, it would have been all the same, the thought was unendurable that you were alive knowing everything and condemning me. I hated you as though you were the cause, as though you were to blame for everything" (269). He returns to murder Zosima.

"And the devil knows what this wishing . . . ," scrawls the Underground Man, leaving his thought unfinished.[143] Indeed: Mikhail's murderous intent is utterly willful, and "at its worst [willfulness] has all the marks which tradition in the West has always associated with the devil" (Lynch, *Hope* 154). Later, Mikhail will credit "the Lord [for vanquishing] the devil in [his] heart" (269). Dostoevsky's word for this devil is *nadryv*, translated here as "laceration." Edward Wasiolek elucidates the voluntaristic destruction signified by the word *nadryv*:

> The word comes from the verb *nadryvat'*, which means—apart from its literal meaning of tearing things apart, like paper— "to strain or hurt oneself by lifting something beyond one's strength." To this must be added Dostoevsky's special use of the word to mean a *purposeful* hurting of oneself, and to this, an explanation of the purpose. *Nadryv* is for Dostoevsky a purposeful and pleasurable self-hurt. . . .
>
> *Nadryv* is for Dostoevsky a primal psychological fact. It is the impulse in the hearts of men that separates one man from another, the impulse we all have to make the world over into the image of our wills. . . . From the Underground Man on, one of the premises of Dostoevsky's mature dialectic has been that the Will will subvert the best and highest motives to its own purposes. *Nadryv* is Dostoevsky's mature pointing to the psychological impulse that works to corrupt everything to its own purposes. (*The Major Fiction* 160)

As Robert Belknap observes, "The *nadryv* causes a person to hurt himself in order to hurt others or, perversely, to hurt others in order to hurt himself" (38). Consumed with *nadryv* Mikhail distorts Zosima's image, and burns to kill his closest friend.

Mikhail cannot recover his true self except *through* another; he can "become [himself] only while revealing [himself] for another, through another, and with the help of another" (Bakhtin, "Reworking" 287). For Mikhail, this other person is Zosima, the man he believes he must kill. When he returns to do so, something miraculous happens:

Suddenly I saw the door open and he came in again. I was surprised.

"Where have you been?" I asked him.

"I think," he said, "I've forgotten something . . . my handkerchief I think . . . . Well, even if I've not forgotten anything, let me stay a little."

He sat down. I stood over him. "You sit down, too" said he. I sat down. We sat still for two minutes; he looked intently at me and suddenly smiled—I remembered that—then he got up, embraced me warmly and kissed me.

"Remember" he said, "how I came to you a second time. Dost thou hear, remember it!" (267)

Mikhail has perceived Zosima as objectifying him with an infernal, Sartrean "look." But in a moment his own sideward glance is smilingly transformed into a Buberian gaze, shared with a "Thou," as "for the first time he addresse[s] [Zosima] with the familiar pronoun."[144]

This moment bears an affinity to that which can occur in any therapeutic or pastoral relation. Lynch defines mutuality as "an interacting relationship . . . from which something new and free is born" (*Hope* 169), and points to "the critical moment" in the doctor/patient relationship when, after much work, the patient begins to see the doctor no longer as an enemy but as someone on his or her side: "The patient had felt the constant need to be alert, but now he enters a new and creative passivity, that acts almost without acting, because it now *wishes with*, not against, and is felt to be *wished with*" by another" (170). As he sits, Mikhail relaxes and releases his ever-alert sideward glance. He grows attentive to Zosima, sees him "as he is, in all his truth" (Weil 43).

Zosima's continuing attention toward Mikhail inspires this release. Zosima exemplifies the kenotic in two ways. First, he symbolically enacts the passage of *kenosis* as he willingly descends from a position above the other to one of equality: "He sat down. I stood over him. 'You sit down, too' said he. I sat down" (267). Second, recalling Christ in "The Grand Inquisitor," he keeps a still and tactful silence in the two minutes in which Mikhail "look[s] intently" at him.[145]

In the two minutes he spends with Zosima, Mikhail mysteriously recovers his "pure I" and his own voice. Before he leaves, he utters a penetrated word of his own, as he charges Zosima to "remember!" this second visit. Zosima does remember: he specifically recalls Mikhail's smile (289), and concludes his story with the solemn cadence of prayerful remembrance: "But every day, to this very day, I remember in my prayer to this day, the servant of God, Mikhail, who suffered so greatly" (291).

But what of prudence, "the skill of seeing the moral point of human situations" (Turner 180)? Doesn't Mikhail's public confession imperil his innocent wife and children? In fact, the townspeople don't believe Mikhail and blame Zosima for his "illness" (268), and in this Zosima sees "God's mercy." But do he and Mikhail fully consider the other possible outcome? St. Thomas Aquinas remarks that "caution is necessary for prudence in order that what is good might be taken in such a way that what is bad is avoided" (*Summa* 2.2.49).[146] Caryl Emerson wonders whether, even after the confession, Mikhail's resulting experience of "paradise" generates "hell" for others ("Mysterious" 169). Mikhail dies joyfully, but, she asks, "What indeed had been gained by this act, in the real world of loving human beings? Absolutely the only thing in its favor is that it was the truth" (162).

But "truth" in this novel proves vital. Prudence can't be separated from truth. For all its alertness to possible outcomes, prudential decision-making can't be reduced to a consequentialist calculus. Nor can those possible outcomes be limited to those we foresee occurring in "small time" ("Mysterious" 172). Ultimately, Caryl Emerson sees Mikhail's story as "indispensable" to Dostoevsky's refutation of the Grand Inquisitor, and defends Mikhail's decision by applying Bakhtin's "theologically inflected" conception of "great time."[147] A sense of great time offers "some fuller future meaning," without which "love would be very difficult" (171). If prudence is infused by the gracious gifts of hope and charity, it must attend to *both* the here and now particulars of "small time" *and* to the eschatological promise of "great time." St. Thomas emphasizes the integral relation of love (*caritas*) to the practice of graciously infused prudence:

> The moral virtues that dispose us to act well in relation to naturally attainable goals can be acquired by human activity without need of charity (and are by many pagans). But the moral virtues that dispose us to act well in relation to our ultimate and supernatural goal must be instilled by God; such virtues are inseparable from charity. Prudence's own right reasoning depends much more on being well adapted to our ultimate goal by charity, than to other goals by the moral virtues. (*Summa*, McDermott trans. 243).

As opposed to the Inquisitor's loveless mystification, Mikhail's decision, fostered by Zosima's guidance, reflects authentic mystery. "*How* this molding of prudence by charity takes place in practice can scarcely be stated, for charity, being participation in the life of the Trinitarian God, is in essence a gift beyond the power of man's will or reason to bestow" (Pieper, *Cardinal* 37; emphasis added). In the drama of Mikhail and Zosima the reader glimpses this participative "molding of prudence by charity" rendered in Dostoevsky's "oblique, artistic form."

For Mikhail, the reality of such gracious "molding" is real, as he avows to Zosima: "The Lord vanquished the devil in my heart. But let me tell you, you were never nearer death" (291). Dostoevsky's "higher realism" recognizes the horizontal and vertical dimensions of reality. Vertical and horizontal lines meet in the form of the cross, the image central to incarnational realism. Grace infuses the silent two minutes the two men sit together. The penetrated word—itself infused from "above"—is spoken by one who wishes *with* the other, who wishes that the other may recover his or her own voice. Grace, as Lynch's commentary elucidates, can be understood in an analogous way:

> The best and the most human part of man is the ability to wish, to say "I wish"; one of the most splendid qualities of the outside world, whether that world be things or God or a teacher or a parent or a doctor, is the ability to communicate help in such a way as to create in others the interior ability to really wish. Grace, therefore, should be understood as the act by which an absolutely outside and free reality communicates an absolutely interior and free existence. The theology of grace has talked mostly of the absolute act and wish of God; it should talk more, as should all of us, of that other absolute to which it is so deeply related, the absolute act and wish of man. (*Hope* 157)[148]

Through the cooperative intervention of Zosima and God's grace, Mikhail makes his public confession and accomplishes what he truly wishes to do. The *authentic* freedom he enacts, however, differs profoundly from the *perverse* freedom he would have asserted had he murdered Zosima. For Dostoevsky depicts two kinds of freedom in *The Brothers Karamazov*: inauthentic and authentic. The inauthentic finds its image in the perverse assertion of will that is *nadryv*, the endless dependence upon "the look" of another, if only to spite it.

Inauthentic freedom scorns mutuality, relation, and grace. Later, in Book 6, Zosima imagines the ultimate, infernal image of this diabolic state:

> There are some who remain proud and fierce even in hell, in spite of their certain knowledge and contemplation of the absolute truth; there are some fearful ones who have given themselves over to Satan and his proud spirit entirely. For such, hell is voluntary and ever consuming; they are tortured by their own choice. For they have cursed themselves, cursing God and life. They live upon their vindictive pride like a starving man in the

desert sucking blood out of his own body. But they are never satisfied, and they refuse forgiveness, they curse God *Who calls them*. They cannot behold the living God without hatred, and they cry out that the God of life should be annihilated, that God should destroy Himself and His own creation. And they will burn in the fire of their own wrath for ever and yearn for death and annihilation. But they will not attain to death. (279; emphasis added)

We recall the "hell" that Alyosha sees in Ivan's heart and head (228) when his brother asserts: "I would rather remain with my unavenged suffering and unsatisfied indignation, *even if I am wrong*" (212). The proud souls in hell know they are wrong: they curse God "in spite of their certain knowledge and contemplation of the absolute truth."[149] In their perverse assertion of freedom they wish against the source of their existence and, thus, themselves. They reject reality, the loophole of divine forgiveness, and usher in self-consuming pain. "The doors of hell are locked on the inside" by persons who "enjoy forever the horrible freedom they have demanded, and are therefore self-enslaved" (Lewis, *Pain* 130). But in Zosima's vision—and that of the novel as a whole—God's loving voice calls even the tenants of hell.

For Dostoevsky, authentic freedom finds its image in Christ. Christ respects the freedom of persons, and calls them to embody potential in decisive action. Authentic and free persons participate in trinitarian *kenosis*: they recognize their own non-sufficiency and that others necessarily assist them in the task of decisive action. Reciprocally, they recognize their calling to assist others in their tasks. "What God asks of man . . . is an effort, however small, to reject his individual self-sufficiency, to resist its impulses, and to will to live as one loving and loved. . . . [T]he new ethos inaugurated by Christ [is] . . . the act of emptying out every element of individual autonomy and self-sufficiency, and realizing the life of love and communion" (53).[150] Mikhail empties himself of self-sufficiency through his attentive looking at the image of the kenotic Zosima—who has himself bowed before his servant, relinquished his gun in a duel, and now sits silently with his friend. Through such a release of self-sufficiency, Mikhail recovers his personhood and is able to enact his wish by signing his deed visibly, publicly. Confessing to the townspeople, Mikhail enacts a further release of self-sufficiency. No one believes him, but Mikhail lets that be and accepts the gift of "God's mercy" to his family (268). He has "done [his] duty" as he tells Zosima. In so doing, he ends his hell of "terrible individualism" (262), as he rightly calls it in the apocalyptic tale that mirrors his own. His incarnational passage opens up the possibility of "joy and peace" (268).

Mikhail's passage underscores that the virtue of *humility* is foundational to incarnational realism. Through *kenosis*, one empties oneself of self-sufficiency to open oneself to the help of another; or, one empties oneself of any egocentric distraction or will to power in order to help another. Both forms of *kenosis* call for a release from pride—and for humility. So too the "both/and" acceptance discussed in the previous chapter. On the one hand, a person justly perceives her possibilities; on the other, she recognizes that she cannot dwell in a sovereign realm of "maybe." In the end, like Mikhail, she must simply act—imperfectly, visibly, humbly. Through his confessional encounter, Mikhail learns humility and enacts the christological passage imaged in the epigraph: "Verily, verily, I say unto you, except a corn of wheat fall into the ground and die, it abideth alone: but if it die, it bringeth forth much fruit."

Zosima as Elder

As an elder, Zosima's actions reflect the humble effort required by "active love." Such love is "hard to acquire, it is dearly bought, it is won slowly by long labor" (275). It involves not "some action quickly over" but a willingness to "hold out long" (270). It is realized through persistent, dutiful work: "Go on educating [the people] quietly," he advises his fellow monks (271) and exhorts them to "work without ceasing. If you remember in the night as you go to sleep, 'I have not done what I ought to have done,' rise up at once and do it" (277). Perseverance and the slow development of habit, not "some action quickly over" (270), characterizes active love. Far from espousing romantic individualism, the elder emphasizes the incarnational, trinitarian reality of a person's life *within* community, and the responsibilities that this reality entails. Intuiting his approaching death, Zosima exemplifies his dependence upon the sacramental life of the church. He states his desire "to confess and take the communion at once," and to receive "the service of extreme unction" (145).[151] Zosima's oft-repeated aphorism, remembered from his brother Markel, insists upon the reality of communal bonds: "everyone is really responsible to all men for all men and for everything" (250).

But *is* Zosima's claim realistic? Responsible for "*all*" and "*everything*"? By encompassing "all," does his maxim eclipse real, limited commitments to *particular* men and women? In fact, Zosima is not counselling a dreamy, vaporous "love for humankind,"[152] as espoused by the easily irritated, secular liberal Miusov. Zosima's re-wording of the maxim emphasizes both particular and universal: "everyone of us is undoubtedly responsible for all men and for everything on earth, not merely through the general sinfulness of creation, but each one personally for all mankind and every individual man" (146). Here the emphasis is both on the "individual" women and men "each" of us encounters in daily life, as well as those we do not know, but with whom we stand in solidarity.[153] God saves persons both individually and communally.[154]

Often—and more accurately—the translation of Zosima's original Russian employs the word "guilty" rather than "responsible." Martin Buber's distinction between responsible, existential "guilt" and neurotic "guilt-feeling" is applicable here.[155] Existential guilt acknowledges responsibility for those things that I have done and left undone, and takes action, if only through small steps. As the sixth-century monastic Dorotheos of Gaza wrote, "The root of all disturbance, if one will go to its source, is that no one will blame himself."[156] In contrast, guilt feeling is self-blame turned inward. It is manifest in paralysis, shame, denial, and, often, reactive, violent *nadryv*.[157]

Zosima's later version of his aphorism raises another question: "Remember particularly that you cannot be a judge of anyone. For no one can judge a criminal, until he recognizes that he is just such a criminal as the man standing before him, and that he perhaps is more that all men to blame for that crime. When he understands that, he will be able to be a judge" (276–77). Does this exhortation blot out the real responsibility of the criminal? Again, no: Zosima accepts the necessity of judgment, but only *after* the one who judges has taken personal responsibility for his or her own evil—"when he understands *that* he will be able to be a judge." Above all, Zosima rejects the pride of self-justification, "throw[ing] [one's] own indolence and impotence on others." Self-justification "end[s] by sharing the pride of Satan and murmuring against God" (276). As a whole, the novel invites the reader to integrate Zosima's "for all" statement with Alyosha's affirmation of Christ's redemptive grace "for all" (213). Grace makes active love, responsibility to all, possible (56).

In his acceptance of ordinary time, Zosima rejects any shortcut to the infinite. Far from seducing his listeners to grasp for the timeless, he reminds them that personal change necessarily takes time. Job's "old grief," for example, "passes *gradually* into quiet tender joy" (252; emphasis added). He affirms "the sacrament of the present moment,"[158] stressing the value of the small sacrifice of time—"an hour a week" spent reading the Scriptures, "if only [to] the children at first." He recognizes the cumulative potential in such small efforts: "the fathers will hear of it and they too will begin to come" (253). Zosima hopes for the day when each person "will long with his whole heart to be the servant of all, as the Gospel teaches" (273), but his hope doesn't blind him to the small deeds one can do now as a step along on the way: "sometimes at least" one might humbly serve tea to one's own servants (274). He warns against utopian dreamers who would build an "edifice" of social equality "by intellect . . . alone, without Christ," for by "denying Christ they will end by flooding the earth with blood" (274). The twentieth century proved the prescience of Zosima's words.

Zosima's mysticism is incarnational. The occasion for ecstasy is literally "down to earth": throwing oneself on the ground, kissing it, watering it with one's tears: "Water the earth with the tears of your joy and love those tears. Don't be ashamed of that ecstasy, prize it, for it is a gift of God and a great one; it is not given to many but only to the elect" (278). Such moments come as sheer gift and are rare. As we see in Alyosha's "Cana" experience, they come only "in the proper time." Before speaking of ecstasy, Zosima counsels his fellow monks to prudently discern *within* time: "Know measure, know the proper time, study that" (278).[159] Zosima's affirmation of mystical experience is always within the context of his encompassing emphasis upon the quotidian and communal. Of all the books of the New Testament, Zosima especially extols Luke: "Don't forget either the parables of Our Lord, choose especially from the Gospel of St. Luke" (254). More than any other gospel, Luke stresses the calling of the Christian to take up his or her cross *daily* (Luke 9:23). *Kairos* emerges in the passage through *chronos*.[160]

Zosima's understanding of our relations with others also underscores his incarnational theology. Zosima extols the power of example, especially upon the young. He speaks of the negative potential of bad example, the way an "evil seed" may be sown in a child if he sees the image of a spiteful adult, one who has not "foster[ed] in [himself] a careful, actively benevolent love" (275). And he speaks of the way the memory of a good example may accrue transformative power, a seed for one's own deeds of benevolence, as did his "lasting impression" of his dying brother Markel.

The narrator introduces Zosima on the first day of the novel, during which he sows good seeds through word and deed. He mediates sacramental healing in his confessional dialogues with visitors to the monastery. As Alyosha stands by silently and observes, Zosima exemplifies the work of Christ-like active love, welcoming them, and attending to their particular needs, balancing both openness and closure. On the one hand, he respects the freedom of each interlocutor, and opens himself up to each person's anguish and desire. But on the other hand, Zosima authoritatively emphasizes the need to take responsibility for one's deeds, to recognize limits, and take decisive action. He shows "that only by staying within this structure of temporality, and moving with it can one gain access to real insight" (Lynch, *Christ* 33). As teacher and confessor, Zosima practices the slow, ordinary work of active love and rejects illusory epiphanies.

Zosima's words in these dialogues are "prosaic": straightforward and direct—as in the root meaning of "prose." He counsels Madame Khokhlakova that change takes time: "Active love is labor and fortitude" (55); to his fellow monks, he insists it's "won slowly by long labor" (275). Zosima offers a vision of personal conversion as incremental, not sudden and apocalyptic.[161] He models the way in which loving attentiveness of another can restore a "good taste of self" in another person. He restores hope in persons—in their capacity to change and take decisive action. Personal change *takes time*, but we don't have forever; thus, the present moment is precious.

Zosima incarnates these truths in the novel's opening scenes, which take place in the late morning of a late August day. Alyosha has dreaded his family's visit to the monastery (34), and his forebodings are realized: once in Zosima's cell, Fyodor almost immediately begins to play the buffoon. Zosima discerns that the old man is driven by shame: "And, above all, do not be so ashamed of yourself, for that is at the root of it all." His words penetrate, as Fyodor responds: "'You pierced right through me, and read me to the core with that remark. . . . Teacher!' he fell suddenly on his knees, 'what must I do to gain eternal life?'"[162]

> The elder, lifting his eyes, looked at him, and said with a smile: "You have known for a long time what you must do. You have sense enough: don't give way to drunkenness and incontinence of speech; don't give way to sensual lust; and, above all, to the love of money. And close your taverns. If you can't close all, at least two or three. And above all—don't lie." (43)

Zosima doesn't decide *for* Fyodor. In his attentiveness to the old man—he has "scrutinized" Fyodor "in silence" (41)—he can see that Fyodor himself knows the right path: "*You* have known yourself for a long time what you must do." He respects Fyodor's capacity to change but also reminds him of his concrete responsibility. Like an astute therapist, Zosima doesn't advise a sudden reversal, an absolute end to Fyodor's previous way of life. Realistically, he counsels that Fyodor start with small steps: "If you can't close all [your taverns], at least two or three." He emphasizes the absolute importance of telling the truth, even as he models a down-to-earth sense of humor: he offers his counsel with a "smile" and, as he departs to visit the women, turns to Fyodor "with a cheerful face" as he chides: "don't you tell lies all the same'" (45).

Outside Zosima then encounters five peasant women. With each he is both empathic yet direct. Aware of his limited time—"I am ill and I know that my days are numbered," he tells the visiting monk (53)—he doesn't dally. In fact, in two instances he turns to a woman even as the other is still talking: "but the elder *had already turned away* to very old woman" (49); "But the elder *had already noticed* in the crowd two glowing eyes fixed upon him" (49; emphasis added). He is not being disrespectful or stinting his attentiveness. Actively empathetic, Zosima enters into each woman's particular experience without ever losing his own place outside her—including his sense of the limits of time. Rather than imposing his authority, he discerns and validates the self-understanding and wishes of the women themselves.

The first encounter is wordless. Zosima simply rests his stole on the "shrieking" woman's forehead, prays, and "she was at once soothed and quieted" (46). The reader recalls the woman who touches the hem of Christ's garment and is healed of her twelve-year hemorrhage (Matt 9:20). Zosima's reflection of Christ's image deepens when the narrator recalls his childhood witnessing of the "strange and instant healing" of frenzied women led before the sacrament of the Eucharist, which his secular parents had dismissed "as pretense and even trickery on the part of the 'clericals.'" Although the narrator now accepts that the healings as genuine, he interprets them naturalistically, as "aroused by the expectation of the miracle of healing and the implicit belief that it would come to pass" (46). In the context of the novel as a whole, however, Zosima's tactile encounter with the shrieking woman suggests less placebo or projection as a genuine mediation of grace, analogous to the grace present in the Eucharist. Zosima teaches that transformation takes time, but Dostoevsky's capacious "both/and" vision leaves room for "sudden"—if temporary—healings like this one. The woman has "been brought to [Zosima] before," and will likely be brought there again. The sacramental life is quotidian.

The second woman bears a profound sorrow that foreshadows Snegiryov's in the latter half of the novel. Nastasya and her husband Nikita have suffered the loss of all four of their children. Their youngest, Alexey, has just died at the age of three. To describe the woman's "ruptured grief,"[163] the narrator uses a form of the word *nadryv* or "laceration": "Lamentations comfort only by lacerating the heart still more. Such grief does not want consolation, it feeds on the sense of its unquenchableness. Lamentations is simply the need to constantly irritate the wound" (47). The woman, however, does not suffer from the kind of *nadryv* we see in Mikhail and others. She "crav[es] to reopen the wound," but not for dramatic effect before the sight of others. Her lacerating grief tempts her to cut herself off from everyone, including her husband, Nikita: "I've done with them all. . . . I don't care to see anything at all!" At first Zosima is too quick to console. He quotes a saint who had counselled a similarly-bereft mother to rejoice, "for thy little one is with the Lord in the fellowship of angels." Zosima believes the words he speaks, but they offer a balm too-quickly-offered, much like her husband's. When Zosima realizes this, he tactfully adjusts, slows down, and accepts her lacerating grief as it is. His next words are not spoken from above, but come across to her as he validates her need to grieve. But he also discerns and enters into her deep wish *not* to be alone and to *not* leave her husband. After all, she has travelled two hundred miles to see Zosima, and has already visited three other monasteries in her "pilgrimage." Further, and especially revealing, she remembers and speaks of "*my* Nikitushka" (48; emphasis added) whom she had left three months earlier. Zosima's concluding words frankly name her spousal desertion as "a sin." But Nastasya senses how deeply Zosima wishes *with* her when he exhorts: "Go to your husband, mother; go this very day." His penetrated word touches her own "deepest I": "I will go, Father, at your word. I will go. You've gone straight to my heart. My Nikitushka, my Nikitushka, you are waiting for me, my dear,' the woman began in a singsong voice, but the elder had already turned away to a very old woman, dressed like a dweller in the town, not like a pilgrim" (49).

This older woman's son is alive. But having heard no word from him for a year, Prokhorovna is tempted to pray for him *as if* he were dead, as if to use God as a means of sending her son a spiritual nudge. Here Zosima's authority takes a sterner form, as the occasion calls for it. He chides her for considering "a great sin, akin to sorcery" (49): the "sorcery" she considers resembles the magic that the Grand Inquisitor misnames as "miracle."[164] Although Zosima admonishes her for confusing the two, he also speaks to her deepest wishes, both as mother and believer. Calling her by name, attending to her personhood, he offers her a promise infused with a glimpse of mystery: "And another thing I will tell you, Prokhorovna: either he will soon come back to you, your son, or he will be sure to send a letter. Go, and henceforward be in peace. Your son is alive, I tell you" (49). When the chastised woman arrives home, she does indeed receive a letter from her son announcing his immanent arrival—an event that comprises what, ironically, Madame Khokhlakova *insists* is "a miracle of prediction" (147).

Zosima's next confessional dialogue concerns a graver matter. He "notice[s] in the crowd two glowing eyes fixed upon him" (49) and invites the young peasant woman to approach. The previous woman had resisted awareness of her guilt, but this woman is almost consumed by hers. Three years ago, she had murdered her abusive husband. Zosima quickly perceives the gravity of the woman's story, and, prudently, draws closer to her. In order to hear her confession, he physically descends, sits beside her to shield her from uttering her sin publicly. Zosima discerns that she is threatened less by her sin—which she has already confessed numerous times—as by her despair that she can ever be forgiven. She has finalized herself *as* her sin. Like any good confessor, Zosima exercises prudential casuistry by attending to the particulars of her situation: She is an abused woman who has committed the sin of murder in self-defense. He assists in restoring her "good taste of self" by recalling her to the reality of God's forgiveness: "There is no sin, and there can be no sin on all the earth, which the Lord will not forgive to the truly repentant! Man cannot commit a sin so great as to exhaust the infinite love of God. . . . Believe that God loves you as you cannot conceive; that He loves you with your sin, in your sin" (50). His words quell her obsessive compulsion to confess. Silently, she accepts his blessing and gift of "a little icon" (50).[165]

In the final encounter, Zosima shows that he is capable of *receiving* a gift as well as giving it (in contrast to Ivan who "bitterly sense[s]" (24) and resists the gifts of others).[166] A healthy "good humored" peasant woman, carrying her baby, has travelled four miles just to see if the elder is healthy, and to extend her good wishes. Satisfied, she confidently—and comically—predicts that Zosima will live for years. Generously, she gives him sixty kopecks for "someone poorer than [she]" (51). Two mornings later, Zosima remembers her "widow's mite" (Luke 21:1), her "onion" when he confirms that Porfiry has imparted the kopecks to "a widow, whose house had burned down lately, and who after the fire had gone with her children begging alms" (246)—the very scene Mitya experiences in his dream of "the babe" (427–28). Zosima accepts her gift with thanks, love, and a blessing before he makes his way to "the separate area set aside for women of rank" (45).

Here he meets Madame Khokhlakova—widowed mother, landowner, self-dramatist, and "lady of little faith." As he did with Fyodor, Zosima discerns in her the corrosive effects of the sideward glance. But he also models the way a good confessor can help turn a confessant from self-enclosed *nadryv* and toward responsiveness to others. Khokhlakova confesses her doubts about the afterlife, and then casts her sideward glance at Zosima. "Oh, God, what will you think of me now!" she cries. (53). Zosima cautions her: "Don't distress yourself about my opinion of you. . . . I fully believe in the sincerity of your suffering." And he advises that her faith will recover through the "labor and fortitude" of active love (55). But—in a preview of Ivan's insistence that Christ-like love is impossible (204–5)—Khokhlakova defensively declares that she is incapable of active love because she demands recognition and thanks for her good deeds. Her tirade concludes with a glare that fiercely demands Zosima to show "approbation for [her] frankness" (55). Even as she *defies* Zosima and asserts her independence from his judgment she reveals her *dependence* upon it. Furious "self-castigation" (54) lies at the root of *both* impulses. Like the Underground Man, Madame Khokhlakova's sense of personhood deteriorates through self-laceration, through the pleasurable, public self-hurt of *nadryv*. She fantasizes becoming a "sister of mercy," but her dreams cease when she considers the prospect of non-appreciation:

> "'Would your love continue, or not?' And imagine, I understood with a shudder: if there is anything that could immediately cool my 'active love for humanity' it's ingratitude. In a word, I work for pay, and demand my payment at once, that is, praise for myself, and love paid for with love. Otherwise I'm incapable of loving anyone."
>
> She was in a very paroxysm of self-castigation, and, concluding, she looked with defiant resolution at the elder. (54)

Her image augurs later paroxysms of perversely "defiant resolution": Mikhail about to kill Zosima; the Grand Inquisitor's with Christ: "Be angry. I don't want thy love" (223); Ivan's before Alyosha: "will you renounce me for that, yes?" (229); and the "proud, fierce" souls in hell who "curse God who calls them" (279).

Calmly, with his characteristic sense of humor, Zosima defuses her fury by telling the story of the doctor who'd come to similar self-knowledge.[167] Simultaneously, he disarms her dramatic flourish—"I'm the worst person ever!"; "No, actually, you're not"—while implicitly suggesting that her "distress" is spiritually healthier than the doctor's cynical and "bitter jest." He acknowledges her unease, but then, with a chilling image, cautions her from continuing to seek his approval: "If you have been talking to me so sincerely, simply to gain approbation for your frankness, as you did from me just now, then of course you will not attain to anything in the achievement of real love; it will all get no further than dreams, and your whole life will slip away like a phantom" (55). Ravenously seeking others' commendation diminishes personhood to phantasm. Zosima's prophecy penetrates her: "You have crushed me!" Zosima continues by exhorting her to remain "on the right road" of active love, "harsh and dreadful" as it may be, and to avoid that which is at the root of the sidelong glance and *nadryv*, "being scornful, both to others and to yourself" (55). Zosima's words prove efficacious, if only for the moment. Madame Khokhlakova weeps and turns her attention to her adolescent daughter: "'Lise, Lise! Bless her—bless her!' she cried, starting up suddenly" (56). She makes a small step of active love.

And in "twenty-five minutes" (56), Zosima has touched the lives of six women.[168]

Zosima and Ivan, Dmitri, and Alyosha

Back inside, Zosima words and silent gestures bring Ivan, Dmitri, and Alyosha to deeper self-knowledge and awareness of the conflict and challenge each will face in the course of the novel. In their encounters with Zosima, the trajectory of Ivan's, Dmitri's, and Alyosha's paths commence and will eventually converge.

When Zosima and Alyosha return to the cell, the others are discussing Ivan's article on the ecclesiastical court. Zosima "look[s] keenly and intently at Ivan Fyodorovich" when Father Iosif describes Ivan's article as an "argument that cuts both ways" (57). We have been told that Alyosha has earlier "dreaded any affront" to Zosima in the form of Ivan's "supercilious half-utterances" (34). Ivan's split utterances suggest his self-division. He won't commit to his own arguments; he resists *signing* for his convictions. Zosima's attentiveness and careful questions foster Ivan's passage toward a more integral sense of self.

Zosima asks if it is Ivan's "conviction" that without faith in immortality, there can be no virtue. Ivan balks at committing himself, and calls it his "contention" (65). Zosima's response respects Ivan's complexity: "You are blessed in believing that, or else most unhappy" (65). Ivan's question reveals his condition: "Why unhappy?" He asks it with a rare smile, without any superciliousness. Neither interlocutor asserts himself above the other. Zosima discerns the appropriate moment, and articulates his insight into Ivan's spiritual struggle. Ivan, "flushing quickly," "suddenly and strangely confess[es]" that he "wasn't altogether joking" in either his articles or his thesis. The word "strange" is applied three times to Ivan in this scene (65). His strangeness—which surprises Alyosha—lies in his growing openness to Zosima. He denies that his utterances are "altogether joking"; his irony may be unstable, but isn't self-consuming.[169] Zosima agrees, but also observes that Ivan's writing may be diverting him from his deeper "despair."

Ivan's despair results from his inability to commit, to say "I believe," or to have the humility to acknowledge his desire to do so, or, like the father of the possessed child, to pray, "I believe, help my unbelief" (Mark 9:24).[170] Zosima sees Ivan's longing: "That question you have not answered and it is your great grief for it clamors for an answer" (61). Ivan's next question reveals his wish to believe, but also his desire that Zosima answer the question for him: "'But can it be answered by me? Answered in the affirmative?' Ivan Fyodorovich went on asking strangely, still looking at the elder with the same inexplicable smile." The elder's authority is rooted in respect for Ivan's personhood, and he proffers no definitive answer. He will not relieve Ivan of his burden of freedom. Instead, Zosima points to the promise of the possible, and thus to the virtue of hope as the exit from despair. Kenotically, he *wishes with* Ivan, and prays for him:

> "If it can't be decided in the affirmative, it will never be decided in the negative. You know that that is the peculiarity of your heart, and all its torment is due to it. But thank the Creator who gave you a lofty heart capable of such suffering; 'of thinking and seeking higher things, for our dwelling is in the heavens.' God grant that your heart will attain the answer on earth, and may God bless your path!"
>
> The elder raised his hand and would have made the sign of the cross over Ivan Fyodorovich from where he stood. But the latter rose from his seat, went up to him, received his blessing, kissed his hand, and went back to his place in silence. His face looked firm and earnest. This action and all the preceding conversation, which was so surprising from Ivan Fyodorovich, impressed everyone by its strangeness and a certain solemnity, so that all were silent for a moment, and there was a look almost of fear in Alyosha's face. (66)

Ivan's confessional dialogue with Zosima restores his "good taste of self." Although he will tack between belief and disbelief, his walk here is not crooked, with his left shoulder higher than his right (230). He doesn't speak in "supercilious half-utterances." His steps are "firm" as—silently, humbly, and resolutely—he walks to Zosima, receives the gift of his blessing, and kisses the holy man's hand. Yes, the epiphanic moment passes. Realism accepts that such moments always do and that it's folly to try to willfully sustain them. Fyodor smears the solemnity of the moment by re-erupting in buffoonery. And Ivan takes note: his silent ride home with his father is chilling and premonitory. But if Zosima's blessing of Ivan is not apocalyptically transformative, its effects are hardly ephemeral. The seed is sown, and its fruits can be seen in Ivan's later dialogues with Alyosha and, in his final scene in the novel: his fractured public confession.[171]

With Fyodor's resurgent buffoonery, Father Zosima's attention turns to the old man's conflict with his eldest son. He "watch[es] them intently as though trying to make out something which was not perfectly clear to him" (68). As he explains to Alyosha the next day, Zosima had discerned Mitya's murderous rage, and anguish that will follow from it:

> I bowed down yesterday to the great suffering in store for him. . . . I seemed to see something terrible yesterday . . . as though his whole future were expressed in his eyes . . . so that I was instantly horror-stricken at what that man is preparing for himself. Once

or twice in my life I've seen such a look in a man's face . . . reflecting as it were his future fate, and that fate, alas, came to pass. (246-47)

"Nothing is more seductive for man than his freedom of conscience, but nothing is a greater cause of suffering," claims the Grand Inquisitor (221). Zosima apprehends Mitya's tormented conscience, his regret for his past cruelties, his anticipation of further violence. Mitya "secretly blame[s] himself for his outbursts of temper with his father on several recent occasions" (34). In Zosima's cell, he painfully recalls his mistreatment of Captain Snegiryov: "I behaved like a brute to that captain, and I regret it now, and am disgusted with myself for my brutal rage" (67). Baited by his father, imploding before Zosima, he reveals his murderous desires: "'Why is such a man alive?' Dmitri Fyodorovich, beside himself with rage, growling in a hollow voice, hunching up his shoulders till he looked almost deformed. 'Tell me, can he be allowed to go on defiling the earth?'" (69) Mitya is "broad" (98), capable of ferocious cruelty and genuine contrition. In that "broadness"—a person's unfinalizable capacity to choose good or evil—lies his freedom of conscience and consequent agony.[172] Zosima foresees Mitya's temptation to kill his father, and the torment of conscience that will follow if he succumbs to that temptation. But unlike the Grand Inquisitor, Zosima doesn't try to strip Mitya of his anguished freedom, to "narrow" (98) him by imposing a course of action. His silent bow is kenotic and prophetic. It reveals Zosima's respect for Mitya's freedom, the gravity of the deed he contemplates, and the path of penitence he foresees:

> The elder rose suddenly from his seat. Almost distracted with anxiety for the elder and everyone else, Alyosha succeeded, however, in supporting him by the arm. The elder moved towards Dmitri Fyodorovich and reaching him sank on his knees before him. Alyosha thought that he had fallen from weakness, but this was not so. The elder distinctly and deliberately bowed down at Dmitri Fyodorovich's feet till his forehead touched the floor. Alyosha was so astounded that he failed to assist him when he got up again. There was a faint smile on his lips.
>
> "Goodbye! Forgive me, all of you!" he said, bowing on all sides to his guests.
>
> Dmitri Fyodorovich stood for a few moments in amazement. Bowing down to him—what did it mean? Suddenly he cried aloud, "Oh God!" hid his face in his hands, and rushed out of the room. (69-70)

Mitya's response, racked as it is, can be read as a counterpart to Ivan's "firm and earnest" receiving of Zosima's blessing. As he did with Ivan, Zosima has actively entered into Mitya's suffering, touched his "deepest I," and mediates the gift of hope. If Ivan can begin to see his way past religious despair, Mitya can see an exit from what seems to be the finality of his Oedipal fate. Zosima has penetrated his self-sufficiency of rage, and opened him to grace, to faith in a "miracle of Divine Providence," as Mitya avows when he confesses to Alyosha in the gazebo later that day (109).

The lovingly attentive quality of Zosima's bow can be more clearly understood when contrasted with Mitya's bow to Katerina. Mitya describes the moment to Alyosha at the gazebo later that day. When Katerina had come to his room to offer herself in order to save her father, Mitya's "broadness" is fully evident. He looked at Katerina with "that hate which is only a hairsbreadth from love, from the maddest love!"; the ice on the frozen window pane "burn[s] his forehead like fire" (103). From one perspective, Mitya renounces himself and refuses to exploit or insult Katerina. Generous, restrained, he simply gives her the money she desperately needs with noble self-restraint and generosity: "I showed the [banknote] to her in silence, folded it, handed it to her, opened the door into the passage, and, stepping back, made her a deep bow, a most respectful, a most impressive bow, believe me!" (103). Mitya's gesture *is* noble; he seeks to follow his ideal of the Madonna and enact a deed of active love. But, broad as he is, his bow is also infected with pride. He casts a sideward glance at Katerina, as if to say, "Do you *see* how noble I am, you who thought yourself so superior?" His bow becomes pernicious, and his "love" soon lacerates:

> She shuddered all over, gazed at me for a second, turned horribly pale—white as a sheet, in fact—and all at once, not impetuously but softly, gently, bowed down to my feet—not a boarding-school curtsey, but a Russian bow, with her forehead to the floor. She jumped up and ran away. I was wearing my sword. I drew it and nearly stabbed myself with it on the spot; why, I don't know. It would have been frightfully stupid, of course. I suppose it was from delight. Can you understand that one might kill oneself from delight? But I didn't stab myself. I only kissed my sword and put it back in the scabbard—which there is no need to have told you, by the way. (103–4)

Ultimately, Mitya wishes *against* Katerina: he asserts his nobility so she can see it and he can gain his point. His help aims to hurt. At the same time, he wishes *against* his own desire to be noble. His narcissistic impulse to stab himself cuts both ways: it reveals both self-hatred and self-congratulation.

He kisses his own sword before sheathing it, and the absurdly symbolic gesture alleviates the tragic reality. After relating this detail, he admits he could have skipped it. The moment is comic—and suggests the sense of humor Alyosha can elicit in Mitya. But with Katerina Ivanovna Mitya never relaxes, never smiles. They begin their vicious dance of *nadryv* as his "sacrifice" elicits her own reactive, resentful bow. From this point on, she will do all in her power to hurt Dmitri, to out-virtue and "save" him, even to the point of destroying them both.

Zosima's bow before Mitya stands in stark contrast.[173] Zosima wishes *with* Dmitri: he wishes that he might be redeemed from "the great suffering in store for him." Later that afternoon, with Alyosha, Dmitri is able to articulate his wish that, with the help of God, he will renounce violence. Three times, he invokes his faith in "miracles": "I believe in miracles. . . . In a miracle of Divine Providence. God knows my heart. He sees my despair. He sees the whole picture. Surely He won't let something awful happen" (110). Zosima's bow participates in the reality of "Divine Providence": Zosima knows Dmitri's heart, "sees the whole picture," including Dmitri's longing to be good. The mysterious, accruing effects of Zosima's bow can be located in this scene and, crucially, two nights later, when Dmitri stands "in the dark," pestle in hand, outside his father's window—and opens himself to grace: "'God was watching over me then,' Mitya said afterwards" (336). The silent encounter with Zosima sows a seed, and Mitya shakily recovers a "good taste of self."

In the days that follow, Alyosha will serve as a gracious presence for both Mitya and Ivan. When his family has departed, Zosima commissions Alyosha for his work "in the world." Again Zosima attends closely to the person's particular situation. Earlier, he'd observed Alyosha's "awkward" smile upon taking Lise's hand, and then, cornered by her flirtatious gaze, the way he'd tried to hide behind Zosima's robe:[174] "The elder turned round and all at once looked attentively at Alyosha" (52). Zosima returns to his sickbed "exhausted," but his gaze still attentive: "He looked intently at Alyosha, as though considering something" (71). As with Ivan and Mitya, Zosima foresees suffering in Alyosha's future.[175] He discerns that "for the time" Alyosha must "serve" in the world, but as a married man, not a celibate monk:

> "And know, my little son"—the elder liked to call him that—"this is not the place for you in the future. Remember that, young man. As soon as it is God's will to call me, leave the monastery. Go away for good."
> Alyosha started.

> "What is it? This is not your place for the time. I bless you
> for great service in the world. Yours will be a long pilgrimage.
> And you will have to take a wife, too, you will have to. You will
> have to bear all before you come back. There will be much to do.
> But I don't doubt of you, and so I send you forth. *Christ is with
> you. Do not abandon Him and He will not abandon you.* You will
> see great sorrow, and in that sorrow you will be happy. Here is a
> commandment for you: seek happiness in sorrow. Work, work
> unceasingly. Remember my words henceforth, for although I
> shall talk with you again, not only my days but my hours are
> numbered." (71; emphasis added)

In the novel (as often in life), personal vocation is discerned through another's beneficial mediation. Zosima discovers his own vocation through his mediatory memories of Markel and humble Afanasy. With Zosima's help, Alyosha painfully begins to discern his own vocation. Like his mentor, Alyosha has been granted "the gift of 'discernment' (*prozorlivost*)—that is, the ability to perceive within the soul of one who is in anguish 'what was in his mind, what he needed, and even what kind of suffering tormented his conscience'" (Connolly, "Confession" 26). Such discernment is integral to the confessor's practice of prudence, which apprehends and responds to the reality of a confessant's particular situation. Zosima grants Alyosha an indelible image of the way a confessor can assist a confessant in discerning and turning toward active love and away from willful destruction of self and others. Like his mentor, Alyosha will serve as a pastoral counselor and confessor—but "in the world" (247). The chapters that follow will trace Alyosha's development in his vocation, his "unceasing work" of helping others to reject lacerating habits, to open themselves to the "hidden ground of love," and practice active love through embodied, responsible action.

Chapter 4

Alyosha's First Three Days

Mentored by Zosima, Alyosha takes up the elder's mantle. The novel's main narrative thread traces his quotidian development as "a monk in the world" (247).[176] *The Brothers Karamazov* transpires over and is structured around six clearly delineated days: Parts One, Two, and Three each comprise one day in late August. Part Four and the Epilogue comprise three days in early November—another trinitarian marker in novel with many: three thousand rubles, Dmitri's three torments, Ivan's three interviews with Smerdyakov, Zosima's odor of corruption that becomes evident "before three o'clock in the afternoon" (285). As the most important number in Christian numerology, the symbolic importance of three is as important to Dostoevsky as it was for Dante.[177] But like Dante, Dostoevsky never allows a symbol to bleach away the literal. Each passing minute, hour, and day presses upon Alyosha.[178] Like his mentor, he is aware of and respects the limits of time.

The narrator-chronicler makes clear that Alyosha is the novel's "hero" (7, 292), but his heroism lies in his daily work of active love, his capacity to quell the destructive impulses of others. The practice of active love takes time, is "harsh and dreadful." Alyosha faces painful setbacks and surprises. But by the end of the third day in August, at the end of Book 7, Alyosha "[rises] up a resolute champion" (312), committed to his calling. Zosima has prepared Alyosha for impediments, and the suffering they bring: "you will go forth from these walls, but will live like a monk in the world. You will have many enemies, but even your foes will love you. Life will bring you many misfortunes, but you will find your happiness in them, and will bless life and make others bless it—which is what matter most. Well, that is your character" (247). Through the daily "misfortunes" and graces of three days, Alyosha grows in maturity and prudence.

From the start, the narrator-chronicler emphasizes that Alyosha respects the personhood of others by refusing to judge, to foreclose their freedom: "There was something about him which made one feel at once (and it was so all his life afterwards) that he did not care to be a judge of others—that he would never take it upon himself to censure and would never condemn anyone for anything" (22). His father tells him: "I feel that you're the only one in the world who has not condemned me" (27).[179] But Alyosha also has good judgment: unlike Prince Myshkin, he can discern the time to take decisive action, and take it. The narrator describes him as "more of a realist than anyone" (28), and we see this as he completes one task to get on with another. Before the action of the novel, he had been moved by a deeply felt intuition to announce his departure to his benefactors—his "accidental family"[180]—and return to the home of his neglectful father. It's not as if he acts from complete certainty: he desires to visit his mother's tomb, but beyond that, accepts the uncertainty of his future: "it is more probable that he himself did not understand and could not explain what had suddenly arisen in his soul, and drawn him irresistibly into a new, unknown, but inevitable path" (24). After he is home for a while, he suddenly announces to Fyodor that "he want[s] to enter the monastery" (26). Here the narrator acknowledges that Alyosha will need to mature in the course of the novel: although he passionately desires to serve "the truth"—and prudence always seeks the truth—his desire to "sacrifice" his life in *this* way will prove impetuous:

> Some will say, perhaps, that Alyosha was stupid, undeveloped, had not finished his studies, and so on. That he did not finish his studies is true, but to say that he was stupid or dull would be a great injustice. I'll simply repeat what I have said above. He entered upon this path only because, at that time, it alone struck his imagination and presented itself to him as offering an ideal means of escape for his soul from darkness to light. Add to that that he was to some extent a youth of our last epoch—that is, honest in nature, desiring the truth, seeking for it and believing in it, and seeking to serve it at once with all the strength of his soul, seeking for immediate action, and ready to sacrifice everything, life itself, for it. Though these young men unfortunately fail to understand that the sacrifice of life is, perhaps, the easiest of all sacrifices, and that to sacrifice, for instance five or six years of their seething youth to hard and tedious study, if only to multiply tenfold their powers of serving the truth and the cause they have set before them as their goal—such a sacrifice is utterly

beyond the strength of many of them. The path Alyosha chose
was a path going in the opposite direction, but he chose it with
the same thirst for swift achievement. (28)

Tellingly, the narrator emphasizes that the monastery serves as Alyosha's "escape": "The monastic path . . . struck him, so to speak, with the ideal escape for his soul struggling from the darkness of worldly wickedness to the light of love" (21). But "worldly wickedness" extends to the monastery, too, as Alyosha will see it in his family's disruptive visit, Father Ferapont's showy and resentful asceticism, the actions of "surly" (148) and fickle monks, and his own rebellion upon the death and dishonor of his beloved elder. Alyosha is not yet ready to embrace the slow, arduous labor required by active love. He wants "immediate action" and "thirst[s] for swift achievement" (28).[181] Nor does he yet discern that holiness manifests itself in others besides Zosima. The elder stands as "a solitary example" (33), and he identifies with him too exclusively, and perhaps with a degree of projection, rejoices in his "fame, in his glory, as though it were his own triumph" (32).

By the end of three long days, Alyosha will experience his own triumph as he gradually embraces his task of "great service" (71) as "a monk in the world" (247), the vocation for which Zosima has blessed him. He learns to better help others anguished by the burden of freedom and self-imposed laceration. He evinces a willingness to persevere *through* the accumulating, often unexpected challenges of everyday life, and the pain wrought by his own mistakes.

Alyosha's First Day: The Oppressiveness of the World

On Alyosha's first day "in the world," "worldly wickedness" nearly overwhelms him. He is saddened by Zosima's commission: "he had a great longing to remain" in the monastery; "It was long since Alyosha had known such anguish" (72). His distress deepens when he receives Katerina's urgent entreaty (92) to see her. Despite his dimly understood "fear of a woman," he refuses to be paralyzed by indecision, for "that was not his way" (92). In this image, we discern not only Alyosha's decisiveness, but the way the novel consistently envisions the way mystery is manifest in the mundane:

Standing still for a minute, he reached a final decision. Crossing himself with a rapid and accustomed gesture, and, at once smiling, he turned resolutely in the direction of his terrible lady. . . .

> [H]e decided to take a short cut by the back-way, for he knew every inch of the ground. This meant skirting fences, climbing over wattle-fences, and crossing other people's back-yards, where everyone he met knew him and greeted him. In this way he could reach Main Street in half the time. (93)

Before making a difficult decision, Alyosha prays. In signing himself with the cross, habitual as that gesture may be, he evinces his wish to be conformed to Christ. He makes a decision, and exercises practical wisdom in his action: time is tight, so he takes a shortcut to Katerina's house.

But *phronesis* entails readiness before the unexpected, and a willingness to revise one's plan. As Alyosha cuts through the garden, he runs into Mitya drinking in the gazebo and thirsting to talk. Alyosha has his plan and grows impatient. But Mitya pleads with him to *listen*: "Listen, Alyosha, listen, brother! Now I mean to tell you everything, for I must tell someone" (95). Alyosha's initial response to Mitya evinces his respect for closure, for "boundaries": he's made a decision and wants to get on with it: "I will do it, but tell me what it is and quickly" (96). But when he discerns the intensity of Mitya's request, he makes himself fully *available* to his brother,[182] who urgently needs to speak. "Alyosha made up his mind to wait. He felt that, perhaps, indeed, his work lay here" (96). Alyosha's decision represents a key moment in his development of prudence, his apprehension of and response to the real.

"Alyosha listen[s] with great attention" (100) to Mitya's "confessions of an ardent heart." When he senses that his brother is evading the truth, he reminds him of his resolution to "tell [him] everything": "Mitya, I know you will tell the whole truth" (103). By the end of his three-part confession, Mitya evinces the accruing, healing effects of others' attention—Zosima's bow, Alyosha's listening presence: three times he avows his belief "in miracles," specifically "a miracle of Divine Providence" (109), his faith "that God will order things for the best, that nothing awful may happen'" (110). But he remains divided: his face "frenzied," he hints at his capacity for parricide, which hours later he comes close to enacting when he hits Grigory, flings Fyodor to the ground and kicks him "two or three times with his heel in the face" (125). Alyosha's intervention at the gazebo is inconclusive, and he departs from Mitya "in deep thought" (110).

Despite his growing sense of oppression, Alyosha sustains his balance of openness and closure during his next stop, his father's house, where Dmitri has requested him to make an appeal. Joining the "controversy" at the table, his father baits him: "'Alyosha, do you believe I am nothing but a buffoon?' 'I believe that you are more than just a buffoon'" (119–20). Like the narrator in the first chapter, Alyosha refuses to finalize his father. He affirms his father's untapped capacities: "Your heart is better than your head" (121). But he also recognizes the responsibility people have for their words and actions. When asked to assess Smerdyakov's defense of apostasy (which Fyodor calls "casuistry"), Alyosha responds "firmly and gravely," "'No, Smerdyakov's faith is not Russian at all'" (117). He reproaches his father firmly for berating Ivan: "'Don't be angry with my brother. Leave off attacking him,' Alyosha suddenly said emphatically" (122). And when Mitya violently bursts inside, Alyosha is commanding: "'Dmitri! Go away at once!'" (125).

Practicing prudential realism, refusing to condemn persons, even as he calls them to responsibility, Alyosha's authentic authority accrues. Consistently, others will approach and confide in him. Even Fyodor "can't resist the way he looks one straight in the face and laughs" (111), and, in one of his best and most honest moments, tells Alyosha that he is "the only one [he is] not afraid of" (126). Ivan too shakes his hand "warmly" and "take[s] the first step toward him" (128).[183] Later in the day, Alyosha will relieve Mitya of suicidal thoughts and inspire his declaration of love for "that little man, my dear little brother, whom I love more than anyone in the world" (136).

Nevertheless, as much as others turn to him for counsel, Alyosha feels overwhelmed by "worldly wickedness." After putting his injured father to bed, he hears Ivan's promise to protect their father even as he nurtures a wish for his death. Ivan's self-division will result in his murderous complicity. Alyosha senses this, and as he leaves his father's house feels

> even more exhausted and dejected in spirit than when he had entered it. His mind too seemed shattered and unhinged, while he felt that he was afraid to put together the disjointed fragments and form a general idea from all the agonizing and conflicting experiences of the day. He felt something bordering upon despair, which he had never known till then. Towering like a mountain above all the rest stood the fatal insoluble question: How would things end between his father and his brother Dmitri with this terrible woman? (128)

Near the end of this first day, Alyosha feels shattered and fragmented. But he perseveres. By the end of his *third* day he will no longer feel as he does now, fearing the need "to put together the disjointed fragments." Instead, in a textual rhyme, a "sense of the wholeness of things" will come to him as a gift, as "fragments of thought [float] through his soul . . . like stars" (309). Alyosha will remain "eccentric" but not as "a particularity and . . . separate element" (7). Rather, as the narrator puts it in his Preface, Alyosha will emerge as one who "*carries within himself the very heart of the whole*" (7; emphasis added).

But he's not there yet. At Katerina's house, the exhibitionist and ma-nipulative power play that she and Grushenka enact leaves him "reeling" (135).[184] Then, in the dark, just hours after Mitya nearly kicks his father to death, he startles Alyosha with his "stick 'em up" antics. With this stunt, Alyosha "beg[ins] to cry" as "something seem[s] to snap in his soul" (136).

The weight he bears corrodes Alyosha's capacities, specifically his will-ingness to keep his word with others. On the way back to the monastery, he promises himself that he will see Mitya the next day: "Tomorrow I will be sure to see him and find him, I will make a point of finding him . . ." (138). He's made other commitments for the following day: he's told his father he will see him in the morning, and has implicitly agreed to see Ivan and Katerina. But upon entering Father Zosima's cell, he longs to remain: "'Why, why had he gone forth? Why had he sent him into the world? Here was peace. Here was holiness. But there was confusion, there was gloom in which one lost one's way and went astray at once . . .'" (138–39). Father Paissy, whom Alyosha has not yet recognized as another mentor, reminds Alyosha that his work is to be found in just such "confusion" and "gloom." Paissy recalls Zosima's commission: "'I blessed him for that work,' he said, 'his place is there, not here, for awhile'" (139). At the end of a hard first day, Alyosha rejects his work. He yearns to remain near Zosima:

> Father Paissy went out. Alyosha had no doubt that Father Zosi-ma was dying, though he might live another day or two. Alyosha firmly and ardently resolved that in spite of his promises to his father, the Khokhlakovas, and Katerina Ivanovna, he would not leave the monastery next day, but would remain with his elder to the end. His heart glowed with love, and he reproached himself bitterly for having been able for one instant to forget him whom he had left in the monastery on his deathbed, and whom he honored above everyone in the world. (139-40)

Having observed his blushed response to Lise's flirtation, Zosima has intuited and told Alyosha that he must "take a wife" (71). Fittingly, it's Lise's letter that unexpectedly calls him to return to his vocation as a monk in the world. Before falling asleep he reads her declaration of love and request that he visit the next day. Her voice recalls him to responsibility—to her and others outside the monastery's walls. Reading it renews his capacity to laugh "softly and happily." Agitation quelled, nearing sleep, he recommences his vocation by praying for "all these unhappy and turbulent souls." He re-members his commitments to others, and entrusts them to God's gracious "mercy" (141).

Alyosha's Second Day: In the Face of Laceration

"Before daybreak," liminally drawn between consciousness and a dream of the previous days' spectacle at Katerina's, Alyosha cries out the word that comprises the title of Book 4, "*nadryv*,": "laceration, laceration, probably applying it to his dream" (164). *Nadryv* marks each encounters that Alyosha faces in the coming day, his second as a monk in the world. The first day demanded "labor and fortitude." So will the second as he again intervenes and strives to interrupt the destructive cycles of others. But in at least two instances—Katerina's and Captain Snegiryov's—Alyosha's interventions seems to *intensify* destructive emotions rather than quell them. In response, Alyosha keenly feels his failure. But he never gives up. By day's end he again hastens back to the monastery. But difficult experience has deepened his prudential capacity. We see signs of his development in his final dialogues of the day—his "Engagement" with Lise and his response to Ivan's "rebellion" at the Metropolis.

Upon awakening from his unsettling dream, Alyosha prefers to remain with his beloved elder. But Zosima insists that Alyosha must begin again his service in the world. Standing beside the elder, Alyosha hears—perhaps for the first time—Zosima's keynote call to responsibility: "every one of us is undoubtedly responsible for all men and for everything on the earth, not merely through the general sinfulness of creation, but each one personally for all men and for all mankind and every individual man" (146). "Attached" to Zosima (21), Alyosha wants to shield himself within the monastery. Zosima perceives this, and his authentic authority restores Alyosha's freedom, his capacity to make—and keep—promises:

> The elder, opening his weary eyes and looking intently at Alyosha, asked him suddenly:
> "Are your people expecting you, my son?"
> Alyosha hesitated.
> "Don't they need you? Didn't you promise someone yesterday to see them today?"
> "I did promise . . . to my father . . . my brothers . . . others too."
> "You see, you must go. Don't grieve. Be sure I shall not die without your being by to hear my last word. To you I will say that word, my son, it will be my last gift to you. To you, dear son, because you love me. But now go to keep your promise."
> Alyosha immediately obeyed, though it was hard to go.
> (151)

Their encounter suggests the paradoxical relationship between authority and freedom. Earlier, the narrator had explained the authority inherent to the position of elder:

> An elder was one who took your soul, your will, into his soul and his will. When you choose an elder, you renounce your own will and yield it to him in complete submission, complete self-abnegation. This ordeal, this terrible school of abnegation, is undertaken voluntarily, in the hope of self-conquest, of self-mastery, in order, after such a long ordeal, to attain perfect freedom, that is, from self; to escape the lot of those who have lived their whole life without *finding their true selves in themselves.* (30; emphasis added)

Zosima's authority is born of his attentiveness to the reality of Alyosha's "true self," his deep wish to serve others. The kenotic authority of his spiritual father fosters resilience—Alyosha's capacity to persevere through setbacks and temporal limits. In the process, Alyosha "grows in strength and wisdom" (cf. Luke 2:40).

A visit with his biological father commences his second day "in the world." Alyosha asks how he is doing after his beating the day before (153). Sensibly, he suggests that he lie down and stop drinking brandy (154). Alyosha's attention contrasts with his father's irritable self-absorption, evidenced by Fyodor's anxious, distracted glances in the mirror (153). Fyodor asks about Zosima's condition, but he "had not even listened, and had forgotten his own question at once" (153). As usual, Alyosha's loving presence diminishes Fyodor's vindictiveness: "Only with you I have good moments"; "I love you even without the brandy" (154). But when Alyosha relates his brother's plea for three thousand rubles, Fyodor responds much as Ivan will at the mention of Mitya: "'I want my money myself, . . . I'll crush him like a cockroach without it. . . . But he will not have Grushenka, sir; anyway, he will not, sir. . . . I'll throw him in the mud.' His anger had returned with the last words" (155). In his competitive rage, Fyodor would destroy his own son to get the woman he lusts after. But his actions are also self-destructive. In his buffoonery at the monastery, he willfully played a role to spite his audience and himself.[185] His raging mimetic rivalry[186] with Dmitri also entails playing a false role. His lies and anger even harden his heart toward Alyosha, the one person who lends him that "good taste of self" which he can least afford to eradicate: "'You can go. There's nothing for you to do here today' he snapped harshly" (155). As he will with each person he encounters during the day, Alyosha responds with love: "Alyosha went up to say good-bye to him, and kissed him on the shoulder" (155). For a moment, Alyosha's silent kiss restores the bitter man's capacity to love. The gratuitous affectionate gesture takes Fyodor by surprise. Out of long habit, he quickly imputes a self-interested motive to a freely given gift: "What's that for?" The moment is telling: So much in this novel returns the reader to this central question: *How do I respond to a gift that is freely given? Do I accept it with humility and gratitude, or do I project my defensive egotism and refuse it?*[187] With a sense of foreboding, his father entreats him to return the next day. But Alyosha's graced kiss will be the last one that Fyodor ever receives. Later, that evening, Alyosha will kiss Ivan in imitation of the kenotic Christ imagined by Ivan in his Grand Inquisitor poem.

In the next episode, Alyosha's non-violent response to little Ilyusha is especially Christ-like. He shields himself from the boy's stones, but refuses to counter with force. At first, his kenotic image allays Ilyusha's violence: "Alyosha stopped two steps in front of him, looking inquiringly at him. The boy, seeing at once from Alyosha's eyes that he wouldn't beat him, became less defiant, and addressed him first" (158). Ilyusha deeply *wants* to speak to Alyosha. He has no one with whom to share his agony about his father's public shaming. He senses that Alyosha will listen, and initiates their dialogue. But by seeing Alyosha only as "a Karamazov," a brother of the bully who shamed his father, Ilyusha's virtuous pride is twisted: his sideward glance senses Alyosha's sympathy, but defiantly *insists* that Alyosha adjust his vision and see him as an autonomous defender of family honor. When Alyosha compassionately observes that he must be hurt by the stones thrown by the other boys, Ilyusha pushes Alyosha's line of vision away from vulnerability to victory: "But I hit Smurov on the head!" He demands that Alyosha see his courage, and sees violence as the only way he can do so. Willfully, he incites Alyosha to attack.

Little Ilyusha is divided between vulnerably desiring love and wanting to appear self-sufficient. But in the boy's words and deeds we see the perspicacity of Zosima's counsel that we ought "care for most people exactly as one would for children" (188). Ilyusha's childish defiance aligns him with Ivan and the Grand Inquisitor. His irritated cry, "let me alone!" echoes the Inquisitor's false and lacerating challenge to Christ, "Why dost thou look silently and searchingly at me with Thy mild eyes? Be angry. I don't want Thy love, for I love Thee not" (223). It foreshadows Ivan's vow to "break off all relations" with Alyosha (508). Ilyusha spurns the person whom he recognizes as most loving and whom he most needs. When Alyosha calmly retreats, Ilyusha taunts—"monk in silk trousers!"—and flings stones, one of them "savagely directed . . . at . . . Alyosha's face." When even that elicits no vengeance, "the spiteful child . . . seized his left hand with both of his and bit his middle finger . . . to the bone" (158).

With his furious bite, the boy tries to obliterate Alyosha's loving image and the agonizing self-division it elicits within him. After each attack, he waits defiantly for Alyosha's counterattack. Alyosha's repeated response, "What have I done to you?" echoes God's reproaches from Micah often read or sung at the Good Friday liturgy: "My people, what have I done to you?" (3:6).[188] Alyosha's response also recalls Christ—and our discussion of the Sinai icon—in its balance of both openness and closure. Alyosha empties himself of countervailing force by remaining receptive to the boy's capacity for reconciliation and peace. But he also calls Ilyusha to take responsibility for his violent deeds. His "gentle eyes" and words pierce the boy: he "stare[s] in amazement" at the unexpected gift of Alyosha's grace, cries, and runs away. His "loud tearful wail" (159) recalls Mitya's cry in response to Zosima's loving bow (64) and presages his "terrible, sobbing wail" (630) when he hears the jury's verdict. In a novel that vibrates with scriptural echoes, Ilyusha's wail evokes St. Peter's in the courtyard (Matt 26:75; Luke 22:62): a cry of remorse that opens up the possibility of change and a cessation of the cycle of defiant violence. But change is hard. We can also hear protest and resistance in Ilyusha's wail. Alyosha's realism, here manifested in the infused virtue of patient courage, sows a good seed in Ilyusha that will bear fruit three months later.

His finger bitten to the bone, Alyosha makes his way to Madame Khokhlakova's where his intervention will not be as serenely offered nor prove as penetrating in its effect. Practical as ever, Alyosha loses no time in getting to his next appointment. He's troubled by Ilyusha's "mystery," but "[h]e made up his mind to find him out as soon as he had time to solve this mystery. Just now he had not the time" (159). Virginal Alyosha must now face an erotic triangle: Katerina loves Ivan, but willfully insists upon being Dmitri's wife. Alyosha needs time to understand this; any helpful intervention will require tact. But his prudence will only develop through experience. Summoned by Katerina herself, he wants to help her, even as he "wish[es] with" both brothers whom he loves. But he feels caught in intractable conflict: "[W]ith which of them was Alyosha to sympathize? And what was he to wish for each of them?" (164). He wants certainty but untangling this knot requires that he patiently endure uncertainty:[189]

> Alyosha's heart could not endure uncertainty, because his love was always of an active character. He was incapable of passive love. If he loved anyone, he set to work at once to help him. And to do so it was necessary to set a goal; he must know for certain what was best for each, and having ascertained this it was natural for him to help them both. But instead of a definite

aim, he found nothing but uncertainty and perplexity on all sides. "It was lacerating," as was said just now. But what could he understand even in this "laceration"? He did not understand the first word in this tangle! (164)

Alyosha wants a clear *telos*, but clarity can take time. Patient receptivity is not passivity. Especially in the role of pastoral counsel, a prematurely defined aim, bereft of forbearing attention, can do more harm than good. The attentive counselor empties herself of her own agenda and nurtures what Keats called "negative capability," "being in uncertainties, mysteries, doubts, without any irritable reaching after fact and reason."[190] Alyosha's love for his brothers is real—but, perhaps, *too* active. He needs to find the wisdom discovered in "letting be." His hasty grasping for a "definite aim" stems partly from his anxiety about sexual relationships. The narrator has described Alyosha's schoolboy "wild fanatical modesty and chastity. He could not bear to hear certain words and certain conversations about women" (23). Before Katerina, "Alyosha felt as it were ashamed of his own thoughts and blamed himself when they kept recurring to him during the last month. 'What do I know about love and women and how can I decide such questions?' he thought reproachfully . . ." (164). Alyosha's anxiety, and self-reproach clouds his capacity for prudence.

Not that willful Katya makes it any easier. Much as the "mysterious visitor" had done with Zosima (266), Katerina pushes Alyosha upon an authoritative pedestal, even as she announces "ecstatically" and presumptuously: "I foresee that your decision, your approval, will bring me peace, in spite of all my sufferings, for, after your words, I shall be calm and submit—I foresee it!" (165). Alyosha has begun to perceive the willfulness that motivates Katerina's commitment to Mitya and her genuine desire for Ivan. But in his impatience, Alyosha doesn't help her in coming to this insight *herself*. She wants to break her engagement with Mitya, to shed this lacerating burden, and commit herself to Ivan. Alyosha sees this, and his response is heartfelt but abashed: "'I don't know what you are asking me," said Alyosha, flushing. "'I only know that I love you and at this moment wish for your happiness more than my own! . . . But I know nothing about such affairs,' he suddenly added hurriedly for some reason . . ." (165). Alyosha wishes all well—Katerina, Mitya, and Ivan. But his embarrassment cripples his capacity to speak words that persuade Katerina to respond with honesty.

Katerina vows that she will never abandon Dmitri. She "crie[s] with an outburst of a sort of pale tormented ecstasy . . . in a sort of frenzy." By the end, she is "breathless" (165–66); she takes sensual pleasure, revels in her proclamation.[191] Her paroxysm provides yet another image of perverse, forced assertion of will: an "irresistible feeling" that "compels [her] irresist-ibly" (165). Her compulsion has its source—*nadryv* always does—in pride perverted by the sideward glance, the overweening concern of one's im-age in the eyes of others. Imperious Katerina *demands* that Dmitri *see* her as noble and self-sacrificing: "I will—I will become nothing but a means for his happiness, or—how shall I say?—an instrument, a machine for his happiness, and that for my whole life, *and that he may see that all his life!*" (166; emphasis added). Katerina presumes to be divine—"a god to whom [Dmitri] can pray." But throughout the novel, the presumption to "man-godhood" actually diminishes personhood (as we will see more fully in Ivan [546]). Of course, so too does forcing oneself to "become . . . a machine." Katerina hates herself for being dependent upon Dmitri's "look," and thus takes perverse pleasure in her own self-objectification. At the same time, she hates Dmitri because she needs him to *see* her as virtuous. She lashes back to hurt him, and would strip his freedom by insisting upon his com-plete intimacy, coercing him to speak: "I will insist on his knowing me and confiding entirely in me, without reserve" (165–66).[192] She would destroy herself and another, and find ecstasy by "gain[ing] [her] point" (166). Her deepest wish is for "real love" with Ivan, but she insists on her "unreal" and false love of Dmitri (168).

Ivan also sees her laceration for what it is. He desires Katya, but his publicly uttered analysis of her is withering—yet also willful. He twists the knife by (unwittingly) speaking words that travesty those spoken by Zo-sima to the grieving mother: "in the end your [mother's weeping] will turn into quiet joy" (48). Ivan tells Katerina that "in the end [your] suffering will be softened and will pass into sweet contemplation of the fulfillment of a bold and proud design" (166). Zosima's penetrated word is infused by Scripture (John 16: 20) and aims to heal a woman whose lacerating grief is a necessary stage through which she must pass. Her grief is real. Kat-erina's is false, but Ivan's ironic word, infected by pride, aims to hurt the woman whom he desires. When Ivan announces his departure for Mos-cow, Katerina's face "suddenly contort[s]," but she summons her pride, puts on her "charming society smile," and makes sure that Ivan sees her as "completely self-possessed" (167) and therefore triumphant. Ivan words are uttered "on purpose" (166); that recurring phrase further suggests his own *nadryv*. Katerina "glad" reply is also spoken "on purpose"—falsely, dramatically, "as in a theater" (167). The lovers cut against the grain of the real by willfully wounding each other. Like the would-be Ophelia who destroys herself in the first chapter, both "*invent* innumerable obstacles to their union" (12, emphasis added).

Throughout her tirade and Ivan's retort, Alyosha remains attentive. And "in a flash" he sees—receives the clarity he'd desired (167). Katerina demands that he speak—"I must have [Alyosha's] decision!" (167). But Alyosha's hasty, embarrassed response fails to halt the vicious cycle of *nadryv* that consumes her. Of course, the fact that Alyosha fails is not sufficient reason to critique his intervention. After all, Zosima's words do not decisively influence Fyodor, for example. Nevertheless, Caryl Emerson's commentary on Bakhtin's concept of "the penetrated word" can help in understanding where Alyosha falters, and her analysis is relevant to any person who seeks to help another find her "own voice": "The penetrated word is informed by authority . . . confident in its power to mean. Its task is to interfere actively in the interior dialogue of another person and 'help that person to find his own voice' [*PDP* 242]; . . . the penetrated word does not stand above or outside the discourse of the characters. *It does not come down but across . . .*" ("Tolstoy" 156–57; emphasis added). As he utters his "broken" words, Alyosha literally stands *above* Katerina:

> "I don't understand myself. . . . I seemed to see in a flash. . . . I know I am not saying it properly but I'll say it all the same," Alyosha went on in the same shaking and broken voice. "What I see is that perhaps you don't love my brother Dmitri at all . . . and never have, from the beginning. . . . And Dmitri, too, perhaps, has never loved you . . . and only esteems you. . . . I really don't know how I dare to say all this, but somebody must tell the truth . . . for nobody here will tell the truth."
>
> "What truth?" cried Katerina Ivanovna, and there was an hysterical ring in her voice.
>
> "I'll tell you," Alyosha went on *with desperate haste, as though he were jumping from the top of a house.* "Call Dmitri at once—I will fetch him—and let him come here and take your hand and take my brother Ivan's and join your hands. For you're torturing Ivan, simply because you love him—and torturing him, because you love Dmitri through 'laceration'—with an unreal love—because you've persuaded yourself."
>
> Alyosha broke off and was silent.
>
> "You . . . you . . . you are a little holy fool—that's what you are!" Katerina Ivanovna snapped. (167–68; emphasis added)

Katerina's "love" for Mitya is indeed "unreal." Alyosha speaks truthfully but imprudently. He lacks confidence and tact. He understands the mangled love affair, but "ashamed of his own thoughts," he denies it: "I don't understand myself . . . ." He speaks with "desperate haste, as though he were jumping from the top of a house." Just before this he "crie[s] suddenly in

distress" and speaks "breathlessly" (167); afterwards he "exclaim[s] frantically" after Ivan (169). Of course, he's only human; as Pieper notes, "the certitude of prudence cannot be so great as completely to remove all anxiety"
(*Cardinal* 18). Nevertheless, by reacting to his anxiety less than mindfully,
Alyosha's capacity for self-possession diminishes.

Before a person can "empty himself" in loving attentiveness to another,
he must first possess himself. Young Zosima shows this when he discerns
when it's the right time to speak to Mikhail, and when to be silent.[193] Fiercely
proud as she is, Katerina requires a quieter, less public word of intercession.
Before Zosima speaks to Mikhail, he pauses and prays. Alyosha rapidly pro-
nounces. Finally, Alyosha's word comes *down, upon* Katerina, not *across to*
her. At the moment that Zosima descends and sits silently with Mikhail,
his silent "word" proves most authoritative. In contrast, Alyosha "g[ets] up
from the sofa" (166), "stand[s] at the table and [does] not sit down" (167).
By standing up, he evinces a well-meaning but frantic desire to "fix" the
situation. But instead of attentively wishing *with* Katerina, he decides *for*
her. He orders her: "call Dmitri, at once." The results are disruptive, not "internally persuasive" ("Discourse" 342). Katerina snaps back not with "her
own voice," but one that sustains the vicious—and absurd—cycle of *nadryv*.
And while Ivan departs with a "forced smile," he also reveals a rare "youthful
sincerity" (168) in his ironic assessment of Katerina's ludicrous pride.

A minor note of humor follows: Katerina recovers herself sufficiently
to commission Alyosha to deliver two hundred rubles to Captain Snegiryov.
Sarcastically she compliments Alyosha on his tact, asking him to offer the
money "'delicately, carefully, as only you know how to'" (169). Alyosha
feels the dig and "blushes." He deeply regrets his earlier outburst. Despite
Madame Khokhlakova's reassurance, he "hid[es] his face in his hands in
an agony of remorse over his indiscretion" (170). Once outside he is "really grieved" and "fearfully ashamed" for having "rushed in like a fool, and
meddled, and in what? In a love affair!" (171).

But the gesture that follows serves as a touchstone in Alyosha's development of prudence. Rather than savoring self-castigation, Alyosha practices a kind of rational-emotive therapy by turning his mind to others who
need his help—to Mitya, and "the little schoolboy" whom he now realizes is
Captain Snegiryov's son:

> Thinking of another subject was a relief, and he resolved to
> think no more about the "mischief" he had done, and not to
> torture himself with remorse, but to do what he had to do, let
> come what would. At that thought he was completely comfort-
> ed. Turning onto the street where his brother Dmitri lodged, he

felt hungry, and taking out of his pocket the roll he had brought
from his father's, he ate it. It made him feel stronger. (171)

Alyosha's simple eating of a leftover roll—living bread for the long day
ahead—represents a small, practical sign of perseverance, of resolution "to
do what he had to" to help Mitya, Snegiryov, and others. It's a crucial step in
Alyosha's prudent practice of active love, "won slowly by long labor" (275).

Alyosha can't find Dmitri, so proceeds to visit Snegiryov in his family's
hovel. Here too Alyosha will learn from failure; for here too his hastily spoken words will intensify the vicious cycle of *nadryv*. Captain Snegiryov has
fashioned his self-presentation around his long subjugation: with lacerating
self-awareness, he suggests that Alyosha call him "Captain Yessirov" (173).
He calls his young visitor "sir" throughout most of their dialogue. Like Fyodor, he compulsively plays his expected part in order to avenge himself
on others. With unstable irony, his tone tacks from servility to aggression.
Unlike Fyodor, he's a devoted father and longs to remove his mask to challenge the injustices wrought by others. But he cringes in anticipation of their
response, as if they were saying: "Fool! You can't change!" Alyosha sees all of
this as he "look[s] attentively at him":

> There was extraordinary impudence in his expression, and yet,
> strange to say, at the same time there was fear. He looked like
> a man who had long been kept in subjection and had submit-
> ted to it, and now had suddenly turned and was trying to assert
> himself. Or, better still, like a man who wants dreadfully to hit
> you but is horribly afraid you will hit him. In his words and in
> the intonation of his shrill voice there was a sort of crazy humor,
> at times spiteful and at times cringing, and continually shifting
> from one tone to another. (173)

Snegiryov is bereft of a "good taste of self," an ability to freely love and
accept the love of others. His sideward glance seeks external validation, but
he lashes back at the other person in frustration for his dependency.

Alyosha's quiet attention will inspire a distinct change in his tone. For
initially, Alyosha remains calm. He responds "thoughtfully" to Snegiryov's
"frenzy" (174). His words come *across* a horizontal plane as he speaks while
"still keeping his seat" (174). Alyosha sees Snegiryov's love for his family,
smiles respectfully in response both to his self-analysis and his sorrow for
his son's condition. In contrast to Snegiryov's daughter's disdain, Alyosha
responds with gentle compassion, and helps the shattered man recover a
"good taste of self." When Snegiryov claims that there "must be someone
able to love even a man like me, sir," Alyosha, deeply moved, affirms this as
reality: "Ah, that's perfectly true!" His daughter Varvara is inattentive and

thus misapprehends her father as "playing the fool" (175). In fact, Snegiryov has begun to trust quiet Alyosha, and is thus willing to show him how his family is suffering from poverty and illness. Tactfully, Alyosha acknowledges their distress: "I see and hear" (176).

Alyosha's respectful presence has a healing effect on Snegiryov. Outside "in the fresh air," in one of the most heart-rending scenes of the novel, Snegiryov describes the anguish of his son, Ilyusha. Straightforwardly, he recounts their sad walks following his humiliation, and honestly, without concern for Alyosha's judgment or the infection of his "Yessirov" role-playing. However, when Snegiryov's plea for divine justice reaches its highest pitch, he again becomes painfully aware of his vulnerable visibility before Alyosha, the brother of the man who had shamed him. His voice fractures and he takes up "his original tone of spiteful buffoonery." Like Ivan at the end of "Rebellion," he returns to his *own* wounds, and an insistence that his "service record" be *seen*:

> "Papochka," he kept crying, "Papochka, darling papochka, how he humiliated you!" And I sobbed, too, sir. We sat shaking in each other's arms. "Papochka," he said, "papochka." "Ilyusha," I said to him, "Ilyusha darling." No one saw us then, sir. God alone saw us, I hope he will enter it on my service record, sir. You must thank your brother, sir, Alexey Fyodorovich. No, sir, I won't thrash him for your satisfaction, sir." (180)

Despite Snegiryov's reversion to his role, Alyosha sees that his presence has helped: "Alyosha felt . . . that he trusted him, and that if there had been someone else in his, Alyosha's place, the man would not have spoken so openly" (180). With deep empathy, Alyosha's "soul . . . tremble[s] on the verge of tears" while listening to Snegiryov's heartrending account of his son's agonized cry to Dmitri—"Let go, let go, it's my papa, forgive him!" (177)—and his subsequent illness.

Snegiryov's speech "in the open air" underscores the novel's most troubling questions: Why do the rich and powerful thrive at the expense of the poor and the weak? Where can justice be found in a world in which innocent children are injured, suffer, and die? Where is God in the midst of such injustice? Why does God permit it? Later that day, Ivan will ask these questions explicitly. And even Dmitri, whose cruelty had planted the "evil seed" (275) that leads to Ilyusha's death, will ask "Why is [the babe] weeping?" But Mitya will also "want to *do* something" (428; emphasis added)—and will thus take a crucial step away from violence and toward active love.

Christ-like active love, rooted in God's grace: this, finally, is Dostoevsky's best answer to the searing reality of suffering. Much suffering stems from natural causes—illness, natural disasters, and mortality itself. But much is caused by people who deform their freedom into willfulness and violence. In the century following the novel's publication, tyrants unleashed horrors beyond imagining.[194] St. Augustine insisted that if love, *caritas*, is ever to counter the temptations of the *libido dominandi*, the virtue of humility must be its foundation. Recalling his youthful presumption, Augustine asks, "Where was the charity which builds on the foundation of humility which is Christ Jesus?" (*Confessions* 7.20.26). Dostoevsky shares Augustine's Christocentric vision, as seen in Zosima's discourse on "humble love" and "loving humility" (275).

Alyosha offers loving humility to Snegiryov. Discerning the appropriate moment, he presents Katerina's gift of two hundred rubles in a manner that again comes *across*, and isn't imposed from above. Tactfully, he clarifies that the gift is not from a Karamazov, but "only from her": "She thought of you only when she had received a similar insult from him—similar in its cruelty I mean. She comes like a sister to help a brother in misfortune . . ." (181). But in the course of Alyosha's entreaty, his tact falters. Perhaps, after failing with Katerina, he is too anxious to succeed? As Alyosha becomes more insistent, the reader can hear his voice rise in pitch:

> She told me to persuade you to take these two hundred rubles from her, as from a sister, knowing that you are in such need. No one will know of it, it can give rise to no unjust slander. There are the two hundred rubles, and I swear you must take them unless—unless all men are to be enemies on earth! But there are brothers even on earth. . . . You have a generous heart . . . you must see that, you must. (181)

Alyosha expresses a profound truth: when people relinquish self-sufficiency, rivalry, and vindictiveness, suffering wrought by violence will diminish. Alyosha "echoes" Mikhail's apocalyptic vision of "terrible individualism" (262). But in that encounter, Zosima kenotically attended to Mikhail's particularity. Here, as previously with Katerina, Alyosha becomes emphatic: "I swear you must take them." (His insistence foreshadows Ivan's "order" that Mitya take money to escape: "He doesn't ask me, but orders me [to escape]. . . . He wants it to the point of hysterics" [503]). Alyosha's enthusiasm approaches hysteria. His apocalyptic image, with its encompassing claim—"unless all men are to be enemies on earth!"—saps his attention to the particular person before him. Alyosha's "direct aim" to make Snegiryov happy detracts from his delicacy, specifically when he adds the "black smear" of Karamazov rubles: "I have money too, take what you want, as you would from a brother, from a friend, you can give it back later. . . .

([Y]ou'll get rich, you'll get rich!)" (193). Later, Alyosha will discern that his offer was perceived as pity bestowed from above, and thus threatened Snegiryov's paternal honor. Furthermore, as he pleads, he appeals less to Snegiryov's humility than to his grandiosity, as he paints an unrealistic dream of the Snegiryovs becoming "rich."

Again, Alyosha's intervention disrupts rather than heals. In a fury of *nadryv* Snegiryov crumples and tramples the money he desperately needs, and with a sideward glance insists that Alyosha "see" his honorable "refusal." He "shriek[s]": "Do you see, sir, do you see, sir?" (183) and his "whole figure expressed unutterable pride" (183). Through painful experience, Alyosha is still learning prudence. He recognizes his failure, which leaves him "inexpressibly grieved" (184).

But again the narrator-chronicler mitigates grief with a minor note of humor. He concludes the chapter dryly: Alyosha returned to "Katerina Ivanovna's to report on the success of his commission" (183). The deadpan tone fosters the reader's sense that despite these fiascoes, Alyosha is slowly developing as a "monk in the world." Scattered throughout the novel, these humble notes of humor offer relief, and help sustain what René Girard calls the "particularly . . . inspired and serene vision" (*Underground* 3) of Dostoevsky's final novel.

The following chapter, "An Engagement," represents another step in Alyosha's development. With Lise's help, Alyosha takes a decisive step away from the monastery and into the world. Indeed, this chapter presents Lise's finest moment as she helps Alyosha, whose vocation is to help all. Alyosha's attentiveness had helped Snegiryov tell his story, and now Lise's helps Alyosha: "Alyosha sat down at the table and began to tell his story, but at the first words he lost his embarrassment and gained the whole of Lise's attention" (186). Her "attention" abets understanding of Snegiryov, and of his "blunder" in offering him his own money (187). He gains understanding *through* their dialogue as opposed to solitary, self-sufficient reflection. It's appropriate that she calls Alyosha's analysis of Snegiryov "ours." She gently cautions Alyosha to resist placing himself in a potentially contemptuous, omniscient position "above" Snegiryov: "Listen, Alexey Fyodorovich. Isn't there in all our analysis—I mean your analysis . . . no, better call it ours—aren't we showing contempt for that poor man—in analyzing his soul like this, as it were, from above, eh? In deciding so certainly that he will take the money?" (188). Bakhtin cites Lise's insight as exemplary when noting the way "artistic finalization," or an anti-polyphonic authorial position in relation to characters, can comprise a form of "violence" ("Reworking" 292).

But Alyosha's analysis is *not* contemptuous. He recognizes his common humanity with Snegiryov, that he's "just the same," and sees that the

father's "soul is . . . full of fine feeling" (188). His salutary "surplus of vision and understanding" ("Reworking" 299) allows him to see Snegiryov's
complexity of circumstance.[195] With prudent foresight, he determines the
best means of fulfilling his goal of helping Snegiryov and his family. His
knowledge is "formed by reality,"[196] and he plans accordingly.

To Lise, Alyosha recalls Zosima's counsel "to care for most people as
one would for children, and for some of them as one would for the sick in
hospitals" (188).[197] Do Zosima's words suggest a condescending pity that
might lead to contempt? Doesn't the Grand Inquisitor, who pities the weakness of humanity, also see them contemptuously as "specimen beings created in jest" (227)? In fact, a stark difference emerges when we consider the
way Zosima ministers to the psychologically tormented, or the way Alyosha
mentors children and cares for the sick (551). Zosima's counsel is one of
love, not condescension or manipulative control. Alyosha aptly remembers
and applies his mentor's words here.

But Lise also helps Alyosha to relinquish his over-reliance upon and
identification with Zosima: "If you knew, Lise, how bound up in soul I am
with him! And then I shall be left alone. . . . I shall come to you, Lise. . . .
For the future we will be together" (191). At least in this conversation, he
finds in Lise a confidante to whom he can even confess his religious doubts
(191). Further, as he and Lise twice kiss and touch hands, Alyosha begins to
accept embodiment and sexual attraction. Unlike Myshkin, he can commit
himself to one person. To Lise's mother, he "declare[s] [it] stoutly" that his
commitment is serious, and that he's ready to wait a year and a half—when,
presumably, she will turn sixteen (192). But within three months, things
have changed. When they next converse, the reader learns that Lise has
broken their engagement, and it will likely remain broken. I will discuss
this scene in Chapter 7, but for now would observe that for all her folly,
Khokhlakova is right to regard their nuptial prospects as doubtful (191).
Despite her comical self-absorption, she does apprehend some things accurately, such as Katerina's *nadryv* earlier that day.

Alyosha leaves Lise's house with a renewed sense of commitment: "It
was getting late, nearly three o'clock. Alyosha's whole soul turned to the monastery, to his dying elder, but the necessity of seeing Dmitri outweighed everything" (192). But in the tavern "Metropolis," to which he's been directed by
Smerdyakov, he finds Ivan, not Mitya. As he did the previous day, he revises
his plan to sit with his brother. He tempers Ivan's *nadryv*. When Ivan concludes his rebellion against God's creation and rejection of Christ, he invites
Alyosha to reject him: "will you renounce me for that, yes?" Alyosha responds
with a silent kiss, a deed of active love that imitates the Christ Ivan has himself
imagined. In response, Ivan speaks in a "resolute" voice of love. Like Zosima's

blessing, the seeds of Alyosha's love remain with Ivan. I will look briefly at their encounter here, and return to it in Chapter 6, which focuses on Ivan.

As "the brothers get acquainted" in the Metropolis tavern, Ivan's fond remembrance of his little brother's love of cherry jam helps Alyosha to relax: "You remember that? Let me have jam, too; I like it still." But increasingly Ivan's influence upon Alyosha becomes lacerating. After a promising start, Ivan begins to reveal his self-division. He declares to Alyosha, "I don't want to corrupt you or turn you from your stronghold, perhaps I want to be healed by you" (204). But in the lacerating "delirium" of his "Rebellion," Ivan aims to hurt Alyosha. Rather than presenting his accounts of children's torture with forthright and justified indignation, he consistently adds bitterly ironic twists in his descriptions: the Turks who shoot babies "are very fond of sweets" (206); the story of Richard, abused by shepherds, which Ivan claims to have found in a "charming pamphlet" (207), travesties the story of Christ's nativity; images of beaten children are described as "charming pictures" (207).[198] Ivan's language twists the knife in himself, as if to flaunt his rebellion before God. But he also twists it in Alyosha, as if to seduce his brother away from his "stronghold" (204) and toward the "beast of rage [and] sensual inflammation" that Ivan sees hidden "in every man" (209).[199] When Ivan asks Alyosha what should be done to the general who has turned his dogs on an eight-year-old boy, Alyosha, "with a pale twisted smile," replies: "Shoot him!" Ivan's response is telling: in a "kind of ecstasy," he declares that there's "a little devil sitting in your heart, Alyoshka Karamazov!" (210). Ivan seems happy to see his brother so possessed. Brought to "a laceration of grief," Alyosha "crie[s] out with a tormented outburst": "'Why are you testing me? . . . Will you finally tell me?" Ivan admits that his intent is, in fact, to wrench Alyosha from faith and toward rebellion: "You are dear to me, I don't want to let you go, and I won't give you up to your Zosima" (211). After Ivan regales Alyosha with his litany of child abuse, he inadvertently emphasizes *his own* wounds as an abused and forgotten child: "I would rather remain with my unavenged suffering and unquenched indignation, *even if I were wrong*" (212). Ivan's rebellion is *personal*. Given his own "unavenged suffering," he'd rather remain with a lacerating lie than accept the "mystery" of non-Euclidean harmony.

But at the end of "Rebellion," it's crucial to observe that Alyosha *also* rejects the "non-Euclidean harmony," the theodicy that posits the suffering of children as "manure" for an eventual eschatological harmony. And Alyosha rightly rejects it: no orthodox Christian theology posits children's suffering as a prerequisite for eventual cosmic harmony. Zosima's protests are adamant and clear: "There must be no more . . . torturing of children" (271); "Woe to him who offends a child!" (275).[200] Ivan presents instances of human violence, willfully imposed upon innocents. "Theodicy" lies when it nullifies the pain of innocent suffering by making it part of a "mysterious" mathematical equation or grand plan. Ivan's picture of divine "mystery"—in which parallel lines converge in infinity—is itself another rationalistic, Enlightenment construction, more akin to that of Leibniz's "best of all possible worlds" theodicy than to incarnational realism. Terrence Tilley has argued that "engaging in the discourse practice of theodicy creates evils, not the least of which is the radical disjunction of 'academic' philosophical theology from 'pastoral' counsel" (*Theodicy* 3). Throughout the novel, Zosima and Alyosha offer such counsel and care. Ivan never does.

Drawing on von Balthasar's *Mysterium Paschale*, Jacob Friesenhahn attempts to heal the "radical disjunction" between theology and pastoral counsel and present a more orthodox understanding of innocent suffering: "The Cross of Jesus Christ is the ultimate historical expression of God's Triune nature, such that by uniting our sufferings to the Cross, we also thereby participate in the inner life of God" (2).[201] Dostoevsky's incarnational realism *does* portray children "participating in the inner life of God": suffering Ilyusha, to whom I'll return in Chapter 7, emerges as an image of Christ. But Zosima's protest remains an imperative. Incarnational realism seeks justice and the protection of innocents, even as it sees their suffering as participating in the kenotic love of God.

Moreover, Alyosha presents an alternative to Ivan's "non-Euclidean" harmony by firmly directing Ivan's attention to the person of Christ, the "Being [who] can forgive everything, forgive all *and for all.*" Christ can forgive all "because he himself gave His innocent blood for all and for everything. . . . and on Him is built the edifice" (213, emphasis in original). Alyosha responds with gratitude to Christ's redemptive act, and with pastoral attentiveness to the suffering of others. He too exemplifies the human calling to participate in Christ's redemptive suffering of Christ by taking on responsibility "for all" through the practice of active love.

Ivan has anticipated that Alyosha will point to Christ: "usually all arguments on your side put Him in the foreground." He responds with his poem, "The Grand Inquisitor." This single chapter has inspired volumes of analysis, but mine will be brief. The Inquisitor (and Ivan behind him) accuses the silent, listening Christ of having placed an intolerably heavy yoke upon human beings in giving them "the fearful burden of free choice" (222). Ivan here returns to a premise he articulated early in "Rebellion" when he claimed that human beings are incapable of loving like Christ: "He was God. But we are not gods" (205). (Note Ivan's use of the past tense; Zosima and Alyosha use the present tense when they point to the risen, living Christ of faith [311].) Ivan points to Christ's love as an ideal impossible for human beings to emulate (204); the Inquisitor emphasizes Christ's exercise of freedom—witnessed most fully in his rejection of the devil's three temptations—as a model beyond the capacity of most mortals:

> There are three powers, three powers alone, able to conquer and hold captive forever the conscience of these impotent rebels for their happiness—those forces are miracle, mystery, and authority. Thou hast rejected all three and hast set the example for doing so. . . . Oh, of course, Thou didst proudly and well, like God; but the weak rebellious race of men, are they gods? (222)

The Grand Inquisitor and his legion "correct" Christ's work. Out of purported "love" for humankind, they found a theocracy "upon miracle, mystery, and authority. And men rejoiced that they were again led like sheep, and that the terrible gift that had brought them much suffering, was, at last, lifted from their hearts" (223). But in his lies to them about heaven, the Inquisitor reveals contempt for humanity, not love. As Roger Cox notes, he offers only "magic, mystification, and tyranny" (210).

Dostoevsky's "oblique," "artistic" answer to Ivan is already present in the silent image of Christ created by his character, Ivan the author. But how are we to interpret Christ's silence before the Inquisitor? Does it represent a refusal to attend to a person in need? Is it cruel? Or is his kiss a sign "of acquiescence," as D. H. Lawrence claimed (128)? I interpret Christ's silence—and his silent kiss—as evidence of love, his respect for the Inquisitor's freedom and personhood. At the beginning of his monologue, the Inquisitor commands Christ not to speak—"Don't answer, be silent" (217). Christ respects his demand, willful as it is. Later the Inquisitor wavers and insists that Christ respond:

> Speak! Did we not love mankind, so meekly acknowledging their feebleness, lovingly lightening their burden, and permitting their weak nature even sin with our sanction? Why hast Thou come to hinder us? Why dost Thou look silently and searchingly at me with Thy mild eyes? Be angry. I don't want Thy love, for I love Thee not. And what use is it for me to hide anything from Thee? Don't I know to Whom I am speaking? All that I can say is known to Thee already. I can see it in Thine eyes. (223)

The Inquisitor refuses Christ's silently offered love and concludes with a vow: "Tomorrow I shall burn Thee, *Dixi*" (226). But, according to Ivan—and here we sense his capacity as a polyphonic artist—the Inquisitor rests firmly in neither his nihilism nor his death sentence. Mikhail gazed at

Zosima and looked longingly for a word from the silent, authoritative other. Perhaps the Inquisitor himself suffers under his own terrible burden of conscience. Perhaps he seeks to flee the agony of his own freedom and find solace in the authority of Christ—even if that "solace" be more monomaniacal rebellion against whatever Christ's "bitter and terrible" word may be.

Christ offers love and respect for freedom, the very gifts the Inquisitor has furiously rejected. Christ's "severe mercy" cuts him like a sword. Christ relinquishes any power to impose his will, including the power of speech; he is similarly silent during his trial, as depicted especially in the Synoptic Gospels—see Christ's silence before the high priests in Matt 26:63 and Mark 14:61, and before Pilate in Matt 27:14 and Mark 15:4. "Harshly dealt with, he bore it humbly, he never opened his mouth, like a lamb that is led to the slaughter-house, like a sheep that is dumb before its shearers never opening its mouth" (Isa 53:7). Christ silently, gently approaches the Inquisitor and kisses him, and the kiss cleaves its recipient:

> "When the Inquisitor ceased speaking he waited for some time for his Prisoner to answer him. His silence weighed down upon him. He saw that the Prisoner had listened intently and quietly all the time, looking gently in his face and evidently not wishing to reply. The old man longed for Him to say something, however bitter and terrible. But He suddenly approached the old man in silence and softly kissed him on his bloodless aged lips. That was all his answer. The old man shuddered. His lips moved. He went to the door, opened it, and said to Him: 'Go and come no more. . . . Come not at all, never, never!' And he let Him out into the dark squares of the town. The Prisoner went away."
>
> "And the old man?"
>
> "The kiss glows in his heart, but the old man adheres to his idea." (228)

The Inquisitor releases the one whom he'd vowed to kill. He's been rent, divided, his "Go!" split between generous release and willful refusal.[202] His willful adherence to his "idea" wars with the glow in his heart. One thinks of St. Thomas the disciple, who, as the narrator ponders, "possibly fully believed in his secret heart even when he said 'I shall not believe except I see'" (28). The Inquisitor now carries a secret heart. As Alyosha perceptively observes, Ivan's poem is ultimately "in praise of Jesus, not in blame of Him (226).[203] Ivan's literary imagination presents a kenotic Christ who listens to and changes the heart of the tyrannical Inquisitor without speaking a word. In depicting the Inquisitor's divided response to Christ's silent kiss, Ivan reveals his own longing that he might turn and be healed by incarnate love.

In a moment of solemn intimacy, like that in which Christ encountered St. Thomas (John 20) or, in Ivan's poem, the Inquisitor, Zosima has
said to Ivan: "If [the question of faith] can't be decided in the affirmative, it
will never be decided in the negative. You yourself know that is the peculiar-
ity of your heart, and all your torment is due to it" (66). Ivan does know this.
Out of his wound of self-division, his "furnace of doubt,"[204] Ivan creates—as
Dostoevsky will in the remainder of the novel—an "oblique" image of redemption. Speaking through the Grand Inquisitor, Ivan articulates the side
of himself that answers the question of faith negatively. But he recognizes
that he can change. Early in their conversation, Ivan had articulated this
affirmative side: "I want to be friends with you Alyosha, for I have no friends
and want to try it. Well, only fancy, perhaps I too accept God . . ." (202). And
he makes an even warmer, more humble revelation: "Dear little brother, I
don't want to corrupt you or turn you from your stronghold, perhaps I want
to be healed by you" (204). But Ivan is also proud and resists fully "deciding in the affirmative." He adheres to his idea, even as he denies the hellish
implications of his adherence: "Why it's all nonsense, Alyosha. It's only a
senseless poem of a senseless student . . ." (228). As Zosima has noted, "The
martyr likes sometimes to divert himself with his despair, as if from despair
itself" (65). Yet Ivan remains capable of hope.

At the end of "The Grand Inquisitor," the image of Alyosha mirrors
that of Ivan's Christ, and Dostoevsky sows another seed in his "oblique, artistic" response. Alyosha has been "all attention" (213). Ivan has claimed
that "another can never know how much I suffer because he is another
and not I" (205), but Alyosha—like Christ entering into the suffering of
the Inquisitor—empathizes with Ivan's suffering, to "the hell" in which his
brother lives in his rebellion. We hear Alyosha's empathy in his "sorrowful,"
"mournful" questions (228). However, like Christ's, his loving attentiveness
is most eloquently expressed in stillness. When Ivan scowls and concedes
the logical, terrible consequence of his ideas—much like the moment when
the Inquisitor admits he is in league with the devil—"Alyosha look[s] at him
in silence":

> "Yes, if you like, 'everything is lawful,' since the word has been
> said. I won't deny it . . . ."
>   "I thought, brother, that going away from here I have you
> at least," Ivan said suddenly, with unexpected feeling; "but now
> I see that there is no place for me even in your heart, my dear
> hermit. The formula 'all is lawful,' I won't renounce—will you
> renounce me for that, yes?"
>   Alyosha got up, went to him and softly kissed him on the
> lips. (229)

In his baiting "yes?" Ivan wills to be rejected by the person he loves most deeply, and who most loves him. The reader can almost hear the gnashing of teeth in that willful "yes?" But when Ivan chooses hell, Alyosha, like Christ, offers love. He embraces Ivan as a free person, and judges it better to relinquish the power of counter-argument. His *contra* is a kiss, drawn from the imagination of the one to whom he attends. Alyosha empties himself of any will to power "in order to receive into [himself] the being [he] is looking at, just as he is, in all his truth" (Weil 115). And if, as Weil claims, attention is "a miracle," Alyosha's proves to be miraculous in a small but powerful way. His attention elicits Ivan's small step toward *metanoia*. He plants a seed that may eventually bear fruit—or at least sprout buds in Ivan's final scene in the courtroom. As he did when he received Zosima's blessing, Ivan, for a moment, finds his own "resolute" voice.

> They went out, but stopped when they reached the entrance of the restaurant.
>
> "Listen, Alyosha," Ivan began in a resolute voice, "if I am ever able to care for the sticky little leaves, I shall only love them, remembering you. It's enough for me that you are somewhere here, and I shan't lose my desire for life yet. Is that enough for you? Take it as a declaration of love if you like. And now you go to the right I go to the left. . . . Goodbye, kiss me once more; that's right, now go." (229)

With "Is that enough for you?" Ivan's pride reemerges and infects his utterance. He wants Alyosha's healing kiss, but also wants him to "go." His command to "go" echoes the Inquisitor's order that Christ "Go and come no more" (228).[205] With Alyosha gone, Ivan can continue to deny his concrete responsibility to his father and elder brother ("'And about brother Dmitri, too, I ask you specially never speak to me again,' he added with sudden irritation"). He walks toward Smerdyakov, with whom that denial will take the concrete form of his departure for Moscow. As Ivan walks, he sways, "his right shoulder looked lower than his left" (230). Here Ivan is again "fruitlessly divided" (Augustine, *Confessions* 2.1.1), "struggling with one part rising up and the other part falling down" (8.8.19). We will return to Ivan—and his affinities to St. Augustine—in Chapter 6.

Active love is harsh and dreadful work. By the end of his encounter with Ivan, Alyosha is shaken. If his dialogue with Lise had restored his sense of commitment with others, the cumulative effect of his dialogue with Ivan seems to corrode it. Again he hurries back to the monastery seeking escape. He runs to Zosima ("*Pater Seraphicus*, he will save me—from him and forever!" [230]) and away from his commissioned service as a monk in the

world. One oversight is especially telling: "Several times afterwards he wondered how he could on leaving Ivan so completely forget his brother Dmitri,
though he had that morning, only a few hours before, so firmly resolved to
find him and not to give up doing so, even should he be unable to return to
the monastery that night" (230). Alyosha forgets Mitya. Upon his return,
Zosima firmly reminds him of his pressing, still-incomplete work: "Make
haste to find [Mitya], go again tomorrow and make haste, leave everything
and make haste. Perhaps you may still have time to prevent something terrible." But, the following day, Alyosha's vocation to "live like a monk in the
world" (247) will be shaken by his own rebellious recoil, and, unexpectedly,
renewed through ironic reversal.

Alyosha's Third Day: The Flowering of Incarnational Realism

The day of Zosima's death is "one of the bitterest and most fatal days of
[Alyosha's] life" (292). During it, the image of the man whom Alyosha loved
above all is humiliated by the premature corruption of his corpse. In the
course of this unexpectedly bitter—but eventually joyous—day, Alyosha
matures as a "monk in the world" in three ways. First, his ardent faith is
educated by irony, incarnated in the human realities of mortality and fickle
judgment. Second, his prudence deepens as he develops an alertness in the
face of unexpected reversals. Third, his fear of sexual attraction further diminishes as he discovers that *eros*, rather than an experience to be rejected,
is a gift to be integrated with self-giving *agape*, and embodied in *caritas*.

In *Images of Faith: An Exploration of the Ironic Imagination*, William F.
Lynch argues that faith needs to be educated by irony—by the unexpected,
by surprises, by life's unfinalizability (102). This is the open, uncertain dimension of life to which our first, fearful reaction is often to *impose* closure.
Closure has its place: the believer trusts God's promises and looks forward
to their fulfillment. In Scripture, God makes a covenant with Abraham, and
Abraham, in his faith, expects God to keep it. But he *never* expects God's order to sacrifice the personal embodiment of that covenant, his son Isaac. But
he willingly obeys God's request, and therein lies faith's open dimension: its
acceptance of and perseverance *through* the unexpected, even the excruciatingly unexpected (*Faith* 126). The poor son of a Nazarene carpenter, Jesus
offers the archetypal instance of faith's link to irony: for "the coming of the
kingdom *had* been expected, but not in the form in which it appears in and
is described by Christ. The ironies of Christ had not been expected" (127).
Drawing on Greek tragedy, Lynch shows the ways in which faith bereft of

irony can produce "fury" and become "a principle of universal mockery; it destroys everything; it becomes diabolical" (102). When, the day before, Ivan's rebellion turns bitterly ironic, "the hell in [his] heart and [his] head" (228) recalls the fury of infernal *nadryv* (279). Ivan's univocal irony, bereft of faith, leaves a "harassing impression" upon Alyosha, and "persistently haunt[s] [his] mind" (293).

Alyosha's faith is not grounded in miracles, but he does univocally "thirst" "for the glory that was [Zosima's] due" (293). Incarnational realism accepts a God of surprises. How do you make God laugh? Tell him your plans. So goes a version of the old Yiddish saw.[206] Ironic occurrences, reversals of human expectation, are woven into the fabric of reality. God's infinite freedom and love are not bound by the schemes and devices of finite creatures. This is not to suggest a voluntaristic god who, willy-nilly, toys with humans "like flies to wanton boys." Rather, Dostoevsky suggests that authentic miracle, mystery, and authority are always directed by a love that can be "great ... and unfathomable" (252)—and, at times, painful. The critical moment experienced by Alyosha—the seemingly unjust shaming of his beloved elder—must be read in the light of Zosima's own assessment of the suffering of Job as "mystery": "The passing earthly show and the eternal verity are brought together in it." "God raises Job again" (252); Alyosha will "[rise] up a resolute champion" (312). The incarnational pattern of descent and ascent will be reprised.

In the wake of Zosima's death, most of the monks and townspeople (like the nervously curious Madame Khokhlakova) expect a miracle. Father Paissy is more mature in his faith: he sees and suspects the "intense expectation on the part of the believers with such haste, ... with such insistence" that a miracle follow Zosima's death, that—like past saintly monks—his body not decompose. Father Paissy chastises some of the monks for their "immediate expectation of something extraordinary." But Paissy too "secretly, at the bottom of his heart, cherished almost the same hopes" (284). Ironically, Zosima's body decomposes more quickly than bodies usually do.

But the repeated specification of the *time* suggests Zosima's linkage with Christ: "But before three o'clock in the afternoon that something took place, ... something so unexpected by all of us and so contrary to the general hope ..." (285); "[B]y three o'clock those signs had become so clear and unmistakable, that the news swiftly reached all the monks and visitors in the hermitage ..." (285). The narrator repeats "three o'clock" three times. However, those who project a preconceived pattern upon reality miss the incarnational, trinitarian recapitulation:[207] to his disciples, Christ's shameful execution and death at three o'clock was utterly, bitterly unexpected. Unreceptive to irony, none discern the possible gift of an unexpected sign. Instead, the reversal of expectation elicits absolutism and fury: those who revered Zosima "were almost mortified and personally affronted by this incident" (286); the self-righteous who envied him show "triumphant satisfaction" (287). Some claim, "it shows God's judgment is not as man's" (287). They miss the irony that their own judgments—projected upon and falsifying reality—leave no room for God's. Ferapont "shout[s] . . . crazily, . . . 'What is your faith?'" blind to the fact that his furious presumption is faith's antithesis. The narrator's critique of Ferapont's irrationality is clear: "the fanatic, carried away by a zeal that outstripped his reason, would not be quieted" (290). Bereft of an education in irony, faith becomes irrational: a travesty marked more by dogmatism and zealotry than *logos* and love. Zosima is savaged for having reasonably recommended a purgative to a monk who was seeing devils (299–300). The faithful elder "[knew] measure" (278); rationally, he has accepted our reality as creatures of flesh and blood. His own mortal body takes the course that dead bodies naturally take. Throughout Book 7, we can discern Dostoevsky's conviction that faith and reason are not only compatible but integral. And, like prudence itself, both are integrally nurtured by experience.

Alyosha does not so much expect the miracle that others seek (292), but he never expects that "the man he loved above everything on earth should be put to shame and humiliated!" (293). As the voices of those who gloat grow strident, he demands to know why God allows such an injustice to occur: "Why did Providence hide its face 'at the most critical moment' (so Alyosha thought it), as though voluntarily submitting to the blind, dumb, pitiless laws of nature?" (293).[208] In the midst of his questioning, "a vague but tormenting and evil impression left by his brother Ivan the day before, suddenly revived again now in his soul and seemed forcing its way to the surface" (293). Rakitin—who exemplifies a reductive irony bereft of faith—arrives on the scene. In response to his scorn Alyosha "crie[s] irritably": "I believe, I believe, I want to believe, and I will believe, what more do you want?" But Alyosha's faith is so challenged by the bitter irony of seeming injustice that he joins Ivan's lacerating rebellion: "'I am not rebelling against my God; I simply "'don't accept his world.'" Alyosha suddenly smiled a forced smile" (294). Ever cynically perceptive, Rakitin observes the uncharacteristic disfigurement of Alyosha's face: "Do you know your face is quite changed? There's none of your famous mildness to be seen in it" (294). Alyosha's trust in the goodness of creation and Creator has been shaken.

Alyosha's "forced" smile strains against his own good nature. It signifies *nadryv*. Before his full emergence as a monk in the world, Alyosha passes through his own brief rebellion. As always with *nadryv*, there's an audience. But Alyosha's sideward glance is aimed not at Rakitin, but at God:

"There was a sudden gleam in his eyes, . . . but not of anger with Rakitin"
(294). In agreeing to the seminarian's series of temptations—sausage, vodka,
an evening visit to Grushenka—Alyosha succumbs not to gluttony or lust,
but to a perverse assertion of will in which he seeks to hurt himself *so that*
he can hurt God. Thus his "forced" smile: to reprise Lynch's phrase, Alyosha
"wishes against" the One whom he most deeply loves.

And yet, with striking ardor, the narrator defends Alyosha at this
"critical moment." He acknowledges Alyosha's too-exclusive love of Zosima,
and the way he forgets his promise to find Mitya and give the rubles to
Snegiryov: "all the love that lay concealed in his pure heart for 'everyone
and everything' had, for the past year, been concentrated—and perhaps
wrongly so—primarily on one being, at least in the strongest impulses of his
heart, his beloved elder, now dead. . . . [A]ll his young strength and energy
could not but turn towards that ideal, even to the forgetting 'of everyone and
everything,'" including Mitya and Snegiryov (292). Curiously, the narrator
advocates for Alyosha by contrasting him with a hypothetical youth "whose
love was lukewarm, and whose mind was too *prudent*" (292; emphasis
added). The narrator here employs the word "prudence" in its oft-misused
sense of "timorous, small-minded self-preservation" (Pieper 4). The narrator contrasts feeble "prudence" with bold love, and closes his defense of
Alyosha with a rhetorical question: "[A]ny man of sense will come back to
reason in time, but, if love does not gain the upper hand in a boy's heart at
such an exceptional moment, when will it?" (293). Prudence and love are,
in fact, inseparable.

The narrator pauses upon "something strange" in Alyosha: "This new
something was the harassing impression left by the conversation with his
brother Ivan, which now persistently haunted Alyosha's mind" (293). As he
"listlessly" answers Rakitin's question about Ivan, his heart is not touched
when he remembers the work he was sent to do:

> [S]uddenly the image of his brother Dmitri rose before his
> mind. But only for a minute, and though it reminded him of
> something that must not be put off for a moment, some duty,
> some terrible obligation, even that reminder made no impres-
> sion on him, did not reach his heart and instantly faded out of
> his mind and was forgotten. But, a long while afterwards, Alyo-
> sha remembered this. (295)

Numbly, yet "on purpose," he allows himself to be led to Grushenka's.
Alyosha will always remember that at this "critical moment" he *forgot* to
remember. Memory is central to the novel's redemptive vision. And, as Josef Pieper observes, prudence and memory are intrinsically related: "The

honesty of the memory can be ensured only by a rectitude of the whole human being, which purifies the most hidden roots of volition" (*Cardinal* 15). Ironically, Grushenka proves to be the means for Alyosha's purification and his recovery of genuine, loving prudence.

The overturning of expectations can hurt—but can also, if only in time, prove joyful. Alyosha learns this at Grushenka's, led by Rakitin, a Judas who expects payment upon delivery. Upon their arrival, Grushenka is unexpectedly genuine and kind. Here Alyosha exercises a key dimension of prudence: *solertia*, an alert openness in the face of the unexpected. Josef Pieper clarifies St. Thomas's conception of *solertia* by calling it

> a "perfected ability," by virtue of which man, when confronted with a sudden event, does not close his eyes by reflex and then blindly, though perhaps boisterously, take random action. Rather, with aid of *solertia* he can swiftly, but with open eyes and clear-eyed vision, decide for the good, avoiding the pitfalls of injustice, cowardice, and intemperance. Without this virtue of "objectivity in unexpected situations," perfect prudence is not possible. (*Cardinal* 16)

The day after Zosima's death is rife with ironic reversals, a day which "long afterwards Alyosha thought of . . . as one of the bitterest and most fatal days of his life" (292). But both the bitterness and joy of this day lie in Alyosha's response to the series of overturned expectations. Throughout Book 7, forms of the words "expected" or "unexpected" appear at least twenty-one times; forms of the word "surprise" at least eleven. The image of Zosima, the man whom Alyosha loved more than any other, has been degraded by the unexpected corruption of his body, and the rabid *ressentiment* of some fellow monks. But the image of Grushenka, the woman he most feared, emerges as Christ-like. In the course of this unexpectedly harrowing, yet ultimately rapturous day, Alyosha's faith matures as it grows more receptive to reality in all its reversals.

In fact, both Alyosha and Grushenka mutually experience the unexpected *in each other*. When he arrives, Grushenka is surprised to see Alyosha, but smiles, "Don't be afraid of me, my dear Alyosha, you can't think how glad I am to see you, my unexpected visitor" (298). In turn, Alyosha "had not expected to see such a kind expression on her face" (299). His brief "listless" bout of *nadryv* is interrupted by an unexpectedly gracious Grushenka. Gradually, his capacity for attention is restored: "He was greatly surprised to find her now altogether different from what he had expected. And, crushed as he was by his own sorrow, his eyes involuntarily rested on her with attention" (299). His dread of sexuality, intensified after witnessing the manipulative display of

Grushenka and Katerina two days earlier, eased by his own encounter with Lise the day before, now diminishes further. When Grushenka nestles on his knee, he finds that he no longer fears "this 'dreadful' woman," but instead feels "the intensest and purest interest, without a trace of fear, of his former terror. That was what instinctively surprised him" (300).

In allowing himself to be led to Grushenka, Alyosha had expected to find Sodom—to use Mitya's image when he agonizes to his younger brother about beauty's "two edged" quality: "I can't endure the thought that a man of lofty mind and heart begins with the ideal of the Madonna and ends with the ideal of Sodom" (98). To his surprise, however, Grushenka, here twice described as "beautiful" (296), presents an image of the Madonna, the face that most resembles Christ's, to borrow words from Dante's *Paradiso* (32.85). Grushenka points up the falsity of Mitya's Sodom/Madonna dichotomy: The Madonna, who bore Christ in her womb, cannot be reduced to an abstract, spiritualized antithesis to fleshly disorder. Mary is herself body and soul, as is her son, Jesus Christ.

Dante's *Commedia* has further relevance here: it tells the story of a man whose soul is risen from the depths by the mediation of a beautiful woman, Beatrice, whom Dante loves, body and soul. So too is Alyosha's soul restored. At first, when Grushenka sits "beside Alyosha on the sofa," Alyosha notices a change in *her* face: "Her lips glowed, her lips laughed, but it was a good-natured, merry laugh. Alyosha had not expected to see such a kind expression on her face . . ." (299). His expectations are further overturned when Grushenka "suddenly skipped forward and jumped, laughing, on his knee, like a nestling kitten, with her right arm about his neck. 'I'll cheer you up, my pious boy'" (300).

When discussing this scene in class the question sometimes arises: "Is Alyosha sexually aroused by Grushenka at this moment?" "Oh no," an earnest student usually replies, and points to the text for support: even with flirtatious Grushenka on his lap, Alyosha

> felt numb. . . . [T]here was nothing in his heart such as Rakitin, for instance, watching him malignantly from his corner, might have expected or fancied. The great grief in his heart swallowed up every sensation that might have been aroused, and, if only he could have thought clearly at that moment, he would have realized that he had now the strongest armor to protect him from every lust and temptation. (300)

But another student may note the next word: "yet." In that "yet" we are reminded that active love in the novel can be understood as *caritas*. At this moment, Alyosha presents an incarnational image of love that integrates both *agape* and *eros*. Here is the passage:

> Yet in spite of the vague irresponsiveness of his spiritual condi-
> tion and the sorrow that overwhelmed him, he could not help
> wondering at a new and strange sensation in his heart. . . . [T]his
> woman, dreaded above all women, sitting now on his knee,
> holding him in her arms, aroused in him now a quite different,
> unexpected, peculiar feeling, a feeling of the intensest and pur-
> est interest without a trace of fear, of his former terror. That was
> what instinctively surprised him. (300)

Alyosha's pure and intense interest is *eros*. He is powerfully *drawn to* Grushenka's beauty—to her female form, but more so to the graceful form with which she responds to Alyosha. She remains flirtatious, but drops the mask of "mannered" "mawkish sweetness" (299–300) and responds to Alyosha's arrival with honesty, hospitality, and kindness.[209] Thus Alyosha's "eyes involuntarily [rest] on her with attention" (299).

But what of Zosima's emphasis on the "labor and fortitude" entailed in active love? Does Alyosha's spontaneous *eros* eclipse the hard work of *agape* to which he's called? Doesn't Zosima's emphasis on "perfect self-forgetful-ness" suggest a kinship to Kant, and his insistence that true love of neighbor ought be bleached clean of any stain of "dear self" and inclination for it to have moral worth?[210] At first glance, Kant's point may seem consonant with the image of the kenotic, self-emptying Christ vital to Dostoevsky's imagi-nation. Doesn't the novel's epigraph itself suggest that "harsh and dreadful" self-renunciation is indeed the novel's prescription: "Except a corn of wheat fall into the ground and die, it abideth alone; but if it die, it bringeth forth much fruit"? Embodied by Christ, such self-giving is called *agape*. Classi-cally, Lutheran theologian Anders Nygren insists that *agape* can have noth-ing to do with *eros*, the human desire by which—in *The Symposium*, for example—the Platonic pilgrim ascends the scales the ladder of love in a quest for immortal, spiritual beauty.

In fact, the organic image from John's Gospel suggests a more complex understanding of the person's participation in divine love. Falling, fertil-izing, bearing fruit—the natural image suggests that desire, *eros*, and its satisfaction has its place in active love. Indeed, an organic image provides the title of this chapter, which comprises the novel's turning point. Alyo-sha's response to Grushenka makes clear that active love partakes of both *agape* and *eros*. Anders Nygren rejects this synthesis; Father Martin D'Arcy and Pope Benedict XVI affirm it. Dostoevsky sees *caritas* as both our most deeply human need and most fully human deed. Dostoevsky works from an incarnational anthropology that understands the human person as created in the image and likeness of God. Sin distorts this image but Christ's redemption restores both spirit *and* body (which Plato called "perishable rubbish" [*Symposium* 95]).[211] Faith in the Incarnation, and the sacramental sense of immanent grace that follows from that faith, fosters trust and "grounded in that gift of trust, *eros* will be transformed but not negated by divine *agape*. That transformation is *caritas*" (Tracy, *Analogical* 432). In Dostoevsky's artistic vision, the person is drawn *to* and *by* beauty to restore her or his divinely endowed image. Indeed, in the Christian tradition, "beauty" is one of God's names.[212] In this chapter, Grushenka and Alyosha become iconic images for each other.

Grushenka's goodness and beauty—her *kalon*—are manifested most fully in her *attentiveness* to Alyosha when she learns of Zosima's death:

> "Good God I did not know!" She crossed herself devoutly. "Goodness, what have I been doing, sitting on his knee like this at such a moment!" She started up as though in dismay, instantly slipped off his knee and sat down on the sofa. Alyosha fixed a long wondering look upon her and a light seemed to dawn in his face.
>
> "Rakitin," he said suddenly, in a firm and loud voice; "don't taunt me with having rebelled against God. I don't want to feel angry with you, so you must be kinder, too. I've lost a treasure such as you have never had, and you cannot judge me now. You had much better look at her—do you see how she has pity on me? I came here to find a wicked soul—I felt drawn to evil because I was base and evil myself, and I've found a true sister, I have found a treasure—a loving heart. She had pity on me just now. . . . Agrafena Alexandrovna, I am speaking of you. You've raised my soul from the depths." (302)

Grushenka is like an icon. Alyosha's radiant response—"a light seemed to dawn in his face"—suggests the transformative power of her beauty, and the spiritual *metanoia* that the icon can inspire in its beholder. The transformation is manifested in the impassioned declaration of Alyosha that follows. His voice, broken earlier by *nadryv*, is now "firm" as he implores Rakitin to "look at" Grushenka as a means of transforming his hardened heart. Alyosha's *metanoia* is then given form by his own confession: "I came here to find a wicked soul—I felt drawn to evil because I was base and evil myself, and I've found a true sister, I have found a treasure—a loving heart." Finally, he acknowledges the manifestation of grace in Grushenka as he tells her: "You've raised my soul from the depths" (302). His "irritable" (294), "listless" (295) voice has decisively changed in tone. Grushenka's authentic piety and respectful attention help him to find his own voice. Providence hasn't hidden its face, but revealed it in Grushenka's.

Grushenka's gesture of crossing herself—a sign she will repeat before the icon at Mitya's interrogation—is fitting. Her attention to Alyosha, even in the midst of her own crisis, reflects the *kenosis* of Christ. She reveals the transfigured glory of the cross: that which seems only forsaken, "harsh and dreadful." Difficult self-renunciation emerges as beautiful. Von Balthasar emphasizes the paradox of beauty in *kenosis*: "To the unity of his humili-ation and exaltation, God brings his own form and proper beauty. Isaiah's phrase, 'he had neither form nor beauty' determines the precise locus from which God's unique beauty radiates . . ." (*Form* 55–56). As von Balthasar stresses, the beauty of kenotic holiness, human participation in God's trini-tarian love, draws us toward other persons and the Other.

Alyosha's prudential receptivity allows him to receive Grushenka's gift. Educated by the irony of gracious surprise,[213] he returns to his work as a more mature monk in the world—beginning with the woman who stands before him. He attends closely to Grushenka's experience, which resonates with his own: "for everything that could shake their souls had just come to-gether in a way that does not happen often in life" (303). Each has surprised the other. Like Alyosha, Grushenka is torn by *nadryv*. Her small gesture of active love—her prayerful response to his grief—mediates his emergence from *nadryv*. Now, in an encounter of mutual healing, Alyosha's attention will help her.

For a short time, Grushenka's *nadryv* has been elicited by her percep-tion of Alyosha's "look," in the dour Sartrean sense of the word: she was convinced that he had "finalized" her as a fallen, wicked woman. She mis-takes his averted gaze—with which he hides his embarrassed concern—as condemnation:

> I wanted to ruin you, Alyosha, that's the holy truth; I quite meant to. . . . And why did I want to do such a thing? . . . Your face haunted my heart. "He despises me," I thought, "he won't even look at me." And I felt it so much at last that I wondered at myself for being frightened of a boy. I'll get him in my clutches and laugh at him. I was full of spite and anger. (304)

Her response is a variation on Mikhail's with Zosima: hatred because he "know[s] everything and condemn[s]" (269). Mikhail had returned to kill the man whose look obsessed him. Grushenka had planned to "ruin" Alyosha by seducing him (304). But as with Mikhail, Grushenka's vengeance dissipates in the face of love. Alyosha looks at her kindly and calls her his "true sister" (302).

For a far longer time Grushenka has been obsessed with the "look" of another, the Polish officer who five years ago seduced and spurned her. To Alyosha she describes her intense desire to *pay the man back*: "At night I used to lie sobbing into my pillow in the dark, and I used to brood over it, I used to tear my heart *on purpose* and gloat over my anger. 'I'll pay him back, I'll pay him back!'" (304; emphasis added). Five years later, she still lacerates herself with "violent, vindictive" fantasies, and since receiving his letter requesting to see her, has "been in such a rage" that she is "worse than [she] was five years ago" (305). She wants the reunion, but flails against the humility it will require. Her wish *for* struggles with her impulse to wish *against*.

Alyosha responds to Grushenka's confession with a calm that had been absent from his responses to Katerina and Snegiryov the day before. He is maturing in prudence, and insists less upon "a definite aim" (164). He relinquishes certainty, and, though confident, is less self-assertive, more kenotically attentive. He understands Grushenka's experience and reflects it back to her. Rather than attempting to decide for her, as he had tried the day before with Katerina, he "wishes *with*" Grushenka. In fact, like Katerina, Grushenka thrusts him into a position of authority. Feeling the agony of freedom, she yearns to be relieved of its burden: "Decide for me, Alyosha, the time has come, it shall be as you say. Am I to forgive him or not?"[214] But now Alyosha relinquishes the temptation to decide for the other person (the Grand Inquisitor's tyrannical practice). Instead, he gently articulates to Grushenka the choice that she has *already* made, as evidenced by her dress and readiness to receive her lover's bidding: "'But you have forgiven him already,' said Alyosha smiling" (306).

Grushenka's immediate response further reveals her desire to forgive. Alyosha's words reveal her to herself, and while they do not immediately bring serenity—she still struggles against her wish to forgive—they enable her to depart with truthful words of resolve. She first responds with self-composure: "'Yes, I really have forgiven him,' Grushenka murmured thoughtfully . . . ." But then, misperceiving her own humility as slavishness, she toasts her "abject heart" and smashes her glass on the floor (306). Yet Alyosha's words have penetrated: "I don't know what he said to me, it went straight to my heart; he has wrung my heart" (307). Here too Alyosha responds to her vulnerability, lowering himself and drawing closer, becoming more "proximate":[215] "'What have I done to you?' answered Alyosha bending over her with a tender smile, and gently taking her by the hands; 'I only gave you an onion, nothing but a tiny little onion, that's all, that's all!'" (307). His gesture will be echoed moments later when Zosima raises Alyosha by the hand and says that he too has only given "one little onion" (311).

Like a "spiritual therapist" (Miller, *Worlds* 86), Alyosha draws out and builds upon the best in Grushenka. She relates the tale of the peasant woman whose single good deed was giving an onion to a beggar. Through narrative, she imagines her own capacity for active love. Alyosha identifies and affirms this capacity, much as he had done when he kissed Ivan. Her "soul," as Alyosha has seen, "is not yet at peace with itself" (305). But she departs with resolve—"only for one instant she stood as though hesitating" (307)—and speaks her last words from her "deepest I," avowing that for "one hour" she truly loved Dmitri without manipulation (308). Comic irony awaits Grushenka in Mokroe: her officer proves to be a dud, and her love for Dmitri more genuine and enduring than "one little hour" (308).

Alyosha now moves with a newly born resolve, toward further joyful surprise: "He walked fast beside Rakitin as though in a terrible hurry" (308). Unintentionally, Rakitin's bitter taunts ironically bespeak the truth: "So you see the miracles you were looking out for now have come to pass!"[216] Alyosha has been opened to the irony of surprise. The healing mutuality he has shared with Grushenka, their exchange of onions, is a miracle. And upon returning to the monastery he will be surprised again by a vision that is *comic* in the deep, Dantean sense of that word.

A last word about the onion: the humble image aptly suggests what is so mysteriously beautiful about the form of *The Brothers Karamazov*: scenes like this, in which repetitions sound, but in slightly different keys, chime throughout the entire novel—much like the chimes in Dante's *Commedia*. As Robin Miller eloquently observes:

> An onion, like a seed, is a living organism . . . . A slice along
> its diameter shows its carefully structured and separate layers;
> to unravel it is to discover that each layer recapitulates all the
> others. *The Brothers Karamazov* embodies these attributes of
> the onion. . . . [C]orrespondences—of which there are literally
> thousands in the novel . . .—give the novel its surprising unity,
> its miraculously open metonymy. (*Worlds* 86)

These correspondences—its countless rhymes and chimes—lend the novel its beauty. Readers perceive and are drawn to this beauty, and often transformed by it.

Like Dante, Dostoevsky sought readerly conversion through the beauty of his art. In the climactic chapter of Book 7 "Cana of Galilee," when Alyosha returns to the monastery and falls asleep beside Zosima's coffin, he receives a vision akin to pilgrim Dante's in *Paradiso*. Beside the elder's coffin, he encounters the risen Zosima who joyfully directs Alyosha's attention to the transfigured, risen Christ. Alyosha awakens after a vision of paradise, a Cana of communal beatitude. Like Dante, he is now ready to embrace his vocation—partly as the author of Zosima's life, but chiefly as "a monk in the world."

A close reading of this brief, poem-like chapter suggests some of the ways in which this avowedly anti-Catholic author nevertheless reveals a deeply "catholic" vision, certainly consonant with his own Orthodox tradition, but revealing its "interior affinity" even to Roman Catholicism, and specifically Dante, similarities to whom I will accentuate here.[217] Moreover, it reveals Dostoevsky's incarnational realism, grounded as his faith is in the Word made flesh. Alyosha, "more of a realist than the rest of us" (P/V 25),[218] perceives the wedding of the finite and eternal. The reverberations of his "Cana" vision remain with him "for the rest of his life" (P/V 363).[219]

Alyosha arrives back in the monastery a little after 9 pm. In a novel in which "triads dominate" and suggest a "Trinitarian theology" (Cunningham 141), the number 9 (which Dante links with Beatrice in his *Vita Nuova*) squares and accentuates the number 3. Zosima's shaming culminates around 3 pm, the hour of Christ death. At about 9 pm, Alyosha will witness Christ's resurrected life. Despite his late arrival, "the gatekeeper let[s] him in by a special entrance"—one among many casuistic loopholes in a novel shot through with scenes of surprising grace. Like the disciples in the upper room after Calvary, Alyosha is "timid" when he opens the door to the room where Zosima's body lies in the coffin. Father Paissy reads from the Gospel of John. Alyosha turns to the right as he enters the room. We recall the night before, as he and Ivan departed from the Metropolis, Ivan had announced that he'd go "left," the sinister direction, while his brother would go right" (229).[220] Now in the corner of the elder's cell, Alyosha kneels and prays. Read in the light of *Paradiso*'s final canto, the "slow and calm rotation" of impressions within Alyosha's soul, the "sweetness in his heart," the "joy singing in his mind," recalls Dante's soul as it rotates "like wheels revolving / with an even motion," "by the Sun and the other stars." Alyosha falls before the coffin "as if it were a holy thing," made sacramental by the presence of the man who lies within. Alyosha "loves" the story of the wedding of Cana, the miracle that Jesus never expected to perform, just as Alyosha never expected to experience a "miracle" with Grushenka (308); these miracles are both gratuitous and purposeful. In what might be called an Ignatian composition of place,[221] Alyosha employs his senses to imagine the scene at Cana: he hears Mary noting the lack of wine, and sees Jesus' "quiet [meek] smile" when he responds by saying "Mine hour is not yet come." But his mother knows that Jesus descended into our human condition, that he "came down ... not just for his great and awful deed" but for just such prosaic events as this one, "the simple, artless merrymaking of some uncouth, uncouth but guileless beings who lovingly invited him to their poor marriage feast."[222]

Mary's mediatory, motherly presence is prominent in Alyosha's comforting, "assuaging" vision, just as it is at the beginning of *Paradiso* 33, and is notable in a novel of brothers bereft of their mothers.[223]

Throughout the chapter, readers can discern a "both/and" vision running through Alyosha's experience of "the wholeness of things" (309).[224] Once the water is made wine, Alyosha feels "the walls of the room opening out." To his surprise, Alyosha sees Zosima at the wedding feast, which is now turned heavenly banquet at which the transfigured, risen Christ presides. Here Dostoevsky's "both/and" imagination can be discerned in three ways. First, Christ is paradoxically presented as both immanent and transcendent. Zosima exhorts Alyosha to be not afraid and to begin his work by looking at the image of the risen Christ: "our Sun, do you see him?" Earlier, he had insisted that if "we . . . did not have the precious image of Christ before us, we would perish and be altogether lost" (276); now he affirms the paradoxical presence of that image: "Awful is his greatness before us, he became like us out of love, and he is rejoicing with us, transforming water into wine, that the joy of his guests may not end." Second, Alyosha's emotional state is marked by both joy and pain, wholeness and self-emptying: "Something burned in Alyosha's heart, something suddenly filled him almost painfully, tears of rapture nearly burst from his soul." Third, as he awakens and gazes for thirty seconds upon the body of Zosima, he recognizes his friend as both dead ("stretched out with an icon on his chest,") and risen, as Zosima's "voice was still sounding in his ears."

Here the symphonic chapter reaches its final movement. "Yearning for freedom, space, vastness," Alyosha hurries outside, and in the starlit August night we discern three more "both/and" moments. First, Alyosha perceives the nuptial union of infinite and finite, the ways "seeds from other worlds" sprout on earth, and how all thus "lives and grows only through its sense of being in touch with other mysterious worlds" (320). Seeing "shining stars," "golden domes," sleeping flowers, he hears the way "the silence of the earth seemed to merge with the silence of the heavens, the mystery of the earth touched the mystery of the stars." Second, Alyosha—like Zosima in his dying moment—both descends and ascends: a profound impulse of love and memory propels him to fall upon the feminine earth in an open-armed gesture that suggests both *eros* ("he long[s] to kiss it, to kiss all of it,") and *agape* ("He wanted to forgive everyone"), the synthesis of which is *caritas*.

Third, and finally, Alyosha's experience is both solitary and communal. No one observes his ecstasy. Father Paissy notices him leaving the elder's room, but tactfully "look[s] away again at once, realizing that something strange was happening with the boy." Alone upon the earth he weeps for his fellow creatures, for "the stars that shone on him from the abyss," and for his fellow human persons: "He wanted to forgive everyone and for everything, and to ask forgiveness, oh, not for himself! But *for all* and for everything, 'as others are asking for me.'" As I have suggested, "for all" provides the linguistic key to the novel, and its continued repetitions forges a both/and unity that suggest both that divine grace is freely given for all (213) and that each of us is responsible for all (276). "For all" links the dual claims of the Christian life, the gift received as task: Christ's work redeems all and we must work responsibly for all. As noted earlier, "for all" is drawn from the Eucharistic prayer in the Orthodox liturgy—"In behalf of all and for all"—as is the phrase "unto ages of ages," repeated three times in this chapter, and again on the final page of the novel. Alyosha's mystical moment in solitude is situated in the communal context of the church.[225]

In "Cana of Galilee" Alyosha has grown fully capable to apprehend and respond to the real. Like Dante, who in his final canto sees that God's light "contain[s] / by love into a single volume bound, / the pages scattered through the universe" (33.85–87), Alyosha senses the integral wholeness of reality, as "those innumerable worlds of God all came together in his soul." Discerning that "grace is everywhere,"[226] he rises up "a fighter, steadfast for the rest of his life," remembering always that "someone visited my soul at that hour." "Three days later" he departs the monastery to begin his work.

In Book 7, Dostoevsky provides a beautiful answer, in "oblique" "artistic form,"[227] not only to Ivan's despair that humans can ever love like Christ (205), but to Dmitri's agonized confession that the beautiful form of literary art has never re-formed him (97). As we will discuss in the next chapter, Mitya is, in fact, re-formed. He becomes a "new man" (503), and the novel's beauty invites the reader to experience a *metanoia* with him, to perceive the reality of things, the way the incarnation has linked the earthly with the infinite. The novel's "prosaics of conversion" doesn't present us with Rilke's impossibly ideal "archaic torso of Apollo." In the novel, the burden of false ideals and self-divinization takes the distorted form of *nadryv*.[228] Instead, the novel's incarnational realism offers the humble, sublime image of Christ in whom Dostoevsky saw "nothing more beautiful."

Christ descends into the limited and particular contours of human life and—in the words of Gerard Manley Hopkins—"plays in ten thousand places,"[229] including the "limbs" and "eyes" and "face" of Grushenka, Zosima, and Alyosha. In the incarnational realism of *The Brothers Karamazov* the salvific image of Christ calls the reader to contemplate this presence and, possibly, be re-formed in the process. In the chapters that follow, we will trace this process in the stories of Mitya, Ivan, and young Kolya.

Chapter 5

Mitya

As Grushenka flies off to meet the man who had seduced and abandoned her, Mitya frantically hopes that he himself might build "a new life" with her (314, 315). He loves Grushenka—not merely "the curve of her body," but "something far higher" (327): her whole image (*obraz*) as a person, one who inspires him to trust, generosity, and salutary shame (327). Ever "broad," Mitya remains hell-bent in his intention to repay Katerina her three thousand rubles. He "grind[s] his teeth" (315, 323) at the prospect of being in her debt. Thus begins an episodic, often comic series of failures. Driven by wishful, even "magical" thinking, Mitya begs Kuzma Kuzmich (Samsonov) to accept the "realism" (319) of his proposal. "Spiteful" Samsonov, seeking to make a fool of him, sends Mitya to Lyagavy "on purpose" (325). Mitya then desires to revenge himself on Samsonov. But he finds a prosaic image of trinitarian love in the three rubles lent to him by "the people of the house who loved him" (321). Mitya finds Lyagavy—who insists upon the name Gorstkin—drunk and asleep, and saves him from carbon monoxide poisoning. Realizing he's been duped, he returns to Skotoprigonevsk and appeals to Madame Khokhlakova, with the "mathematical certainty that this was his last hope" (328) to secure three thousand rubles. But she detests Mitya and, in "Gold Mines," obliviously extols her brand of "realism" to him (329). Now at rock bottom, Mitya returns to his father's house, walks with pestle in hand past the closed door into the garden, and stands before his father's bedroom window. Repelled by Fyodor's visage, he rages "in the dark" on the verge of murder.[230]

Mitya's explanation for what happens next is completely consistent with the novel's vision of incarnational realism: "God was watching over me then" (336)—or, as he puts it the next morning to his interrogators, "my guardian angel saved me, that's what you have not taken into account" (403). Mitya does not murder his father. "Broad" as he is, however, he has not yet renounced violence: as he runs away, he strikes his foster-father Grigory and, after soaking his handkerchief in an attempt to stanch the elderly man's bleeding, leaves him for dead. When he learns that Grushenka has in fact "gone to Mokroe, to her officer" (338), he again chooses violence. Reaching "some new determination," he resolves to see Grushenka one last time, if only to "step aside" (339) and, come dawn, "put [a] bullet in [his] brain" (343). With the fifteen hundred rubles he's kept hidden in the amulet around his neck, he orders supplies, retrieves his pistols, and rushes to Mokroe.

In fact, Mitya still "want[s] to live." He "love[s] life" (344). Indeed, he feels an incipient desire for active love, for "a higher order" (346), a yearning "to bless God and His creation" (347). But he confuses genuine self-sacrifice with self-immolation, a self-imposed "punishment" for his past life of "disorder" (346). Purgatorial cleansing and various forms of "giving way" must be practiced in community. Despite Mitya's "sudden decision" for the isolation of suicide—for "the gallows," not the cross, to use Ivan's formulation (549)—his words and actions suggest that he remains uncertain. When he recalls "pulling the captain's beard," he feels salutary guilt (347). He promises Fetya and Pyotr Ilych that he has no intention of using his pistols to kill Grushenka and her lover, and asks Fenya's forgiveness for having "hurt" her, even if it's "all the same now" (348).

Desperate, Mitya encounters an earthy image of hope: Andrey, the peasant coach driver. Mitya's conversation with him during their "twelve mile" (350) troika ride to Mokroe chimes forward to two scenes in which main characters happen upon peasants: Ivan with the "drunken little peasant" (522) and Kolya with the "not quite sober" peasant (448). Mitya's moving dialogue with Andrey bears close analysis as it elicits vital signs of a "new man" arising.

Their conversation begins when Mitya expresses anxiety that Grushenka may already be asleep—and in the arms of her lover, the thought of which puts him "beside himself" (351). Andrey assures him that they're likely awake, playing cards, but then expresses his own qualms of conscience: is he serving as an accomplice to murder? In response, Mitya seizes Andrey by the shoulders and, haltingly, strives to be clear: he intends to punish *himself* in order to stop running over other people and "ruining" them with his violence. Like a good confessor, the peasant Andrey "keeps up the conversation" by reflecting back and reinforcing Mitya's best sentiments with prudent peasant wisdom: if creatures are created by God, no creature should be "forced" beyond its capacity, not even a horse. Mitya's *non-sequitur* is apt: Forced along . . . "to hell?" he asks. Mitya already knows that by punishing himself through suicide he would *forcefully* strain himself toward hell, and cut against his deepest wish for life. He turns to Andrey as a spiritual authority when he pleads, both passionately and formally: "Andrey, simple soul, will Dmitri Fyodorovich Karamazov go to hell, or not, what do you think?" (352).

Andrey's threefold response resonates with Zosima's orthodox wisdom. First, Andrey responds by reminding Mitya of his divine gift of freedom: "I don't know, dear man, it depends on you." Secondly, he reminds Mitya that Christ's death, descent into hell, and subsequent resurrection freed "all" sinners infernally "tormented." Like Alyosha (213), Andrey avows that Christ enacted his salvific descent and ascent "for all." And thirdly, Andrey distinguishes Mitya from the self-enclosed proud and "mighty of the earth," who will visit hell, at least until "Christ come[s] again" (352). In contrast to these, Andrey and his cohorts see Mitya as "a little child." Their perception is prudent: Mitya *is* childlike in his unabashed dependence on others, like Andrey. Reminded of his inter-creatural humility, Mitya is able to call upon God's offer of forgiveness. As will Kolya when he converses with his peasant, Mitya asks if Andrey will forgive him—adding, in a phrase understandably baffling to Andrey—"for everyone." Mitya turns their troika into a confessional, and Andrey fulfills a sacerdotal role: Mitya arrives at Mokroe praying fervently for God's forgiveness and for the continued capacity to love, for the strength to respect Grushenka's freedom and to release her honorably. And if he *were* to commit suicide and go to hell, he promises to love God there forever. Mitya thereby presents another image of "hell with a loophole," joining those offered by Zosima and Grushenka: "Lord, receive me, with all my lawlessness, and do not condemn me. Let me pass by Thy judgment, . . . do not condemn me, for I have condemned myself, do not condemn me, for I love Thee. O Lord, I am a wretch, but I love Thee. If Thou sendest me to hell, I shall love Thee forever and ever. . . . But let me love to the end . . ." (352). Mitya's prayer prepares him for the ironic reversal and unexpected grace he will receive in Mokroe: the joy of Grushenka's love and the purgative torments of interrogation.[231]

Before turning to those torments, a word about Mitya's temptations to suicide—both before and after he arrives at Mokroe. The narrator has alerted us to the fact that Mitya's wild ride "perhaps" transpires at the same time as Alyosha's mystical experience in "Cana of Galilee." On Mitya's drive, "the big stars shining in the sky" are the same ones that Alyosha sees when he apprehends the silent conjoining of finite and infinite (312). In fact, the brothers' simultaneous experiences can be read as conjoined: for both brothers, the beatific image of Grushenka inspires sanctified *eros* and hope. Earlier that evening, Alyosha did not feel lust for the beautiful woman who had nestled on his lap, and "yet . . . could not help wondering at a new and strange sensation in his heart, a feeling of the intensest and purest interest without a trace of fear" (300). Similarly, Mitya yearns for Grushenka with "his whole being," yet feels "not the slightest jealousy of this new man, new rival, this officer . . ." (350). Like Alyosha in "An Onion," Mitya will experience a radical overturning of expectation, a joyful *peripeteia,* for it is *he* who proves to be the "new man" and rightful lover, and the officer no lover at all. Grushenka loves Mitya; earlier she has declared her love for Alyosha "with all [her] soul," but "in a different way" (301). Alyosha had gone to Grushenka with his own self-immolating intention of throwing away his new vocation as "a monk in the world" in order to spite God. Similarly, Mitya plans to "meet the first warm ray of 'golden-haired Phoebus'" with a bullet in the brain, an aesthetically-crafted exit. But as he rides, yearning for Grushenka, he sees through his plan's theatrical falsity: even by committing suicide he "could not be rid of the past, of all that he had left behind and that tortured him" (357), including Grigory, whom he's left lying in blood on the ground. He's tempted to have Andrey stop so he can "make an end of everything without waiting for the dawn" (350). But the "fearful specters" of immediate self-destruction "[fly] by like a spark" when Mitya thinks again of Grushenka, and "long[s] to look upon her, if only for a moment, if only from a distance." Again, as throughout the "Onion" chapter, Grushenka's imperfect beauty[232] mediates grace in surprising ways: "Never had this woman, who was such a fateful influence in his life, aroused such love in his breast, such new and unknown feeling, surprising even to himself, a feeling tender to devoutness, to self-effacement before her! 'I will efface myself!' he said in rush of almost hysterical ecstasy" (351).

Unlike Alyosha's, Mitya's ecstasy is not "firm and unshakable" (312). In three successive sentences, the narrator repeats that Mitya lacks the capacity to "reason" (350). And yet, inchoately, Mitya has determined that suicide would be willful and wrong. He recognizes this again in Mokroe, after he *knows* Grushenka loves only him, and in the "delirium" that ensues—somewhere between Sodom and Cana—he feels the guilt of Grigory's blood. He prays to God to "let this cup pass" and to restore Grigory's life (372). His prayer seems to be answered: his suicidal impulse dissipates. (Later, Mitya tells his defense attorney that his mother, Adelaida Ivanovna, had been praying for him at this moment [616].) As we've seen earlier, the word "yet" signals the dispersal of darkness and "damnation": "Yet it was as if some ray of some kind of bright hope shone to him in the darkness. He jumped up and ran back to the room—to her, to her, his queen forever!" (372). He finds her and kisses her. Grushenka also feels guilt and seeks punishment: "Beat me . . . oh how I deserve to be tormented. Stop, wait, afterwards, I won't have that . . .' She suddenly thrust him away" (374). Though both are drunk, the lovers discern and accept the limits imposed by conjugal form, the proper *obraz* for their union. Mokroe isn't the site to consummate their sacramental love: "'Don't touch me . . .' she faltered in an imploring voice. 'Don't touch me, till I'm yours. . . . It's nasty here.'" Mitya responds respectfully: "I'll obey you! I won't think of it. . . . I worship you." Though inebriated, she acknowledges his generosity, and pleads: "Let us be honest, let us be good . . ." (376). Mutually, they vow to begin again, together. Sustained by Grushenka's love, Mitya is prepared to face "the torments" of his interrogation.

Mitya's Torments

Moments later, legal representatives arrive and place Mitya under arrest. Throughout their interrogation, they consistently hold their suspect in contempt. They refuse their attention. Perhaps one should expect as much in the investigation of a violent crime, especially when all outward signs point to the suspect's guilt. Mitya himself recognizes that their positions are unequal: "I don't pretend to be on equal terms with you" (391). Prosecutor Ippolit Kirillovich tells Mitya: "you have a perfect right not to answer the questions put to you now, and we on our side, have no right to extort an answer from you" (397). But he and the district attorney, Nikolay Parfinovich, subtly exert their power to extort. "Continental pretrial procedures aim to elicit a confession; hence the inquisitor's curiosity legally extends to every aspect of a suspect's personal life" (Weisberg 47). As such, the situation is one in which Mitya is "circumstantially forced to speak" (Fogel 225–26). Amy Ronner analyzes Mitya's interrogation (165–74) and observes that his interrogators "employ nearly every trick in the book to coerce and deliberately elicit information out of their suspect, and these old fashioned Russian tactics prefigure the ones in the pre- and post-Miranda tool kit" (165).[233] Criminal interrogation hardly offers an ideal site for confessional dialogue. The relation of Ippolit Kirillovch and Nikolay Parfenovich to Mitya is *not* that of Zosima to Mikhail.

But the novel may inspire the reader to ask: might Mitya's questioners *approach* such a relation? Might they protect law and order *and* serve as "monks in the world"? In a section of her essay, "Forms of the Implicit Love of God," Simone Weil suggests such a possibility.[234] She envisions a "supernatural virtue of justice," which consists of behaving exactly as though there were equality when one is the stronger in an unequal relationship. Exactly, in every respect, including the slightest details of accent and attitude, for a detail may be enough to place the weaker party in the condition of matter, which on this occasion naturally belongs to him; just as the slightest shock causes water that has remained liquid before freezing point to solidify. (143)

Weil describes the more typical situation, in which "contempt . . . the contrary of attention" (153) defines the law's relation to the criminal:

Everything combines, down to the smallest details, down even to the inflections of people's voices, to make him seem vile and outcast in all men's eyes including his own. The brutality and flippancy, the terms of scorn and the jokes, the way of speaking, the way of listening and of not listening, all these things are equally effective. (154)

Contempt toward the suspect or criminal reifies and reduces him to "the condition of matter." In contrast, attention never denies the criminal's or suspect's responsibility for his actions, but entails treating him as a person, not "a thing. It means wishing to preserve in him the faculty of free consent" (153) and "obtaining from the magistrates and their assistants the attention and respect for the accused that is due from every man to any person who may be in his power . . ." (155).[235] Weil's "supernatural" conception of justice is akin to Zosima's, who calls for an even more radical "respect for the accused": Zosima claims that "no one can judge a criminal, until he recognizes that he is just such a criminal as the man standing before him, and that he perhaps is more than all men to blame for that crime" (276–77). Justice based "on reason alone, but not with Christ" (272) cannot reach such a level of solidarity with and attentiveness toward the suspect or criminal. Neither Weil nor Dostoevsky (through Zosima) disavow reason or justice. They imagine justice refracted through the prism of Christ's love.

At first, Mitya seems eager to cooperate with his questioners, and seeks "attention and respect" from them in return. Initially, he believes they have come to arrest him for the murder of Grigory: "I un-der-stand!" (419). He never expects that he might be a suspect in *Fyodor's* murder. When accused of it, he forthrightly avows his innocence: "Not guilty. I am guilty of the blood of another man, but not of my father's" (389). When he learns that Grigory is in fact alive, he thanks God for the "miracle," crosses himself three times. He remembers the way Grigory served as his surrogate father, and declares to his interrogators "in one minute you have given me new life, resurrected me!" (390). Now he wants to assist his questioners, hoping to "put an end of it in one moment" (391). Throughout the questioning, he expects them to respect his human freedom. When he sees them carefully recording his testimony, he responds first with surprise, then with his "consent"—the word Weil emphasizes—and his direction:

> "Well write it; I consent, I give my full consent, gentlemen, only . . . do you see. . . . Stay, stay write this. Of disorderly conduct I am guilty, of violence on a poor old man I am guilty. And there is something else at the bottom of my heart, of which I am guilty, too—but that you need not write down" (he turned suddenly to the secretary) "that's my personal life, gentlemen, that doesn't concern you, the bottom of my heart, that's to say. . . . But of the murder of my old father I'm not guilty." (391)

Increasingly, however, Mitya realizes that his questioners do not care about his "consent" or the "feelings" he wishes to keep private (391), or his desire that they share "mutual confidence" and refrain from "rummag[ing] in [his] soul" (394). "A man is not a drum," Mitya insists. But he grows progressively and painfully conscious of the way they beat on him as a thing, purely instrumental to their goal of solving the crime. He notices the prosecutor winking to the district attorney "on the sly" (392), and pleads with them to "drop that regulation method of questioning" (396) which aims to sneak up on the suspect. He compares his situation to that of a hunted beast: "I'm a wolf and you're the hunters" (399).

Certainly Mitya shares the blame for his situation. His past behavior warrants his interrogators' suspicion. Further, Mitya petulantly refuses to answer any questions as to why he needed three thousand rubles when he already had fifteen hundred: "'Oh, gentlemen, you needn't go into details, how, when, and why, and why just so much money . . .'" (395); "that's my private life, and I won't allow any intrusion into my private life" (397). His insistence denies the matter-of-fact reality that he must reveal these details if he wishes to be exonerated. He insists on "realism" (399), but lacks it himself. His past actions have done little to earn the trust of others. He justly asserts his right to be respected as a human being, but refuses to cooperate by not confessing his shameful theft. He himself falls short in the balancing of openness and closure necessitated by incarnational realism. But, in my reading, his inquisitors fall shorter. They insist upon hearing Mitya corroborate the reality that they have already constructed, and resist opening themselves to the complexity of Mitya's situation. They won't allow Mitya to surprise them; they've already made up their minds.

There is, however, one exception: "The good-natured police captain," Mikhail Makarovich. Once the captain allows himself to be surprised by

Grushenka's "gentle soul" and enters into her suffering (394), he is able to speak to Mitya with a "look of warm, almost fatherly, feeling for the luckless prisoner." He confesses that he had been "unfair" to Grushenka when he called her a "harlot" who was "most to blame" (389). By saying this and "a great deal that was irregular," he personifies Weil's conception of "the supernatural virtue of justice" in his own natural way: "Supernatural virtue, for the inferior thus treated, consists in not believing that there really is equality of strength and in recognizing that his treatment is due solely to the generosity of the other party. That is what is called gratitude" (Weil 143). The captain's solicitude elicits Mitya's deep gratitude and restored resolve: "Mitya jumped up and rushed toward him. 'Forgive me, gentlemen, oh, allow me, allow me!' he cried. 'You've the heart of an angel, Mikhail Makarovich, I thank you for her. I will, I will be calm, cheerful, in fact'" (394). Could the captain's exemplary attention and "irregular" words (394) ever become more regular in police interrogations?[236]

The prosecutor and district attorney do not follow the police captain's example. Even when "it was evident that [Mitya] was trying more than ever not to forget or miss a single detail of his story" as he describes himself "in the dark," outside his father's window, "both attorneys listened . . . with a sort of awful reserve [and] looked coldly at him" (400). Mitya senses them laughing at him after he has "softly" describes the way "the devil was conquered" at that moment (400). Mitya is indignant at their indifference and refuses to believe that grace intervened at that moment: "But, you see, I didn't murder him, you see my guardian angel saved me—that's what you have not taken into account. And that's why it's so base of you, so base!" (403). Their strictly empirical realism leaves no room for spiritual reality. Remaining detached, they require Mitya to strip. Naked, Mitya "was almost ready to believe himself that he was inferior to them, and that now they had a perfect right to despise him" (409). Their cold closure toward him as a fellow person keeps him from revealing his relationship to Katerina: "And you expect me to be open with such scoffers as you, who see nothing and believe in nothing . . . and to tell you another nasty thing I've done, another disgrace . . . !" (411).

The prosecutor responds "with the most frigid and composed air" to Mitya's righteous fury (411) and exhorts Mitya "to enter into our position" (413). But he refuses to enter into Mitya's. Even when Mitya finally reveals his great disgrace, the prosecutor smiles coldly when Mitya insists on the "vital difference" between a thief and a scoundrel (416). He smirks at Mitya's anguished explanation of why he couldn't possibly go to Katya for money (418). Both prosecutor and district attorney "[laugh] aloud" when Mitya tries to explain his "base" reserving of the remaining fifteen hundred rubles

(417). By the end, Mitya has made a full confession. But he despairs when his listeners respond to it with, in Weil's words, "the terms of scorn and . . . jokes" (154):

> "I have made you an awful confession," Mitya said gloomily in conclusion. "You must appreciate it, and what's more, you must respect it, for if not, if that leaves your souls untouched, then you've simply no respect for me gentlemen, I tell you that, and I shall die of shame at having confessed it to men like you! Oh I shall shoot myself. Yes, I see, I see already that you don't believe me. . . ." In despair he hid his face in his hands. (418–19)

Mitya seems reduced to "the condition of matter" (Weil 143): "His face now expressed complete, hopeless despair, and he sat mute and passive as though hardly conscious of what was happening" (421). Finalized as "a closed case," he forecloses his own possibilities, and again considers suicide (421).

But the thought of Grushenka gives him hope, and her testimony— like those spoken earlier by Markel Makarovich—proves restorative. Grushenka gives her truthful evidence, and claims that she always "had faith in [Mitya's] noble heart." Her avowal of faith inspires Mitya to request "one word" with Grushenka:

> "Agrafena Alexandrovana!" Mitya got up from his chair, "have faith in God and in me. I am not guilty of my father's murder!"
>
> Having uttered these words Mitya sat down again on his chair. Grushenka stood up and crossed herself devoutly before the icon.
>
> "Thanks be to Thee, O Lord," she said, in a voice thrilled with emotion, and still standing, she turned to Nikolay Parfenovich and added: "As he has spoken now, believe it! I know him. He'll say anything as a joke or from obstinacy, but he'll never deceive you against his conscience. He's telling the whole truth, you may believe it."
>
> "Thanks Agrafena Alexandrovana, you've given me fresh courage," Mitya responded in a quivering voice. (427)

Here Mitya and Grushenka exchange "penetrated words" that nurture their mutual faith. Mitya grounds his avowal of innocence in faith in God, as if calling upon God to infuse his own words with grace. His words pierce Grushenka. In turn, her voice is "thrilled with emotion," and grounds her response in prayer. She crosses herself, as had Mitya upon learning that Grigory was alive (390), and as she had done earlier that evening when she heard of Zosima's death (302). She directs her response to Nikolay

Parfenovna, but her testimony of faith in her beloved's innocence gives Mitya "fresh courage." Both make vows, the solemnity of which is reflected as they rise to their feet to speak. Mitya's words secure Grushenka's faith in him; her words heal him of despair and assist him in recovering hope.

With Grushenka's healing intervention, Mitya emerges as a "new man." As he tells Alyosha three months later, "I've taken her soul into my soul and through her I've become a man myself" (501). But even here in Mokroe he evinces a "good taste of self": aware of his past misdeeds, he takes public responsibility for them, even as he looks ahead to his future opportunities to help, not hurt others. His dream of "the babe" proves the agonized counterpart to Alyosha's joyful dream of Cana. Both dreams signify *metanoia*.

Exhausted, Mitya falls asleep and dreams of the weeping babe and the suffering peasants. Like Ivan, he asks "why?" He asks "foolish," "persistent" questions—"[W]hy are they crying? . . . [W]hy are people poor? Why is the babe poor? . . . Why don't they feed the babe?" He senses that he *must* speak, as if speech were a necessary step that must precede his actions to help those who suffer: "And he felt that, though his questions were unreasonable and senseless, yet he wanted to ask just that, and he had to ask it in just that way" (428). In a different key, Mitya's dream reprises and affirms the value of the harrowing questions Ivan had asked in "Rebellion." But a crucial difference lies in Mitya's will to *act*:

> And he felt that, though his questions were unreasonable and senseless, yet he wanted to ask just that, and he had to ask it just in that way. And he felt also that a passion of pity, such as he had never known before, was rising in his heart, and he wanted to cry, that *he wanted to do something for them all*, so that the babe should weep no more, so that the dark-faced, dried-up mother should not weep, that no one should shed tears again from that moment, and he wanted to do it at once, at once, regardless of all obstacles, with all the Karamazov recklessness. (428; emphasis added)

Mitya wants to *do* something about the suffering of the poor and vulnerable and weak. Ivan never makes such a resolution or acts upon it—until, perhaps, he cares for the peasant he's almost killed, and shows up at court the following day to testify at Mitya's trial. Granted, Mitya's insistence on "immediate action" (28, 55)—"at once"!—suggests love in dreams. He's a suspect in custody, and his powers to help are limited. But it's a crucial beginning. Mitya awakens to the sound of Grushenka's "tender voice" avowing her commitment to him, and discovers a pillow placed anonymously under his head—another small loving gesture, another onion. Ecstatic, he perceives it as "some great kindness." And he's right to do so: incarnational realism sees power in the smallest of deeds, in every "mustard seed" (117) thrown. He cries out his joyful gratitude to *all* (428) and, moments later, is "impelled by uncontrollable feeling" to "pronounce" a public confession (429).

Through this confession, and his subsequent plea that others forgive him—"Grusha" and all the "good people"—Mitya "offers . . . his hand" to all. His words forge a little community, albeit imperfectly. Nikolay Parfenovich "hide[s] his hands behind his back" (430) when Mitya offers his. But others respond with pleas that they too be forgiven: "'Forgive me at parting, good people!' Mitya shouted suddenly from the cart. 'Forgive us too!' he heard two or three voices" (431); Kalganov runs up to the cart, to shake hands and shares "good-byes" with Mitya as he is taken away (431).[237] And twice after their "penetrated" dialogue, Grushenka utters two potent "performative utterances" to Mitya.[238] When he awakens, she vows, "I won't leave you now for the rest of my life," and her promise fills him with a great longing for life and light (428). Just before he is taken away, she repeats her vow, "I will follow you forever." Her words elicit in Mitya the capacity to ask her—and all—for forgiveness.[239] Naturally, counter-voices sound: Mavriky Mavrikyevich "snap[s] out savagely" at Mitya (431); Mitya himself shouts "from resentment" at Trifon Borisich (432). But the words at the end of Book 9 resonate with the "joy" (429) of a new man. Mitya will summon "labor and fortitude" to sustain the voice he has found by the end of his tormenting descent and ascent at Mokroe.[240]

Mitya's Discernment of Responsibility

In his public confession before the people at Mokroe, Mitya articulates a newly achieved insight that speaks to the novel's crucial themes of personal responsibility and suffering. In matchless Mityan style, he claims his personal responsibility "for all": "We all make men weep, and mothers, and babes at the breasts, . . . of all I am the lowest reptile!" And he admits his past misdeeds: "I've sworn to amend every day of my life, beating my breast, and every day I've done the same filthy things." His words offer an implicit response to Ivan's rebellion in the face of human suffering. Yes, humans do "filthy things" and cause innocent children to suffer. But Ivan sees only the injustice, and bitterly rebels; Mitya recognizes that suffering can be the catalyst for human growth. As Leon Bloy once noted, there are "places in the heart that do not yet exist, and into them enters suffering, in order that they may exist."[241] Suffering can shock one out of persistent irresponsibility. It can purify, expiate, and assist one in acting responsibly. As Mitya puts it: "I understand now that such men as I need a blow, a blow of destiny to catch them as with a noose, and bind them by a force from without. Never, never should I have risen of myself! But the thunderbolt has fallen. I accept the torment of accusation, and my public shame, I want to suffer and by suffering I shall be purified" (429).

About three months later, in November, Mitya still sees his suffering as a form of grace. He's a "new man," he tells Alyosha, and wants to embody his new sense of responsibility by suffering for others. Mitya sings his remarkable "hymn":

"I must pour out my heart to you. Brother, these last two months I've found in myself a new man. A new man has risen up in me. He was hidden in me, but would never have come to the surface, if it hadn't been for this blow from heaven. I am afraid! And what do I care if spend twenty years in the mines, breaking out ore with a hammer? I am not a bit afraid of that—it's something else I am afraid of now: that the new man may leave me. Even there, in the mines, underground, I man find a human heart in another convict and murderer by my side, and I may make friends with him, for even there one may live and love and suffer. One may resurrect and revive a frozen heart in that convict, one may wait upon him for years, and at last bring up from the dark depths a lofty soul, a feeling, suffering creature; one may bring forth an angel, resurrect a hero! There are so many of them, hundreds of them, and we are all responsible for them. Why was it I dreamed of that 'babe' at such a moment? 'Why is the babe poor?' That was a sign to me at that moment. It's for the babe I'm going. Because we are all responsible for all. For all the 'babes,' for there are big children as well as little children. All are 'babes.' I go *for all* for somebody must go *for all*. I didn't kill father, but I've got to go. I accept it. It's all come to me here, here, within these peeling walls. There are numbers of them there, hundreds of them underground, with hammers in their hands. Oh, yes, we shall be in chains and there will no freedom, but then, in our great sorrow, we shall rise again to joy, without which man cannot live nor God exist, for God gives joy: it's His privilege—a grand one. Ah man should be dissolved in prayer! What would I be underground there without God? Rakitin lies! If they drive God from the earth, we shall shelter Him underground. One cannot exist in prison without God; it's even more impossible than out of prison. And then we men underground will sing

from the bowels of the earth a tragic hymn to God, with Whom
is joy. Hail to God and His joy! I love Him!"

Mitya was almost gasping for breath as he uttered his wild
speech. He turned pale, his lips quivered, and tears rolled down
his cheek. (499; emphasis added)

Mitya's hymn articulates a dimension of suffering vital to incarnational
realism: suffering can be sacrificially offered to God *on behalf of others*, in
participation with the suffering of Christ (Col 1:24).[242] Somehow Mitya has
heard and embraced Zosima's dictum that we are each responsible "for all."
He sees Siberia as the place providentially set before him to offer up his
suffering on behalf of a fellow convict, and to practice active love. He rejects
Rakitin's reductive realism, which would diminish his spiritual ecstasy to
the firing of synapses, to a purely biological process, "not at all because I've
got a soul, and that I am some sort of image and likeness" (497).[243]

But Mitya also shares a secret with Alyosha: Ivan is arranging for his
escape. "[Ivan] doesn't ask me, but orders me" (503). Like the Grand Inquisitor, Ivan's authoritarian command would relieve his brother of the burden
of his conscience (and salve his own, as co-inheritor of his father's money).
But Mitya's conscience remains anguished. He knows that if he escapes he
can stay with Grushenka, the woman through whose mediation he's become
a "new man." But he fears that escape will result in his "los[ing] God" (496).

After the trial, in which the peasants "stand up for themselves" against
Fetyukovich, the "adulterer of thought," Mitya's conundrum is reprised in
the chapter entitled "For a Moment, the Lie Becomes the Truth." This penultimate chapter poses a problem for both Mitya and the reader: *Should* Mitya
escape with Grushenka to America and flee twenty years imprisonment
in Siberia? Given the novel's ethos—Zosima's insistence upon personal responsibility and the laborious practice of active love, and Mitya's avowed
desire to embrace this ethos—is his decision to escape defensible? Dmitri is
the chief actor in the novel, and yearns throughout for reformation. Alyosha
has inherited the mantle of Zosima, and, as a monk in the world, serves as a
confessor to many. Thus, at stake in answering this question is Dostoevsky's
artistic response to Ivan's claim that Christ-like love is impossible for human
beings (205).

Readers are divided on the question of Dmitri's escape. (In my "formal" defense of his escape, I'll use Dmitri Fyodorovich's more formal first
name, as opposed to the affectionate "Mitya" that I've used throughout most
of this book.) When I ask my students what Dmitri should do, the class is
often split down the middle. I divide the groups and ask them to debate the
question. They take positions articulated more fully in critical commentary

on the question. In fact, Gary Rosenshield, and I have ourselves publicly debated the issue, playing the roles, if you will, of Dmitri's prosecutor and advocate. In *Western Law, Russian Justice: Dostoevsky, The Jury Trial, and the Law*, Rosenshield presents a cogent argument outlining why Dmitri could not and would not escape. Given the theological vision presented by the world of the novel, what *should* Dmitri do? Given his character and situation, what *would* Dmitri do—especially if Dostoevsky had continued the novel, or written its sequel? Carol Flath (Apollonio) joins Rosenshield in *prosecuting* any plan for escape. Given the central place of Christ's image in the novel, Flath argues, "[I]t is inconceivable that Dmitri should accede to the pressure to flee to America; instead he must go into Siberian exile, go below the earth (in an analogy to Christ's time spent in the tomb, or perhaps to his entire life spent 'below,' here on earth)." If Dmitri rejects this Christological pattern, then Alyosha, by supporting Dmitri's decision to escape, "becomes a tempter" (595). In fact, Dmitri labels Alyosha's defense of the escape-plan "Jesuitical," a term that seems to link Alyosha to Smerdyakov and Fetyukovich, the novel's chief casuistical tempters—and liars.

But, Alyosha insists to Dmitri, "I must tell you the truth" (636)—and in defending his brother's decision, he *does* tell the truth. Ironically, Alyosha employs the Jesuitical practice of casuistry to arrive at the truth. Like other practices in the novel (confession [31], psychology [609]), casuistry is "two edged" and "cuts both ways." As used by Smerdyakov and Fetyukovich, casuistry takes the form of sophistry that seeks, above all, to please its audience and deny genuine guilt. As Albert R. Jonsen and Stephen Toulmin explain in their comprehensive study of the practice, classical casuistry deteriorated, and justly became the object of scorn when it placed baroque ingenuity and, in confessor's manuals, univocal solutions to complex problems. Casuistry became insufficiently attentive to *both* overarching principles *and* particular cases (155–57). As employed by Alyosha and Zosima, however, casuistry returns to its classical form as it cuts in the direction of *both* personal responsibility *and* redemption, justice *and* mercy. At its best, casuistry attends to the intricate circumstances of particular persons. In brief, it requires the virtue of prudence, and entails "receptivity of the human spirit, to which the revelation of reality, both natural and supernatural reality, has given substance" (*Cardinal* 9). Alyosha fosters Dmitri's realism, his receptive sense that considerations of proportion and readiness must enter into his decision: Though guilty of much, Mitya is innocent of the murder of his father. Twenty years in Siberia, bereft of Grushenka, would be a disproportionate punishment, and, given his impulsive character, an imprudent burden for him to shoulder. In his fledgling desire to serve he is unready for such a burden. In his last discourse, Zosima exhorts, "Know measure, know the proper time, study that" (278): Alyosha discerns measure and timeliness when he "studies" Dmitri's case. Indeed, the novel's Christian vision of responsibility and active love demands discernment, prudence in the midst of complicated circumstances. Responsibility demands casuistry in its classic form.

But how could Dostoevsky—called "the greatest enemy of the Society of Jesus that had arisen since Pascal"[244]—endorse casuistry? The answer can be found in his appreciation for prosaic detail, and his belief that persons enact their freedom in complex circumstances. Each case has a particular "face," each human but different from the other. As Gary Saul Morson observes, when in *A Writer's Diary* Dostoevsky defends legal cases like that of Ekaterina Kornilova—who, while pregnant, "threw, [without harm], her little six-year-old stepdaughter from a fourth-story window" (*Diary*, 641)—"he preaches casuistry, reasoning by cases. Real ethical consciousness never reasons from the top down but from the bottom up. It proceeds from the particularities of each incident and not from the system of norms into which the case might be made to fit" ("Introduction" 100). James P. Scanlan rightly qualifies Morson's point: Dostoevsky was sensitive to particulars, but "[h]is ethical thinking is founded on and dominated by an absolute moral law—the Christian law of love—which is nothing if not universal" (103).

In fact, classical casuistry weds *both* the universal *and* the particular (another incarnational both/and form). As Jonsen and Toulmin demonstrate, casuistry always links an affirmation of universals with an attention to circumstances. Casuistry reached its apex with the Jesuits, and "the premier Jesuit casuist was Juan Azor (1535–1603)" (153), who examined cases of conscience with a commendable methodology: "The general principle [always grounded in the absolute moral law of the Ten Commandments] is first exhibited in an obvious case and only then in other cases in which circumstances make its application increasingly less clear" (155). As William O'Malley observes, early Jesuits like Azor recognized that "circumstances differ from instance to instance," but "[t]he study of cases was meant . . . to facilitate the application of general norms like the Decalogue to different sets of circumstances according to consistent principles. . . . [T]he basic impulse behind casuistry was the desire to clarify complicated moral issues, to sort out claims of seemingly conflicting moral absolutes *down from* the high heavens of abstraction to the *more lowly* human reality of 'time, places, and circumstances'" (144; emphasis added). O'Malley's description of casuistry suggests an incarnational pattern of descent, an analogy to the Word made flesh. The Christological pattern emphasized by Flath presents, in fact, the best defense of Dmitri's decision to escape. His decision to escape bespeaks incarnational realism.

As Zosima articulates it, the work of active love is marked by slow, painstaking effort, attentiveness to particular persons, and a keen sense of both grace and one's limits. In contrast, love in dreams is marked by envisioning a single, grand gesture of martyrdom, done on behalf of an abstract "humanity," "rapidly performed and in the sight of all" (55). When, through Alyosha's casuistical assistance, Dmitri chooses to go America with Grushenka, he chooses the cross of *agapic*, active love, and integrates it with his erotic love for Grushenka. He relinquishes the martyr's cross, which, for Mitya, would likely prove to be a self-destructive "love in dreams."

Gary Rosenshield and I share three crucial points of agreement. First, Dmitri must take responsibility for his actions. If Dmitri has not killed Fyodor he has desired his death, and has brutally beaten both his biological and adoptive fathers. He has publicly shamed the father of Ilyusha (and is thus indirectly responsible for the child's illness and eventual death), and has wounded and betrayed Katerina. Second, in Dostoevsky's vision, suffering itself can be understood as a mode of responsibility with expiatory potential not only for oneself but for others—especially so, I would add, in the light of the novel's recapitulated phrase "for all" and the Orthodox emphasis on *synergy*, the human call to be "fellow workers" with Christ (Ware 215). Catholics and Orthodox share an understanding that faithful human suffering can *participate* in Christ's salvific suffering on the cross. Third, as this very point suggests, and as Rosenshield writes, "mysticism"—or what I, with Zosima, would call "mystery" (252), and which the novel ultimately affirms, along with miracle and authority—"is not only part of life but its essence" (222).

This sense of mystery at the heart of reality, grounded in the incarnation, manifests itself in at least three crucial ways: First, the recognition that "grace is everywhere" inspires the consequent cataphatic (as opposed to apophatic) insight that the humblest things—an onion, a pillow, a pound of nuts, pancakes after a funeral—can bear grace, and serve as analogs of divine love. Second, faith is educated by the irony of the unexpected: the surprising event of a saint's body decaying prematurely and a presumed sinner's raising a rebel's soul from the depths. Third, given Zosima's insistence that "all is like an ocean" (299), such an encompassing, mystical sense accepts that we live and move and have our being within the hidden ground of trinitarian love. Responsibility *is* our reality: each is responsible to all and for all. These are all tenets of incarnational realism.

But from these points of commonality, Rosenshield and I disagree on at least three crucial points: the role of casuistic speech; the relation between faith and reason; and the necessity of Grushenka for Dmitri. Employing the novel's vision of incarnational realism, I will here defend and advocate

Mitya's decision to escape to America. I hope my casuistic defense is more persuasive and—more importantly—more reflective of Dmitri's reality, than his novelistic advocate Fetyukovich!

Rosenshield writes, "Alyosha's words [defending escape] are essentially a paraphrase of the Devil's (Fetyukovich's) words on spiritual resurrection" (*Western Law* 211). In fact, the casuistry of those two work in very different ways. Fetyukovich's words—inattentive to Dmitri, manipulative of Scripture—are perverse and serve to adulterate thought. First, Fetyukovich is wrong about Dmitri. Mitya's immediate response to the jury's verdict is not marked by resentment and hatred (627). Rather, at the end of the trial, "[h]e seemed as though he had passed through an experience that day, which had taught him for the rest of his life something very important he had not understood till then. His voice was weak but he did not shout as before. In his words there was a new note of humility, defeat and submission" (627). When the verdict is announced, he tearfully declares that all in the court are his "brothers" and "friends" (630), as if discerning that the verdict were part of the "blow from heaven" (499) through which he must suffer and become "a new man" (499). Second, Fetyukovich is profoundly inattentive to Scripture.[245] I'll mention only three examples. By arguing that Fyodor is not, in fact, a father, and that the murder cannot be called a parricide, he denies the irreducible fact of fatherhood, and, implicitly, the cataphatic name for God that Christ gives when he teaches people how to pray in the "Our Father." Second, in John's Gospel, Jesus does not call himself "the Good Shepherd" "on the eve of His Crucifixion" (621). Third, when, in Luke's Gospel, Christ says, "What measure you mete, it shall be measured unto you again," the second measuring is the prerogative of God, not human beings. By interpreting this as a counsel to return violence with violence Fetyukovich assumes a stance of demonic rebellion. Rosenshield argues that without the salvific act of Dmitri going to Siberia, the trial itself would not make much sense. In fact, the trial's conclusion shows the people's discernment in rejecting Fetyukovich's "adulteration of thought," his corrosive casuistry. Trial by jury is a *flawed* but *necessary* instrument of justice.[246]

In contrast to Fetyukovich, Alyosha speaks an authoritative, penetrated word when he affirms his brother's decision to escape. In Bakhtin's conception, the authority of the penetrated word is rooted in the self-emptying attentiveness to both the person to whom it is spoken, and to God, often through the mediation of Scripture. In this union of the particular and the universal, the penetrated word can be understood as casuistic. Casuistry was developed to help confessors, "doctors of the soul," in their work with confessants. The manuals were imperfect, but at their best, descriptive rather than prescriptive. They fostered the confessors' pastoral prudence, and exercise of tactful authority. Recall our earlier discussion of the penetrated word, the authority of which comes across and is not imposed—à la the Grand Inquisitor—from above. One indication that Alyosha has spoken such a word in his casuistic approval of Dmitri's escape lies, for example, in his gentle reflection back to Dmitri of his own words, the phrases which suggest Mitya's own deepest hopes and wishes. We see this earlier in the novel when, for example, Fyodor confesses his fear of hell and its infernal hooks, and Alyosha responds, "'But there are no hooks there,' . . . looking gently and seriously at his father" (27); when Ivan, in a fit of *nadryv*, invites his beloved brother to reject him, Alyosha "softly kiss[es] him on the lips" (229) in imitation of Ivan's narrative image of the kenotic Christ; when Grushenka falls on her knees before Alyosha "in a sudden frenzy," he bends over her gently taking her by the hands" and says, "I only gave you an onion" (307). We see it here when Alyosha exhorts Mitya to "remember that other [new] man always." Then Mitya points out that they've been talking like a couple of Jesuits, Alyosha replies, "Yes," and "smile[s] gently" (636). As always, Alyosha reveals his authority "gently." Fetyukovich and Smerdyakov never speak gently—or authoritatively. Dostoevsky hints his approval of Alyosha's casuistry when he describes Dr. Varvinsky's gentle, and "not quite legal" indulgence in placing Mitya in a separate room because he knew that Mitya needed to grow accustomed to the company of criminals "by degrees" (634).

Rosenshield further argues that the "mystical" notion of responsibility that Dostoevsky developed in the last seven years of his life is incompatible with the rational workings of legal justice, in which, "the punishment fits the crime" (215). He argues that Dmitri's punishment "cannot be understood in terms of rational commensurability [and] is by definition irrationally commensurate and mystical" (215). Thus in 1862, writing *Notes from the House of the Dead*, Dostoevsky thought Ilinsky's ten years in Siberia were served "in vain": "From the perspective of 1862, the wrongly convicted parricide not only did not benefit from his prison experience, he probably was permanently crippled by it" (208). But in 1862, Dostoevsky was arguing from the perspective of *chronos*, ordinary time; by 1880 he sees twenty years in Siberia more fully in the light of *kairos*, time mystically charged (214). Rosenshield observes—and I agree—the novel represents less the locale of utopia than of *chronos* and everyday irony. Dostoevsky's incarnational realism—with its faith in God's entrance into ordinary, human time—enables him to see *chronos* as sacral, and human reason itself as one means by which God's will can be discerned. As I've emphasized throughout this work, I believe the "irrational" dimension of Dostoevsky's faith has been overstated, and am persuaded by James Scanlan's demonstration that "Dostoevsky's position on faith and reason in matters of religious belief is in some ways similar to that of the Roman Catholic Church he so despised" (56). Even in 1854, Dostoevsky testified that he knew nothing "more reasonable" than Christ. The mystery of the incarnation, the Word made flesh, lies at the heart of Dostoevsky's imagination. But his exemplars of faith are realists—and reasonable. As a young confessor, Zosima insists that his mysterious visitor confess his crime and face the legal consequences. As an elder, he embraces monastic prayer, discipline, and sacramental practice (*pace* Sergei Hackel)—the communal life of the church (145). He rejects the hallucinatory extremes of Ferapont. In his treatment of others, be they upper class or lower, he exemplifies and counsels moderation: "Know measure, know the proper time" (278). And Zosima allows for the possibility that one can "make oneself responsible for all men's sins" even when serving as a judge or on a jury (277). Alyosha sustains this responsible—and reasonable—legacy. As he tells Mitya, crime and punishment are commensurable: "If you had murdered father, it would grieve me that you should reject your cross. But you are innocent and such a cross is not for you" (636).

Third and finally, Rosenshield points to two key reasons why Dostoevsky could never envision sending Dmitri to America. First, as Rosenshield writes, "Dmitri represents Russian earth; he cannot receive salvation by watering with his tears the soil of America, the quintessential symbol of materialistic individualism. In *Crime and Punishment*, going to America, as Svidrigailov makes explicit, means committing suicide" (211). Second, the plot of husband and wife escaping to America and returning to Russia incognito is drawn from Chernyshevsky's *What Is to Be Done*, which Dostoevsky had parodied in earlier works, and does so here to emphasize "the patently ridiculous [quality]" (211) "of Dmitri's hypothetical escape to America" (212). Granted, the plan *is* a bit comical, especially as Dmitri describes it: "So to the country of the *Last of the Mohicans*, and there we'll tackle the grammar at once, Grusha and I. . . . [W]e shall speak English like any Englishman" (637). But this makes it consistent with the novel's many gently comic ironies, and its underlying joyful tone.[247] Alyosha simply listens, and replies with tactful, taciturn approval, "not wanting to contradict" his brother (637). But in the crucial moment that precedes this, Alyosha speaks emphatically, at just the right moment. The two have been speaking about Ivan, but the subject suddenly switches to Grushenka:

> A silence followed. Something very important was tormenting Mitya.
>   "Alyosha, I love Grusha terribly," he said suddenly in a shaking voice, full of tears.

"They won't let her go out *there* to you," Alyosha put in at
once. (636)

Alyosha speaks authoritatively with words that reach across to his
brother and enable him to find his own decisive voice. Alyosha articulates
that which Mitya already deeply knows: Grushenka has become an icon
for Mitya, a Christ-bearing image (*obraz*) that reflects and mediates divine
love and, like the Orthodox icon, is vital to the re-formation of Mitya's own
image as a person. Recall that when Mitya is at his lowest point near the
end of the interrogation, and just before his salvific dream of "the babe,"
Grushenka "crosses herself devoutly before the icon," thanks God, attests
to the truth of Mitya's words, and gives Mitya, in his words, "fresh courage"
(427). As he tells Alyosha in prison: "I've taken all her soul into my soul
and through her I've become a man myself" (501). Like Dostoevsky, Mitya
"hates" America, but he'll bear his cross there, for it is there, and not Siberia,
that he will be with Grushenka. "All are babes," including Americans—and
America will be the site of Mitya's purifying, purgative pain.[248]

Rosenshield relates two encounters that Dostoevsky had with his
young friend Soloviev. Once, when Soloviev was depressed, Dostoevsky
suggested the antidote of forced labor in Siberia. Another time, on the occasion of praising Soloviev, Dostoevsky told him that he was good man,
but that three years of forced Siberian labor would make him "a completely
beautiful and pure Christian" (223). Here, Rosenshield sees Dostoevsky
"expressing his mystical view of suffering and responsibility in what might
seem to some a half-serious or even joking manner" (222). I agree: good
friends inspire each other's sense of humor. And humor keeps one humble,
brings one down to earth, the *humus* from which the Christian believer
recognizes the stuff out of which he's created, and that which his Redeemer
embraced in the humility of the incarnation.

By the end of the novel, Alyosha and Mitya have become good friends.
Mitya laughs and accuses the two of them of talking like Jesuits. Alyosha
smiles and agrees—he has a sense of humor and humility. This note of humility defines the novel's penultimate chapter—and lends it its sublimity.
Mitya accepts his limitations through Jesuitical casuistry—and for a moment, in an ironic, parabolic surprise,[249] that "lie" too becomes "the truth"!
As I'll discuss in Chapter 7, Mitya and Katerina embrace in mutual forgiveness, and for a moment the "lie" of their love becomes "the truth." From this
moment both draw a capacity to offer small gestures of active love: Mitya
implores Alyosha to comfort Katerina, stricken with shame before Grushenka; Katerina has sent flowers for Ilyushechka's coffin and asks Alyosha to
tell the Snegiryov family that she will "never abandon them" (639).

These are imperfect, offstage gestures of active love. In moments like this—and in what Robin Feuer Miller sees as the onion-like recapitulations of these moments (*Worlds* 85)—Dostoevsky provides an answer, "in oblique artistic form," not only to Ivan's despair regarding Christ-like love, but to Mitya's agonized confession that the beautiful form of literary art has never re-formed him: "I always read that [Schiller] poem about Ceres and man [and the need to cling to Mother Earth]. Has it ever reformed me? Never! For I'm a Karamazov" (97). By the end of the novel Mitya *is* reformed, is a "new man." And the novel's beauty invites us to change with him.

Chapter 6

Ivan Fyodorovich Karamazov

O n the day before the trial, when Alyosha visits Mitya in prison, he avows his faith in his brother's innocence:

> "I've never for one instant believed that you were the murderer!" broke in a shaking voice from Alyosha's breast, and he raised his right hand in the air, as though calling God to witness his words. Mitya's whole face was lit up with bliss.
> "Thank you!" he articulated slowly, as though letting a sigh escape him after fainting. "Now you have given me new life. Would you believe it, till this moment I've been afraid to ask you, you, even you. Well, go! You've given me strength for tomorrow. God bless you! Well, go along! *Love Ivan!*" *was Mitya's last word.* (503–4; emphasis added)

Alyosha's impassioned words give "new life" to Mitya: they restore his "good taste of self" and enable him to turn his attention to his brother, Ivan. Mitya utters a penetrated word, makes his own gesture of active love: "Love Ivan." The words intensify Alyosha's concern for Ivan, whom he is now on his way to see (504).

In my discussion of Alyosha's dream of Cana, I pointed to Dantean resonances. In my analysis of Ivan, I will draw on a work that serves as a kind of companion to the *Commedia*, Augustine's *Confessions*. Like René Girard, I have found over years of teaching that all three works—*Confessions, Commedia, Karamazovs*—share "the structure of the incarnation" (*Resurrection* 72). Ivan, proudest of the Karamazov brothers, recalls the youthful Augustine[250] in his intellectual gifts, pride, and divided will. Young

Augustine didn't see his intellect as a gift: "You know, Lord my God, that quick thinking and capacity for acute analysis are your gift. But that did not move me to offer them in sacrifice to you," he writes as an older, wiser man (4.16.30). Nor does Ivan acknowledge his intelligence as a gift. In fact, the narrator is careful to observe that Ivan resisted accepting gifts. Here Ivan is radically unlike Alyosha, who "never cared at whose expense he was living. In that respect he was the complete opposite of his elder brother Ivan Fyodorovich, who struggled with poverty for his first two years in the university, fed himself by his own labor, and had from childhood bitterly sensed that he was living on the bread of [his benefactor, Yefim Petrovich]" (24). Recall that at the monastery, the elder Zosima had recognized Ivan's gifts as well as his anguish, but exhorted him to be thankful to God for giving him "a lofty heart" (66). Zosima's blessing of Ivan recalls the dream of Augustine's mother Monica, who counters her son's twisted interpretation with accurate understanding: "Where you [Monica] are, there will [Augustine] be also" (3.11.20). Where Zosima is, Ivan will be also: recall the way Ivan rises and approaches Zosima in order to receive his blessing.

Ivan's "affirmative" side is fostered by Alyosha in their long conversation at the Metropolis tavern (discussed in Chapter 4). Alyosha confidently declares that his older, imperious brother is "just a young and fresh and nice boy, green in fact!" Ivan responds "warmly and good-humoredly," and affirms to Alyosha his "thirst for life": "I love the sticky little leaves as they open in spring. I love the blue sky, I love some people, whom one loves you know sometimes without knowing why" (199). Ivan's love for life in its sensuous splendor recalls the note of childlike wonder the aged Augustine strikes near the end of City of God: "How could any description do justice to all these blessings? The manifold diversity of beauty in sky and earth and sea; the abundance of light, and its miraculous loveliness, in sun and moon and stars; the dark shades of woods, the colour and fragrance of flowers; the multitudinous varieties of birds, with their songs and their bright plumage ..." (22.24). For Augustine, the "small physical size of a child" is emblematic of Christ's humility (1.19.30). When Ivan is at his most childlike, as in "The Brothers Get Acquainted," he reveals his nascent humility, his desire to accept the help of others and for abundant life: "'I don't want to wound my little brother who has been watching me with such expectation for three months. . . . Of course I am just such a little boy as you are. . . . I want to be friends with you, Alyosha, for I have no friends and want to try it. Well, only fancy, perhaps I too accept God,' laughed Ivan, 'that's a surprise for you, isn't it'" (202).

But even here, Ivan reveals a divided self, as we discussed briefly in Chapter 4, and will expand upon here. On the one hand, Ivan humbly expresses his longing for life and love. On the other, he asserts an antithetical impulse driven by pride, a desire to hurt others and himself. He declares it likely that he will "dash the cup to the ground" when he is thirty and commit suicide (229). When Alyosha reports that Katerina is ill, in one breath Ivan declares that he "must find out" if she is all right, and in another "I won't go to her at all" (201). When Alyosha asks how the dreadful conflict between their brother Dmitri and their father Fyodor will end, Ivan lashes back by evoking the biblical figure who, for Augustine, ushers in all the violence that characterizes the "city of man":[251] "'You are always harping upon it! What have I to do with it? Am I my brother Dmitri's keeper? . . . Well, damn it all, I can't stay here to be their keeper can I?'" (200). Ivan echoes Smerdyakov (196), and echoes Cain.

Ivan's self-bifurcation was evident on the first day of the novel. Anticipating further violence between his father and Dmitri, he promises Alyosha: "Be sure, I shall always defend [Fyodor]." Then he confides: "But in my wishes I reserve myself full latitude in this case" (128). In Bakhtin's cogent analysis, "Ivan . . . wants his father murdered, but he wants it under the condition that he himself remain not only externally but even *internally* uninvolved in it. He wants the murder to occur as an inevitability of fate, not only *apart from his will*, but in opposition to it" (*Problems* 258). While conversing in the Metropolis, Ivan tells Alyosha he has rejected God's world because he cannot accept any image of harmony and reconciliation founded upon the suffering of innocent children. With savage irony, he regales Alyosha with gruesome stories from the newspapers, detailing the torture and murder of children. As we have seen, Ivan's rebellion is rife with *nadryv*, a self-lacerating bitterness stemming from his own memories of a traumatic childhood, which he directs at his father, Fyodor, Father Zosima, and, finally, God.[252] By the chapter's end, Ivan speaks as a child who was *himself* forgotten and hurt: "I'd rather remain with *my unavenged suffering* and unquenched indignation, *even if I am wrong*" (212; emphasis added). Each day our own news stories present images of suffering innocents. The reader sympathizes with Ivan's protest against the violence inflicted upon them. But, as noted earlier, Ivan's rebellion *in the name of his own suffering* gives us pause. Ivan will himself hurt a child (Lise). Furthermore, he offers no assistance to children, unlike Alyosha throughout Book 10.

As noted earlier, Alyosha *also* rejects Ivan's non-Euclidean theodicy. But Ivan's willfully solitary stance denies the possibility of reconciliation and forgiveness.[253] He takes the very path of pride against which Zosima cautions (276), and skirts the hell of despair. Moreover, Alyosha reminds Ivan that in the Christian vision, the divine gift of reconciliation doesn't take the form of a rationalistic theodicy, or a purchased "entrance ticket."

The gift takes the form of a person (213), in the precious image of Christ (276). Christ is the redemptive cornerstone and sanctifying sustainer. From Zosima and hard experience, Alyosha learns that the human response to Christ's gift must be "Christ-like" (205) active love, which entails our own "labor and fortitude" (55), and a recognition that we are, in fact, "each responsible to all and *for all.*" Sustained by grace, "Christ-like love" *is* possible (205). Grace is offered *for all*; each is responsible *for all.* The novel gives artistic form to Jesus' exhortation: "Freely you have received, freely give" (Matt 10:8). The repeated phrase that links both claims—"All and for all"—suggests the synergistic relationship between Christ's sacrifice "for all" and the believer's sacrificial response to that gift. In Dostoevsky's novel, responsibility is encompassing—"for all"—but takes particular form within the fluid reality of our particular relationships. Active love is hard work, but its ripple effects transcend our control: "all is like an ocean, all is flowing and blending; a touch in one place sets up movement at the other end of the earth" (275).[254] Its effects are "incalculably diffusive" in George Eliot's beautiful phrase (*Middlemarch*, Chapter 87). For Dostoevsky, to accept the reality of our responsibility "for all," and to respond with active love, is to conform to the kenotic pattern of Christ.[255]

Of course, Ivan is ready for what may at first seem to be Alyosha's all-too-easy Christian response. He responds with an imaginative narrative of his own, "The Grand Inquisitor" who rejects Christ's "gift" of freedom as intolerable for the majority of humankind: freedom imposes the anguish of decision upon weak human beings and they respond with the blight of sin. But as even Ivan himself admits, the Inquisitor is a liar. Truth, as embodied in the Gospels, takes the form of a *person*—"*I* am the way, the truth, and the life" (John 14:6)—and informed by that person's command to "go and do likewise" (Jn. 10:37) all persons are called to embody the truth in love (Eph 4:15). In his poem, Ivan rightly portrays Christ's loving attentiveness and respect for human freedom, even when the Inquisitor twists his own freedom into the form of perverse willfulness. But Ivan shows his own capacity as a polyphonic novelist by depicting *both* the perverse Inquisitor and the silent, loving Christ. Ivan's image of the kenotic Christ inspires Alyosha to participate in that love: like his Inquisitor, Ivan perversely invites rejection—"Will you renounce me for that, yes?"—and Alyosha responds by "softly kiss[ing] [Ivan] on the lips" (229). In his little brother, Ivan discerns an analogy of Christ. He accepts his gift, a seed, that will gradually take root.

But only gradually—and here we turn to Ivan's decisions and development later in the novel. In the two pivotal chapters that follow "The Grand Inquisitor"—"For a While a Very Obscure One" and "It's Worthwhile Speaking to a Clever Man"—Ivan seeks release from responsibility, and thus from his human calling to conform to the pattern of Christ—to make oneself "responsible for all" and to participate in Christ's redemptive love "for all." In his pride and desire to be blameless, he is akin to Augustine the Manichaean, who blamed evil on the "alien nature" of matter: "It flattered my pride to be free of blame and, when I had done something wrong, not to make myself confess to you that you might heal my soul" (*Confessions* 5.10.18). But Augustine soon doubts the Manicheans and, like him, Ivan is haunted by "a deep conscience" (551) that torments him.[256]

Ivan shares responsibility for Fyodor's murder. He has taught Smerdyakov that if there is no immortality then "all things are lawful," and inspires his "student" to pound a paperweight into his father's skull. He chooses to leave his father's house when he senses danger looming. Smerdyakov insinuates that Fyodor will be at risk if Ivan leaves. But instead of following through on his promise to defend their father, Ivan announces "loudly and clearly" to Smerdyakov that he will leave the following day (237); the next morning, he announces it again: "'You see . . . I am going to Chermashnya,' broke suddenly from Ivan Fyodorovich. As on the day before, the words seemed to drop of themselves, and Ivan laughed, too, a peculiar, nervous laugh. He remembered it long after" (241). The "full latitude" he has taken in his fantasy life—his wish that his father were dead—has withered the vigor of his vow to defend his father. Announcing his departure to Smerdyakov further entangles him in the next day's murder. Ivan's refusal to commit himself has concrete ramifications for which he must ultimately face responsibility. His ironic mode becomes insidiously self-consuming as it battles with his gnawing consciousness that he cannot escape responsibility. His gait reflects his self-division, which Alyosha observes as Ivan walks home to meet Smerdyakov: "He suddenly noticed that Ivan swayed as he walked and that his right shoulder looked lower than his left" (230). After his talk with Smerdyakov, "[Ivan] moved and walked as though in a nervous frenzy" (237).

After Fyodor's murder, Ivan's anguish intensifies as he grows increasingly conscious of the degree to which his words and actions have provoked murder. A pattern emerges: guilty consciousness, rejection of those who elicit such consciousness, denial, and, consequently, further excruciating self-division. On his first day back from Moscow, he visits the imprisoned Mitya, and is insulted by Mitya's rebuke that "it was not for people who declared that 'everything was lawful,' to suspect and question him" (509). Afterwards he goes to Smerdyakov's, and detects "an insulting significance" in his half-brother's parting words, "'I shall say nothing of that conversation of ours at the gate'" (513). He "[feels] as though he wanted to make haste to forget something" (514). But forgetting proves impossible. Two weeks later he began to be haunted by the same strange thoughts as before. It's enough to say that he was continually asking himself why it was that on that last night in Fyodor Pavlovich's house he had crept out on the stairs like a thief and listened to hear what his father was doing below. Why had he recalled that afterwards with repulsion; why, next morning, had he been suddenly so depressed on the journey; why, as he reached Moscow, had he said to himself "I am a scoundrel"? (515)

Thus haunted, he abruptly stops Alyosha "in the street," and demands that his little brother answer his question: When Ivan spoke of "'reserv[ing] the right to desire'" did Alyosha believe that Ivan desired his father's death and was "even prepared to help bring that about"? When Alyosha admits that he did, Ivan rejects his brother because he has pricked his conscience: "From that time Alyosha noticed that Ivan began obviously to avoid him and seemed to have taken a dislike to him, so much so that Alyosha gave up going to see him" (515). As he had done two weeks earlier with Mitya (509), he leaves the brother who challenges him toward responsibility and goes directly to Smerdyakov's, where he persists in denial. When Smerdyakov himself expresses his belief that Ivan was "very desirous of [his] parent's death," he lashes back furiously: "Ivan Fyodorovich jumped up and struck him with all his might on the shoulder, so that he fell back against the wall" (517).

After this second interview, however, Ivan agonizingly gropes toward discerning the extent of his responsibility. To Katerina he "pronounce[d] this strange sentence: 'If it's not Dmitri, but Smerdyakov who's the murderer, I share his guilt, for I put him up to it. Whether I did, I don't know yet. But if he is the murderer, and not Dmitri, then, of course, I am the murderer, too'" (520). Fearful of Ivan being implicated, Katya shows her beloved the letter in which Mitya had drunkenly inscribed his intent to murder. Ivan is "convinced" of Mitya's guilt (521). But the evidence does not relieve his "deepest I" of a true sense of his own guilt: "Something *very deep down* seemed burning and rankling in his soul" particularly the question as to whether he himself is "a murderer at heart!" (521; emphasis added).

Is Ivan a murderer? In one of the most dramatic moments of the novel, Alyosha tells him unequivocally that he is not.[257] When Ivan asks Alyosha who he believes the murderer is, Alyosha "pronounce[s] in a low penetrating voice": "'You know who.'" Upon Ivan's further, "fierce" questioning, Alyosha responds:

> "I only know one thing," Alyosha went on, still almost in a whisper, "*it was not you* who killed father."

"Not you! What do you mean by 'not you'?" Ivan was thunderstruck.

"It was not you who killed father, not you!" Alyosha repeated firmly. . . .

"You've said so to yourself many times, when you've been alone during these two dreadful months," Alyosha went on softly and distinctly as before. Yet he was speaking now, as it were, not of himself, not of his own will, but obeying some irresistible command.

"You have accused yourself and have confessed to yourself that you are the murderer and no one else. But you didn't murder, you are mistaken: you are not the murderer. Do you hear? It was not you! God has sent me to tell you so." (507)

Clearly, Alyosha's words are portrayed as "penetrated": he speaks as if "obeying some irresistible command." And his words penetrate, but not in a way that quickly brings Ivan peace and resolution. Ivan is "in a frenzy" after he hears them, and, "with a cold smile" "break[s] off all relations with [Alyosha] from this moment and probably forever" (508). Alyosha's words penetrate Ivan's conscience like a thorn, thus his resistance to and rejection of Alyosha.

Alyosha's words throw Ivan into the human experience of self-examination and discernment: if he is not completely guilty, then he must discern the *degree* of his guilt. Alyosha's words are authoritative and true: Ivan did not kill Fyodor, Smerdyakov did. But if Smerdyakov is the murderer, Ivan must face responsibility for their "conversation at the gate" and his careless pronouncement in Smerdyakov's presence that "Everything is lawful"— *scenes of which Alyosha lacks knowledge.* Alyosha's authority cannot relieve Ivan of guilt for these deeds. His is not the false authority of the Grand Inquisitor who "allows" his "pitiful children" to sin (225).[258] But Alyosha's words will assist Ivan in discerning the *degree* of his guilt.

As we saw in Alyosha's "Jesuitical" advocacy of Mitya's decision to escape, prudence attends to the reality of the situation, in all its particulars, and responds with an awareness of degree and proportion. Ivan is romantic, proud, "very fond of being alone" (508). He would rather hold up the bold, dialectical extremities of "either/or" than discern within more messy "both/ and" territory, the grey area that lies between. Ivan would prefer something like this: "Either I am innocent and detached from this ugly mess or I am the murderer." But by saying "I am the murderer," Ivan detaches himself in another way: he refuses to recognize the responsibility of another—his half-brother Smerdyakov—with whom he has been *in relation.* Ivan spurns relation—especially with someone as lowly as his illegitimate half-brother—and thus rejects the domain of discernment: the muddy middle that comprises our tangled ties with other persons.[259] As the devil later tells him, Ivan fashions himself a "man-god, even if he is the only one in the whole world, . . . stand[ing] [at] the foremost place" (546). He would thus prefer total responsibility to partial, the "mediocre."[260] But signing for one's actions does not necessitate taking *total* responsibility: "Signing an act does not mean accepting all blame or assuming absolute control over it" (Morson and Emerson, *Prosaics* 69). Such a univocal maneuver denies the reality of our relations with others. Signing means locating and embracing our responsibility *within* the nexus of our relationships, not with the intentions of finding a loophole, but by honestly determining where our obligations lie. Thus the *prosaic* wisdom of Zosima's exhortation that all are responsible, "each one personally for all men and *every individual man*" (emphasis added).[261] Ivan's either/or refuses to ground his responsibility in his relations with others. He thus flees true discernment.

A further point on Ivan's romantic impulse to take *all* of the blame. He knows that on the following day he will be called upon to testify, before the public, at the trial. And where there is pride, and a shaky sense of self, the sideward glance usually follows. Ivan is intensely sensitive to becoming "visible" before the public that will perceive him. His devil—whom Ivan is conscious of as his double[262]—makes an accurate observation:

> You are really angry with me for not appearing to you in a red glow, with thunder and lightning, with scorched wings, but have shown myself in such a modest form. You are wounded, in the first place, in your aesthetic feelings, and, secondly, in your pride. How could such a vulgar devil visit such a great man as you! Yes, there is that romantic strain in you . . . . (544)

With such a romantic strain, Ivan would rather go to court and be perceived by the spectators as a daring nihilist father-slayer, than admit the more "modest" degree of his guilt in all its shabbiness. Thus Smerdyakov[263] wrongly predicts that Ivan will not "give evidence," but rightly observes: "You like to be respected, too, for you're very proud; . . . you care most of all about living in undisturbed comfort, without having to bow to anyone."[264] In proud anguish, Ivan resists bowing, even after Alyosha has spoken his penetrated word.

The destructive consequences of Ivan's pride are imaged in the next scene. Halfway to Smerdyakov's—to whom Ivan turns for a third time after his conscience has been pricked by one of his brothers—he "suddenly came upon a solitary and drunken little peasant." The peasant sings a song—"Ach,

Vanka's gone to Petersburg"—that likely reminds him of his own guilty flight
to Moscow.[265] Ivan reflexively responds to the peasant with "intense hatred":

> Suddenly he realized his presence and felt an irresistible impulse
> to knock him down. At that moment they met, and the peasant
> with a violent lurch fell full tilt against Ivan, who pushed him
> back furiously. The peasant went flying backwards and fell like
> a log on the frozen ground. He uttered one plaintive "Oh-oh"
> and then was silent. Ivan stepped up to him. He was lying on
> his back without movement or consciousness. "He will freeze,"
> thought Ivan, and he went on his way to Smerdyakov's. (522)

Ivan's raging refusal to discern and embrace responsibility leads to
another potential murder, this time one for which he would be directly
responsible.

By the end of his third interview with Smerdyakov, in which he learns
the real story of Fyodor's murder, Ivan shows that he retains a capacity for
discernment. In contrast, Smerdyakov denies his freedom and casts himself in the role of a theatrical tool:[266] "You murdered him; you are the real
murderer, I was only your instrument, your faithful servant, Licharda, and
it was following your words I did it" (524).[267] But in a moment, Smerdyakov
articulates words that *do* reflect reality, and point to that for which Ivan *is*
responsible: his philosophical pronouncements and his refusal to speak at
the crucial domestic moment: "'You were bold enough then, sir. You said
"everything was lawful," and how frightened you are now'"; "[The murder]
was done in a most natural way, following your very words, sir" (526); "by
your consent you silently sanctioned my doing it" (528).

As he listens, Ivan inches toward responsibility. Initially, he lashes out
with the violence and egotism he has shown throughout the novel: "Listen,
you miserable, contemptible man! Don't you understand that if I haven't
killed you, it's simply because I am keeping you to answer tomorrow at the
trial." He resists—"No, no, I didn't urge you on!"—but then gropes toward
accountability. By the end of their conversation, he avows before God that
he will testify what he knows, and will confess those details that implicate
him—if not legally, than morally:

> "God sees," Ivan raised his hand, "perhaps I, too, was guilty; per-
> haps I really had a secret desire for my father's . . . death, but I
> swear I was not as guilty as you think, and perhaps I didn't urge
> you on at all. No, no, I didn't urge you on! But no matter, I will
> give evidence against myself tomorrow, at the trial. I'm deter-
> mined to! I shall tell everything, everything. But we'll make our
> appearance together. And whatever you may say against me at

the trial, whatever evidence you give, I'll face it, I am not afraid of you. I'll confirm it all myself! But you must confess, too! You must, you must, we'll go together. That's how it shall be!"

Ivan said this solemnly and resolutely, and from his flashing eyes alone it could be seen that it would be so. (530–31)

By the end of this utterance, Ivan has channeled his fury into solemn resolution.

Upon his departure, Ivan's "unbounded resolution" guides him to saving a person's life. His "bold" steps turn "staggering," but he senses "something like joy . . . springing up in his heart." He "stumble[s] against . . . the peasant he had knocked down" earlier, who is now near death. He carries him to the police station, pays for a doctor, and sees that he is cared for (532). The image suggests Luke's Parable of the Good Samaritan (Lk. 10:25-37) and counters those that link Ivan to the murderous, detached Cain.[268]

But upon further consideration, the scene suggests more of a travesty of Jesus' parable—and recalls a very different one: that of the self-justified Pharisee who speaks a prayer of gratitude "to himself," and stands in contrast to the humble tax collector who prays, "O God, be merciful to me, a sinner." The tax collector leaves the temple "justified" (Luke 18:9–14). Yes, Ivan provides "a liberal hand for the expenses," and spends "a whole hour" at the police station to ascertain that a doctor attends to the peasant. Ivan compliments himself for his actions. He doesn't, however, confess to the police that it was his own "irresistible impulse" that drove him to push the peasant to the ground "furiously," with the full knowledge that "[h]e [would] freeze" (522). Bursting with self-satisfaction, Ivan departs the police station assured of his autonomy: "'I am quite capable of watching myself, by the way,' he thought at the same instant, with still greater satisfaction, 'although they have decided that I am going out of my mind!'" (532).

Ivan's "staggering" steps prove telling. Never in the course of the novel does Ivan ever fully "make an end of the wavering that had so tortured him" (532) and humbly accept his place as a person within the community. The virtue of humility is integral to recovering one's "deepest I" and a "good taste of self." Bakhtin sees "enclosure within the self as the main reason for the loss of one's self . . ." ("Toward" 287). Humility—and incarnational realism—entails accepting one's "non-self-sufficiency." As a person opens himself to help another, so he becomes more receptive to another's help. Again, St. Augustine sheds light on Ivan: "The acknowledgement of dependence, and with it, the capacity to be grateful, does not come easily, in Augustine's opinion" (Brown 326). Surely it doesn't for Ivan, who feels no gratitude for the sheer good luck—or grace—of having run into the peasant, saved his life, and avoided culpability for murder. Instead, he asserts his autonomy. In reviewing his own life, Augustine had come to realize "if denial of guilt was the first enemy, self-reliance was the last" (Brown 176).

Self-reliant pride infects Ivan's resolve, and propels his flight from reality. Ivan rightly sees the link between his decision to testify and his helping of the peasant, but is blind to the "non-self-sufficiency" integral to both acts. By separating "himself" from "them," he corrodes the very foundation of his earlier resolve: an acceptance of his responsibility to others. If there is anything that the reality of the situation is calling Ivan to do, it is to go *directly* to the prosecutor's with the new information and evidence he now holds, and to do so before Smerdyakov commits suicide. Ivan himself realizes this. He halts his self-satisfied musings and stands still before the court of his conscience:

> Just as he reached his own house he stopped short, asking himself suddenly whether he hadn't better go at once now to the prosecutor and tell him everything. He decided the question by turning back to the house. "Everything together tomorrow!" he whispered to himself, and, strange to say, almost all his gladness and self-satisfaction passed in one instant. (532–33)

Ivan procrastinates. He retreats to his habits of self-enclosure and rejects the claims of those for whom he bears responsibility. He denies the "daily" demands of time.[269] Tomorrow will be too late to save Dmitri—or Smerdyakov, whose looming suicide Ivan has intuited (531). But Ivan is thinking of neither. He wants his day in court "to say what he had to say boldly and resolutely and 'to justify himself to himself'" (533). Never is Ivan more "Pelagian" than in his desire to achieve his own justification.[270] From an Augustinian view, the consequence of such exalted self-assertion is a plunge into nightmare. As Augustine writes, "Nothing is superior to God; and that is why humility exalts the mind by making it subject to God. Exaltation, in contrast, derives from a fault in character, and spurns subjection for that very reason. Hence it falls away from him who has no superior, and falls lower in consequence" (*City* 572). Ivan denies his creatural limitations, and justifies himself. Hence his devil's midnight visit.

As Deborah Martinsen observes, Dostoevsky "sets up a series of implicit comparisons between Christ's incarnation and the devil's. Whereas Christ takes on human form to redeem the sins of the world, Ivan's devil takes on human form to attend a cocktail party" (210).[271] Such "comic contrasts" suggest travesty, a concept implicit in Augustine's conception of evil. Early in *Confessions*, Augustine reflects extensively on his youthful theft of the pears, recognizing it as "an assertion of possessing a dim resemblance to omnipotence" (2.6.14). In the theft he sees a creatural travesty of God's power, and a rejection of an analogical imitation of his love: "In their perverted way all humanity imitates you . . . and exalt themselves against you. But even by thus imitating you they acknowledge that you are the creator of all nature and so concede that there is no place where they can entirely escape from you" (2.6.14). Augustine sees evil as parasitic upon a Good God who has created all as good. If we see Dostoevsky's depiction of the devil as a travesty of the incarnation, we can correct the occasional claims that Dostoevsky holds a "Manichaean" view of equally oppositional good and evil.[272] In fact, as Augustine observes, evil is an absence, with no reality of its own: "The theft itself was a nothing" (2.8.16) for "as long as [things] exist, they are good. Accordingly, whatever things exist are good, and the evil into whose origins I was inquiring is not a substance, for if it were a substance, it would be good. . . . For our God has made 'all things very good' (Gen. 1:31)" (7.12.18). Dostoevsky's vision is similarly non-dualistic: as a creature, the devil was created as a good angel by a superior, loving Creator; in his habitually perverse assertion of will, the devil's capacity for good has deteriorated—much like those characters entrapped in habitual displays of buffoonery, *nadryv*, or "terrible individualism" (262).[273] In fact, the devil's conflicting claims regarding his reality point up his aim: to bring Ivan himself to nothing, to the willful attempt at self-annihilation that is suicide.[274] In a travesty of Zosima's blessing, the devil admits as much: "But hesitation, suspense, conflict between belief and disbelief—is sometimes such torture to a conscientious man, such as you are, that it's better to hang oneself at once. . . . I lead you to belief and disbelief by turns, and I have my motive in it" (542). The devil's motive is to impel Ivan toward the Judas-like path Smerdyakov takes—hanging himself upon the gallows.

Toward the end of his tirade, the devil confronts Ivan with the proto-Nietzschean ideas that had inspired Smerdyakov: "all things are lawful"; "since there is no God and no immortality anyway, the new man may well become the man-god."[275] Now ashamed of his words, Ivan tries to shut his ears, furiously resisting responsibility for them and the actions they've inspired: "Ivan sat with his eyes on the floor, and his hands pressed to his ears. . . . [He] suddenly snatched a glass from the table and flung it at the orator" (546). Even when Alyosha arrives, Ivan continues to resist. He quotes the devil's exhortation to spurn conscience and become a god, and insists "It was he who said that, it was he who said that!"

Earlier that day, Alyosha had whispered, "'*It was not you* who killed father'" (507, emphasis in original). But now he challenges Ivan to face that for which he *is* responsible: "'And *not you, not you*?' Alyosha could not help shouting, looking frankly at his brother" (549; emphasis added). When paired, Alyosha's two utterances of the phrase "*not you*" can be read in tandem as an invitation to Ivan to discern and humbly accept his *partial* guilt. He must refrain from either of two prideful extremes: taking on all of the blame (a form of pride that denies his shameful tutelage of and manipulation by Smerdyakov, the real murderer) or rejecting guilt for any of it (as Manichaeism enabled Augustine to do). Ivan needs to avow responsibility for his proto-Nietzschean ideas. Alyosha's pastoral mediation, rooted in incarnational realism, helps Ivan to see his guilt for what it is, to "give it a name," and show up the next day in court.[276]

Just before falling asleep, Ivan promises Alyosha that he will be present in court the next day: he will refuse the "gallows" path that Smerdyakov has taken in his suicide, and will choose the cross of responsibility. "Tomorrow the cross, but not the gallows. No, I won't hang myself" (549), Ivan declares. He keeps his promise. But when he arrives at the court the next day, it's clear that Ivan's commitment to "the cross"—presenting the 3,000 rubles as evidence, and humbly confessing his involvement in Fyodor's murder—is not yet wholehearted. He shows up: this is significant in itself, given his earlier flights from responsibility. But his condition resembles Augustine's in the Milan garden: his "soul hung back. It refused and had no excuse to offer" (8.7.18). Ivan has been called before the court. But he hangs back, "owing to an attack of illness or some sort of fit" (575). In retrospect, Augustine saw that "my madness with myself was part of the process of recovering health, and in the agony of death I was coming to life" (8.8.19). Similarly, when Ivan finally walks into the courtroom, "there was an earthy look in [his face], a look like a dying man's" (575). To bear fruit, the corn of wheat must fall to the ground and die.

Like Augustine, Ivan's divided will manifests itself bodily. Augustine "made many physical gestures of the kind men make when they want to achieve something and lack the strength" (8.8.20). Ivan slowly enters the courtroom, listlessly responds to the questions, then turns to leave "without waiting for permission":

> But after taking four steps he stood still, as though he had reached a decision, smiled slowly, and went back.
> "I am like the peasant girl, your excellency . . . you know. How does it go? 'I'll stand up if I like, and I won't if I don't.' They were trying to put on her sarafan to take her to church to be married, and she said, 'I'll stand up if I like, and I won't if I don't.' . . . It's in some book about our folklore." (576) [277]

He is like Augustine facing his own decision of whether or not to accept the Christian cross: "I was neither willing nor wholly unwilling. So

I was in conflict with myself and was dissociated from myself" (8.10.22). Unable yet to enact what he truly wishes, Ivan is capricious. He would voluntaristically assert his will rather than make a decision humbly grounded in reality.

Ivan's comparison of himself to a peasant girl draws from specifically Russian tradition, but reveals an important link between Augustine's conversion and Ivan's confession. In both Orthodox and Catholic tradition, marriage entails not only a mutual exchange of vows, but a mutual gift of grace that undergirds the unity forged in the sacrament. Like any sacrament, matrimony entails both human free will and the gift of God's grace, a gift beyond the power of any person to control. Further, in a marriage, grace is mediated by the gathered community. For both Augustine and Ivan, communal mediation proves vital: for Augustine, the words and presence of Monica, Ambrose, and Alypius; for Ivan, the prayers of Katerina (506), and Alyosha, who reflects upon and prays for his brother the night before: "'The anguish of a proud determination. A deep conscience!' God, in Whom he disbelieved, and His truth were gaining mastery over his heart, which still refused to submit. . . . 'Either he will rise up in the light of truth, or . . . he'll perish in hate, revenging on himself and on everyone his having served the cause he does not believe in,' Alyosha added bitterly, and again he prayed for Ivan" (551).

With his first resolute utterance before the court, Ivan "rise[s] in the light of truth." He presents the monetary evidence to the President of the court, and precisely confesses his culpability: "I got [the money] from Smerdyakov, from the murderer yesterday. . . . I was with him just before he hanged himself. It was he, not my brother, who killed our father. He murdered him, and I incited him to do it. . . . Who doesn't desire his father's death?" (576). But in the pause of that ellipsis, Ivan casts a sideward glance at the gazing public, feels ashamed, and, in a vain attempt to flee responsibility and judgment, grabs a proto-Freudian loophole as if to say: "I'm just like everybody else."[278] The "revenge" that Alyosha feared marks the "contemptuous" and "snarl[ing]" utterances that follow.

But Ivan does *not* "perish in hate." Yes, he is dragged from the courtroom "yell[ing] and scream[ing] something incoherent"—a far cry indeed from the liberating, luminous peace Augustine experiences when he reads Romans 13! But like Augustine, Ivan remains in the *process* of being healed by grace. Ivan is ill, but his final, seemingly mad words can be explicated, if not by his interlocutors in court, then by the attentive reader. His words reveal a person wrestling with and finally cooperating with grace, choosing the humility of Christ, the "Godman," and rejecting the pride inherent in his previous aspirations to "man-godhood," his declarations that "all things are lawful." We see the first shift from pride to humility when Ivan retreats from accusation to confession and avowal of dependence: "It's a spectacle they want! 'Bread and Circuses.' Though I am one to talk! Have you any water? Give me a drink for Christ's sake!' He suddenly clutched his head" (577). In his self-critical pause, Ivan senses the folly of his pride and, albeit angrily, asks for a symbolically suggestive form of help—a drink of water. Terras notes that Russian commentators locate here "a symbol of the 'living water' of faith," and that Ivan "here for the first time invokes the name of Christ" (410). Unknowingly, he invokes Christ's promises which suggests that he may be moving from rebellion to discipleship: "And whoever gives only a cup of cold water to one of these little ones to drink because he is a disciple– amen, I say to you, he will surely not lose his reward" (Matt 10:42).[279]

Then, Ivan "confidentially" reveals his belief in the devil and, implicitly, his desire to believe in God. Here are Ivan's final words in the novel— allusive and deeply revealing:

> He [the devil] is here somewhere, no doubt—under that table with the material evidence on it, perhaps. Where should he sit if not there? You see, listen to me. I told him I don't want to keep quiet, and he talked about the geological cataclysm . . . idiocy! Come, release the monster . . . he's been singing a hymn. That's because his heart is light! It's like a drunken man in the street bawling "Vanka went to Petersburg," and I would give a quadril- lion quadrillions for two seconds of joy. You don't know me! Oh, how stupid all this business is! Come, take me instead of him! I didn't come for nothing. . . . Why, why is everything so stupid?
> . . . . (577)

Conclusively, Ivan spurns his "Geological Cataclysm" as "idiocy." In that poem, he'd posited the "need to destroy the idea of God in man," so that, "Man will be lifted up by a spirit of Titanic pride and the man-god will appear" (546). Instead, he embraces an alternative vision of humility to which he had given form in a fantasy he'd composed at seventeen: A de- ceased atheist refuses to accept the beatific vision "on principle" and is given a purgatorial prescription: he must "walk a quadrillion kilometers in the dark" before arriving at "the gate of heaven" where "he will find forgiveness" (541). In protest, he lies down for a thousand years. Then gets up. He begins his long walk home. The moment he arrives in paradise, he "crie[s] out that those two seconds were worth walking not a quadrillion kilometers but a quadrillion of quadrillions, raised to the quadrillionth power!" He sings "Hosannah!"—to the point of comic excess (542).[280] Ivan now declares *his* desire to take this expiatory walk: "I would give a quadrillion quadrillions for two seconds of joy. You don't know me!" No longer is Ivan so "very fond of being alone" (508). Intensely, he now wishes to be known by others, which suggests a kenotic emptying of his self-sufficiency. As Christos Yannaras writes: "What God asks of man, existentially alienated and degraded as he is, is an effort, however small, to reject his self-sufficiency, to resist its impulses and to will to live as one loving and loved. . . . It is the *kenosis* put into practice by Christ as man: the act of emptying out every element of individual autonomy and self-sufficiency and realizing the life of love and communion" (52–53). Ivan here takes this "first step" of *kenosis* (52). Like Mitya singing his "Hymn," he wants to give his life for another, for Mitya, his innocent brother: "Come, take me instead of him! I didn't come for nothing. . . . Why, why is everything so stupid? . . ." (577).

Ivan sees all as "stupid" because his spiritual and psychological state is shattered. However, I see Ivan as suffering less from a brain-fever-induced breakdown as undergoing an experience of being broken down by God. Recall Alyosha's prayerful reflection from night before: "God in Whom he disbelieved, and His truth were gaining mastery over his heart, which still refused to submit" (551). Like Augustine in the garden, Ivan struggles against, and gradually submits to God's truth. Recall Mitya's words: "A new man is risen up in me. He was hidden in me, but would never have come to the surface, if it hadn't been for *this blow from heaven*" (499; emphasis added). In Ivan's last tormented words and screams, the reader can discern that Ivan is experiencing a healing, restorative "blow," especially when she hears the Lukan echo that concludes the scene.

Ivan tries to gain control, to gather his stupefied wits by "slowly, and as it were reflectively, looking round him again." He is not expecting the bailiff to seize his arm:

> "What are you doing?" he cried, staring into the man's face, and suddenly seizing him by the shoulders, he flung him violently to the floor. But the police were on the spot and he was seized. He screamed furiously and all the time he was being removed, he yelled and screamed something incoherent. (577–78)

Victor Terras notes, "in the original, *zavopil neistovym voplem* is clearly biblical language, bringing to mind the screams of the possessed healed by Jesus and the apostles (e.g., Luke 8:28, Acts 8:7)" (*Companion* 410). With this echo in mind, we can see Ivan's final, frenzied exit as an exorcism, a healing in process, and an answer to both Alyosha's prayer and Ivan's plea "Give me a drink for Christ's sake." As in Augustine, free will and grace work cooperatively. Ivan's fractured words have enacted a kenotic outpouring of his old, diabolical pride. At the same time, his pride is being emptied by God through a healing exorcism. Ivan does not finally "perish in hate." Fitfully, he opens himself to helping, and being helped by others. He thus approaches an imitation of the *kenosis* imaged by the cross. At the same time, he is visited—brutally, healingly—by the person who hung there.[281]

Like so much in *The Brothers Karamazov*, Ivan's future is left open-ended. Mitya's words—"He will recover" (635)—resonate,[282] but Alyosha seems less sure: "'I too believe there is every hope that he will get well,' Alyosha observed anxiously" (636). At the end, he describes Ivan to the schoolboys as "lying on death's door" (644). No one in the courtroom—not even Alyosha—has discerned that a healing is taking place. They see a young man descending into "brain fever" and collapse—an apparent evil. So too many readers: Vladimir Kantor, for example, writes: "Ivan identifies himself with Smerdyakov and the truth of repentance becomes a demonic farce, definitively confirming Mitya in the murder" (217). Ivan's confession ushers in the evil of Katerina's subsequent testimony, in which she frantically tries to protect Ivan by producing the letter that falsely incriminates Dmitri. Where is God's presence and grace in the midst of this brokenness? This is the question that haunts Alyosha: "Does the spirit of God move above that force [of the raging Karamazovs]?" (191). It is also the question that torments Ivan when he rages against the suffering and death of children.

But perhaps Ivan's confession will bear fruit in "great time," to retrieve the Bakhtinian phrase we employed in our discussion of Mikhail in Chapter 3. Great time is *not* the equivalent of Ivan's conception of eventual harmony, of parallel lines meeting, a pyramid-like "edifice" built upon the tears of an innocent child. Both Ivan and Alyosha have rightly rejected this theodicy. Ivan's non-Euclidean theodicy, which he presents as "Christian," turns out to be all-too-rational in its presumptuous claim that suffering will produce harmony; it reduces "great time" to formulaic cause and effect. In the novel, the oceanic realities of authoritative miracle and mystery abide. Great time is "unpremeditated and often unexpected" (Emerson, "Zosima" 171). Graham Pechey suggests that great time can discern "miracle" and usher in "the order of grace: the future neither hoped for nor feared but in which our completion as finite beings lies."[283] Great time lends form to Augustine's promise in his *Enchiridion*: God, "the supremely Good [can turn] to good account even what is evil" (116). This is the "order of grace" glimpsed by the reader in the final scene of *The Brothers Karamazov*: a Eucharistic community founded upon the memory of a dead child, to which we turn in the next, final chapter. For the reader, the ascent to glimpsing the order of grace always arrives after a difficult descent. Such is the demand of Dostoevsky's final novel, composed in the christological spirit and form memorably voiced by Saint Augustine: "Descend that you may ascend, and make your way to God."

Chapter 7

Alyosha's Three Days in November

After his late-August experience of Cana, we next see Alyosha in early
November. He has clearly matured—he remains deeply committed to
being available and attentive to others, but is calmer, firmer, and more confident despite the sadness and stress that surrounds him. He seems to have
found the answer to that searing question he had asked Lise three months
earlier: "Where is God?" We have seen the mediatory role Alyosha's presence plays with Ivan and Mitya. In this final chapter, I will look closely at his
interactions with children, and especially two adolescents, Kolya and Lise,
and will focus upon Book 10 and the Epilogue.

Near the start of Book 10, Kolya wonders why, when his brother is
about to go to trial, Alyosha is spending his time with children (444). Some
readers ask the same thing: Why this book-long detour from the central
plot? Truthfully, I can't imagine the symphonic whole of the novel without the music of Book 10. Robin Feuer Miller calls it her "favorite in the
novel" (99), and it may be mine, too. This study emphasizes the image of
Christ, and we recall that he too was a child who "advanced in wisdom
and age" (Luke 2:52). As an adult, Jesus exhorted children to come to him
(Matt 19:14) and pointed to them as examples: "Unless you become like
a little child, you will not enter the kingdom of heaven" (Matt 18:3). The
presence of children fosters the virtue of hope, and inspires our readiness
to sow good seeds when we're near them. As Zosima stresses in his final
words: "Love children especially. . . . Woe to him who offends a child! . . .
You may have sown an evil seed in him, and it may grow, and all because
you were not more careful before the child, because you did not foster in

yourself a careful, actively benevolent love" (275). Dostoevsky was keenly aware of his own responsibilities to children—to his own, and to members of the younger generation, whom he feared being influenced by corrosive contemporary ideas. He set aside time aside to meet and counsel them, even as he struggled to complete his final novel.[284]

The eight stages of life posited by neo-Freudian Erik Erikson are applicable here.[285] Alyosha's stage of intimacy—which in "real life" would take years—might be seen as symbolically transpiring over three chapters: "Engagement" with Lise, with its hidden love letter and chaste kiss, and more robustly, in his encounter with Grushenka in "An Onion" and its ecstatic aftermath in "Cana." In a sense, "Cana of Galilee" represents Alyosha's own wedding feast, akin to Jesus' meeting with the woman at the well, which some see as analogous to a "betrothal type scene" (John 4:1–42).[286] The union, however, is ultimately with Christ. Father Zosima mediates the "wedding"—"Do you see our Sun, do you see Him?" (311)—just before Alyosha vows to begin his work as "a monk in the world." In Book 10, we see Alyosha commencing his vocation in earnest, mentoring young people with a commitment to what Erikson calls "generativity," even as he guides his brothers and the women they love.[287] Come November, Alyosha has become a rather natty dresser. But he never seems more like a celibate priest.[288] The Preface suggests Dostoevsky's plans to write a sequel, and he imagined writing about the further complexities of Alyosha's relationship with Lise. But by the end we have reason to believe that the only two erotic bonds sustained beyond the book's bindings are those of Dmitri with Grushenka and Ivan with Katerina. Wherever Dmitri goes, Grushenka will follow, and the narrator makes clear that Ivan's "mad and consuming passion for Katerina Ivanovna . . . left its mark on all the rest of his life: this would furnish the subject for another tale, another novel, which I may perhaps never write" (514). The reader may sense Dostoevsky's premonition of his own nearing death, but she closes the novel with every reason to believe that Mitya's prophecy regarding Ivan is accurate: "He will recover" (635).

Kolya

Kolya represents the impressionable youth of Dostoevsky's time. He is a lot like Ivan, but uniquely himself: precocious, charming, imaginative, rebellious, tyrannical, capable of love. To use Erikson's terminology, he's in the identity-formation stage, and is thus *especially* sensitive to the ways in which he is perceived and judged by others. He *insists* that others see him as intelligent, *au courant*, and brave—even as he recoils before their gaze, especially

Alyosha's, for whose good opinion he yearns. At any stage of life, accepting the fact that we are *visible* before the eyes of others is vital to the process of "human maturation" and "human flourishing" (Williams 117). Human reality is inextricably social; other people inevitably see and evaluate the way we act in the world. For Sartre, this means other people are "hell" as their gazes reduce and finalize us to our worst qualities. As noted earlier, Bakhtin sees a gift in the gaze of the other person as it offers the gift of "rhythm" and integral form. Being "visible" to the other grants us a sense of ourselves unavailable in solitary introspection. If the other offers a compliment, one may receive it with gratitude; if a critique, one may respond with a responsible willingness to change. In both cases, the gaze of the other offers blessing, not curse, and fosters a secure sense of "internality."[289] But if a person becomes anxiously dependent upon another's external validation, hyper-alert to others' judgment, the person will attempt to manipulate that judgment, thus denying not only the freedom of the other, but diminishing one's own through compulsive willfulness. Leslie Farber's therapeutic insight is deeply Dostoevskian:

> the consequence of willing what cannot be willed is that we fall into the distress we call anxiety. And since anxiety, too, opposes such willing, should we, in our anxiety, now try to will away that anxiety, our fate is still more anxiety. Within this impasse, meaning, reason, imagination, discrimination fail, so that the will is deprived of its supporting and tempering faculties. Under these reduced circumstances a [person] is, in a sense, all will. Or nothing but will. His disability is willfulness, meaning the state of being "governed by will, without yielding to reason," which is Webster's definition. (79)

No longer recognizing that one *can* change, one falls into what Bakhtin calls a "vicious circle," a compulsive attempt to control the other person's view, or willfully seek revenge (*Problems* 229).

Such is Kolya's adolescent condition when we first meet him on a cold November day. He's named his dog "Perezvon," which means "chime," and Kolya's character "chimes" with our memories of some of the most divided, even demonic characters in the novel: not only Ivan, but also that dark creation of Ivan's consciousness, the Grand Inquisitor, and the devil who visits Ivan at night. But by the end of Book 10, Kolya is more like Mitya than Ivan: confessing, tearful, and repentant. Alyosha's generative presence nurtures Kolya's incipient virtues. Alyosha fosters Kolya's "good taste of self," and his capacity to speak with his own voice, from "the pure deep *I* from within [himself]" (Bakhtin, "Reworking" 294). Like his mentor, Kolya grows more prudent, more capable of accurately apprehending, and responsibly responding to reality.

We get a sense of Kolya's capacity for virtue in the first chapter. For all of his flaws, especially his vanity, recklessness, and habit of "look[ing] down upon everyone" (435), he is capable of self-restraint and perceiving "that last mystic limit beyond which a prank became disorder, rebellion, and lawlessness" (436). Although he never oversteps this limit, he walks a razor's edge. He skirts death by lying beneath a roaring train. He earns his sought-for "reputation" among his peers as a "desperate character" (437), but, simultaneously, grows unabashedly affectionate to and respectful of his mother (recalling Zosima's young brother Markel with *his* mother). When she hears of his train "exploit," she is horrified and, in response, Kolya promises to relinquish his "pranks": "he swore on his knees before the holy icon, and swore by the memory of his father, at Mrs. Krasotkin's insistence, and the 'manly' Kolya burst into tears like a boy of six, from 'feelings,'" and in the days that follow, "he had become more silent, more modest, sterner, and more thoughtful" (438). In Dostoevsky's imaginative world, tears usually signal *metanoia*, a turn toward receptivity to reality and responsibility. Of course, like so much in the novel, "tears" can cut both ways. Fyodor's tearful sentimentality can be wicked, his unearned emotion willful and false (26). In contrast, naive Kolya sees *any* expression of deeply felt emotion witnessed by others—affection, compassion, remorse, grief—as "sheepish sentimentality" (436). Kolya wants control, and shuns vulnerability. But his authentic emotions often rise up unbidden. When acknowledged and accepted, emotions are simply an integral part of mature experience. But bereft of his father, Kolya lacks a male model of emotional integration. Alyosha will provide that model.

A further indication of Kolya's capacity for virtue can be seen during his babysitting of eight-year-old Nastya and seven-year-old Kostya during which he "plays horses with the little lodgers at home" (439). As we'll see when he arrives at the Snegiryov home, Kolya's capacity for beneficent play—playing in such a way that it invites others into the "simple, artless merrymaking" (310)—is one of his best features. Of course, he "haughtily parrie[s]" when the story of his play reaches his schoolmates (439–40). If Kolya *must* be visible, he demands respect! After delaying for months, he's finally ready to visit little Ilyusha, if only to make his grand dramatic entrance—willful, not playful—with a trained "Perezvon," Zhuchka "risen from the dead." Even as he plays with the "kids," he's champing at the bit to do so. Late for his appointment with eleven-year-old Smurov, still awaiting Agatha's return—"she must have broken her leg" (441)—Kolya announces to the "kiddies" that must leave them to fend for themselves.

But he doesn't leave. He stays, and listens to the children's theories of human reproduction. Nastya's explanation comically rhymes with Ivan's tragic decision, and highlights the good decision Kolya has just made: "thinking and thinking of it [a baby] will produce pregnancy" echoes Ivan's "full-latitude" (128) wish to see his father murdered, which takes embodied form when he leaves for Chermashnya.[290] The comical child's tale mirrors the tragic reality. Both Ivan and Kolya experience—in varied degrees—the anguish of freedom: "Should I stay or should I go?" Kolya's departure would have entailed a similar dereliction of responsibility by leaving others vulnerable. He apprehends reality and delays departure. Ever the dramatist, he "sensationally" demonstrates his miniature cannon to the kids (441) even as he yearns to perform even more sensationally before Ilyusha and his friends. When "the kids" expose their weakness—"we sha-all cry" (442)—he decides to stay. Like Ivan, he flourishes literary allusion: "'Oh, children, children, how fraught with peril are your years!"[291] But in his decision to stay, Kolya differs crucially from Ivan: "There's no help for it, chickens, I shall have to stay with you I don't know how long" (442). Of course, Kolya's responsible act has muddled motivations: he relishes presenting Perezvon's "performance" and, when Agatha finally returns, he theatrically (but comically) plays the inquisitorial tyrant: he demands that she "swear on [her] eternal salvation to care for the children" and chastises "Granny" for teaching them "old woman's nonsense" (443). He infuriates Agatha, but intent upon sustaining his *shtick* ignores her. The narrator begins the next chapter "But Kolya did not hear her."

This transitional sentence rhymes with an earlier, very different scene of transitional human encounter and shifts of attention: Zosima's movement from one peasant woman to another: "but the elder had already turned away" (49); "but the elder had already noticed" (49). Both characters respond practically to the pressure of limited time. But Zosima's shifts of attention are pragmatic: he only has so much time. More precisely, they are *prudential*, as Zosima brings each encounter to graceful closure at the right time, just after each woman has found peace and a renewed sense of purpose.[292] In contrast, Kolya shifts his attention from one peasant to another, aiming to elicit "disorder," his playfulness sliding into willfulness: he misnames and angers the "market women" (446) and leaves the man with the pockmarked face in a frenzy of confusion with his "saucy pranks" (446). In these encounters, Kolya evokes the Grand Inquisitor: he gazes down on all and cultivates meretricious "mystery" (445) with his sudden announcement that he will visit Ilyusha. Kolya secretly intends to perform a sham resurrection of Zhuchka, the dog. The Grand Inquisitor is a liar, but most terribly when he lies to the people about their deepest hope, "that we shall all rise from the dead, and shall live, and see each other again" (646). The Inquisitor admits to Christ: "we shall entice them with the reward of heaven and eternity" but "beyond the grave they will find nothing but death" (226). Thus the Inquisitor's willful atheism: he has witnessed Christ raise the girl from the dead, but he willfully refuses to believe in the reality of eternal life. Given his "beastly willfulness" (469), Kolya is tempted toward similar refusal.

Kolya next encounters Matvey, whose name he happens to guess. He lies about being "thrashed" in order to satisfy what he condescendingly projects to be the peasant's expectations (446). Repeatedly, Kolya has claimed to have been "thrashed"—with "the kids" (442), with Smurov (443), and later with Bulkin (461). He echoes Ivan's terrible—and true—stories of child abuse, but also raises the troubling possibility of precocious children making false claims.[293] Moments like these are comical for the reader, but perhaps our laughter implicates us: Kolya's fabrications leave people in a state of disorder (446). We recall the tragic valence in Ferapont's crazed offense "against good order" (289) and Lise's perverse desire for destructive "disorder" (490). As Kolya "march[es] along with a triumphant air," proudly knowing he's stirred up "fools" (448) among whom "there'll be a hubbub . . . all day" (448), we may remember the Inquisitor's contempt for the multitude of "geese" whom he dupes (227). When Kolya incites the peasant to gratuitously kill a goose, he recalls Smerdyakov, and not only by hurting an animal: like Smerdyakov with Ivan at the gate, Kolya insinuates and winks "on purpose,"[294] manipulating the peasant to do his will (462). But Kolya is also like Ivan, the "intelligent man" who has tutored Smerdyakov in his "everything is permitted" philosophy. Finally, like both Ivan *and* Smerdyakov, Kolya denies responsibility. In court, he claims to the justice of the peace that he'd "only stated the general proposition, had spoken hypothetically" (462). The reader laughs at the mess Kolya makes, but may also remember the murderous forms disorder can take.

Impudent Kolya misapprehends and manipulates reality. But throughout Book 10, his expectations and projections are overturned through characters who serve as foils to his folly, such as the third peasant whom Kolya assumes to be a "stupid" "blockhead" (448). The peasant may be tipsy, but his simple responses destabilize Kolya's autonomy. The peasant's astute utterances emphasize that reality is a divine gift, and that all are called to share, non-competitively, in that gift. Their comical encounter emerges as a parable:

> "Hey, good morning peasant!"
> "Good morning, if you are not laughing at me," he said deliberately in reply.

"And if I am?" laughed Kolya.

"Well, a joke's a joke. Laugh away. I don't mind. There's no harm in a joke."

"I beg your pardon, brother, it was a joke."

"Well, God forgive you!"

"You forgive me, too?"

"I quite forgive you. Go along."

"I say, you seem a clever peasant."

"Cleverer than you," the peasant answered with the same gravity.

"I doubt it," said Kolya, somewhat taken aback.

"It's true though."

"Perhaps it is."

"It is, brother."

"Good-bye, peasant!"

"Goodbye!"

"There are all sorts of peasants," Kolya observed to Smurov, after a brief silence. "How could I tell I had hit upon a clever one? I am always ready to recognize intelligence in the peasantry." (448)

Of course, it is the prudent peasant who "recognizes" and articulates the truth. Disconcerted before the younger Smurov, Kolya defensively boasts of his just willingness to give deserving peasants their due. His sententious claim reeks of Rakitin's reductive "realism," one that labels human beings according to biological laws or binary sociological categories: "clever" and "unclever" peasants. Reductive realism denies the complex reality of *persons*; incarnational realism attends to the reality of personhood and responds responsibly.[295]

The peasant's every utterance suggests the incarnational realism embodied in Dostoevsky's novel—thus the encounter's parabolic resonance, its pitch-perfect blending of "gravity" and levity. His tone is "deliberate" and "grave." He intuits Kolya's mockery, and nevertheless responds (like Matvey) with a willingness to respectfully encounter another person with common civility: "good morning." His addendum—"if you're not laughing at me"—is motivated less by self-protection, as by a desire to help heedless Kolya. With a characteristic swagger, Kolya admits that, yes, he is mocking the man. The peasant accepts that truth, and demonstrates that while spiteful humor can humiliate, such humbling can offer an occasion to practice humility: "well, a joke's a joke. Laugh away. I don't mind. There is no harm in laughter." The reader might ask: Could I respond to a stranger's insult with humble laughter? As a whole, the novel invites such self-examination.

The peasant's words chime with those uttered by characters more obviously authoritative:[296] at the dinner, the Father Superior "gladly bears" (83) Fyodor's absurd taunting. Like Kolya, Fyodor "could not restrain himself" (82). And in both scenes, the victim of mockery responds freely, without resentment, but with creatural humility and even gratitude. In contrast to Miusov's compulsive reactions to Fyodor's "vileness" (82), the Father Superior accepts Fyodor's pettily demonic disparagement as a gift: "'Pardon me,' said the Father Superior suddenly. 'It was said of old, "Many have begun to speak against me and have uttered evil sayings about me. And hearing it I have said to myself: it is the correction of the Lord and He has sent it to heal my vain soul." And so we humbly thank you honored guest!' And he made Fyodor Pavlovich a low bow" (82). His bow bespeaks neither masochistic self-abnegation nor "sanctimoniousness," as Fyodor misnames it (82). Likely drawing on patristic example,[297] the Father Superior's response is a traditional yet sincere expression of gratitude, the fruit of disciplined practice. This is incarnational realism in action: neither fanciful nor a disguised assertion of the will to power, Father Superior's response recognizes that "all is gift"—or "tout est grâce" as Dostoevsky's contemporary, St. Therese of Lisieux put it.[298] Spoken from a position of inter-creatural confidence, the Father Superior's words have a penetrative capacity to disrupt the mocker's blinkered self-confidence. In contrast, Fyodor, in his "paroxysm of simulated feeling," musters false emotion and blurts lies: Fyodor refuses to recognize the real.

Although Kolya's willful pranks are less frenzied than Fyodor's, they bear similarities. Fyodor "was so carried away by simulated emotion, that for one moment he almost believed it himself. He was so touched he almost wept. But at that very instant he felt it was time to draw back" (83). Simulated tears stimulate false emotion, whereas genuine love is anything but the "sheepish sentimentality" to which Kolya would reduce it.[299] Fyodor and Kolya share both the buffoon's compulsivity and comic sense of limit. Kolya admits "there is no stopping me now"; of Fyodor, the narrator notes that "he had no clear idea of what he would do, but he knew that he could not control himself, and that a touch might drive him to the utmost limits of obscenity, but only to obscenity, to nothing criminal, nothing for which he could be legally punished. In the last resort, he would always restrain himself and had indeed marveled at himself on that score" (80). Kolya too knows where "to draw the line" (436). "Habit is the great motive power" (445), but Book 10 suggests that, with the generative help of Alyosha, young Kolya has the youthful capacity to change.

Let us return to the peasant's incarnational realism: When Kolya admits that his greeting was, in fact, "a joke," the peasant responds not with an assertion of his *own* power to forgive, but an acknowledgment of his inter-creatural dependence upon God's grace: "'Well, God forgive you.'" Kolya re-sists this deference to divine reality, and demands a self-assertive response: "'do you forgive me, too?'" he asks, more as challenge than plea. "I quite forgive you. Go along.'" The peasant doesn't interrogate Kolya's motive, but simply participates in the divine grace of mercy. But rather than responding with gratitude, Kolya retorts with condescension: "I say, you seem a clever peasant." The peasant's ready response—"cleverer than you"—further un-settles Kolya's preconceptions. The peasant isn't competing here: he simply recognizes that Kolya's foolish assertion of will is, in fact, not very clever. Where Kolya spreads confusion, the peasant sows clarity. "Taken aback," Kolya retorts in the only way he yet knows, competitively: "I doubt it." The peasant calmly re-affirms the truth: his receptivity to the real is indeed more "clever." Prudence is "'the intelligent prow' of our nature which steers through the multiplicity of the finite world toward perfection"[300] Kolya re-veals prudential *potential* as he opens himself to the peasant's possibility: "Perhaps it is [true]." The peasant confirms it—with a reminder to Kolya that despite their differing capacities, he and the boy remain responsibly related as fellow creatures: "it is, brother." If all are adopted brothers and sisters of Christ, then *each* is his or her brother's or sister's keeper. We are, like Christ, each responsible "for all." The two bid each other farewell, and the resonantly comic scene comes to a close.[301] Aware that Smurov has wit-nessed his humbling, Kolya is nonplussed. And when the sensible younger boy suggests that he go inside and meet Alyosha, Kolya returns to his "des-potic tone," playing the role of one who insists that others do *his* bidding.

Before turning to Kolya's transformative encounter with Alyosha, a word about sensible Smurov The left-handed schoolboy (157) is one of the most luminous and lovable characters in the novel. Although he's three years younger and "never dreamed of putting himself on a level with [Kolya]" (444), he has much to teach the older boy. Smurov "was the one who told Alyosha Karamazov about Ilyusha" during the stone-throwing episode (443) and is like Alyosha in three interrelated ways: his prudence, his insistence upon truthful speech, and his honest emotion. As soon as Smurov sees Kolya, he "stolidly" (443) observes that the older boy is late, and corrects him, making clear that he is "never thrashed" (443). He ex-horts Kolya not to "provoke" the peasant Matvey (445). In his compassion for Ilyusha, he exercises a bit of practical casuistry: might they not *pretend* that Perezvon is Zhuchka? Showing no awareness of his own hypocrisy, Kolya rejects the idea with Kantian *hauteur*—"Shun a lie . . . even with a good object"—even as he cloaks his own deceit. Smurov sighs, anticipating with clear-eyed *solertia* (prudent anticipation of the future) that a new dog will not comfort Ilyusha. Over the course of the preceding weeks, Alyosha had artfully reunited the boys with Ilyusha. Kolya calls it "sentimentality." Quickly Smurov rejects this misnaming and points out that Kolya is himself going to Ilyusha to "make it up" (444). With "sudden warmth," much as Alyosha will do later, Smurov chides Kolya for his delay in joining them: "Why was it, why was it you wouldn't come all this time?" Smurov's question and intonation recalls that of both Martha and Mary to Jesus: "Lord, if you had been here, my brother would not have died" (John 11:21, 32). But in his pretension to "resurrect" Zhuchka, Kolya is a Christ-manqué, an analog of the deceitful Inquisitor.

Kolya has heard about Alyosha, his generative "influence" upon and "use to" the "younger generation" (450). He is strongly drawn to Alyosha even as he fears his opinion. When he sees Alyosha's face for the first time, he is relieved by its expression of joy. The reader hasn't seen Alyosha since his dream of Cana; three months have gone by, and he has traded his novice's cassock for stylish layman's clothes (450); his always "good-humored" face has matured and relaxed: "there was a gentleness and serenity in his good humor." When he greets Kolya, he situates himself as one *among* the group of boys: "How anxious *we've* been to see you!" (450; emphasis added). And he names Ilyusha's condition as it really is: "he is certainly dying." When he sees the dog, like Smurov, he asks, pitifully, "not Zhuchka?" (450).

Outside and alone with Alyosha, we can observe a halting transformation: Kolya's recovery of a voice authentically his own, not determined by external validation. Like Mikhail the "mysterious visitor" confessing to Zosima, Kolya tacks between forthright acknowledgment and a willful attempt to control the confessant's judgment of him. He relates the complex story of his relationship with Ilyusha, and exposes the ways in which he has acted far more like the Grand Inquisitor than the Elder Zosima. He has generative instincts akin to Alyosha's: when he sees Ilyusha being bullied, Kolya says he "gave it to them hot," and "beats" the other kids who nonetheless "adore" him (450). He protects Ilyusha, whom he wishes to "teach" and "develop" (450). But, as with the Inquisitor's jaundiced "love," his tutelage is marked less by attention than by contempt. "I was cool in responding to [Ilyusha's] endearments. And so, in order to train him properly, the tenderer he was, the colder I became. *I did it on purpose . . .*" (451; emphasis added). Again, the phrase "on purpose" reveals a violent, theatrical assertion of the will, cutting against the grain of reality. And as it does in varying ways throughout the novel, such perverse purposefulness—willfulness—damages others. Ilyusha is vulnerable, and, like the Inquisitor, Kolya treats him like a dog to be trained, "licked into shape." When Ilyusha confesses to Kolya that at Smerdyakov's instigation, he had fed Zhuchka a pin inside the bread, Kolya rejects him, "excommunicates" him, employing the act that Zosima had declared anathema to the Christian call of love (61). Even though Ilyusha confesses and weeps with remorse, Kolya is "determined to give him a lesson" (451), treats Ilyusha as a "scoundrel," and "giv[es] him the silent treatment." When Ilyusha rebels, Kolya "treat[s] him with contempt." Ilyusha reacts by stabbing him with the penknife. The contrast between this scene and that of Ilyusha's biting of Alyosha's finger couldn't be sharper. In pain, both remain calm. But whereas Alyosha responds to Ilyusha's vicious bite with a loving call to the boy to take responsibility, Kolya "look[s] at him contemptuously" (452).[302] Three months later, Kolya is penitent, and confesses all to Alyosha: "it was stupid of me." But even here, anticipating Alyosha's judgment, he snatches a loophole, sets up a defense, as if to say: "you see, I already know that I was stupid, so *you* can't call me stupid."

Alyosha responds with the prudence of a good confessor. He wishes that he'd sought out Kolya earlier, and thus have relieved Ilyusha of his guilt for "kill[ing] Zhuchka": "and if the dog were found and proved to be alive, then, perhaps [Ilyusha himself] might even be resurrected by joy" (452). But, like Ivan before the devil's visit, Kolya has procrastinated. He has missed the opportunity to bring healing and truth to the ill boy because he craves the spotlight, a "trick," a "theatrical performance" (454) "with all looking on and applauding as though on stage" (55). He savors love in dreams, not hidden, active love. And so he waits. "Waiting" cuts both ways: Ivan's deferral in going to the prosecutor, Kolya's delay in seeing Ilyusha, are destructive. In contrast, Alyosha has learned the art of *constructive waiting*, the tactful delay that conforms to the contours of reality. Early on, he waits for Ivan and, in time, "his brother [makes] a step toward him, as he long desired" (128); when Dmitri needs him he delays his errand, and "[makes] up his mind to wait" (96). In the weeks that follow, Alyosha slowly, patiently reconciles the boys with Ilyusha, without drama, such that the boys barely recognize the role Alyosha has played: "several boys were sitting with Ilyusha and, though all of them like Smurov were prepared to deny that it was Alyosha who had brought them and reconciled them with Ilyusha. All the art he had used had been to take them, one by one, to Ilyusha, without 'sheepish sentimentality,' appearing to do so casually, and without design. It was a great consolation to Ilyusha in his suffering" (454). Prudence entails the capacity to feel things out, to improvise along the way. A theatrical mass-visit would have overwhelmed Ilyusha. Not that "theater" itself is necessarily bad—it too cuts both ways. As Alyosha explains to Kolya, who listens "intently," children's "make-believe games of soldiers and robbers in their playtime are also art in its first stage" (453). In his Fifteenth Letter, Schiller claims that "It is exactly play, and *only* play, that makes [a human being] complete"

(*Aesthete Education* 55). Indeed, as Carla Arnell demonstrates, play proves therapeutic in Book 10. Alyosha employs "art" in gradually reconciling the boys with Kolya because, like children playing, he improvises and is "the actor [himself]" (453).

In fact, Alyosha takes his part in this "theodrama." Playful as theater may be, the stakes here are life and death. In the novel's vision, the "resurrection" of Ilyusha for which Alyosha had hoped can be understood in the light of the risen Christ; Ilyusha's experience participates in that incarnational reality. Even Ilyusha's death, heart-rending as it is, will be represented in the light of Christ's salvific passion, death, and resurrection, seen most fully in the finale, the speech at the stone.

"At Ilyusha's Bedside," Alyosha realizes that Kolya has in fact delayed visiting the sick boy simply to keep his private, gnostic secret, in order to perform a pseudo-resurrection of Zhuchka before the eyes and applause of all. In a rare moment of judgment,[303] Alyosha chastises him firmly. His rebuke recalls that of Zosima to the woman who would magically manipulate God to wrench a response from her son (459). Like the Inquisitor, Kolya's "mystery" is "mystification," his miracle a magic trick, and his authority contemptuous tyranny. In fairness, Kolya *is* trying to help the other suffering person. Of course, the Inquisitor claims that he too acts out of love (223). Kolya wants to "help" on his own dramatic terms—and thus hurts the one he aims to help. As he sits with Ilyusha, for a moment, he obeys the better angels of his nature: "*Something* moved Kolya to raise his hand and pass it over Ilyusha's hair." When the narrator uses "something" or "someone" as the subject of his sentence, he usually does so to denote a benevolent impulse integrally cooperating with divine grace, or divine grace cooperating with human freedom.[304] Notice also the narrator's emphasis upon *the real*: "in reality [Kolya] had to do his utmost to control his feelings, not to burst out crying like a 'child'" (457).

But feeling vulnerable, Kolya retreats to the role of Inquisitor, sadistically shaming Ilyusha and rejecting Alyosha's prudent effort to intervene. Snegiryov asks, "you were so kind as to come with Alexei Fyodorovich?" Kolya responds brutally:

> "No. . . . I came with Perezvon. I've got a dog now, called Perezvon. A Slavonic name. He's out there. . . . If I whistle, he'll run in. I've brought a dog too," he said addressing Ilyusha all at once. "Do you remember Zhuchka old man?" He suddenly fired the question at him.
>
> Ilyushechka's little face quivered. He looked with an agonized expression at Kolya. Alyosha, standing at the door, frowned and signed to Kolya not to speak of Zhuchka but he did

not or would not notice. "Where . . . is Zhuchka?" Ilyusha asked in a broken voice.

"Oh well, my boy, your Zhuchka's lost and done for!"

Ilyusha did not speak, but he fired an intense gaze once more on Kolya. Alyosha, catching Kolya's eye, signed to him vigorously again, but he turned away his eyes pretending not to have noticed.

"It must have run away somewhere. It must have died after an appetizer like that," Kolya pronounced pitilessly, though he seemed a little breathless. "But I've got a dog, Perezvon. . . . A Slavonic name. . . . I've brought him to show you." (457–58)

Kolya would kill the one whom he'd come to help. His "breathless" state in the throes of willfulness recalls the "breathless" *nadryv* of Katerina, who declares her devotion to Dmitri while willfully ignoring Alyosha (166). Kolya's psychological state when he makes "pitiless" pronouncement recalls Ivan's "delirium" (211) when he twisted the knife in Alyosha with his sadistic stories of children. Kolya insists upon competing. He refuses to simply accept and give the gift of love. Thus he loses his sense of integral personhood. Kolya's willfulness begets a willful reaction in the younger boy: "'I don't want him!' cried Ilyusha with a mournful laceration in his voice" (458). Kolya insists, saying he "brought him *on purpose*": the recurring phrase unmasks Kolya's willful desire to re-open the wound. Kolya would will Ilyusha's descent to his lowest point so that he can spring his theatrical "surprise" to the greatest effect.[305]

"Surprise" too cuts both ways: when Alyosha and Grushenka exchange onions, their mutual "surprise" is beneficial and healing. Their gift exchange is marked by receptivity to grace, with no need for an audience. Here, however, the self-orchestrated "surprise" aims at an ovation, and wins its longed-for cries of "bravo," "Krasotkin is great!" (459)—a travesty of the novel's final, grace-imbued scene. The drama proves poisonous: "Ilyusha could not speak. White as a sheet, he gazed open-mouthed at Kolya, with his great eyes almost popping out of his head. And if Krasotkin, who had no suspicion, had known what a disastrous and fatal effect such a moment might have on the sick child's health, nothing would have induced him to pay such a trick on him. But Alyosha was perhaps the only person in the room who realized it" (458).[306] Perhaps the narrator is too generous in his assessment of Kolya; Alyosha is justly critical: "'Can you really have put off coming all this time simply to train the dog?' exclaimed Alyosha, with an involuntary note of reproach in his voice. 'Simply for that!' answered Kolya, with perfect simplicity. 'I wanted to show him in all his glory'" (459).

Having reveled in self-exaltation, Kolya briefly lets go of his self-con-sciousness. This presents a glimmer of hope: Kolya *can* lose himself in play that genuinely desires to bring happiness to others.[307] Now that he's on a roll, Kolya presents his cannon, improvising and ready to forego theatrical timing: "'you are all happy now,' he felt, 'so here's something to make you happier!' He was perfectly enchanted himself" (460).

But gradually Kolya becomes aware of the reality of Ilyusha's suffering, that he has made *himself* the inappropriate focus of attention with his sham resurrection, and hurt Ilyusha by doing so: "though he assumed an uncon-cerned air as he talked he still could not control himself and was continually missing the note he tried to keep up" (461). He begins to worry that Alyosha holds him in contempt—"I believe you are laughing Karamazov?"—though he's "reassured" by Alyosha's equanimity, his "good-natured" avowal that he's listening (462).

With bravado, Kolya tells his audience the story of the dead goose and again recalls Ivan. He displays his intellectual *bona fides*, professes his "faith" "in the people" (462).[308] He parades his judiciousness with a Latin phrase. By presenting a hypothesis that incites his pupil to violence, Kolya had con-temptuously seen the young peasant as a "fool." He mused, "I am wondering what the goose thinks about," and asked him "if that cart were to move on a little, would it break the goose's neck or not?" So had Ivan tutored Smerdya-kov in his "everything is permitted" philosophy, all the while assuming his student to be "stupid" (532), "a prime candidate [or 'cannon fodder'] when the time comes" (118).

In fact, Smerdyakov proves to be diabolically clever, and Kolya's articu-lation of the *specific* way the goose's neck might be broken—"*if* the cart . . .'" (emphasis added)—also recalls the role-reversal in which Smerdyakov the pupil manipulates Ivan the would-be teacher. Smerdyakov convinces Ivan to leave for Chermashnya, thus allowing his father to be murdered. At the time, Smerdyakov had continuously used the word "*if*"—"if I should be laid up with a fit, sir" (235)—and depicted a course of murderous action that gives "flesh" to Ivan's "general proposition." Smerdyakov manipulates Ivan, who leaves the conversation as if hypnotized: "He walked and moved as though in a nervous frenzy" (237). When Ivan departs, Smerdyakov as much as "winks" at him when he stares at him "penetratingly" and declares "it's al-ways interesting speaking with an intelligent man" (241). When the peasant and Kolya are taken before the justice of the peace, the scene suggests the weirdly fluid identity shared by Smerdyakov and Ivan. As in Smerdyakov's denial of responsibility—"you murdered him. . . . I was only your instru-ment. . . . It was following your words I did it" (524)—the peasant claims, "it wasn't me. . . . It was he who egged me on" (462). Kolya responds "with the utmost composure" and denies his responsibility: "I simply stated the general proposition, had spoken hypothetically" (462). The justice smiles at the precocious prankster, but the story has deadly resonance: as an adult, Kolya *could* become part of the revolutionary intelligentsia, holding "the people" in contempt, and persuading them to murder, and to serve as "prime cannon fodder . . . when the time comes."[309] As Joseph Frank has shown, Dostoevsky was increasingly concerned with young people and their future; in the uncertain futures of Ivan and Kolya, he depicts that concern.[310]

After telling the tale of the goose, Kolya alludes to his secret knowledge about the founding of Troy. Kolya's self-consciousness before Alyosha deepens and he acts much like Ivan inviting his brother to reject him—"will you renounce me for that, yes?" (229)—or the Grand Inquisitor willing Christ to reject him: "I don't want Thy love" (223). In his vanity, Kolya "began by degrees to have a wrangling fear that Alyosha was silent because he despised him, and thought he was showing off before him. If he dared to think anything like that, Kolya would . . ." (463). The ellipsis suggests Kolya's anticipation of the rebellious *nadryv* by which he would cut himself off from the man whose mentorship he needs. Kartashov's eager announcement that he too knows who founded Troy interrupts his impulse to *nadryv*, and Kolya returns to his tone of "haughty superciliousness" (463). Like the peasant woman in hell who insists "it's *my* onion" (303; emphasis added), Kolya holds tightly to *his* "secret knowledge" of Troy as it elevates him above others who wish to join him. But such clutching and kicking away others only breaks the onion, and Kolya descends further into the pettily demonic distress of vanity and the prison of the sideward glance. When he insists upon a positivist pedagogy that would allow only "mathematics and natural science" he's painfully aware that he "was showing off and he stole a glance and Alyosha; his was the only opinion he was afraid of there. But Alyosha was still silent and still serious as before. If Alyosha had said a word it would have stopped him, but Alyosha was silent and it might've been the silence of 'contempt' and that finally irritated Kolya" (464).

Kolya's sideward glance, of course, *projects* contempt upon Alyosha, who stands silently attentive, like Christ before the Inquisitor. Like the Inquisitor, Kolya confronts Alyosha—"you seem to disagree with me again, Karamazov?"—and Alyosha responds with good-humored frankness: "'I don't agree,' said Alyosha with a faint smile." Kolya persists, "breathless[ly]": he would dispense with classical languages "because they stupefy the intellect, . . . that's my entire opinion of them, I hope I shall never change it,' Kolya finished abruptly. His cheeks were flushed" (464). His blushing assertion recalls Ivan's challenge to Alyosha to reject him (229). Further, just as Ivan's words influence others, so too do Kolya's: Smurov affirms the older boy's

ideas "in a ringing tone of conviction." But Alyosha rejects neither Ivan nor
Kolya. He listens, smiles, asks for clarification, and then asks aptly, without
condescension: "why who taught you all this?" Kolya responds defensively,
"I am capable of thinking for myself without being taught" (464). We soon
learn that his tutor, his "adulterer of thought," is Rakitin, the reductive realist. At this moment, the pompous, narcissistic doctor arrives and Kolya and
his new, much-needed mentor step outside.

The next chapter, "Precocity," presents one of the most moving interpersonal encounters in the novel. As in the story of Zosima's "Mysterious
Visitor," we see how loving attentiveness can elicit *metanoia* in the one who
receives its gift. Alyosha's attention helps Kolya recover his own voice, and
he emerges as a kind of older brother, even a father to the fatherless Kolya.
Alyosha directs Kolya's attention to reality: "Ilyusha will die. I think that
is certain,' answered Alyosha mournfully" (465). Alyosha sees how Kolya
longs to express his warmth toward him, "smile[s] and presse[s] his hand."
Alyosha's loving attention inspires Kolya to articulate his "respect" for Alyosha but, "faltering and uncertain," he shields his desire for relationship with
intellectual self-assertion, half-digested literary references, and claims for
his atheistic superiority. Kolya prescribes Rakitin's brand of atheist realism
like the pompous doctor prescribing an unrealistic cure at "Sy-ra-cuse" to
the impoverished Snegyirovs: "I know you are a mystic but . . . that hasn't put
me off. Contact with real life will cure you. . . . It's always so with characters
like yours" (466). Throughout their conversation, Alyosha is "calm," smiles
"warmly," but his response here is "rather astonished": "Cure me of what?"
"Oh, God, and all the rest of it." Kolya draws on his skimpy familiarity with
Belinsky, and fears that Alyosha will "think he was trying to show off his
knowledge and to prove that he was 'grown-up'": "'I haven't the slightest
desire to show off my knowledge to him,' Kolya thought indignantly. And
all of a sudden he felt horribly annoyed" (466). Kolya is infuriated not only
by his overweening concern for Alyosha's judgment, but also by his own attempts to lie to himself. He reveals a capacity for salutary self-criticism that
Fyodor can no longer summon, habituated as the old man is to believing his
own lies. Crucially, Kolya is capable of embracing the truth: When Alyosha forthrightly cites the German maxim about Russian schoolboys, "no
knowledge and unbounded conceit" (469), Kolya responds with defenseless
delight: "Truthissimo! Exactly so." In Dostoevsky's last novel, Christ and
truth are envisioned as synonymous, never hypothetically opposed as they
were in his 1854 letter to N. D. Fonvizina.

Kolya is learning to accept the truth of his human vulnerability, but
such acceptance takes time. In his mentorship, Alyosha's relinquishes any
will to dominate, and generatively encourages the boy to articulate his

radical views by responding "quietly, gently, and quite naturally, as though he were talking to someone his own age, or even older"—treating him, that is, as if he were "on a higher footing" (188). Discussing Voltaire, Kolya appreciates the way Alyosha respects his freedom, "leaving the question for him, little Kolya, to settle" (466). But "serenely and modestly" (467) Alyosha also observes that young Kolya has been influenced by others. When Alyosha refers to Kolya's age as "only thirteen," Kolya "interrupt[s] him hotly," accusing Alyosha himself of being a kind of Inquisitor: "come, you want obedience and mysticism." But when Kolya asserts that Christ would have played a prominent role among the revolutionaries, Alyosha discerns a more forceful response to be appropriate: "'Oh, where, where did you get that from? What fool have you made friends with?' exclaimed Alyosha" (467). Alyosha's exclamation is not born out of a competitive desire to win the argument, but simply out of his love for Christ, a bond shared by his creator Dostoevsky, who, even as a young radical became tearful when he spoke of Christ.[311]

Alyosha's avowal, born of his relational love for Christ, again stirs Kolya's incipient desire for truth. He confesses that he has, in fact, been swayed by others: "come, the truth will out! It has so chanced that I often talked to Mr. Rakitin, of course, but . . . Old Belinsky said that too, so they say." In the latter half of the novel, Rakitin's friendship is identified as poisonous. Later that day Alyosha will confront Mitya (who, like Kolya, has been "thirsting" [495] for the living water of Alyosha's friendship) and ask him bluntly, "why does [Rakitin] come here so often? Surely you are not such great friends?" Mitya denies it—"such people . . . . [n]ever understand a joke, and their souls are dry, dry and flat; they remind me of prison walls . . ." (495). So too Kolya defensively distances himself from the seductive rationalizing of Rakitin: "Please don't suppose I am such a revolutionist. I often disagree with Mr. Rakitin" (467–68). Kolya is young and impressionable, a would-be revolutionary like those who would assassinate Czar Alexander II about thirteen years after the events transcribed in the novel, and only months after its publication. But Alyosha's mediatory influence pours living water where Rakitin had left scorched earth.

The devil of Kolya's vanity takes time to exorcise; active love always takes time and can never take the form of a "quick deed."[312] Kolya admits he hasn't yet read a classic, Pushkin's *Eugene Onegin*, although he "want[s] to read it" (468), and in his desire "to hear both sides" (468), suggests his ear for polyphony. But when he senses that he has become visibly vulnerable, he lashes out, much like Snegiryov who, after describing to Alyosha the tears he and his son shared at the stone, falls back into his "spiteful" "Yessirov" role (180) or like Ivan, inviting Alyosha to reject him (229). Here is Kolya's defensive recoil:

> "Tell me Karamazov, have you an awful contempt for me?" Kolya rapped out suddenly and drew himself up before Alyosha, as though he were on parade. "Be so kind as to tell me, without beating about the bush."
>
> "I have a contempt for you?" Alyosha looked at him wondering. "What for? I am only sad that a charming nature such as yours should be perverted by all this crude nonsense before you have begun life." (468)

Alyosha would not only inoculate Kolya from "perversion," but also, more importantly, free the adolescent from his fear of being seen—as small, young, a show-off—and to accept the reality that, as social creatures, we will *always* be seen by others. But, as Alyosha demonstrates, we *can* look at others with loving attentiveness. Kolya "fancies that Alyosha is smiling at him with contempt," and Alyosha explains "that [his] smile meant something quite different": he was recalling the German witticism about Russian schoolchildren. He inspires Kolya's playful "truthissimo!" and his laughter. Incarnational realists—unlike Rakitin—intuit the link between humility and humor, and can laugh at themselves.

Humbly, Kolya begins to make his confession. Self-accusingly, Kolya recalls and repeats the words that Ilyusha's sister Ninochka had just spoken to him: "'why didn't you come before?' And in such a voice, so reproachfully!" Ninochka's reproach recalls Alyosha's, which recalls Martha's and Mary's to Jesus: Kolya's visit a few weeks earlier might have saved her brother. The Johannine echo suggests Kolya's capacity to fulfill the human calling to conform to the image of Christ, "without which we should be undone and altogether lost" (276). For any person, however, descent into humility—especially in the form of confession—must precede such conforming. Alyosha repeats Ninochka's reproach—"yes, it's a great pity"—but also notes how Kolya will become better for having befriended the Snegiryovs, and how his "charm" has inspired and "influenc[ed]" the "noble" Ilyusha (469).

Kolya's "charm," his beauty and goodness, have been deformed, "distorted" by his capricious assertion of will. Kolya's willfulness elicits the anxiety that follows any strained effort to will that which is can't be willed.[313] But it's hard for Kolya to admit this. When Alyosha reminds him that his delay has had a baleful effect on Ilyusha, Kolya recoils, then confesses: "Don't tell me! You make it worse! But it serves me right. What kept me from coming was my conceit, my egoistic vanity and the beastly *willfulness* which I can never get rid of" (469; emphasis added). Alyosha's loving attentiveness balances both openness (by affirming Kolya's gifts and capacity to change), and closure (by reminding Kolya of the deeds for which he remains responsible). In confessing, Kolya begins to relinquish his "beastly," even demonic willfulness. He admits that he had "thought . . . [y]ou despised me! If only you know how I prize your opinion!" Alyosha had discerned Kolya's "sensitivity"—his anxious eye for judgment—and the reader recalls the sideward glance of other confessants: Madame Khokhlakova and Mikhail with Zosima, Grushenka with Alyosha. Like these characters, Kolya emphasizes Alyosha's capacity for *looking*, his own desire for "display" and concomitant fear of "contempt," and his deeper and more truthful yearning to be truly seen, heard, and loved:

> What an eye you've got, I say! I bet that was when I was talking about the goose. That was just when I fancied you had a great contempt for me for being in such a hurry to show off, and for a moment I quite hated you for it, and began talking like a fool. Then I fancied—just now, here—when I said that if there were no God he would have to be invented, that I was in too great a hurry to display my knowledge, especially as I got that phrase out of a book. But I swear I wasn't showing off out of vanity, though I really don't know why, out of joy, yes, I believe it was from joy. . . . Though it's perfectly disgraceful for anyone to be gushing with joy . . . . (469–70)

Kolya's confession has a loophole: "I swear I wasn't showing off out of vanity." But if imperfect, his utterance retains truth: he vainly boasts at Ilyushechka's bedside, yet is *also* sincerely joyful. Again the novel represents complex human reality more as a "both/and" rather than an "either/or." Moreover, Kolya is ashamed of his joy because it makes him vulnerably receptive to the gift of community for which he deeply longs. But he also admits his longing to see Alyosha, and his regret at not having visited Ilyusha much earlier. As in Augustine's *Confessions* and Dante's *Commedia*, conversion transpires as a temporal process, not a single epiphany. Kolya is slowly changing from a "desperate character," an individual "looked at" by others with approbation, to a person whose true vocation can be found only in community, in responsible relation to others.[314]

The sideward glance, which spies the other person as threatening competitor or contemptuous judge is born of the demonic. The open, attentive gaze exemplifies Christ-like humility. In Jesus' acceptance of shameful crucifixion, he accepts looking "ridiculous" and being vulnerable to the ridicule of others. Alyosha exemplifies this humility in the rich colloquy that follows, a good-humored forging of friendship that forecasts Alyosha's final dialogue

with Mitya. As will fourteen-year-old Lise later that day, Kolya discloses that
he loves disorder and tormenting others:

> "Oh, Karamazov, I am profoundly unhappy. I sometimes fancy
> all sorts of things, that everyone is laughing at me, the whole
> world, and then feel ready to overturn the whole order of things.
> . . . I torment everyone around me, especially my mother.
> Karamazov, tell me, am I very ridiculous now?"
>
> "Don't think about that, don't think of it at all!" cried Alyo-
> sha. "And what does ridiculous mean? Isn't everyone constantly
> being or seeming ridiculous? Besides nearly all clever people
> are fearfully afraid of being ridiculous, and that makes them
> unhappy. . . . Nowadays the very children have begun to suffer
> from it. It's almost a form of insanity. The devil has taken the
> form of that vanity and entered into the whole generation; it's
> simply the devil," added Alyosha without a trace of the smile
> that Kolya, staring at him, expected to see. (470)

Alyosha is deeply serious here. His generational insight coheres with
the novel's larger vision in which the demonic is yoked to the fear of being
seen as "ridiculous."[315] Recall Smerdyakov's words to Ivan, later that night:
"you'll be too much ashamed, sir, if you confess it all" (531). Ivan leaves him,
and is, in fact, too ashamed to go to the prosecutor. Instead he meets the
devil. Ferapont wants to be seen as a super-ascetic, and sees—ridiculous-
ly!—devils everywhere (150). Alyosha exhorts Kolya to "not be like everyone else" in fearing ridicule and affirms his being "not ashamed to confess
to something bad and even ridiculous" (470). But Alyosha goes further: he
models humility when, with "sly happiness," Kolya observes that Alyosha is
himself blushing, that he's "a little ashamed" at their "declaration of love":

> "It was you made me blush," laughed Alyosha, and he really did
> blush. "Oh, well, I am a little ashamed, goodness knows why, I
> don't know . . ." he muttered almost embarrassed.
>
> "Oh, how I love you and admire you at this moment just
> because you are rather ashamed! Because you are just like me,"
> cried Kolya, in positive ecstasy. His cheeks glowed, his eyes
> beamed.
>
> "You know, Kolya, you will be very unhappy in your life,"
> something made Alyosha say suddenly.
>
> "I know, I know. How you know it all beforehand!" Kolya
> agreed at once.
>
> "But you will bless life on the whole, all the same."
>
> "Just so, hurrah! You are a prophet. Oh, we shall get on to-
> gether Karamazov! Do you know, what delights me most, is that

you treat me quite like an equal. But we are not equals, no, we're not, you are better! But we shall get on. Do you know, all this last month I've been saying to myself, 'either we shall be friends at once, forever, or we shall part enemies to the grave!'"

"And saying that, of course, you loved me," Alyosha laughed gaily.

"I did. I love you awfully. I've been loving and dreaming of you. And how do you know it all beforehand?" (470–71)

Kolya's "Hurrah!" presages the last word of the novel, and the encounter parallels three other scenes in the novel. In "An Engagement," Alyosha's discussion with Lise presents similar phrases—"just like me," "being on an equal footing," "knowing it all beforehand" (187–88). Alyosha's hopeful "prophecy" recalls Zosima's to Ivan, who torments himself with an idea that "will never be decided in the negative" (65–66). And their conversation also looks ahead to the Epilogue, when Alyosha assists Mitya to accept his decision to escape, and Mitya points out that they sound like a couple of Jesuits. Alyosha agrees with a gentle smile, and Mitya laughs joyfully. Especially in these later scenes with Kolya and Mitya we see how Alyosha's capacity for friendship has deepened.

An additional "chime": in both scenes, both Alyosha and his interlocutor grow closer in shared humility and humor. But, as always, the epiphanic glow dims and the slow work of active love begins again: Minutes after he and Mitya have shared their Jesuitical laugh, Mitya rebukes Grushenka for not forgiving Katya instantly. In response, Alyosha "cri[e]s hotly": "Mitya, don't dare to blame her; you have no right to!" (639). Here, the departing doctor makes it clear that compassion "is not [his] business" and Kolya threatens to sick Zhuchka on the "apothecary" (472). Alyosha's retort is equally stern: "'Kolya, if you say another word, I'll have nothing more to do with you,' Alyosha cried peremptorily." Kolya obeys Alyosha's prudent and authoritative command.

The next chapter is aptly titled "Ilyusha" as it is the dying child who "unite[s]" all in community (646). The chapter resounds in scriptural echoes, beginning with sorrowful Snegiryov's appeal to the indifferent doctor: "Your Excellency, for Christ's sake. But can nothing absolutely nothing save him now?" Throughout the novel, invocations of Christ's name—even when uttered profanely—resonate.[316] In Ilyusha's suffering, and the unity forged from it, the little boy himself emerges as the image of Christ in the chapter that bears his name:

The sick boy was holding [Kolya's] hand in calling his father. A minute later the captain, too, came back.

> "Papa, Papa, come . . . We . . ." Ilyusha faltered in violent
> excitement, but apparently unable to go on, he flung his wasted
> arms around papa and Kolya, uniting them in one embrace, and
> hugging them as tightly as he could. The captain suddenly began
> to shake with dumb sobs, and Kolya's lips and chin twitched.
> (472)

This tableau is heartbreaking. But through her tears, the reader may
discern an image of the Trinity: father, son, and spirited friend, lovingly
bound in a *kenosis* of sorrow, participating in God's triune life of love.[317]

Of course, the human experience bears only an analogical relation to
the Divine. Nevertheless, it *participates* in that life. In a way that is congruent with Dostoevsky's Orthodox imagination, Pope John Paul II writes that
human suffering, united to Christ's, carries creative potential:[318]

> For *whoever suffers in union with Christ*—just as the Apostle
> Paul bears his "tribulations" in union with Christ—not only
> receives from Christ that strength already referred to but also
> "completes" by his suffering "what is lacking in Christ's afflic-
> tions" [Col 1:24]. This evangelical outlook especially highlights
> the truth *concerning the creative character of suffering.* The
> sufferings of Christ created the good of the world's redemp-
> tion. This good in itself is inexhaustible and infinite. No man
> can add anything to it. But at the same time, in the mystery of
> the Church as his body, Christ has in a sense opened his own
> redemptive suffering to all human suffering. In so far as man
> becomes a sharer in Christ's sufferings—in any part of the world
> and at any time in history—to that extent *he in his own way
> completes* the suffering through which Christ accomplished the
> Redemption of the world. (*Salvifici Doloris* 24)

The triune tableau encapsulates the twinned "for all" theme I have
emphasized throughout this book. Christ's redemption is "for all," as Alyosha reminds Ivan (213); the graced gift is real. But the work continues, as
we, in response, become responsible *for all*, and complete Christ's work in
community—a cosmic, universal church embodied in the parochial and
quotidian.[319] If Alyosha founds a "church" upon Ilyusha's rock with his gathered twelve disciples, so too does Ilyusha himself—suffering with his dear
father, forgiving Kolya, and bringing unity to all three in his loving embrace.

On the cross, Christ calls out for his father—"*Eli, eli, lama sabach-
thani!*" (Matt 27:45–46)—much as Ilyusha cries out here, "Papa, papa! How
sorry I am for you, papa!" (473). Like Christ, Ilyusha is the corn of wheat
who falls into the ground and dies to bring forth fruit—the good fruits of

Kolya's *metanoia*, a restored community of boys, and his dear father's relinquishing not only of alcohol (at least for now) but his lying role of "Yessirov." Here, Snegiryov speaks, laments, and protests in his true paternal voice. But as always in this novel, the graced connection—"they were all three silent, still embracing"—is quickly eclipsed by the demands of the ordinary.[320] When Kolya runs outside weeping and unashamed, Alyosha—very much like the authoritative Zosima—"emphatically" (473) insists that Kolya "keep his word" and return to the poor home that evening.

Virtues become habit only after long practice. Snegiryov is not ready to accept the scriptural mystery that Zosima has earlier explicated: "But how could [Job] love those new [children] when the first children are no more? When he has lost them? Remembering them, how could he be fully happy with those new ones, however dear those new ones might be? But he could, he could" (252). Zosima emphasizes that the movement from grief to joy transpires, slowly, over time. God's work of grace, infusing and energizing the human work of active love, moves *through* time. In the molten heart of lacerating grief "tragic phrases . . . comfort the heart" (310), and are apt: "'I don't want a good boy! I don't want another boy,' he muttered in a wild whisper, clenching his teeth. 'If I forget the Jerusalem, may my tongue . . . .' He broke off with a sob and sank to his knees" (473). The image of Snegiryov recapitulates "Rachel of old" (48). Now is not the time for comfort. But even in his state of laceration, Snegiryov recalls Psalm 137, and utters words that Kolya will never forget: "What was that he said about Jerusalem? . . . What did he mean by that?" Alyosha explains, "'It's from the Bible. "If I forget thee Jerusalem," that is, if I forget all that is most precious to me, if I let anything take its place, then may . . . .'" Kolya cuts him off: "I understand, that's enough! Be sure you come!" Kolya is moved, but his peremptory command forecasts a moment in Alyosha's immanent visit with another adolescent, Lise, who, in a menacing voice, will command Alyosha to deliver her letter to Ivan, "today!" (494).[321] Visiting Lise one of the "great many things Alyosha has to do" on this November day (481).

Lise

The chapter "A Little Demon" can be read as a narrative diptych alongside Book 10. Both narratives focus on troubled youths, each about fourteen years old. Both contain references to Judaism, though in severely differing registers. In "Ilyusha," Dostoevsky cites the Hebrew Bible with reverence. The heartrending echoes of Job and Psalm 137 suggests the author's respect for the Jewish tradition, which he encountered in his childhood, his lifetime reading of Scripture, and his own Orthodox liturgical practice. As an adult, Jewish intellectuals were among Dostoevsky's many correspondents and respected interlocutors. However, Alyosha's encounter with Lise is more tortured than that with Kolya, and—for a moment—blighted by the anti-Semitism that disfigures so much of Dostoevsky's nonfiction. Lise asks, "Alyosha, is it true that in Easter the yids steal children and kill them?" Alyosha answers, "I don't know." The reader's heart sinks. Couldn't Dostoevsky's most convincingly Christ-like character have corrected and dispelled Lise's anti-Semitism, the way any responsible spiritual guide would today, with the memory of the Shoah seared in our consciousness? Is it anachronistic to expect more of Dostoevsky who wrote during a period of history rife with anti-Semitism? Perhaps. But the scene must also be read in the light of Dostoevsky's repulsive anti-Semitic statements in *The Diary of a Writer* and letters. James Scanlan presents this evidence, and persuasively shows how Dostoevsky's anti-Semitism is the mirror image of his Russian nationalism.[322] Dostoevsky's prejudice extends, of course, to other forms of Christianity: for him, Russian Orthodoxy seems to be the only kind of Christianity worth emulating—superior to both authoritarian Catholicism and schismatic Protestantism. But while Dostoevsky recognizes that Jews have been victimized, much like the Russians, he sees them as the opposite of Russians in their denial of Christ. Thus Dostoevsky's references to "yids," and his epistolary descriptions of Jews as egotistical, resentful, and insular. This is my biggest stumbling block when reading Dostoevsky, and I suspect I'm not alone.

But what if Dostoevsky had lived to witness the Shoah—to see for himself where demonic prejudice like his had led? Source of spiritual sustenance that it is, *The Brothers Karamazov* inspires me to imagine the Russian author's penitence, even his public penance for the sin that besmirched his life and even, in this one small moment, the novel that represents his most persuasive artistic expression of an orthodox, catholic Christian vision. I like to imagine that Dostoevsky's Christian faith would have given him the courage to renounce his sins of anti-Semitism and chauvinistic nationalism. Given the incarnational realism that gives form to *The Brothers Karamazov*, I would like to believe that Dostoevsky would have evinced the courage that Martin Heidegger so disturbingly lacked. Even in the years following the Shoah, Heidegger never publicly repented for his support of the Nazi regime. Perhaps part of the reason lay in the way his imagination—and his character?—was formed by romantic poetry. Dostoevsky's incarnational, narratival imagination would, perhaps, have been more receptive to *metanoia* had he had witnessed the twentieth century.[323] Emmanuel Levinas lost most of his family in the Shoah, but built his ethical philosophy in large part upon Zosima's mantra that we are each responsible for all. Anti-Semitism certainly taints the history of my own Catholic tradition—before, during, and after the period in which Dostoevsky wrote. But I'm grateful that in 1965, Vatican II promulgated *Nostra aetate*, which made clear the sinfulness of anti-Semitism, and for the statements that followed, including Pope John Paul II's 1998 public apology for the church's past failings.

My wishful imagining does not exculpate Dostoevsky. But it is worth noting the narrative *context* of this scene. Lise utters her anti-Semitic question and hideous fantasy in a psychological/spiritual state of rebellion and sin. (Similarly, Fyodor Karamazov's anti-Semitic language is presented as part of his habitual, willfully ignorant sinfulness.) I'm aware that Dostoevsky indicated plans for Alyosha to marry Lise in his sequel, but at this point in this novel I doubt that Alyosha would have done so, even if such a sequel had been written. Their broken engagement doesn't come as a surprise. Early on, Alyosha tells Lise, "Zosima tells me I must marry," but admits "I haven't had time to think about it" (162). After all, Lise is only fourteen— roughly Kolya's age (sixteen was the youngest a girl could be married in Russia at this time). She has recently made a sexual proposition to Ivan (her version of lying down on the tracks?). Given her age, Alyosha's relationship with Lise ultimately recalls that with Kolya. Alyosha's presence is generative, even parental, filling a role that Lise's flighty mother often vacates.

The parallels between the two young people are numerous: Like Kolya, Lise reads "unsuitable" (436), even "nasty books" (491), declares her love of disorder (490), and is keenly sensitive to Alyosha's "look." Like Kolya, she recalls Ivan and seems drawn to the "hell in his heart" (228), akin to her own. As with Ivan, Alyosha makes himself fully, non-judgmentally "available" to Lise.[324] Like Ivan in "The Brothers Get Acquainted," Lise is divided. Alyosha observes that she is "spiteful *and* open-hearted" (489; emphasis added). On the one hand, she falsely declares her contempt for Alyosha and her delight in their broken engagement. On the other, she pleads with him to "come and see me more often" (492); minutes later, she pleads with him to "save" her (493). On the one hand, she empathizes with the suffering child, "[shaking] with sobs all night . . . fancying how the little thing cried and moaned." On the other hand, she imagines herself as the torturer, devouring "pineapple compote" while watching the child suffer and die (492). The sick fantasy fills her with self-loathing, a hunger to hurt herself. Earlier, Ivan has said, "In every man, a beast lies hidden, a beast of rage, a beast of sensual inflammation from the tortured victim" (208). In saying this, Ivan was seeking Alyosha's healing (204); so too is Lise, who yearns to be released from her "devil"—spawned in part by her perverse relation with Ivan. Inter-creatural relation is vital, but it too cuts both ways. The Ivan-Lisa relationship cuts toward a Sartrean hell marked by contempt rather than attention. Alyosha understands that Ivan holds Lise in contempt, much as he holds himself: "If he doesn't believe in people, of course, he does despise them" (493), an echo of Zosima's "One who does not believe in God will not believe in God's people" (254). In Ivan, Lisa has recognized a kindred spirit who protests the suffering of children and, at the same time, tells the stories of their torture with a sadistic twist of the knife—consumed with contempt for both his listener and himself. After Ivan's tirade, Alyosha reminds him of the Christ who came "for all"; Ivan retorts with the Grand Inquisitor, who demonically relieves people of the burden of freedom—the very burden with which the adolescent Lise now struggles. After rejecting Alyosha, visiting Smerdyakov, and deferring responsibility, Ivan will be revisited by the devil, whose "special method" (537) jerks Ivan back and forth, toward faith and then away, to the point of self-division and destruction. Lise, too, is torn by this divisive "back and forth."

Later this cold November night, Ivan's final words will comprise a promise: "tomorrow the cross, not the gallows." Lise faces the same existential divide, the same "either/or." She describes to Alyosha her dream in which—like Ferapont (150)—she sees "devils all over the place" (491). Just before they "see" her "I suddenly cross myself and they all draw back, though they don't go away altogether, they stand at the doors and in the corners, waiting. And suddenly I have a frightful longing to revile God aloud, and so I begin, and then they come crowding back to me, delighted, and seize me again and I cross myself again and they all draw back. It's awful fun, it takes one's breath away" (492). Lise reviles the loving source of her existence. Her question to Alyosha suggests this: she knows she is committing "the greatest sin" (490), that of despair, the sin against the Holy Spirit (Matt 12:31–32). She willfully chooses self-destruction—"the gallows" chosen by Smerdyakov—and by Kirillov (*Demons*) and Svidrigailov (*Crime and Punishment*). She threatens suicide (493, 494). In her "dream"—which Alyosha admits having had, too (492)—Lise clings to the cross, but treats it like a magic wand, first drawing the devils near her and then crossing herself to cast them back. She statically acts out her own self-division. Like Ivan and Kolya, she wills Alyosha's rejection so as to justify her own hateful lashing back: "You do despise me though!" (491).[325] Perversely, she sets out to destroy the relationship she most treasures.

Ultimately, however, she recognizes her need for the Christ-like Alyosha, and for the grace he mediates: just before she utters another blasphemy, she turns and begs him to save her: "[S]he suddenly jumped from the couch, rushed to him and seized him with both hands. 'Save me!' she almost groaned" (493). In imagining this open-ended novel's possible future,

I foresee Lise continuing to need Alyosha as a spiritual guide. But not as a husband. Their final embrace suggests a relation marked more by spiritual guidance than marital intimacy. As with Kolya, Alyosha is more of a generative mentor to Lise than anything else.

Their encounter ends—much like Ivan's confession in court—with fractured hope. After Lise declares that she no longer wishes to live and "loath[es]" (493) everything, she reaches frantically for an onion: "'Alyosha, why don't you love me in the least?' she finished in a frenzy" (493). Alyosha has listened to her without judgment. When she asks, "What will they do to me in the next world for the greatest sin?" Alyosha responds directly and clearly: "God will reproach you." He does not say "God will *condemn* you." Instead, like Zosima, Alyosha affirms a God who does not "excommunicate," but calls *all*, even those in hell (279). But Alyosha also makes clear that God will hold her responsible, and will not relieve her of her freedom. Throughout their talk, Alyosha is reminds Lise of her freedom, helping her to understand that she is locking her infernal prison *from the inside.*[326] She can choose to do otherwise.

Toward the end of their encounter, she shows signs of symbolically nudging the door open, even as, literally, she slams it. She thanks Alyosha, and while her "go!" (493) echoes the Inquisitor's to Christ, it resonates with less finality. Lise's "go!" is more like the one she has uttered to her mother the night before (488): she had pushed her mother out the door, but only after kissing her, much as she has earlier hugged and kissed Yulia's feet after she had slapped her (which itself recalls Zosima's penitent embrace of Afanasy) (258). These are images of hope, and suggest Lise's willingness to welcome Christ who stands at the door knocking (Rev 3.20), not spying (489). But she remains divided: "menacing[ly]" she demands that Alyosha give the letter to Ivan, and threatens suicide if he doesn't. Ivan will tear up the unread note and "honorably" (493) sever their hellish entanglement. Perhaps Lise "offers herself" (506) to Ivan in the spirit of "sacrifice" in which Katerina has "offer[ed] herself" to Dmitri (103). Sacrifice cuts both ways: any sacrificial "offering" that reifies personhood as a thing to be simply used by another exemplifies *nadryv*. It's difficult to know *why* Lise offers herself to Ivan—to hurt Alyosha, to help Ivan, to erotically yoke their mutual infernos, to prove herself as mature as Kolya, whom she admires as a "lucky fellow" (491) for having risked shedding blood on the tracks? In any such case she would—to use Kantian language—be using herself solely as a means to an end, just as Katerina would make herself "a *means* for [Dmitri's] happiness, . . . an instrument, a machine," making sure "that he will *see* that for all his life!" (166; emphasis added). The demand for an audience always indicates *nadryv*. And yet Lise also extends her care to Mitya and genuinely wants

Alyosha to see him before the prison doors close. She gives him his hat and "almost forcibly" pushes him out the open door before slamming it shut.

On her own finger. What of this image of self-harm? Well, she doesn't (like Kolya) do it for an audience; if only for that her act is not *nadryv*. If Ivan's confession in court is a fractured exorcism in process, Lisa's willfully self-imposed penance may be seen as a fractured *step toward* penitence, a de-formed effort to reach purgatory by herself. As Dante's second *cantica* continuously reveals, penitence requires grace mediated by a community of persons, courteously assisting each other in the gradual process of conform-ing to Christ's image.[327] True penitence has no place for the self-loathing Lise exhibits as she gazes at her bloodied, blackened finger and repeats, "I am a wretch" (494). As Fetyukovich observes (a rare moment in which he gets it right) "despair and penitence are very different things" (619): penitence bespeaks the cross; despair bespeaks the gallows. Like Ivan, Lise is some-where between the two—"halfway to heaven and just a mile out of hell."[328] She recalls impetuous Mitya, pistol packed and on the way to Mokroe, who thinks that purgatively "making way" demands a bullet in the brain (350)— or who, after the trial, believes that "self-purification" entails Siberian exile for a murder he didn't commit (502). Dostoevsky's language is "subtle."[329] He doesn't preach Christ like a child but depicts the possibility of Christian life in its complexity, in "oblique artistic form." Like Mitya, Lisa needs to hear a voice that counters Ivan's (who "orders" Mitya to go to Siberia [503]), a voice like Alyosha's that offers love. This gift must come from another. We cannot justify—or purge—ourselves.[330] Indeed, there is a suggestion at the end of the novel that Lisa has heard and accepted the gift of Alyosha's loving voice: along with Katerina she sends flowers for Ilyusha's funeral (640). This organic image of hope links both women. If only symbolically, they partici-pate in the funeral service that emerges—paradoxically—as an analogy to the heavenly banquet, a Cana-like marriage feast of paradise, to which all are welcome and onions don't break, to which invitations are extended "for all."

Epilogue

In the Epilogue, we walk with Alyosha through his final day in the novel. This last November day is as demanding as any he's experienced,[331] but he works through each encounter with grace and authority. Just before he vis-its Mitya in prison, he visits Katerina, tortured by shame for her role in securing Mitya's conviction. Here too Alyosha enters into Katya's situation and discerns that he isn't the one to whom Katya must confess, "though her conscience was impelling her to." Rather, she must confess to Mitya, whom she has grievously wronged through her false testimony. Katya fears Mitya's look. Alyosha realizes, she "hates [Mitya] at moments" because she feels guilty before him (633). Alyosha thus prudently insists that Katya *must* agree to Mitya's request to visit and be "visible" before him:

> "I must . . . but I cannot . . ." Katya moaned. "He will look at me. . . . I can't."
>
> "Your eyes ought to meet. How will you live all your life, if you don't make up your mind to do it now?"
>
> "Better suffer all my life."
>
> "You must go, you *must* go," Alyosha repeated with merciless emphasis.
>
> . . .
>
> "Have pity on *me*!" Katya said, with bitter reproach, and she burst into tears.
>
> "Then you will come," said Alyosha firmly, seeing her tears. "I'll go and tell him you will come at once." (634)

Alyosha is not being coercive. The reality is that Katya and Mitya *must* look at each other—not with sideward glances, or the rival taunts of their past, but with clear-eyed acknowledgement of their guilt before each other. As Alyosha observes to her, only after her willful betrayal has Mitya come to understand "how he has offended you . . . he had never grasped it before so fully" (633). Katya's tears suggest that she realizes this herself. Alyosha's words carry authority, and penetrate, not because they are emphatic, but because they grow out of a discerning attentiveness to Katya's "deepest I," her genuine wish to reconcile with Mitya.

And Alyosha's authoritative words bear fruit. When Katya arrives at Mitya's room, it is as if their meeting fulfills *each other's* deepest wish. For a moment—"at that moment it was all true" (638)—they share a gaze and words that bespeak love. But it's a combustible mixture of charitable and erotic love that "confounds" Alyosha, and leaves him "speechless" (638). It's not that he's embarrassed by their passionate embrace, as he would have been earlier, but is working to understand how the "lie" of their love has suddenly seemingly become "the truth." In fact, their ecstatic declaration of mutual love does not dismiss the need for "labor and fortitude" to be sustained. Even as they embrace, each must resist proud, destructive impulses:

> "I have forgotten that I came here to punish myself," she said, with a new expression in her voice, quite unlike the loving tones of a moment before.

"Woman, yours is a heavy burden," broke, as it were, involuntarily from Mitya.

"Let me go," she whispered. "I'll come again. It's more than
I can bear now." (639)

Sometimes in life one thinks, "I've had all that I can take." But then
there's more. So too now for Katya: Grushenka walks in the door. The moment is potentially incendiary, but both Katya and Grushenka[332] strive to
keep it from becoming so. When she's outside, Katya's pride flares as she asserts to Alyosha: "I asked her forgiveness because I wanted to punish myself
to the bitter end. She would not forgive me. . . . I like her for that!" she added,
in an unnatural voice, and her eyes flashed with fierce anger (639). Katya's
"unnatural" voice of is one of *nadryv*. Her struggle will continue—as will
that of every character beyond the novel's bounds (yes, "and we . . . ourselves,
too" [13] after we read the final page). But a moment earlier Katya had be-
seeched Grushenka; she "moaned softly, almost in a whisper: 'Forgive me!'"
and spoken in a voice of genuine contrition. Humiliated, Katya nevertheless
practices the "labor and fortitude" of active love (55). She does the best she
can, and again the Epilogue offers a small image of hope: Katerina pays for
the grave where Ilyusha will be buried (643).

Funeral, Remembrance, Resurrection

The two parts of the final chapter—"Ilyushechka's Funeral. The Speech at
the Stone"—comprise the most symphonically recapitulative ending in any
literary work that I know. The chapter reprises every tone in the novel: grief,
anger, rebellion, yearning, acceptance, hope, humor, joy, love. This chapter
chimes with all of the novel's major themes and events;[333] it forms a unity
that resonates with the whole.[334] Alyosha's speech at the stone must be heard
within the circumstance of excruciating grief depicted in the first half of the
chapter. "Out of the depths I cry to you, O LORD" (Ps 130:1) the psalmist
sings, and the novel echoes the psalm by suggesting that the Lord answers
with "steadfast love" (130.7). Ascent follows descent, resurrection springs
from death. The major chord of incarnational realism that I have emphasized throughout this work—that Christ has died and risen *for all*; we are
responsible *for all*—resonates throughout this chapter, even as Dostoevsky's
"subtler language" does not explicitly invoke Christ. The scene is both incarnational and trinitarian in its vision of what Metropolitan John Zizioulas
calls "being as communion": the hidden ground of God's inter-relational
love, the chimes of which can be heard in the diverse yet ultimately unified
voices of the Snegiryov family, the twelve boys, and Alyosha.

These rhymes and chimes invite the attentive reader to participate in a redemptive act of remembrance. The funeral service gives ritual form to convulsive grief, and that form is a gracious gift meditated by tradition, rooted in the community: there's "something ancient, eternal . . . something good" in "eating pancakes" and salmon after a funeral, as Alyosha says, with laughter (646).[335] With parochial precision, the nameless landlady suggests the goodness of that which is simply given, not earned: in this case, the Orthodox tradition into which Ilyusha was born and baptized, which provides the consecrated place in which he'll be buried:

> "What an idea, bury him by a heathen stone, as though he had hanged himself," the old landlady said sternly. "There in the churchyard the ground has been crossed. He'll be prayed for there. One can hear the singing in the church and the deacon reads so plainly and verbally that it will reach him every time just as though it were read over his grave." (641)

Her words echo Ivan's promise on the night before the trial: "Tomorrow the cross, . . . not the gallows" (549); Ivan will choose the active love imaged by the cross not the "terrible individualism" (252) chosen by Smerdyakov on the gallows. The community will pray for Ilyusha, even as it sees *him* as part of a "great cloud of witnesses" (Heb 12:1) praying for *them*. Recall Alyosha's insight at the end of "Cana": "others are praying for me" (312)— including the risen Zosima, whom he's just encountered in his dream. In that dream, Zosima tells Alyosha that Christ "is expecting more guests" (311); now Alyosha exhorts Snegiryov not to spoil the flowers, the "onion" he'd first clutched as "mine" and now, penitentially, yearns to give to his wife: "mamochka is expecting them" (643). The grieving father had "pressed his forehead to the stone floor" (642) recalling Zosima, who "touched the floor with his head" in his bow to Mitya (69). The novel presents an incarnational vision of church as the body of Christ, extending through place and time, and embodied in actions shared by both the living and the risen dead.

Throughout the funeral service and Alyosha's speech, the formal, centripetal closure wrought by liturgical form is interrupted by the messy, centrifugal reality of both sincere grief and egoistic assertion (the two-edged sword of "laceration"). And yet the recurring note in the chapter is one of unity and gracious surprise. For example, "strange to say, there was practically no smell from [Ilyusha's] corpse": a gratuitous, minor miracle, like water turned to wine, a reminder of the disruption set off by the 3 pm decomposition of Zosima's body, and a sign that the perishable will be clothed by the imperishable. Ilyusha's "beautiful" hands hold "white roses" (641) "sent early in the morning by Liza" and Katerina (640): their small gift recalls the onion, pillow, and pound of nuts (640). The flowers conjure Ivan's setting for "The Grand Inquisitor": in Seville, Christ raises the little girl, who "sits up in the coffin and looks around . . . holding a bunch of white flowers they had put in her hand" (216–17). Christ's words—"Maiden, arise!"—resound in Alyosha's speech: "Yes, we shall all rise again" (646). Gentle Ninochka's last kiss on her brother's lips (641) recalls Christ's to the Inquisitor, and Alyosha's reprise of that kiss to Ivan (229).

The funeral scene is occasionally marked by centripetal outbreaks of chaos, as if to remind the reader that, this side of paradise, the Christian story does not wipe away every tear nor open every closed fist. In his crazed grief Snegiryov attempts to will order upon that most dis-ordered event imaginable, so contrary to the natural order: the suffering and death of his own little child. His efforts have been noble—especially his stalwart refusal to succumb to the consolation of drink—but his rage for order is less than blessed in its refusal to make room for others. When "mamochka," also "crazy with grief," asks for a white flower from Ilyusha's hand, Snegiryov refuses and "cries callously, 'they are his flowers, not yours! Everything is his, nothing is yours!'" (641). In his grief, Snegiryov would give all to his dead son, but in refusing to share with others, especially his wife and Ilyusha's mother, he recalls Grushenka's wicked woman in hell: "it's my onion, not yours!" (303). He may have wanted Ilyusha buried by the stone where they had walked, but he naturally attends the traditional funeral service. During the liturgy, he fussily wills order—adjusts the wreath and cover of the coffin—and so topples a candle, which he also fumbles over. He joins the singing, until he can't, then falls to his knees and bows his head to the ground. Like his daughter, he kisses Ilyusha "on the lips" (642), then remorsefully remembers Mamochka. The onion doesn't break, and he runs weeping, stumbling through the snow with the flowers she'd wanted. Again the kenotic movement of descent—falling to the ground in humble grief and contrition—augurs the ascent of reconciliation and redemption.

Throughout, Dostoevsky reminds us of the constraining limits of time, and the never-ceasing call to "perfect self-forgetfulness" (54). Alyosha arrives late for the funeral service, and the boys and Ilyusha's family decide to carry the coffin "to the church without him" (640).[336] The twelve boys are "glad" to meet him along the way, but Kolya, self-assertive as ever, wants to stand out among the rest: "'How glad I am you've come, Karamazov!' he cried, holding out his hand to Alyosha" (640). His greeting echoes Alyosha's to him six days earlier, but Alyosha had situated himself *within* the community: "How anxious *we've* been to see you!" (450; emphasis added). In his tête-à-tête with Alyosha before the liturgy, we see Kolya slowly maturing. As always, he presents himself with dramatic flair, with the exaggeration redolent of love in dreams, or what Zizioulas calls "the 'passion' of individualism, of the separation of the hypostases [persons]" (51): "I haven't slept for the last four nights for thinking of [whether Mitya's is guilty]." When Alyosha affirms Mitya's innocence—Smurov, pure of heart, has known it all along—Kolya proclaims with dramatic grandeur: "Oh, if I could sacrifice myself someday for truth. . . . To die for all humanity!" (640). It's easy to add Kolya's unspoken thought here: "with all looking on and applauding as if on stage" (55). Kolya claims that he doesn't care about the "disgrace" of his name, but, after the liturgy, he's quick to silence anyone who presumes to steal his limelight or intrude upon his private dialogue with Alyosha, to whom he confides his deep wish for Ilyusha's resurrection and prudently suggests a return visit that evening (644). For all his progress, Kolya is still clinging to his onion, here in the form of the attention granted from Alyosha, whom he worships.

The sinister potential of such egotism emerges as the group approaches Ilyusha's stone and Kolya questions the Orthodox tradition of eating pancakes after a funeral. Shy but exuberant Kartashov overhears and chimes in: "'They are going to have salmon too,' the boy who had discovered Troy suddenly observed in a loud voice." Kolya responds like the prissy nihilist he could someday become:

> "I beg you most earnestly, Kartashov, not to interrupt again with your stupidities, especially when no one is talking to you and no one cares to know whether you exist or not," Kolya's snapped out irritably. The boy flushed crimson but did not dare to reply. Meanwhile they were strolling slowly along the path and suddenly Smurov exclaimed: "there is Ilyusha's stone, under which they wanted to bury him!"

Kolya is part of this little "church"—along with the landlady and her sister, he'd insisted on Ilyusha being buried in holy ground (641)—but he hasn't yet joined the chorus. He insists on singing solo, and misapprehends others' help as competition, sees their gift as threat. Like Ivan, his assertions of autonomy breed contempt for others, even to the point of willfully wishing to blot out their existence. Recall Ivan's image of "one most entertaining set of sinners in a burning lake" who sink to the bottom, and whom "'God forgets'—an expression of extraordinary depth and force" (214). In Zosima's vision, shared by Dostoevsky, God forgets no one and remembers all.

Fittingly, it's Smurov's blessed, exuberant voice—"There's Ilyusha's stone!"—that heralds the second half of the final chapter. A moment earlier, Smurov had a hurled a stone at the sparrows. The boys had been chasing after Snegiryov who had flung away his hat, and, in deep remorse, had rushed from the grave to "mamochka" with the flowers he had refused her earlier. "Smurov picked [the hat] up and carried it after him. All the boys were crying, and Kolya and the boy who discovered Troy most of all, and though Smurov, with the captain's hat in his hand, was crying bitterly too, he managed, as he ran, to snatch up a piece of red brick that lay on the snow of the path, to fling it at the flock of sparrows flying by" (643).[337] When we had first met him, Smurov was throwing stones at Ilyusha (157); now he's throwing them at Ilyusha's sparrows. Smurov's lacerating gesture cuts against any sentimental sense of closure inspired by the image of birds[338] eating bread on Ilyusha's grave. Smurov's brick misses the birds, but the image preserves a place for Ivan's protest: "what *do* children have to do with it, tell me please? . . . *Why* should they suffer . . . ?" (211; emphasis added). Righteous anger, Rachel's lacerating tears: both remain fitting responses to a child's death. So too does the cry for justice, for human actions to protect the innocent, as Zosima insists: "There must be no more . . . torturing of children, rise up and preach that, make haste . . . !" (271). The stone commemorates *both* Ilyusha's brave plea for justice, the way "he stood up for his father" (645) *and* his Christ-like response to illness and death, which bears fruit in community. It's fitting that clear-eyed Smurov *sees* Ilyusha's stone and calls their attention to it (644).[339]

In the final pages, Alyosha founds a joyful community, a little church of twelve, upon this rock of Ilyusha's stone. The uncanny irony is that this "harmony" seems to be built upon the memory of a child who has suffered and died. As Robin Feuer Miller observes "their brotherhood is cemented by the very mortar that Ivan had earlier so eloquently refused to accept—the unjustified suffering of a child" (133). Sometimes on our last day of class, after seven weeks of discussing the novel, just before we re-enact the speech at the stone with our class-selected Alyosha, I read Robin's words aloud. A chill runs down my spine and that of others: Has Dostoevsky closed with an image of heavenly harmony built on Ilyusha's tears? Has he accepted Ivan's "non-Euclidean" theodicy?

No. The novel's final image of communal harmony does not reflect that theodicy which *both* Ivan *and* Alyosha rightly reject. As mentioned earlier, theodicy itself is a modern and suspect construct whether it takes the form of Leibniz's defense of this as the "best of all possible worlds" or John Hick's argument that suffering is necessary to "soul-making." Theodicy imposes a humanly constructed, rational purpose upon horrific, painful death. Ilyusha's suffering and death—and the promise of his resurrection—finds its meaning in a more "ancient, eternal" (646) understanding of suffering, grounded in Scripture and tradition, and founded upon the faith that the human person *participates* in the Paschal mystery of Christ's salvation.

Thus St. Paul's exhortation that his readers make their "minds like that of Christ," who kenotically accepted our human condition: childhood, suffering, death—and eventual resurrection (Phil 2:5–12).

Kolya has claimed "if it were only possible to resurrect him, I'd give anything in the world to do it" (644); Alyosha shares Kolya's yearning. Three months earlier, Alyosha had momentarily shared Ivan's lust for violent retribution: "'shoot him!' Alyosha said softly, lifting his gaze to his brother with a somehow pale, twisted smile" (210). But then Alyosha remembered that justice, happiness, and harmony rest neither on our acts of vengeance *nor* on the "manure" (211) of suffering, innocent children. He remembers that the foundation is the hidden ground of love made incarnate in Christ: "there is a Being and he can forgive everything, *and for all*, because he gave his innocent blood for all and everything. You have forgotten him, and on him is built the edifice, and it is to him they cried aloud 'Thou art just, O Lord, for thy ways are revealed!'" (213) In the speech of the stone, Christ's way is revealed in Alyosha's "subtle" affirmation of Ilyusha's—and every person's—invitation to participate in Christ's suffering, death, and resurrection. If the Trinity participates in the *mysterium paschale*, so too do we as persons, made in the Trinity's image and likeness.

We have come full circle. Early in the novel, Zosima had entered into the experience of the grieving mother, who had left her husband Nikitushka. Here, Alyosha sees and accepts the natural laceration of familial grief: "let them weep" (644). But Zosima had also called the suffering woman to responsibility, specifically to her bond of marriage: "go to your husband, mother; go this very day" (49). So too Alyosha here encourages broken Snegiryov to return to *his* spouse: "you'll spoil the flowers. . . . And mamochka is expecting them, she is sitting crying because you would not give her any from Ilyusha before. Ilyusha's little bed is still there . . ." (643). Christ's redemptive act is offered *for all*, yet our responsibility *for all*—especially to those closest to us—never ceases, even in grief. The person's graced capacity to love actively is Dostoevsky's answer to what seems like senseless suffering.[340]

Alyosha's responsive prudence is shown in his improvised response to Smurov's exclamation, "Here's Ilyusha's stone, under which they wanted to bury him!":

> They all stopped silently by the big stone. Alyosha looked in the whole picture of what Snegiryov described to him that day, how Ilyusha weeping and hugging his father had cried: "Papochka, papochka, how he insulted you," rose it once before his imagination. Something seemed to shake in his soul. With a serious and

> earnest expression he looked from one to another of the bright,
> pleasant faces of Ilyusha's school fellows, and suddenly said to
> them:
>
> "I should like to say one word to you, here at this place."
>
> (644)

Alyosha remembers the injustice done to Ilyusha and his father, looks at
each particular face "of Ilyusha's schoolfellows." "Suddenly" he declares, "I
should like to say one word to you, here at this place." His improvised speech
comprises the novel's second climax. In "Cana," "*someone* visited [Alyosha's]
soul" (312); here "*something* seemed to shake in Alyosha's soul." Both times,
Alyosha receives a gift from Another, unseen yet real. Josef Pieper notes that
"Christian prudence . . . means . . . the inclusion of new and invisible realities within the determinants of our decisions" (*Virtues* 37)—or, in Zosima's
words, "a precious, mystic sense of our living bond with the other world"
(276). The "higher, heavenly world" offers grace that lifts humans from the
earth, the *humus* from which we're made, into which the grain of wheat
falls, into which Ilyusha is buried.

Alyosha responds to the gift of infused prudence with charitable service. Alyosha's extemporaneous "homily" is Eucharistic: it both remembers
and participates in Christ's death and resurrection. Memory is essential to
prudence: Alyosha remembers the Calvary shared by father and son, the
father's cry for justice, and his plea for his son to show mercy to Mitya, the
malefactor who knew not what did when he shamed father before son.[341]
When Christ institutes the Eucharist, he emphasizes: "do this in remembrance of me" (1 Cor 11:24; Mark 14:22; Luke 22:19). Alyosha repeats varia-
tions of the word "memory," and assures the boys that "one good memory
may keep [them] from great evil" (645). At the Divine Liturgy, they've sung
"Eternal Memory";[342] improvisational as it is, Alyosha's speech *sustains* the
liturgy as it not only remembers but manifests God's incarnate love. Christ
takes bread and wine and says, "This is my body. This is my blood." The final
chapter is book-ended by images of bread. Before the burial, the mourners
bring bread for the birds; after the speech they go off together to eat pancakes. In Catholic, Orthodox, and some Protestant traditions, the bread and
wine are transformed and make present Christ's body and blood. As "source
and summit of the Christian life,"[343] the Eucharist makes present the church
itself as the mystical body of Christ. Christ establishes his church on Peter,
Petros: "upon this rock I will build my church." Analogically, the boys are
united as *ecclesia* at the stone of Ilyusha,[344] just as the deceased boy himself
has participated in the suffering, death, and resurrection of Christ. In the
Roman rite, the Memorial Acclamation of the Eucharistic prayer avows

Christ's death, resurrection, and restorative return: "Christ has died. Christ is risen. Christ will come again."

Also integral to prudence is "farsightedness," the poised readiness in the face of the unexpected.[345] Alyosha had displayed this with Grushenka in "An Onion". The boys are themselves poised for Alyosha's unexpected request "and at once [bend] attentive and expectant eyes upon him" (644). Alyosha sees their readiness to promise that they'll "never forget . . . how good it was once here, . . . all together, united by a good and kind feeling, which made us, for the time we were loving that poor boy, better perhaps than we are" (645). How can we "better than *we are*"? Alyosha suggests that their experience is one of self-transcendence,[346] a brief recovery of their creaturely likeness to their loving Creator, fully recovered only in *theosis*. "Cana" offers another example: in Alyosha's dream, the "simple, artless merrymaking of some obscure and unlearned beings" is transfigured to become an image of communal beatitude. In Ilyusha's funeral, the many become one through "the Being [who] can forgive everything, all and *for all*" (213). As opposed to the meretricious "mystery" imposed by the Grand Inquisitor, Alyosha gives witness to the real mystery: participation in the trinitarian love of God. Alyosha implores his twelve listeners to remember their participation—to "be kind, then honest," and to "never forget each other" (645). He assures them that "one good memory may keep [them] from great evil" (645). Alyosha promises that he will always remember this moment and, in the true form of active love, he emphasizes the *particular* faces and names of the boys whom he addresses, and welcomes the way they are looking at him as their *gift* to him:

> I give you my word, gentlemen, that for my part I'll never forget one of you; every face looking at me now I shall remember for thirty years. Just now Kolya said to Kartashov that we did not care to know "whether he exists or not." But I cannot forget that Kartashov exists and that he is not blushing now as he did when he discovered Troy, but is looking at me with his nice, kind, happy little eyes. Gentlemen, my dear gentlemen, let us all be generous and brave like Ilyushechka, intelligent, brave, and generous like Kolya (though he will be ever so much more intelligent when he is grown up), and let us all be as bashful but also as smart and sweet as Kartashov. But why am I talking about these two! You are all dear to me, gentlemen, from this day forth, I have a place in my heart for you all, and I beg you to keep a place in your hearts for me! Well, and who has united us in this kind, good feeling which we shall remember and intend to remember all our lives, who, if not Ilyushechka, the good boy,

> the dear boy, the boy precious to us now and unto ages of ages!
> Let us never forget him, and may his memory be eternal and
> good in our hearts now and unto ages of ages! (646)

"Unto ages of ages" sustains the liturgical form of the scene. The conclusion of Alyosha's speech is infused with the promise of resurrection,
restoration, and reunion. We recall, early in the novel, the narrator's image
of the doubting St. Thomas who believed in his "secret heart" in the reality of Christ's resurrection; here, at the end, "doubting Kolya" serves as the
catalyst for the communal affirmation of eternal life. The boys have ecstatically, cheerfully declared their love for Ilyusha and Alyosha, have prayed
that "the dead boy's memory live eternally." Kolya then asks, with hope, not
haughtiness:

> "Karamazov!" cried Kolya, "can it really be true what religion
> says, that we shall all rise from the dead and shall live and see
> each other again, everyone, and Ilyushechka?"
> "Certainly we shall all rise again, certainly we shall see each
> other and gladly, joyfully will tell each other all that has hap-
> pened," Alyosha answered, half laughing, half ecstatic.
> "Ah, how good it will be!" broke from Kolya. (646)

At this point, readers may find themselves echoing Kolya's spontaneous
words of yearning, "Ah, how good it will be!"

Dostoevsky wrote with the hope of such a response. The attentive
reader will "hear" the ways in which the chimes of the chapter inspire a
sense of cosmic wholeness, unity, integration. In earlier chapters I have
noted affinities between the novel and Augustine's *Confessions* and Dante's
Commedia. Here, as during "Cana," the final canto of *Commedia* again
comes to mind. Dante discerns an "eternal Light," and in its depth "gathered
and bound / By love in a single volume, all we have found / On single pages,
scattered throughout our world" (Raffel trans. 33.86–88). In the novel's beginning, the narrator promises that Alyosha "carries within himself the very
heart of the whole" from which others have been "torn . . . as if by a gust of
wind" (7). In the novel's end all that was scattered—Snegiryov's trampled
rubles, Mitya's ragged pouch, Smerdyakov's copy of St. Isaac the Syrian left
on his nightstand—*all* the lacerating losses are recovered and re-membered
by love. Zosima has promised Mme. Khokhlakova that the practice of active
love will convince her of the reality of the resurrection, and here the active
love of Alyosha and the boys has borne fruit not only in an affirmation of
eternal life, but an experiential taste of it. Ivan has denied the resurrection
(120), but imagined the eschatological joy the end of the quadrillion me-
ters (577); such joy is imaged here. Mitya sings his "hymn"; Alyosha and

the boys sing theirs at the stone. Alyosha affirms the salvific effect of one memory, and we recall the angel remembering the wicked old lady's single onion (303). Lying in his coffin, little Ilyusha recalls Zosima in his, but also Zosima's appearance at Cana, and its promise of abundant new wine.

Throughout the novel, the gritty work of active love precedes epiphany, and epiphany precedes the prosaic: Alyosha reminds the boys that they must "finish talking and go to the funeral dinner" and readers too must descend from this ecstatic taste of eternal communal joy. In the climactic moment in *The Confessions*, Augustine and Monica gaze out the window in Ostia and glimpse eternity. Then they reenter the quotidian demands of daily life. On the last page of Dante's *Commedia*, the pilgrim Dante sees our human image inscribed in the Trinity, feels "the Love that moves the sun and the other stars." He then becomes the exiled poet who faces the hard task of writing his lifework.[347] Readers close *The Brothers Karamazov* with an image of communal beatitude, but, possibly, too, with the resolve to begin again the slow, graced work of active love, recalling the gift given *for all*, and the responsibility each bears *for all*. So too the dismissal at the end of the liturgy must be understood as "the starting point" of our work of active love, for "the word 'dismissal' has come to imply a 'mission.'"[348]

Read slowly and attentively, the last chapter often elicits salutary tears in the reader. And in the novel, tears can suggest a change of heart, a tender *metanoia*: Zosima before his servant Afanasy, Grushenka before Alyosha, Alyosha watering the ground with his tears, Mitya's dream of "the wee one" and discovery of a pillow beneath his head. If the reader weeps, and remembers those earlier tears, she or he may vow to do better, to be better, to respond to the hidden ground of Christ's love "for all" with active love "for all." In its symphonic recapitulations and call to love, "The Speech at the Stone" invites its reader to accept the novel's vision of incarnational realism as true, and to bring it to fruition in real and ordinary life.

So, like the child who called out to St. Augustine in the Milan garden, I exhort you, "Pick up and read!" Or, better, reread. Share your reading experience in conversation with others—the ways in which Dostoevsky's novel has given you food for the journey, and the ways his words might be made flesh in your own ordinary lives.

Afterword

Alyosha, His Life and Afterlives

—CARYL EMERSON—

"Where else would you find Russian youth like this, men radiant in spirit . . . who have withdrawn to the white monastery of Gallipoli to bear closed, pure witness? . . . Green is our garden, precious our Russian hope, our Russian youth, our novice Alyosha, the third and youngest of the brothers, who will come to replace us all, even the cold, mad Ivans, who are the devil's kin, and the Don Quixote Mityas who squander their souls, and the abominable Smerdyakovs. The third brother, our dear Alyosha, behind whom, whitewashed in a deluge of blood and pus, stands the third Russia."[1] Thus wrote the émigré Russian writer Ivan Lukash (1892–1940) in a short piece of fiction, "The Scattering of Stars" [Rozsyp' zvezd], published in the Bulgarian capital Sofia in 1922 and based on his own experience during the Russian Civil War. The story is set in 1921, among the defeated anti-Bolshevik Whites now interned at Gallipoli. Its genre is that rare type of prose lyric, the military idyll. Soldiers and their families are awaiting the end, without violence or bitterness. Gallipoli, Lukash writes, has become home to thousands of Russian students, who are performing there a "monastic feat."

Lukash does not clarify what precisely the Third Russia would inherit under the chaplaincy of the third brother. For his part Dostoevsky, shortly before his death, is reported to have said that in his planned sequel to *The Brothers Karamazov* Alyosha would leave the monastery, become an anarchist, and kill the tsar. But the actual afterlife of this irresistible fictive personality has been closer in spirit to Lukash than to projections of his original author. By the 1920s, Alyosha Karamazov was already a luminous

beacon for those exiles (soon to become émigrés) who hoped to see Russia restored to faith when the godless Bolsheviks fell from power. The Bolsheviks did not fall, and the official literary policy of the new regime—the
Second or Soviet Russia—was unsympathetic to Dostoevsky. Reading him
was not encouraged. His heroes were too unhealthy: hysterical, ideologi-
cally unreliable, selfish in their violence and pious in their conversions. Such
undisciplined energies, which relied as much on God as on humanity and
scientific progress, could not build socialism. Creative interpretations of the
most spiritually complex of the great novels, *The Brothers Karamazov,* took
place abroad during the interwar period, in the new and more culturally
liberal Slavic countries.

In 1928, for example, the Czech composer Otakar Jeremiáš (1892–
1962), working with the Symbolist dramatist and novelist Jaroslav Maria as
librettist, premiered their opera *Bratři Karamazovi* in Prague. In a pan-Slavic
nationalist spirit, set to music reminiscent of Wagner, Richard Strauss, Berg,
Smetana, and the late tonal language of Janáček, the libretto distilled Dostoevsky's plot to its secular, erotic, sensationalist outer sequence of events.
Its three acts are entirely Mitya-centered (Act I is the murder; Act II, the
Poles and Grushenka at Mokroe; Act III is divided between courtroom and
jail cell). Of metaphysics there is none: no Elder Zosima, no Grand Inquisitor, and only a hint of Ivan's devil. Alyosha, a lyric tenor, is characterized
by a static, chromatic-diatonic musical motif—and his role in the drama is
passive, almost iconic, activated only in the final scene. Mitya is reconciled
with Katerina Ivanovna in the prison cell. When Grushenka arrives, the betrothed couple sings a culminating duet on faith, hope, and love in Siberian
exile, which is blessed by Alyosha. It would appear that this third brother
interests Jeremiáš and Maria largely as a symbolic anchor, a dispenser of
grace after the necessary trials have been confronted and true love has tri-
umphed. Their Czech Alyosha is a radiant but somewhat mechanical figure
of redemption, not uncommon for Decadent Catholic art of the Symbolist
period. But it has little in common with the modest, prudent, constantly
present and continually anxious brother celebrated by Paul Contino.

For an operatic version closer to Contino's Alyosha, we move ahead
eighty years to Aleksandr Smelkov's *Bratya Karamazovy,* which premiered
at St. Petersburg's Mariinsky Theater in 2008 under Valery Gergiev.[2] This
second musicalized example differs from the earlier Czech opera in almost
every respect, beginning with its genre. Smelkov and his librettist Yuri
Dimitrin called their composition an *opera-misteriia* or "opera-mystery
play," alluding to the conventions of staged medieval Christian allegory.
Not every Russian nineteenth-century novel written during the Age of
Realism could be recast as liturgical drama, but this one could. The time

of both Decadent Symbolism and atheistic Soviet communism had passed. Ascendant in Putin's Russia was an aggressive chauvinism (very much in Dostoevsky's vein) and a resurgent official church. Such a re-consecration of unity between Russian Orthodoxy and the Russian imperial state, familiar since the time of Peter the Great, has its undeniably ominous side.[3] But it did encourage therapeutically creative interpretations of Dostoevsky, as a confused, humiliated, and impoverished populace sought a moral compass in the spiritual vacuum left by the collapse of communism and the invasion of robber-baron capitalism.

The opera's topography, as befits a mystery play, is laid bare in the opening and closing tableaus. Past and future are simultaneously present. This outer frame (Prelude and Postlude) is set in the medieval city of Seville during the Spanish Inquisition, and it comes with a *figura:* a children's choir singing of a parallel case in which resurrected spirit confronts misguided law, Dmitri Karamazov's trial. The twenty scenes in between, labeled by quotes from Dostoevsky's chapters and unfolding in linear time, are divided into two Parts. Of the twelve scenes of Part One, Alyosha appears in eight of them—first as novice, but then ever more actively as witness, confidant, intercessor, and confessor. Two scenes, #13 and #16, reprise the Grand Inquisitor's encounter with a returned Christ. The second iteration of Seville also contains echoes of the imminent murder trial. It is followed by a solo scene, "Mitya's Prayer"—for in this opera, arias as well as physical gesture can be rendered as prayers. The final curtain closes with Christ's kiss on the Inquisitor's bloodless lips.

Alyosha has a prayer too: scene #11, pleading for Grushenka not to use a knife against her Polish officer at Mokroe. But Smelkov is careful to keep under control the piety inherent in the mystery-play form, playing up rather the pain and doubt. The essential solo scene for the third brother is not a prayer but #21, "Alyosha's Dream." This, of course, is the novel's famous "Cana of Galilee" episode (chapter 4 of Part III, Book Seven, "Alyosha"), which takes place in that hazy hypnogogic time-space of a sacrament, Father Païssy intoning Scripture over the body of the deceased Zosima. Alyosha falls asleep to the rhythmic reading of John 2:1–12, Jesus's first miracle. In his pre-sleep vision he recognizes his Elder at the wedding feast, who calls on him to rise, rejoice, and look on Christ, "on our Sun." But Alyosha "dares not look." Zosima does not insist. New guests are always welcome and always expected, he assures Alyosha; there will be bread and wine enough for all. This vision becomes Alyosha's liberation from crisis-time and scandal-space, and the rapture that follows marks the end of his disbelief.

In Smelkov's operatic equivalent of this pivotal spiritual episode, matters are less ecstatic, far more frightening and tentative. Scene #21, "Alyosha's

Dream," takes place not at the Wedding at Cana but at the center of a pulsating shaft of light, Dostoevsky's sign of divine grace.[4] The Elder Zosima draws near to Alyosha but utters no reassuring words of mercy or encouragement. He repeats only one three-word phrase: *Gdye ty, Alyosha?* [Where are you, Alyosha?] As if struck blind, the indistinct silhouettes of Mitya, Ivan, Fyodor Pavlovich, Smerdyakov, Grushenka, and Katerina Ivanovna move toward the third brother with the same question, *where are you?* Then these restless shades dissolve, having received no answer. Thus the opera reproduces the disturbed texture of Alyosha's own conflicted consciousness as Contino has described it: earnest, honest to a fault, hands-on, everywhere well-intentioned, sought out by all but fixed in the present, never certain that he is in the right place at the right time or even whether his attempts to help his family are welcome. Alyosha might be everyone's unacknowledged mediator and servitor, but his pilgrimage through the opera is painful and obscure.

One final "incarnation" of Dostoevsky's last novel will clarify the challenge of representing, on the performance stage, the reality of Alyosha and the spiritual realm that sustains him. In 2013, Boris Eifman adapted *The Brothers Karamazov* for his St. Petersburg Ballet Company.[5] The Eifman Ballet is post-classical (that is, with admixtures of modern dance, mime, vocals) and devoted to the expressive body. To communicate in dance, this body must be heightened and stylized. But Alyosha (unlike his father and brothers) does not lend himself to exaggeration or caricature. His body and mind are simply *healthy*—or as Contino expands on Dostoevsky's idea, his person is "prosaic" in its virtues and modest in its daily acts. The ballet is not wholly lacking a metaphysical dimension; in Act II, built off the novel's Book Five, Ivan becomes the Inquisitor and Alyosha his Jesus, dancing out their opposing worldviews. But the core of what is danced by the family is the relentless, depraved sensualism of "Karamazovism." To a musical pastiche of Rachmaninoff, Wagner, and Musorgsky, all three brothers are equally tormented by the flesh, wrestling with their demons. Alyosha appears alternately in a white and a black cassock, sometimes with his torso stripped bare. Bodies in the ballet are exclusively tensed; they do not find resolution or relief anywhere, and do not intercede for one another. Understandably, Eifman's choreography contains no Elder Zosima. In the final tableau, Alyosha spirals upward, dreamlike, to embrace a crucifix mounted high above the stage. This might be powerful staged art, but nothing about that desperate, isolated reaching-up recalls Alyosha at the funeral stone, rallying the survivors below in communal rejoicing.

⌘

Paul Contino's variation on the "Alyosha phenomenon" is also an interdisciplinary interpretation of Dostoevsky's final novel—although not, of course, danced or sung. But there are parallels between Contino's study and the narratives created by opera or ballet. First, one must already know the novel reasonably well going in, because Contino, like the librettist and choreographer, spends no time re-telling its story. A great classic is a cultural given and its parts can be freely re-arranged. Even an audience that is literate in Dostoevsky, however, must understand how a libretto works (its conventions of aria, recitative, and ensemble), just as ballet fans must be conversant in the symbolism of dance choreography. Contino's equivalent medium—that which provides the underlying momentum and rhythm, the connective tissue and necessary cadence to his argument—is the New Testament. Going in, it helps enormously to have that classic text under one's belt as well, for often the reader is given only a tiny toehold on the relevant passage, two or three words. Contino has not written a concordance, of course, but something closer to a palimpsest. To make its layers legible, he equips his reader at the start with larger interpretive frameworks: the analogical imagination, confessional dialogue, kenotic attentiveness, the Thomist virtue of *prudentia*—and embracing them all, incarnational realism. These organizing principles guide our experience of Dostoevsky's plot. And it is helpful never to forget Contino's ecumenical vision. Although his personal perspective is Roman Catholic, many of his core ideas are deeply consonant with Russian Orthodox tradition, especially the "spiritualization of matter" as celebrated by Dostoevsky's close friend and Russia's greatest philosopher, Vladimir Soloviev.[6] The task of the human body, Soloviev argues, is to mediate between the realm of the spirit and material form; thus these two intertwined components of personhood must not be declared hostile to each other or incommensurable. Matter is not lifeless, accursed, or irrational; it too is a manifestation of the absolute. Revelation and consciousness follow embodiment.

A second parallel with the staged arts, then, can be seen in Contino's radical deployment of incarnation as a spiritualized concept—even though he is analyzing a novel. We cannot imagine ballet or opera without embodiment. Singing, acting, and dancing are physical affects literally produced in the body and communicated by means of bodies. In contrast, verbal narratives, if so structured, can be processed solely as a sequence of ideas, devoid even of intonation. (Try imagining a film of "Notes from Underground" that really stays inside the Underground Man's head. It's been tried, and in the most honest adaptations, the speaking face ends up dissolving in a grey blur. This is a voice that does not wish to be seen by the outside.) Contino will have none of this incorporeal moving around of words and ideas. He encourages us to visualize *The Brothers Karamazov* as a species of morally marked performance art, as (literally) an ensemble incarnated in time and space, disharmonious now but aware, if only in flashes, of the path toward concord. This might seem obvious, but it is not. Great interpreters of Dostoevsky, such as Mikhail Bakhtin, have analyzed his prose formally, that is, in terms of *how words work* inside it. Within this functional framework, physical events (say, a spectacular murder) are necessary in order to put words and ideas in circulation. A fictional hero (what Bakhtin calls an "idea-person") exists to give voice to these ideas. Contino draws deeply on Bakhtin, but as much on his early philosophical essays, grounded in spatial metaphors, as on his Dostoevsky monograph, where the distinctiveness of Dostoevsky has already moved from the embodied scene to the dialogized verbal encounter. It takes serious work to recuperate an ethical system, not to mention a fully christological framework, out of dialogue, polyphony, and multi-voicedness understood solely as verbal-compositional devices. In principle, one set of ideas is as "equally-weighted" as any other, and arguably the health and freedom of humanity requires as many voice-viewpoints as possible. This is one reason why Bakhtin, a believing Christian, has been so successfully integrated into sociological, Marxist, and relativizing postmodernist worldviews.

To discipline those dynamics in a personalist direction and a moral hierarchy, Contino adds a firm scriptural subtext. Incarnational realism, as the reader has come to know it in these pages, is not an intellectual doctrine. Although it is at all points reasonable (that is, not irrational), its primary expressive medium is not ideas. Ideas are forever contradictory, subject to rhetorical manipulation, and flourish when allowed to proliferate on their own—as we know from their prime advocate in *The Brothers Karamazov*, the second brother Ivan. The medium for incarnational realism, rather, is the speaking and acting body, which must answer for its immediate effect on other bodies and for all accidents of timing and misidentification. To be sure, we are dealing with a novel; words remain the aesthetic medium for these transactions. But Contino asks us to feel Dostoevsky more as sacred theater, or in the words of Hans Urs von Balthalsar, as "Theo-drama."[7] Although conflict and temptation is everywhere, nothing is "equally weighted" in Dostoevsky, any more than it is in the options that Aleksandr Smelkov bodied forth in his mystery-play opera.

There is one crucial difference, however, between Alyosha in Dostoevsky's novel and in his various stage versions. As Contino shows, part of

Alyosha's "prudential realism"—and a major ingredient in Zosima's concept of active love—is its utter *non*-theatricality. In a novel full of ecstasy, hysteria, psychic lacerations and public display, the prudent person prefers listening to declaiming. He does not move forward by a script, but by the sense that whoever needs his presence or attention this minute, has it. Alyosha can be insulted as well as flirted with, but he does not lose his head over either. His first intuition is to trust a person. When he is hurt, what he feels is not anger or resentment, but sadness. Despair sets in only when he senses a need in a person and cannot see a direct path toward helping or alleviating that need. Thus he learns how to let go of situations that cannot be improved upon by his intercession. In all these traits, Alyosha is the opposite of prideful Ivan—the brother that Contino probably likes the least.[8] (Dmitry's ecstatic irrationality and behavioral excess is tolerated far better in this book, forgiven and even celebrated.) Starting in Chapter 4, Contino takes the reader through the six days of Alyosha's novelistic journey. In no sense are these days triumphant. How quickly the failed, awkward, anti-climactic moments pile up! Although this youngest brother becomes everyone's confidant, he proves unable to plan, plot, or keep a confidence (whoever asks the whole story from him, receives it). Yet all these setbacks do not become part of Alyosha's defining profile or essential plot. There is a privacy about him that is almost spooky.

Because of this privacy, spontaneity, and the attendant unstageable, unplottable nature of his behavior, the Alyosha personality-type is hard to define by its appetites or acts. It is more a set of responsive attitudes and faith patterns, whose success is never guaranteed (least of all to Alyosha himself) because, as Robert Belknap noted long ago, "delay in the operation of grace is a central theme of the novel."[9] Rowan Williams, in his 2011 study of Dostoevsky, had the following to say in support of this open-ended image of the youngest Karamazov brother: "Alyosha's faith . . . will not turn out to be an affirmation that cosmic process will necessarily justify or heal; all he will really know is that change happens and that it is not dependent on human resource."[10] Healing happens to others under Alyosha's attentive person; they sense he is a conduit for energy that has its source in other worlds. But unlike his brothers and father, Alyosha is disinclined to preach what he lives by. Several times in the novel Alyosha is associated with a holy fool (by the narrator in the introduction, who refutes it, and then by Katerina Ivanovna [168]). But more prominent in the novel are Alyosha's qualities as seeker, mediator, and healer. He seeks, as an agent in the world, practical ways to heal what is broken in others, while being true to a precious lost thing.

⌘

Are we of the twenty-first century living in the time of the Third Russia? Not, surely, as the first diaspora envisaged it. But some of the most adventurous writers in Russia today are taking the longest possible view of the Russian tradition, which inescapably brings us to the monastery and to eschatological themes. A salvific image of Alyosha—novice, Christian seeker, healer taken for a holy fool—has worthy descendants in the contemporary Russian historical novel, many of which are now post-secular: beyond the postmodernist, but not yet post-humanist. Wondrous examples have begun to reach the Anglophone readership. Consider Evgeny Vodolazkin's global bestseller *Laurus* (published in Russian in 2012 as *Lavr* and subtitled "a non-historical novel"), set in the medieval northern princedom of Rus' of the fifteenth century, frozen and starving for half the year, ridden with plague for the rest.[11] Labeled a "postmodernist saint's life," it was welcomed by many as a profound renascence of national spirituality and mocked by others as a sign of Russia's failure to progress beyond her own dark ages. The End of Time is expected in 1492. The hero Arseny, an orphan and herbal healer, has been an Alyosha type from childhood: gentle, other-directed, in harmony with nature (both animals and plants), able by his mere presence to calm others and turn their impatience into insight, their self-pity into gratitude. As a very young man, he failed to save the life of his beloved Ustina in childbirth and, of equal awfulness, had kept her hidden, deprived of church communion, thus jeopardizing her soul and that of their stillborn child. Elder Nikandr from the nearby monastery administers lifesaving advice to Arseny: you are to blame for her bodily death, he says, but you can "give her your own life," by which Nikandr meant: not by dying, but by loving. "Love made you and Ustina a united whole, which means a part of Ustina is still here. It is you. . . . You have a difficult journey, for the story of your love is only beginning."[12]

Throughout the remainder of the novel, in his speaking and silent years spent in Rus' as well as during an arduous pilgrimage to Jerusalem, Arseny constantly addresses Ustina, this departed but immortal part of himself. She does not respond. In the hope that somehow and at some point she will, Arseny re-focuses his love, lifting it out of the usual trappings of the erotic plot—courtship, carnal possessiveness, jealousy, a narrowing of one's focus to hearth and family. Exhausted and often sorrowful, Arseny spreads this love over many needy people and a vast territory. As one Russian critic noted, *Laurus* is a "deep and passionate love novel in which love has been taken out of the narrative. It serves as the internal mainspring that sets the entire novelistic mechanism in motion, making the main hero walk, talk, and move, but at the same time this hero remains chaste and mysteriously hidden from the readers' eyes."[13] Losing a beloved and losing an elder are of course very different bereavements, but Arseny forges for himself the same chaste spiritual bond with Ustina that Alyosha has with his departed Zosima, one that turns an outer person into a living inner text. There is a blurring of lines between types of love (Eros, Philia, Storge, Agape), and all take on the same empathetic urgency. At the Empty Tomb in the Holy City, in an hour of despair that bears comparison with the night that Alyosha feared he had betrayed Zosima, Arseny begs for some sign that he is on the right path toward Ustina, so that he might move forward with that knowledge. The elder at the Tomb responds: "What sign do you want and what knowledge?" All journeys are dangerous. "So you say faith is not enough for you and you want knowledge too. But knowledge does not involve spiritual effort; knowledge is obvious. Faith assumes effort. Knowledge is repose and faith is motion" (297).

The effort of this ever-shifting faith-in-motion produces active love. As in the Zosima model, its deeds are not always understood. Upon his return to Rus', administering to plague victims and burdened with rising fame as a doctor, Arseny resettles in his birth village and enters a monastery. But his fame follows him, since his healing and predictive powers approach the miraculous; his life—and the expectations surrounding his death—begin to resemble the Elder Zosima's. Arseny, now called Amvrosy, becomes the hermit Laurus. In the last stage of his journey, he finally loses track of forward-moving time. And in the novel's final astonishing chapters, it is revealed to us that if we openly confront an error, or a sin, or simply an unspeakable accident in profane linear time, it will cycle round again and test us, until we are allowed to make it right.

In July 2016, Rowan Williams gave a Ted Talk on Vodolazkin's *Laurus*, defining Arseny's task as "coming to terms with his own powerlessness." His task was to live his life in such a way "as to give room to that lost other person." This is a "self-stripping," but not a self-annihilation. The quest for a stripped-back self results not in negation, William notes, but in a flowering of the right sort of relationship, tentative, attentive, receptive, and "all the great novels of Dostoevsky are of this sort." Williams has spoken in several venues on *Laurus*, usually tracing its "mysterious and impenetrable" personalism back to Dostoevsky, the writer in whom "the creative potential of every person is an abyss of risk and danger."[14] As Paul Contino has intimated in this book, personalism is not individualism. The person comes on the scene already embedded in community. In an Orthodox Christian framework, personhood [*lichnost'*] is itself communal [*sobornaia*], an idea originating in the Trinity and precious to Dostoevsky. And because the actively loving self is not the autonomous Cartesian self (an entity unknown to Eastern Orthodox Christianity), but rather the person as part of a community, it can diminish itself only so far. Persons do not dissolve. Since an Orthodox worldview acknowledges no void (by definition, no space is empty), this worldview requires both a self and an other as minimal structural necessities. When my eyes look out, others' eyes are already looking in—whether or not I see them. What is "out there" are relationships still latent, whose potentials have not yet been realized.

Laurus is certainly a saint's life. But can we also see it as an Alyosha tale, in the terms that Contino has laid out in this book? To some extent we can. The fifteenth century is not, to be sure, Dostoevsky's nineteenth. Vodolazkin unobtrusively weaves into his novel what might look to us like miracles: holy fools and elders walking on water, a chunk of monastery bread that does not diminish in Laurus's cave, month after month. Neither the narrator nor his depicted characters are surprised in the least by these witnessed or soberly reported facts. Within the worldview of *Laurus* they are shared realities, along with the constancies of painful death, plague, disasters of weather and lethal dangers of travel. The horrific everyday life of Pskov province is related in a crisis-free intonation, "a most sympathetic narrative full of gentle humor, inner calm and quiet love."[15] In a word, the story is not only about an Alyosha type, but it is related in Alyosha's prayerful, scripturally-saturated zone. This zone, free from panic or fear, persists in the reader's mind throughout *Laurus*, although Vodolazkin's startling shifts in stylistic and linguistic register can be at times as disorienting as the unreliable antics of a Dostoevskian narrator.

Prudence and incarnational realism, therefore, have a narrative tone as well as a roster of deeds. And among the benefits of Contino's book, for all its copious scholarly apparatus, is that it encourages us to supplement the sophisticated research industry surrounding *The Brothers Karamazov* with a simple, slow, close re-reading of what we already know. What we learn about "The Third Son, Alyosha" (Part I, Book One, Chapter 4) bears repeating, in today's moral climate more than ever. Alyosha is not a fanatic, not a mystic, he just loves people and wants to help them. He doesn't talk much—and although he is often made sad by events, he cannot be surprised or frightened by anything, rarely passes judgment, and never remembers an offense. The most varied people, from buffoons to cynics to the novel's panoply of resentful injured egos, end up desperately wanting him around. Perhaps the most striking thing about Alyosha, as Dostoevsky lays out his hero, is the complete fusion in his person of the sacred and the profane, the metaphysical and the mortal. "Incarnational realism," we realize, is fully compatible with what the outside world calls miracles; it can also be made compatible with many humanistic varieties of materialism.[16] Contino's concentration on Alyosha as the incarnation of *prudence* performs the same integrative work. Josef Pieper, in his discussion of the virtues, calls prudence "the mold and 'mother' of all the other cardinal virtues," however strange and evasive this might seem to the contemporary mind, raised on conventional theatrical heroism; only a prudent person, Pieper writes, "can be just, brave, and temperate," and we are good and act well only in so far as we are prudent.[17] The Alyosha model, again, does not protect the self against failure. All it does is enable the self to act in a way that does not add to the failure. Denys Turner, summarizing Thomas Aquinas, calls *prudentia* the "skill in seeing the moral point of human situations, what true desires are to be met within them."[18] It can be fairly said that Alyosha's mission in *The Brothers Karamazov* is to help define, for each of the other major characters, what their "true desire" is. As we have seen in Contino's account of the novel's half-a-dozen days, broken down by brother, this could be a thankless mission. Only a "Zosima within" could help Alyosha bear it.

⌘

If the third son Alyosha is Russia's hope and a "Christ among the Karamazovs," then for decades, Paul Contino has been the Roman Catholic among American Dostoevsky scholars. All of us who admire and love Paul are a bit surprised how this came to pass. Dostoevsky despised Catholics (to be sure, this was not the only ethnic or religious group he despised, but Catholicism was consistently featured in utterly unflattering venues, such as the Inquisition in Spain). Contino takes a less dogmatic, more ecumenical and deed-centered view of the Russian writer, along the lines of Rowan Williams in his *Dostoevsky*. In his Series Introduction to that book, Williams ponders the "current rash of books hostile to religious faith," concluding that the authors of such books routinely attend to the wrong things. They fail to see religious belief as one of many "systems of meaning" (including those that we "unreflectively think of as science"), all of which "seem to operate by allowing us to see phenomena in connected rather than arbitrary ways."[19] All functional meaning-systems utilize metaphor and creative imagination. Some even establish laws, although each system differs in its degree of dependence on quantification and verifiable reproducibility of results. What polemically anti-religious books "normally fail to do," Williams notes, "is to attend to what it is that religious people actually do and say"—that is, they scrutinize exclusively the doctrine, which may or may not strike them as illogical, without attending to the "repertoire of resources" available to a person who has chosen to see and connect phenomena in a certain way.

A close look at one fictive person's "repertoire of resources" has been the task of this book on Alyosha Karamazov. As Paul Contino is at pains to emphasize in his Epilogue, taking us step-by-step through Alyosha's last day, Ilyusha's fate in the novel is awful and undeserved. Dostoevsky rejects out of hand the idea of embedding it symbolically in a theodicy—the framework favored in the novel by brother Ivan and cruelly aestheticized by him. "Theodicy imposes a humanly constructed, rational purpose upon horrific, painful death," Contino writes. This cannot and should not be done. Recall the wisdom that the pilgrim Arseny, in *Laurus*, receives from the elder in Jerusalem: "Knowledge is repose and faith is motion." As Contino reworks this idea, prudence, always moving forward into unknown particulars, must be "farsighted," the "poised readiness in the face of the unexpected." Contino glosses Thomas Aquinas for this notion, which I paraphrased through Denys Turner as a "true desire," so let me close on a quote from an earlier page of Aquinas's masterwork, his illuminating discussion of the virtues. "Prudence is knowing what to want and what not to want," Aquinas writes, after which the mind can deliberate reasonably and the will can make choices.[20] The passion and spectacle of *The Brothers Karamazov*—which includes Dostoevsky's novel, its incarnated adaptations for the stage, and its legacy in later fiction from Lukash to Vodolazkin—lies in each character learning slowly true desires, what to want and what not to want, in the presence of other persons to whom they are answerable. Alyosha's gift, Contino writes, is to "infuse prudence with charitable service" to these other persons. If these others are capable of growth at all, they will grow into accepting this gift.

Endnotes to the Afterword

1. Ivan Lukash, *"Rozsyp' zvezd,"* in *Goloe pole (Kniga o Gallipoli)*, 1921 [The Naked Field (A Book about Gallipoli), 1921] (Sofia, Pechatnitsa Balkan, 1922), 55–70. In English see Ivan Lukash, "A Scattering of Stars," trans. Bryan Karetnyk, in *Russian Émigré Short Stories from Bunin to Yanovsky* (New York: Penguin Classics, 2017) 124–37. Quote on p. 129.

2. For a gallery of 120 photographic stills from the opera, see https://vk.com/album-3988573_92716578.

3. See John Garrard and Carol Garrard, *Russian Orthodoxy Resurgent: Faith and Power in the New Russia* (Princeton: Princeton University Press,

2008). Their chapter 5 ("Irreconcilable Differences: Orthodoxy and the West") surveys the split between Catholicism and the Eastern Church from a perspective sympathetic to today's conservative believing Russians—and is thus a useful (if not ecumenical) guide to reading patriotic-religious narrative art in twenty-first-century Russia.

4. For more on this symbolism, see the (still unsurpassed) discussion of sunlight, grace, and non-judgmental silence in relation to Alyosha in Robert L. Belknap, *The Structure of* The Brothers Karamazov [1967] (repr., Evanston, IL: Northwestern University Press, 1989), 39–42.

5. For select footage of the balletic Eifman *Karamazovs*, including a glimpse of Alyosha's final ascent, see the *Stage Russia* official trailer from 2019: trailerhttps://www.youtube.com/watch?v=GD7lv7L_iAQ.

6. For a lucid overview of this central tenet in the Sophianic tradition, see Oliver Smith, *Vladimir Soloviev and the Spiritualization of Matter* (Boston: Academic Studies Press, 2011), especially his discussion on "The Material World," 31–36. Opposing the duality between idea and matter that "had been the starting point for much idealist and religious philosophy after Plato" (the Cartesian separation of *res extensa* and *res cogitans*), Russian Orthodox thinking tended to emphasize "a moral imperative to act toward the sowing of the ideal in the real" (35, 31).

7. See Hans Urs von Balthasar, *Theo-Drama. Theological Dramatic Theory, I: Prologomena*, trans. Graham Harrison (San Francisco: Ignatius, 1988). Especially suggestive in any discussion of incarnational realism is Part III, B on "Role as the Acceptance of Limitation."

8. However Ivan's intellectual arguments might impress scholars and academics—for he has our skill set—Contino is probably right in his criticism. As Antony Johae has argued, Ivan's Christ is an isolated Romantic figure, an individual seeker who can realize his truth alone, but for Dostoevsky (unlike Tolstoy), "fullness of life in oneself alone is self-destructive and negates the essential unity of parts with the whole"; "ultimately Dostoevsky does not come down on Ivan's side because he understands only too well that a man without a center (the intersecting points of the cross) loses his hold on life and becomes, as it were, parallel lines in space, full of unrestrained energy, but reaching out into an inexplicable and deadly void." See Antony Johae, "Idealism and the Dialectic in *The Brothers Karamazov*," in *F. M. Dostoevsky (1821–1881): A Centenary Collection*, ed. Leon Burnett (Colchester, UK: University of Essex, 1981), 110 and 114.

9. Belknap, *The Structure of* The Brothers Karamazov, 66.

10. Rowan Williams, *Dostoevsky. Language, Faith, and Fiction* (Waco, TX: Baylor University Press, 2011), 39.

11. Eugene Vodolazkin, b. 1964, a medieval historian by profession and student of the great Soviet medievalist Dmitry Likhachev, wrote his *Lavr* in a patchwork of stylized Old Russian and contemporary speech.

12. Eugene Vodolazkin, *Laurus*, trans. Lisa C. Hayden (London: Oneworld, 2015), 90–91. Subsequent page number given in text.

13. Galina Yuzefovich, discussing *Lavr* for *Itogi* No. 8, Feb. 24, 2014, "Eto kniga, o kotoroj priyatno govorit' i dumat'. . ." [This is a book that it's pleasant to talk and think about . . . ." https://evgenyvodolazkin.ru/632_galina-yuzefovich-lavr-eto-kniga-o-kotoroj-priyatno-govorit-i-dumat/. Accessed 27 Jan. 2020.

14. See, for example, Rod Dreher's review "The Wonder-Working *Laurus*," which quotes at length from his interview with Williams, in *The American Conservative*, October 27, 2015.

15. This comment belongs to Vyacheslav Kuritsyn in his review of *Lavr* in "Odnako," 29 Jan. 2013, "Vsyo zhe, uvy, o kontse sveta" [Again, alas, about the end of the world].

16. Instructive and inspirational in this regard are the opening chapters of Terry Eagleton's *Materialism* (New Haven, CT: Yale University Press, 2016), which rescues the category from the barren caricature of positivist "dialectical materialism" in doctrinaire Marxism and re-attaches it to Thomist Aristotelianism, Spinoza, and other enlightened thinkers who "take the material world with unswerving seriousness. . . . To be a materialist in this sense is to invest human beings with a degree of dignity by seeing them as part of a material world which is identical with the Almighty. . . . There is, then, an ethical dimension to materialism as well as a political one. In the face of hubristic humanism, it insists on our solidarity with the commonplace stuff of the world. . . . What makes us moral beings is not our autonomy but our vulnerability, not our self-enclosure but our open-endedness" (4–5). Eagleton, arguing from an illuminated Catholic perspective, does not discuss Russian Orthodoxy, but there are intriguing points of contact between his rehabilitation of matter and Oliver Smith's [n.6].

17. Josef Pieper, *The Four Cardinal Virtues: Prudence, Justice, Fortitude, Temperance* [1954–59] (South Bend, IN: University of Notre Dame Press, 1966), 3–4.

18. Denys Turner, *Thomas Aquinas: A Portrait* (New Haven, CT: Yale University Press, 2013), 180.

19. Rowan Williams, *Dostoevsky,* vii–viii.

20. Opening sentence of the entry on Prudence in St Thomas Aquinas, *Summa Theologiae. A Concise Translation*, ed. Timothy McDermott (Thomas More Publishing, 1997), 376.

Appendix I

Testimony from an Array of Catholic Readers of *The Brothers Karamazov*

Martin Sheen: "I was in Paris, during that very, very sensitive period, I ran into an old and very dear friend, who became my mentor, really, and that was Terrence Malick, who was living in Paris, very kind of underground. He was on the same kind of journey I guess I was. But he saw in me this struggle and he, I guess for lack of a better term, became for me a spiritual advisor. . . . [H]e would give me material along the way. Say, "Well, Martin, I think you're ready for this." And he'd give me material. We'd talk about that. And then he'd give me another book. And the final step, I guess, in my journey was *The Brothers Karamazov*, yeah. And that did it. It got me in ways that I could not have imagined. I stayed up nights. It took me a week to read it. It was over 1,000 pages. [*laughs*] And then I finished it on—I mean, I remember very specifically, May Day in Europe is a big celebration. It's like our Labor Day. And I had [time] off from work that day. I'd finished it the night before, and I knew that I had to respond to this need within me that was now at a very critical crossroads. And that is, all right, where do you go from here? And I walked—I was living in the Left Bank at that time, and I walked over to this little Catholic church. It's the only English-speaking church in all of France, I discovered later. And it was the church where Oscar Wilde converted. I learned that later. [*laughs*] I said, "Well, I think I came to the right place." Yeah, and I came back to Catholicism, and it was the single most joyful moment of my life, because I knew that I had come home to myself. In deeply personal ways, this satisfaction has lasted all these years. I'm still on the honeymoon. [*laughs*] Go figure."[349]

Dorothy Day: "Sometimes life is so hard, we foolishly look upon ourselves as martyrs, because it is almost as though we were literally sharing in the sufferings of those we serve. It is good to remember—to clutch to our aching hearts those sayings of Fr. Zosima—'Love in practice is a harsh and dreadful thing compared to love in dreams.'"[350]

Thomas Merton writing to fellow Catholic poet Czeslaw Milosz: "The answer—the only answer I know—is that of Staretz Zossima in *The Brothers Karamazov*—to be responsible to everybody, to take upon oneself *all* guilt—but I don't know what that means. It is romantic, and I believe it is true."[351]

Walker Percy on *The Brothers Karamazov*: "Perhaps the greatest novel ever written."[352]

Hans Küng on *The Brothers Karamazov*, which he calls Dostoevsky's "greatest work": "Here too perhaps this psychologically and theologically uncannily clear-sighted author saw more deeply than others the significance of Jesus."[353]

Malcolm Muggeridge: "Supposing one were asked to name a book calculated to give an unbeliever today a clear notion of what Christianity is about, could one hope to do much better than *The Brothers Karamazov*?"[354]

Romano Guardini: "For Dostoevsky the word 'people' expresses the epitome of everything humanly authentic, deep, sustaining, etc. The people is the primordial sphere of human life, rooted, strong, and worthy of reverence. . . . Despite all its misery and sin the people constitutes the genuine human being. . . . The human being who belongs to the people relates to it through the circulation of blood, open to all that flows from the common life of family, community, and humanity."[355]

Henri de Lubac: "The mysticism of *The Brothers Karamazov* is the mysticism of the resurrection. It is eschatological. It is that of the Fourth Gospel but also that of the Apocalypse. Dostoevsky does not dream of some sort of eternity grasped in an instant. . . . Nobody had less patience for that 'impatience of limitations' (to quote Stanislas Fumet), the only effect of which is to enslave us more harshly. But no one, perhaps, has given us so much hope that one day we may be freed from them."[356]

Appendix II

Names in *The Brothers Karamazov*

Russians have three names: a first, or given name; a patronymic; and a last, or family name. Patronymics are derived from the first name of the father and are modified according to gender. A son acquires his father's first name with the ending -ovich / -evich; a daughter acquires her father's name with the ending -ovna / -evna. For example, the Karamazov brothers each have a first name—Dmitri, Ivan, and Alexey—and all receive the patronymic Fyodorovich from their father, Fyodor. He in turn received the patronymic Pavlovich from his father, whose first name must have been Pavel (Russian for Paul). If there were a Karamazov sister, her patronymic would be Fyodorovna. Family names, like patronymics, are declined according to gender. Liza Khokhlakova's deceased father would have used the name Khokhlakov (without the feminine ending); a Karamazov sister would bear the name Karamazova.

Character Names

Karamazov

Kará is the Turkish root for *black*. The Russian root *maz´* signifies tar or grease; *mazat´* means to smear, coat, paint, or soil. The name Karamazov thus means roughly "black smear." It may also evoke the Russian word *chernomazyi* (swarthy). The Russian root for *black* is *chern*, so Ilyusha's mother is translating from Turkish to Russian when she calls Alyosha "Chernomazov" (see p. 175).

Fyodor Pavlovich Karamazov

Fyodor is the Russian form of Theodore (derived from Greek meaning "gift of God").

Dmitri Fyodorovich Karamazov (Mitya, Mitka, Mitenka)

The name Dmitri is derived from the ancient Greek goddess of agriculture, Demeter. Dmitri is a popular Russian name, associated with saints worshipped in the Eastern Orthodox Church and with many figures from Russian history.

Ivan Fyodorovich Karamazov (Vanya, Vanka, Vanechka)

Ivan is the Russian form of John.

Alexey Fyodorovich Karamazov (Alyosha, Alyoshka, Alyoshechka, Lyosha, Lyoshechka)

Alexey is the name of one of the most beloved saints in the Russian Orthodox Church. (see p. 48.)

Pavel Fyodorovich Smerdyakov

Smerd has several meanings in Russian: a bad smell, a man of low origins, a slave or serf. Smerdet' means to stink.

Sophya Ivanovna

Sophya means divine wisdom in Greek. It can also be pronounced Sophya, with end stress; this sounds more sophisticated to Russian ears and is closer to the Greek pronunciation.

Agrafena Alexandrova Svetlova (Grushenka, Grusha)

Svet is Russian for light, bright; grusha means pear.

Katerina Ivanovna Verkhovtseva (Katya, Katenka)

Verkh means upper, supreme, proud in Russian; verkhovnyi means supreme.

Liza Khokhlakova (Lise)

Khokhol means the crest of a bird or a topknot in Russian. Lise is the French form of Liza; upper-class Russians like the Khokhlakovs often spoke French at home and adopted French versions of their names.

Mikhail Rakitin (Misha)

Rakitnik means broom bush in Russian.

Il*yu*sha Snegir*yov* (Il*yu*shechka)

Ilyusha and Ilyushecka are nicknames for Il'ya (Russian for Elias or Elijah). *Sneg* means snow in Russian; *snegir'* means bullfinch.

H*er*zenstube

Pronounced "Gertsenshtube" in Russian. *Herz* is heart in German; *Stube* is room or chamber.

Fetyu*k*ovich

The name implies *blockhead* in Russian.

Zo*s*ima

Pronounced "Za*s*ima" in Russian. A great elder and ascetic, Zosimas of Palestine (c. 460–560; also spelled Zosimus or Zosima) is recognized as a saint in Eastern Orthodox Christianity. While fasting and praying in the desert in preparation for Lent, he encountered St. Mary of Egypt (see p. 254).

*Kol*ya Kra*sot*kin

Kolya is the short form of Nikolai (Nicholas). Kra*sota* means *beauty* in Russian.

Grig*ory* Vasil*'yev*ich Ku*tu*zov

The name Grigory (Russian for Gregory) is derived from Greek meaning watchful or awake. Russian readers would associate the name Kutuzov with Field Marshal Mikhail Kutuzov (1745–1813), the military hero whose tactics contributed to Russia's defeat of Napoleon in 1812.

*Mar*tha Ig*nat'* yevna Ku*tu*zova

Her name may allude to the Martha in the Gospels: see John 11.1–28. (All references to the Bible are to the King James Version.)

Ma*x*imov

P*yo*tr Ale*xan*drovich *Miü*sov

Per*kh*otin

Appendix II
Nicknames

Russian is rich in nicknames and diminutives. Papa and mama, for example, yield a variety of forms, such as *papenka/mamenka* and *papasha/ mamasha*. The longer the nickname, the more intimate and affectionate it is: for example, Mitenka and Ilyushechka are more diminutive and inti- mate than Mitya and Ilyusha.

Place Names

Cher*mash*nya
Stems from the Slavonic word for vermillion or red. Dostoevsky's father bought a village named Chermashnya in 1832.

*Mo*kroe
Means wet in Russian.

Su*khoi* Pos*y*olok
Means dry hamlet in Russian.

Skotopri*gon*'evsk
Based on the word *skotoprigonka* (stockyard) derived from *skot*, Russian for cattle or livestock.

Endnotes

1. Here are Pope Francis's remarks about Orthodoxy and Dostoevsky, drawn from the press conference he gave after the 2013 World Youth Day in Brazil: "In the Orthodox Churches, they have retained that pristine liturgy, which is so beautiful. We have lost some of the sense of adoration. The Orthodox preserved it; they praise God, they adore God, they sing, time does not matter. God is at the centre, and I would like to say, as you ask me this question, that this is a richness. Once, speaking of the Western Church, of Western Europe, especially the older Church, they said this phrase to me: *Lux ex oriente, ex occidente luxus.* Consumerism, comfort, they have done such harm. Instead, you retain this beauty of God in the centre, the reference point. When reading Dostoevsky—I believe that for all of us he is an author that we must read and reread due to his wisdom—one senses what the Russian soul is, what the eastern soul is. It is something that does us much good. We need this renewal, this fresh air from the East, this light from the East. John Paul II wrote about this in his Letter. But many times the *luxus* of the West makes us lose this horizon." http://w2.vatican.va/content/francesco/en/speeches/2013/july/documents/papa-francesco_20130728_gmg-conferenza-stampa.html.

2. Wil van den Bercken summarizes much of this recent scholarship in the first chapter of his book, as does Malcolm Jones in the second chapter of *Dostoevsky and the Dynamics of Religious Experience.*

Preface: *The Brothers Karamazov* as Transformational Classic

3. For an illuminating study of the way the novel took serial form in *The Russian Messenger*, see William Todd's essay.

4. In his Pushkin speech, Dostoevsky said that Pushkin had "diagnosed [our] ailment he also gave us great hope" (*Diary* 1272). Dostoevsky points to one specific image of hope, the "literary type" of the Russian monk that Dostoevsky himself had recently formed into the character of Father Zosima, and the monk's "indisputable, humble, and majestic spiritual beauty" (*Diary* 1290). In his novel, Dostoevsky writes "the history of a certain little family" (11). In *The Love of Learning and the Desire for God*, Jean Leclercq describes the "practical," edifying purpose of western medieval *historical* chronicles: "to instruct in order to do good, and to do this in two ways. The first way is by praising God; one writes for the glory of God and in order to stimulate the reader to praise the Lord. Odericus Vitalis [one such monastic historian], without any hesitation, says several times that one must 'sing' history like a hymn in honor of Him who created the world and governs it with justice. Moreover they wanted to propose examples to be imitated if good, to be avoided if bad" (158). Although he wrote in a very different genre and context, I believe that Dostoevsky wrote his final novel with a similar intention.

5. Here and throughout, unless otherwise noted, my references to the novel will be by page number in parenthesis, using this edition: Fyodor Dostoevsky, *The Brothers Karamazov*, Norton, Second Critical Edition. Edited by Susan McReynolds Oddo.

6. See *The Analogical Imagination*, 108. For Tracy, events and persons can also be classics. As Stephen Okey notes, in Tracy's later work, such as *Fragments and Filaments*, he "seeks to overcome" some of the "elitist connotations" of the term classic. Indeed, his emphasis upon "the fragment" helps us understand Dostoevsky's "Author's Preface" in which the narrator-chronicler emphasizes the "fragmentary" quality of his hero, Alyosha, and of the novel itself, even as he points to "the heart of the whole."

7. Lest my avowal of literature's transformative capacity appear too glibly sanguine, I present two provisos. The first has been classically articulated by George Steiner: "I find myself unable to assert confidently that the humanities humanize. Indeed, I would go further: it is at least conceivable that the focusing of consciousness on a written text, which is the substance of [the humanities scholar's] pursuit, diminishes the sharpness and readiness of our actual moral response. . . . The death in the novel may move us more potently than the death in the next room" ("Educating" 61). Mikhail Mikhailovich Bakhtin saw this danger, too—but also a way through it. From the *Oxford Handbook of Religious Thought*, here is the beginning of

Caryl Emerson's essay on that Russian thinker: "In the summer of 1924, the twenty-nine-year-old Mikhail Bakhtin (1895–1975), already invalided by a chronic bone disease and without regular employment in the new Soviet state, delivered a lecture to his study circle in Leningrad on that category of religious experience he called 'grounded peace'. Prayer was key to it. The task of a philosophy of religion, Bakhtin argued, was to understand 'the form of a world in which prayer, ritual, and hope' could have validity for consciousness. Peace of mind is the product either of complacency, or of trust. Aesthetic tranquility—our mind coming to rest in a well-formed work of art—tends to be complacent. What liberates us from complacency is uneasiness or anxiety [*bespokoistvo*], which develops into repentance, a principled 'non-coincidence' of self with self. Whenever this internal bifurcation occurs, I need a Third, someone who can witness and evaluate, 'Someone who needs me to be good' and whom I can address. Thus 'the true being of the spirit begins only when repentance begins' (Pumpiansky 1923–1925, 207–9)" ("Bakhtin"). Bakhtin's insight comprises my second proviso: Realistically, a transformative encounter with literature—and the "grounded peace" that may follow—is unlikely without repentance, prayer, and action. The aesthetic experience must be followed by the theo-drama of active love. Trust in the presence of Bakhtin's "Third" grounds my hope that we can "become better people" by reading books like *The Brothers Karamazov*.

8. Ivan's telling phrase, "full latitude" (128).

9. Dorothy Day offers one prominent example: As she extended radical hospitality to the broken and homeless, she carried *The Brothers Karamazov* with her for ready inspiration. In 1976, during my senior year at Monsignor Farrell High School, I was blessed to meet and converse with Dorothy. Decades later, I visited Marquette University's archival collection of her books and perused her personal copy of the novel, with its markings. Zosima's words on active love were well marked.

10. The title of Reinhard Hütter's fine "Thomistic Study in Eschatology and Ethics." Drawing upon the work of theologian Maurice de la Taille, Michon Matthiesen's eloquent reflection is relevant: "The perfect, trinitarian state of friendship with God does not occur 'in plenitude' in this life. The journey of the contemplative is a long one, perpetually involving the willing and painful sacrifice of yet unpurified love" (237).

Chapter 1: The Analogical Imagination and Incarnational Realism

11. For an excellent, extensive discussion of this subject, see George Pattison, *God and Being*.

12. The nominalist departure from the scholastic analogical conception of being is well told, in varied ways, in a number of books, notably by Barron, Dupré, Gillespie, Gregory, Milbank, and Pfau. In brief, for the nominalist, God is pure will, not *logos*. In this sense persons are utterly separated from God, in an alienated condition of equivocal difference. Paradoxically, nominalism denied the existence of universals, yet, reductively, defined God as a being among other beings. Both moves corrode the analogical imagination in which creaturely, finite existence participates in the infinite love of the Creator.

13. "The Definition of Chalcedon." See *Documents of the Christian Church*, 54–55.

14. The "both/and" approach suggests a "Chalcedonian orientation," Mark Noll's phrase, in *Jesus Christ and the Life of the Mind*. Such an orientation accentuates "doubleness" as an intellectual disposition grounded in faith in the incarnation. The view of "doubleness"—a "both/and" approach— "seek[s] the harmonious acceptance of the dichotomy" (Noll 49), and thus discerns what I am calling, via Thomas Merton, "the hidden wholeness" of reality. Along with "doubleness," Noll points to contingency, particularity, and self-denial as integral to the Christian intellectual life. Of course, when they are experienced, none of these three realities may immediately elicit an epiphanic sense of wholeness. But incarnational realism recognizes that epiphanies emerge only with a slow passage through duration and difficulty. See also Sammon: "[A]nalogy is a principle that identifies the mutual interpenetration or harmonious togetherness of unity and diversity, of identity and difference" (144). Analogy thus fosters an approach to reality more "both/and" than "either/or" in emphasis.

15. P. H. Brazier sees in Dostoevsky more of an "either/or" than the "both/and" emphasis of my analogical approach. See especially in his emphasis upon a "dialectic between faith and reason" (80) and his claim that his "dialectics are rooted in theodicy" (81, 151). Brazier does, however, acknowledge that *The Brothers Karamazov* "presents a more balanced understanding of the human condition" (66).

16. See Leslie Farber on willingness vs. willfulness (79). For a valuable discussion of "both/and" see Terrence W. Tilley, *Inventing Catholic Tradition:* "The most general characteristic of the analogical imagination is to treat dilemmas or paired types as 'both/and' in contrast to the 'either/or' of the digital imagination" (126).

17. See Thomas Aquinas, *ST* I, q.1, a.8, ad.2: "Grace does not destroy nature but perfects it."

18. See Alan Jacobs' fine discussion of *kenosis* in *A Theology of Reading* (101–12). Jacobs quotes Dostoevsky's 1864 reflection on the death of his first wife, in which he wrote of "annihilating the self" as "the fullness of the development of the self" (105). He rightly contrasts this with Bakhtin's insistence that ethical responsibility precludes "self-evacuation" (109). Bakhtin does, however, deeply value an "ascetic self-discipline that does not eradicate the self but chastens it," and this "owes its character to the passage from Philippians in which the term *kenosis* appears" (108). I see the later Dostoevsky who composed *The Brothers Karamazov* and the early Bakhtin as fairly congruent in their validation of *kenosis*.

19. Again, Thomas Merton's helpful phrase, from his prose poem "Hagia Sophia." "There is in all visible things an invisible fecundity, a dimmed light, a meek namelessness, a hidden wholeness. This mysterious Unity and Integrity is Wisdom, the Mother of all, *Natura naturans*" (included in Lawrence Cunningham, *Master* 258). My sense of the "hidden wholeness" in Dostoevsky's novel accords with Ksana Blank's analysis of the role of "antinomy" in his work, in which "two ideas are juxtaposed as contradictory but are at the same time united into a single conceptual whole." However, whereas Blank underscores the dialectical, I emphasize the analogical. Blank turns to the Russian Orthodox theologian perhaps most noted for Sophiology: "Sergei Bukgakov clarifies this point: 'An antinomy testifies to the equal significance, equal strength, and at the same time, to the inseparability, unity, and identity of contradictory assumptions'" (14–15). Although, as Blank acknowledges, Dostoevsky did not know Chinese philosophy, her use of the Taoist yin/yang symbol as a heuristic resonates with my sense that prudential active love must incorporate the Taoist spirit of *wu wei*, a doing that is not doing. For a discussion of *wu wei*, see my essay on the Taoist philosopher "Zhuangzi."

20. The Lutheran theologian Anders Nygren rejects the *caritas* synthesis and dialectically opposes divine *agape* and human *eros*. More analogically inclined Catholics and Orthodox affirm this *caritas* synthesis. See, for

example, Martin D'Arcy, *The Mind and Heart of Love*. D'Arcy's understanding of the relation between *agape* and *eros* is closer to Dostoevsky's: "The proper way to state the problem [of the interrelation between God's *agape* and human *eros*] is surely this: that God must act with sovereign power and freedom, and we know from the New Testament and all Christian teaching that God has freely offered to man a way of life which is His own, the way of what Nygren calls Agape. God, therefore, has the initiative and by His grace does lift man up into an order of love that is above that which Nygren delineates in terms of Eros. But God does this without constraint or defiance of what is best in human nature; He makes man a co-heir with His own Divine Son without destruction of his freedom or his human personality. Grace perfects nature and does not undo it. How this can be so is precisely the mystery" (83). Catholic David Tracy writes, "As grounded in that gift of trust, *eros* will be transformed but not negated by divine *agape*. That transformation is *caritas*" (432). And Pope Benedict XVI's 2005 encyclical, *Deus Caritas Est* insists: "*Eros* and *agape*—ascending love and descending love—can never be completely separated. The more the two, in their different aspects, find a proper unity in the one reality of love, the more the true nature of love in general is realized" (7). Orthodox theologian, Vigen Guroian writes: "Eros united to agape belongs to the original image of God in humanity" (*Incarnate Love* 42).

21. As Denys Turner observes, opposition between "either/or" and "both/and" is *itself* a dialectical stance. A "true Catholic theology must be *both* 'either/or' and 'both/and'" (154).

22. In the medieval pictorial tradition, the cross is often represented as the tree of life. See, for example, the apse mosaic in the church of San Clemente, Rome or Taddeo Gaddi's fresco in the refectory Santa Croce, Florence. Dostoevsky, of course, lived in Florence for a number of months in 1868–69. I imagine that Ivan has the church of Santa Croce in mind when he confesses to Alyosha that he will visit the tombs of the great, "will fall on the ground and kiss those stones and weep over them" (199). The nave of Santa Croce holds the tombs of Galileo, Michelangelo, Machiavelli—and an empty cenotaph memorializing the exile Dante. Santa Croce's Bardi chapel is decorated by a series of late-Giotto frescoes depicting the life of St. Francis of Assisi. For an excellent account of Dostoevsky's journeys in Italy and throughout Europe, see Supino.

23. In *The Analogical Imagination*, David Tracy identifies two "cultural and ecclesiastical traditions" in Christianity (371). On the one hand, "the

route of manifestation" emphasizes the myriad ways in which grace is mediated in the world, "disclosed everywhere, in each particular" (382). On the other hand lies "the route of proclamation," in which "God comes as eschatological event, as unexpected and decisive Word addressing each and all," and which stresses that "only if God comes to disclose our true godforsakenness and our possible liberation can we be healed" (386). *The Brothers Karamazov* evinces both the route of manifestation and the route of proclamation. But, I would argue, the route of manifestation predominates: "The illumination and participation motifs of Eastern Christianity, the patristic vision of the natural goodness of all existence, the radical immanence of God in all nature, the sense of each human being as *imago Dei*—all these classic and often half-forgotten symbols of the tradition take on a new life in the theologies of the concrete, the ordinary, the everyday" (381).

24. Fred Niedner opened my eyes and ears to these complexities. See "How the Bible Handles Hatred: The Judas Factor" (1992). Available in audio link http://audio.holdenvillage.org/node/16708.

25. Von Balthasar, *Epilogue*, 122. See also C. S. Lewis, *The Great Divorce* for another modern image of hell with the possibility of an exit. Hans Urs von Balthasar discusses the orthodoxy of both Lewis's and Dostoevsky's vision of hell in *Dare We Hope . . . That All Men Are Saved?* (56–59). See also related books by David Bentley Hart and Robin Parry.

26. Hedgehog and fox is, of course, Isaiah Berlin's touchstone antithesis in *Russian Thinkers*. Marilyn McCord Adams's words are relevant here: "Because every created nature is essentially a way of imitating the Divine, each is a natural sign of some aspect of God's glory. Because each is 'almost nothing' in relation to the Infinite and Eternal, God creates the universe according to the principle of plenitude—maximum variety with maximum unity—to maximize its collective Godlikeness" (140). "Living unity" is a phrase used by Pope Francis, drawing on Romano Guardini, when describing the ways in which *The Brothers Karamazov* imagines a way of life marked by willing union as opposed to willful isolation: "By accepting with simplicity existence in the hand of God, personal will transforms into divine will and in this way, without the creature ceasing to be only a creature and God truly God, their living unity is brought about." See: http://www.vatican.va/content/francesco/en/speeches/2015/november/documents/papa-francesco_20151113_romano-guardini-stiftung.html.

27. In *Christ and Apollo*, Lynch writes: "[I]n our terms of analogy the act of existence has descended and keeps descending into every created form and possibility, adapting itself to every shape and form and difference. Is it true or not that the natural order of things has been subverted and that there has been a *new creation*, within which the one, single, narrow form of Christ of Nazareth is in process of giving its shape to everything? To think and imagine according to this form is to think and imagine according to a Christic dimension. It would also make every dimension Christic. However, like analogy itself, this would not destroy difference but would make it emerge even more sharply" (250). Lynch opposes the analogical to both the "univocal" and the "equivocal." The univocal imagination "reduces everything to a flat community of sameness," "it tends in its various ways to eliminate the unlike, the different, the pluralistic, as a kind of intractable and even hostile material" (160). The equivocal, on the other hand, sees "reality" only in its varied fragments and difference: "it . . . believes that in the whole world of reality and being no two beings are in the same sense; everything is completely diverse from everything else. . . . [D]ifference, and only difference, reigns everywhere" (176). William C. Spohn helpfully links the ways in which both Lynch and David Tracy understand the analogical imagination. As Spohn writes: "Unlike the analogical imagination, romanticism and Manicheanism fail to take particular realities seriously" (56); "The command of Jesus to 'go and do likewise' makes sense when Christians approach scripture through the analogical imagination" (60). In conversation, Mikhail Epstein and I have noted affinities between the analogical imagination and twentieth-century Russian thinker Yakov Abramov's theory of "unidiversity."

28. See, for example, Dostoevsky's notes on Katerina Ivanovna "A person fails to live throughout his life but invents himself" ("From the Notebooks", 666).

29. "Indispensable minus": this is the term that Ivan's devil employs when he defends refusing to praise God and "stick[ing] to his nasty task" in order to prevent "everything on earth [being] extinguished at once." The devil's view of reality is Manichaean and a lie. He claims to practice "good sense" but presents a buffoonish travesty of prudence (545).

30. "The Transtheoretical Model (also called the Stages of Change Model), developed by Prochaska and DiClemente in the late 1970s, evolved through studies examining the experiences of smokers who quit on their own with those requiring further treatment to understand why some

people were capable of quitting on their own." See http://sphweb.bumc.
bu.edu/otit/MPH-Modules/SB/BehavioralChangeTheories/BehavioralCh-
angeTheories6.html.

31. A recurring theme in the novel: Ivan's devil says, "'I am a sort of
phantom in life who has lost all ends and beginnings, and who has even
forgotten his own name." He gives the same sideward glance to Ivan that
Madame Khokhlakova gives to Zosima: "You are laughing—no, you
are not laughing, you are angry again" (emphasis added; 540). It is this
overweening anxiety about one's image in the eyes of another that Zosima
claims could cause Madame Khokhlakova's life to "slip away like a phantom" (55) and that Alyosha will describe to Kolya as "a sort of insanity. The
devil has taken the form of that vanity and entered into the whole generation; it's simply the devil" (470).

32. C. S. Lewis's point is similar: "the doors of hell are locked on the
inside" (*Pain* 130). Platonically, Hart questions that any rational person
could knowingly and willfully choose hell: "for a rational spirit to see the
good and know it truly is to desire it insatiably and to obey it uncondition-
ally, while not to desire it is not to have known it truly, and so never to
have been to choose" (*Universal* 79–80).

33. "Cuts against the grain": Ivan's devil twice uses this phrase to justify his
irrational and willful actions, and I will employ it throughout this study.
See Louis Dupré on modernity's shift from ontology to epistemology:
"Epistemology became a substitute for metaphysics. It failed to address
the fundamental ontological questions raised by the new function of the
subject: How does that subject's constitution of meaning and value affect
the very nature of the real?" (*Passage,* 161).

34. Servais Pinckaers, O.P. sees the perverse "freedom of indifference"
as characteristic of modernity and, like others, notes its genesis in the
thought of William of Ockham's late medieval nominalism. He contrasts
the nominalist notion of freedom with St. Thomas's realism. For Thomas,
free will unites "reason and will, knowledge and love in the act of choice.
This places the image of God in the power humans have to act on their
own, in mastery and moral responsibility" (137). In contrast, "The image
of God in humanity now consists in the sheer self-determined voluntarism
that characterizes freedom of indifference. Like God and confronting God,
this man takes his stance by his own will in a free act. But this independent
stance is precisely what isolates human freedom from the freedom of God,
and from every other freedom, leaving him in *isolation*" (142; emphasis

added). The last words could have come from Mikhail's speech to Zosima (261–62). Pinckaers' distinction between "self-determined voluntarism" and St. Thomas's realism is consonant with Dostoevsky's contrast between the self-assertion of the "god-man" and the theosis of Godmanhood. See also Michael Martin's critique of "postmodern nominalist degradation" of personhood (33), and his alternative proposal of "Catholic Sophiology."

35. But, with David Tracy, "I do not believe that *only* the Catholic theological and artistic imagination is an analogical one" (*Filaments* 16; emphasis added).

36. George Pattison observation is helpful: "These 'Russian' features are mostly received positively by Dostoevsky's religiously-minded readers, even Western ones, although other 'Russian' themes, such as the idea of Russia as a 'God-bearing nation' are more controversial. It is true that *Demons* presents this idea as having been taught by Stavrogin the arch-'demon' (*Demons*, II, 1.7), but *The Diary of a Writer* shows Dostoevsky embracing a strong view of Russia's divine vocation, culminating in the declaration that 'Constantinople will be ours', i.e., that, as the historic defender of Orthodoxy, Russia is providentially destined to rule Constantinople (1876, June: Ch. 2 and 1877, March: Ch. 1). This political fantasy seems hardly to fit with the humility of the Russian Christ said to have passed through Russia in the incognito of a peasant, yet myths of national abasement and violent rhetoric are often interwoven in modern political discourse. But whilst we certainly cannot deny the challenge of interpreting the connection between Dostoevsky's Christianity and his politics, it would be an injustice to portray him as a blind nationalist who was unappreciative of Western European civilization. His own literary and intellectual debts to that civilization were great and were acknowledged. Yet, clearly, he believed that the West had taken a wrong turn in its religious development and that Russia was uniquely called to amend this." ("Dostoevsky"). I believe part of Dostoevsky's antipathy toward Catholicism was inspired by Vatican I's conciliar declaration in 1870 of the pope's infallibility in matters of faith and morals. For a helpful discussion of the infallibility issue, see O'Malley, *Vatican I*.

37. For Bakhtin's later reflections on "outsideness" see his "Response to a Question from *Novy Mir*," in which he writes: "Creative understanding does not renounce itself, its own place in time, its own culture; and it forgets nothing. In order to understand, it is immensely important for the person who understands to be located outside the object of his or her

creative understanding—in time, in space, in culture" (*Speech Genres* 7). See also Chapter 5 in Caryl Emerson, *The First Hundred Years*. Gadamer discusses the inevitability and possible fruitfulness of "prejudice" in *Truth and Method*, 269–77; "we are always situated in traditions" (282). George Pattison's observation is germane: "Like other great writers, Dostoevsky can be different things to different readers. A literary text is not a scientific research paper from which we might expect well-defined and unambiguous outcomes. As a field of manifold literary, existential, and spiritual possibilities, neither internal nor external differences derogate from its value or from its trans-cultural significance. On the contrary, they may be integral to it. It is because Shakespeare is richer with diverse possibilities than Webster that he remains more read and more performed—and much the same can be said of Dostoevsky and many of his Russian and non-Russian contemporaries" ("Dostoevsky").

38. Formula of the Fourth Lateran Council (1215).

39. I draw here from Chapter Two of Smith's *What Is a Person?* This chapter outlines Smith's "three key critical resources" for his "theory of personhood: critical realism, philosophical personalism, and an anti-naturalistic phenomenological epistemology" (91); the chapter's footnotes alone comprise an invaluable resource for anyone who wishes, as did Dostoevsky, to reflect deeply on "the person in the person."

40. David Bentley Hart's reflections on human consciousness are apt: "We could never know the world from a purely receptive position. To know anything, the mind must be actively disposed toward things outside itself, always at work interpreting experience through concepts that only the mind itself can supply. The world is intelligible to us because we reach out to it, or reach beyond it, coming to know the endless diversity of particular things within the embrace of a more general and abstract yearning for a knowledge of truth as such, and, by way of an aboriginal inclination of the mind toward reality of a comprehensible whole. In every moment of awareness, the mind at once receives and composes the world, discerning meaning in the objects of experience precisely in conferring meaning upon them; thus consciousness lies open to—and enters into intimate communion with—the forms of things" (*Existence* 238–39). Similarly, for Jacques Maritain, "when it comes to knowledge of sensible objects, for example, the mind has both a passive role (receiving sense impressions) and an active one (constructing knowledge from these impressions)." See: https://plato.stanford.edu/entries/maritain.

41. In his *Notes*, Dostoevsky wrote: "With full realism, to find the man [or the human] in the man. . . . They call me a psychologist: not true: I am only a realist in a higher sense, i.e., I depict all the depths of the human soul" (cited by Fanger, 215). Peter Winsky notes that "in his letter of August 16, 1839, Fyodor Mikhailovich wrote to his brother Mikhail Mikhailovich that "the person is a mystery. . . . I am studying that mystery because I want to become a person." F. M. Dostoevsky, *Polnoe sobranie sochinenii v tridsati tomakh*. vol. 28(I), ed. Bazanov et al., (Leningrad: Nauka 1972–90), 63. Translation is Peter Gregory Winsky's ("'To Uncover the Secret of the Person, While Preserving the Secret as a Secret'—A Review of the Bulgarian Dostoevsky Society's International Symposium *The Anthropology of Dostoevsky*" https://bloggerskaramazov.com.

42. While Malcolm Jones calls these words "vitally important" (*Dynamics* 129), I agree with Rowan Williams that Dostoevsky does more than "leave the door clearly open to 'minimal religion'" (*Dostoevsky* 211). Robert Belknap wisely encourages Karamazov scholars to attend to "the literary density of the strong passages" (*Genesis* 90) and this is certainly one such passage.

43. Joseph Frank's commentary is helpful: "Dostoevsky rather incautiously spoke of the utterances of Zosima in Book 6 as having been designed specifically to answer the accusations of Ivan against God, but he did so to pacify the fears of Pobedonostsev that the reply would not be as powerful as the attack. Later, however, in an entry in his notebook set down after the work had been completed, he wrote that 'the *whole book*' was a reply to the Legend of the Grand Inquisitor [and, we might add, 'Rebellion'] (27:48)" (*Writer* 850; emphasis added). The idea of "the whole" is a crucial recurring image, pointed to by Father Paissy (152) and Father Zosima (278).

44. Title of John D. Zizioulas's book.

45. See the work of Dostoevsky's younger, more ecumenical friend Vladimir Soloviev, who emphasizes the reality of coinherence and wholeness (in Russian *tsel'nost*). My thanks to Caryl Emerson for this connection. "Coinherence" also translates the key theological term *perichoresis*, which "has variously been rendered in English as 'interpenetration,' 'coinherence,' 'mutual indwelling,' and 'mutual immanence' . . ." (Twombly 1). In his study, Alexandar Mihailovic notes the ways in which Bakhtin refers "to the patristic concept of perichoresis that figures in a number of post-Chalcedonian discussions of the Trinity" (138) and "the parallels between Solovyov and Bakhtin" in this regard (141).

46. Since I will refer to Zosima's phrase "precious image of Christ" throughout the book, I will not repeat the page reference (276), except as needed.

47. Zosima's emphasis on "measure" is congruent with that of Thomas Aquinas, who "expressly compares, under the aspect of 'measure,' the relation of reality and knowledge and the relation of the practical reason to concrete moral action. Both relations are symbolized by the image of the relation of the artist and his work" (Pieper, "Reality" 164). Relatedly, Maritain emphasizes prudence as integral to artistic creation in *The Responsibility of the Artist* (1960). https://maritain.nd.edu/jmc/etext/resart.htm.

48. According to his editor William Shannon, Merton used this phrase in a lecture at Smith College on April 13, 1967. Merton spoke of "the happiness of being one with everything in that *hidden ground of love* for which there can be no explanation." Shannon continues: "These words which see God not as a being among other beings but as the ground of all beings, and even more precisely the ground of love in which all beings find their identity and uniqueness, provide a most appropriate title for this volume" ("Introduction" *Love* ix). Merton's phrase suggests the grounding for Dostoevsky's incarnational realism, and I will employ it from time to time in this study.

49. See Gary Saul Morson, "The God of Onions." Morson describes Dostoevsky's final novel as evincing "the mythic prosaic" or "Christianized prosaics."

50. For a reading of the "doubting Thomas" (John 20) that is quite close in spirit to his friend Dostoevsky's, see Vladimir Soloviev's "Seven Paschal Letters" in which he writes: "If the unbelief of Thomas had resulted from a crude materialism which reduced all truth to sensory evidence, then having been convinced palpably in the fact of the resurrection, he would have invented for himself some kind of materialistic explanation and would not have exclaimed, 'My Lord and My God!'" (96). Soloviev contrasts Thomas's "conscientious unbelief," "thirsting only for a complete and final attestation in perfected truth" with the "cunning belief" which is "consciously indulged to excess with various half-truths out of a hostile fear before the full truth" (97). In my reading of the novel, Rakitin, the "seminarian on the make" (in Pevear/Volokhonsky's translation) stands in stark contrast to Alyosha, and represents this latter, willful "cunning unbelief." Relatedly, Liza Knapp demonstrates, Dostoevsky believed that only eternal life could offers an alternative to the materialist teachings that posit only "universal

inertia and the mechanization of matter" and "death" (2). However,
"[w]hile the theoretical choice between the alternatives was easily made
in favor of God and the 'true philosophy' [of faith], the 'annihilation of
inertia' that would result in eternal life was not easily effected. Dostoevsky
rejected materialism as a teaching, but he understood that man, as a material creature, is subject to the laws governing the matter in the universe,"
including the law of death. In the incarnation, of course, Christ "becomes
matter," dies, and rises bodily. Knapp rightly observes that Zosima is no
Platonist in his attitude toward the body, but "represents what has been
called the 'biblical understanding of man as a soul and body, which will
both be saved as a unit' . . . and is in keeping that part of the Orthodox
[and orthodox!] tradition that had emphasized the integral role of the
body in salvation" (*Inertia* 200).

51. "[Rakitin's] kind of 'seeing' . . . has nothing at all in common with
Zosima's deep perspicacity, his sagacity, his prophetic intuition . . ." (Buzina
71).

52. Victor Terras writes: "A 'realist,' according to Dostoevsky, is a person
who lives and thinks in terms of an immediately, or intuitively, given
reality. The opposite, then, is the 'theoretician' (*teortetik*), who seeks to
create and to realize a subjective world of his own." (*Companion*, 137).
Dostoevsky's distinction between "realist" and "theoretician" is analogous
to Gary Saul Morson's opposition of "prosaics" to "theoretism." William
Lynch's distinction between the analogical and univocal imaginations, and
his sharp and simultaneous affirmation of difference within similarity may
remain a vital alternative to critical reductiveness. See my essay, "William
Lynch's *Christ and Apollo* and the Field of Religion and Literature" for
further discussion of these ideas. Also relevant here is Rowan Williams's
appreciation of von Balthasar's analogical imagination: "[W]hat then is
analogy? It is the active presence of the divine liberty, love and beauty precisely within the various and finite reality of material/temporal reality. 'The
divine' is not present in creation in the form of 'hints of transcendence,'
points in the created order where finitude and creatureliness appear to
thin out or open up into a mysterious infinity, but in creation itself—which
includes, paradigmatically, creation being itself in unfinishedness, time-
taking, pain and death. The crucified Jesus is, in this context, the ground
and manifestation of what analogy means. . . . Here is a theological
language which can make some claim to have gone beyond the sterile opposition of undifferentiated presence/identity on the one hand [what, with

Lynch, I call the univocal] and unthinkable difference [what, with Lynch, I call the equivocal] on the other." ("Balthasar" 80; 82).

53. Dreyfuss and Taylor call theirs a "pluralist, robust realism" and rightly point out that naturalist explanations like Rakitin's have a place within a fuller understanding of reality. The incarnational realism Dostoevsky portrays in this novel "need not conflict with the laws of physics and chemistry" (159). Rakitin's reductive realism, however, denies such a robust "both/and" vision.

54. Randall Poole observes, "Confession is the act in which I realize that I am not adequate to myself, that I cannot complete myself. . . . A confession is made, Bakhtin repeatedly says, in penitent tones ("A&H" 57, 128, 141ff.) With this, he introduces the key apophatic image of repentance. In Vladimir Lossky's words, 'the apophatic way of Eastern theology is the repentance of the human person before the face of the living God'" (*MTEC* 238). On this point there is indeed a striking similarity between Lossky and Bakhtin" ("Apophatic" 165).

55. "Evidently [Dostoevsky] often doubted in the sense of being unsure; but he does not say that he ever *disbelieved*, only that he is a child of age of disbelief and doubt. A plausible reading of the text is that he is lamenting his frequent lack of confidence in his religious beliefs, not the absence of the beliefs themselves; his 'thirst for faith' is a search for the kind of perfect certainty in which 'the truth shines through.' Similarly, when in a late notebook he writes of his Christian convictions that 'my *hosanna* has come through a great *furnace of doubts*', we need not interpret that statement as indicating a loss of belief at any time; the hosanna may have weakened but it survived the furnace. And when in *A Writer's Diary* he speaks of having taken Christ into his soul 'anew' through his contact with the common people in prison, he explains that he is referring to 'the Christ whom I had known . . . as a child but almost lost when in my turn I became a European liberal'" ("Immortality," Scanlan 2).

56. While in prison, Dostoevsky closely read and marked his New Testament, a gift of N. D. Fonvizina, and, as Brazier notes, "a large group of markings relate to resurrection—one of Dostoevsky's central concerns" (44).

57. From the *Catechism of the Catholic Church*: "*Prudence* is the virtue that disposes practical reason to discern our true good in every circumstance and to choose the right means of achieving it; 'the prudent man looks

where he is going' (Prov. 14:15). 'Keep sane and sober for your prayers'
(1 Peter 4:7). Prudence is 'right reason in action,' writes St. Thomas Aquinas, following Aristotle (*Summa* II-II, 47,2). It is not to be confused with
timidity or fear, nor with duplicity or dissimulation. It is called *auriga vir-
tutum* (the charioteer of the virtues); it guides the other virtues by setting
rule and measure. It is prudence that immediately guides the judgement
of conscience. The prudent man determines and directs his conduct in accordance with this judgement. With the help of this virtue we apply moral
principles to particular cases without error and overcome doubts about the
good to achieve and the evil to avoid." (Section 1806) http://www.vatican.
va/archive/ccc_css/archive/catechism/p3s1c1a7.htm.

58. Wittgenstein's phrase in *Philosophical Investigations* (sections 106–7)
when discussing the need to return to "the subjects of our everyday thinking" and ordinary language: "We want to walk: so we need friction. Back
to the rough ground!" http://topologicalmedialab.net/xinwei/classes/read-
ings/Wittgenstein/pi_94–138_239–309.html. The phrase lends the title
to Joseph Dunne's *Back to the Rough Ground: "Phronesis" and "Techne" in
Modern Philosophy and in Aristotle*.

59. Catholicism has traditionally emphasized the interdependence of
faith and reason, "the two wings of the human soul," as Pope John Paul II
called them in his encyclical, *Fides et Ratio*. In this sense, I see a distinctly
"Catholic" dimension in Dostoevsky's art. As Frank notes, "for Dostoevsky
[Catholicism] was not true Christianity" (337), and he intended "The
Legend of the Grand Inquisitor" to be "directed 'against Catholicism and
the papacy'" (*Mantle* 438). In a personal letter dated November 26, 1996,
Professor Frank generously responded to my query regarding what I dis-
cerned in Dostoevsky's final novel as a "Catholic" appreciation of practical
reason and its relation to faith. Here is part of Professor Frank's kind letter:
"As for the *BK*, I agree with you that Dostoevsky now wanted to show
Christian morality in more practical, but not utilitarian, terms. The reason
is that it was being accepted once again by the radicals, who had tried to
replace it in the 1860s with 'rational egoism' and that battle had been won.
Dostoevsky's aim now was to show that such morality—which he felt to be
that of the Russian people—could not be *really* accepted without accepting
a supernatural God as well, just as the people did. You are right about the
shift in accent, but I'm not sure that it involves any new theological position. Aleksey may be rational, but it is a rationality that comes from an
irrational faith; it is this faith that helps him to see the *truth* that Dimitry is
innocent. Without the faith, he would reason like Rakitin."

60. My emphasis upon the communal dimension of Dostoevsky aligns with Catholic theologian Romano Guardini: "If [Karl] Barth and [Eduard] Thurneysen found in Dostoevsky an almost Kierkegaardian individualism, Catholic readings, such as those of Romano Guardini, found the Russian's emphasis on community to be key to his importance" (Pattison "Dostoevsky").

61. David Tracy aptly writes: "Catholic analogical theologians use apophatic language as an always-already necessary but not sufficient aspect of all analogical theology. . . . Analogy is an alternative to equivocal language, a danger for all radically apophatic language without a corresponding cataphatic element" (*Fragments* 372-73).

62. See Nel Grillaert's essays and Malcolm Jones (*Dynamics* 139-46) on the theme of silence in Dostoevsky. See also John Givens (50-58). Denis Zhernokleyev, for example, reads the "Cana of Galilee" chapter with a much greater apophatic emphasis—and more caution toward the cataphatic—than do I: "The latest of the four gospels to be composed, the Gospel of John is permeated with awareness of the aesthetic danger that is inherent to incarnational truth of Christology. The apophaticism of Johannine theology, therefore must be seen as a reaction to the potential for aestheticization inherent to the synoptic gospels. The miracle at Cana of Galilee is where the 'apophatic logic' of the Johannine text manifests itself most obviously. By announcing resurrection at the outset of the gospel, the miracle at Cana places the fullness of a religious experience outside the narrative and therefore in a negative relationship to it." (I draw here from Denis's book-in-progress, *Dostoevsky's Apophatic Novel*. I am very grateful to Denis for sharing a chapter of this most promising book with me.) See also Denis's essay on "Mimetic Desire in *The Idiot*."

63. In that letter, Dostoevsky also famously wrote: "if someone succeeded in proving to me that Christ was outside the truth, and if, *indeed*, the truth was outside Christ, then I would sooner remain with Christ than with the truth" (*Letters* 68). Czeslaw Milosz criticizes this claim: "Those who would choose the truth are probably more honorable, even if the truth appears on the surface to deny Christ (as Simone Weil argued). At least they are not relying on their fantasy and not constructing idols in their own image" (*To Begin* 283). (Milosz is one Catholic who admits to not trusting Dostoevsky, largely, he admits, due to the author's rabid anti-Polonism, which especially mars the Mokroe scene in *The Brothers Karamazov*.) See "Dostoevsky" in *Milosz's ABC's*. James P. Scanlan, however, insists that Dostoevsky's

claim in this letter is "far from an unqualified rejection of rational demands. The full statement consists of three clauses, the second of which is
typically overlooked: '[1] If someone were to prove to me that Christ were
outside the truth, and [2] it *really* were the case that the truth is outside
Christ, [3] I would prefer to remain with Christ than with the truth.' . . .
By the second clause Dostoevsky requires in effect that it genuinely be *true*
that the truth lies outside Christ before he will choose the latter—a confused and no doubt unintentional bow to the authority of truth even when,
in a transport of religious enthusiasm, he sought to dramatize his devotion
to faith by sacrificing truth to it. And of course he did *not* think that the
truth lay outside Christ" ("Immortality" 17).

64. See Frank, *Writer* 399–401.

65. Dmitri decries Rakitin's reduction of personhood to brain chemistry:
"I see and think because of those tails [nerve endings], not at all because
I've got a soul, and that I am some sort of image and likeness" (497).

66. My understanding of Dostoevsky's valuing of practical reason is consonant with A. Boyce Gibson's reading. In *Crime and Punishment*, Gibson
distinguishes "between *razsudok* and *razum*, . . . theorizing and good
sense. . . . The distinction between *razsudok* and *razum* serves the purpose
of bringing practice together within the bounds of reason without destroying its distinctiveness as practice" (99).

67. Like Kaplan and Coolman, Andrew M. Greenwell cites Nichols' book
on Newman, and notes further: "The illative sense is what allows us to take
our concrete human experiences—whether they be of nature's beauty, of
the demands of conscience (the feeling of guilt, the pangs of remorse, the
search for forgiveness), of the sense of the contingency of life, of the peace-
ful joy elicited by the shallow breathing of your sleeping child beside you
in bed, of the honor given to a soldier who sacrificed his life for his fellows,
of the haunting beauty of the second movement of Schubert's Piano Sonata
in A major, of the pathos of G. M. Hopkins' poem "Spring and Fall," of
indeed any created good or beautiful thing—and come to the conclusion
that there must be a transcendent reality behind it all, ultimately, He whom
we call or know as God." http://www.catholic.org/homily/yearoffaith/story.
php?id=48296.

68. See Reinhard Huttar's emphasis upon the communal character of
beatitude in Aquinas (437–45). Huttar writes: "Charity, the love of friendship with God, is the cause of the love of friendship with the neighbor, that

is, all the other blessed. What begins in the life of the *viator* by sanctifying grace, is completed in the eternal life in the *comprehensor* by the light of glory. . . . The *communicatio* or *conversio* constitutive of the heavenly friendship ceaselessly flows in the beatific vision from the life of the triune God that is charity to the blessed and returns as charity to the triune God, including in the charity shared among the heavenly *communio* of the blessed. Like the resurrection body, the companionship of friends does not increase beatitude, but rather extends beatitude into the fully embodied and comprehensively communal existence of all the blessed" (*Bound for Beatitude* 441–42). Huttar's discussion of prudence (164–74) is also very helpful.

69. Nietzsche said that "Dostoevsky was the only psychologist from whom I have learned anything," although he did not read *The Brothers Karamazov*. Dostoevsky did not know the work of Nietzsche, but I concur fully with Berdyaev's claim in his book on the Russian novelist: "Dostoevsky knew everything that Nietzsche knew but he also knew something that Nietzsche did not know." I use Robert Louis Jackson's translation from *Dialogues* 328, n.1). For more recent work on Nietzsche and Dostoevsky see Maia Stepenberg's fine study and the collection of essays edited by Jeff Love and Jeffrey Metzger.

70. René Girard also observes the affinities among these three great works of the Christian imagination and, implicitly, emphasizes the novel's "incarnational realism": "Honest realism and true realism triumph over the chimeras of the underground" (*Resurrection* 72). Further, Dostoevsky "regard[s] himself as a sinner" and the experience he represents "does not differ essentially from that of Saint Augustine or Dante. This is why the structure of *The Brothers Karamazov* is close to the form of *The Confessions* and *The Divine Comedy*. It is the structure of the Incarnation, . . . [t]he form of the incarnation . . . becomes identical with the work itself" (*Resurrection* 73). (My thanks to former student and scholar Jessica Hooten Wilson for this reference to Girard.) Deborah Martinsen also notes connections between *The Brothers Karamazov* and *Confessions* and *Commedia* (*Surprised* 16). Joseph Frank justly places *Karamazov* alongside other great works—*King Lear*, *Paradise Lost*, and *Faust*—but its Christocentric vision links it especially to those of Augustine and Dante. Harriet Murav draws on John Freccero's analysis of the pattern of conversion in Dante, and observes a similar pattern in *The Brothers Karamazov*, specifically in its repeated pattern of descent and ascent, which she links to the structure of certain icons. She calls the novel a "narrative icon in which the stories

of the brothers and the structure of the novel mirror each other. The icon consists of three parts: *katabasis*, or descent into hell; trial; and resurrection, or ascent" (135).

71. The "retrieval" to which Auerbach points finds an analogue in Rémi Brague's affirmation of scholastic realism in *Curing Mad Truths*. He writes: "a) If we think of God on the analogy of a rational being, creation will become less opaque and unintelligible. We will find in ourselves an equivalent of the creative act whose presence we suppose in him. . . . b)We can become the dialogue partners of a rational Being. His will underlies the whole show. Not a blind desire, not a whim, but a benevolent, reasonable will, suffused with wisdom and logos, that has put us and, together with us, whatever led to our being, from the remotest galaxy to our parents, into being out of sheer love. We will be, literally, on speaking terms with God. Prayer will become a meaningful enterprise, and together with it intellectual inquiry into the logic underlying an intelligible world, that is, science. . . . Freedom is the unfolding of what we really and essentially are, in the core of our being" (65–66).

72. Pedgrag Cicovacki claims that "the well-educated Ivan knows that Goethe uses Pater Seraphicus as a character in his *Faust*—Ivan is more familiar with foreign tradition than his own" (*Affirmation* 283). Cicovacki notes that "of all Goethe's works, *Faust* made the most profound impression on Dostoevsky. He read it in German for the first time when he was seventeen" ("*Faust*" 153).

73. This is not to say that icons do not present narrative. Numerous narrative icons exist, such as those of the Nativity or Saint's lives. But these icons remain consistent in their stylized representation of a transfigured reality, rather than the naturalistic, though grace-infused representation of prosaic reality typical of Giotto and others. An icon of "Our Lady of Sorrows" hung in Dostoevsky's study, but so too did a copy Raphael's "Sistine Madonna" which, according to his wife Anna, was "the painting he considered the finest manifestation of human genius" (quoted by Miller, *Unfinished Journey* 9). The Raphael was a treasured birthday gift from his wife Anna, presented to her by his ecumenical friend Vladimir Solovyov, himself an inspiration for the character of Alyosha. Despite his virulent attacks on the West and Catholicism, Dostoevsky's artistic imagination evinced both Orthodox and Catholic tastes.

74. St. Ireneaus on recapitulation: "[Christ] recapitulates in Himself all the nations dispersed since Adam, and all the languages and generations of men, including Adam himself" (von Balthasar, *Incarnation* 64).

75. Numerous figural patterns are observed by Nina Perlina: "The authority of the Bible subordinates and structures the entire sum of individual 'moralities' in *The Brothers Karamazov*. . . . Within the framework of Erich Auerbach's theory [articulated in his essay "Figura"], Biblical narrative, the most authoritative and universal text that has ever existed, engulfs all the individual discoveries made by Dostoevsky's heroes. A figural interpretation of the novel tends to saturate occurrences of everyday life with the spirit of eternity" (12–13). Diane Oenning Thompson also sees the image of Christ as central to the novel, and the foundation of figural and recapitulative readings. She emphasizes the vital role of memory in the process of conversion, and contrasts Dostoevsky's realism with that of his contemporaries (*Memory* 223). Rowan Williams argues that the christological dimension of the novel is integral to its dialogic form. Like David S. Cunningham, Bruce Ward observes the novel's trinitarian form and writes: "*The Brothers Karamazov*, in particular, can be regarded as a sort of 'hymn' to the Trinity: it is indeed one of the most significant expressions of Trinitarian thought to be found in any modern text" (*Redeeming* 202). In Christian theology, christological reflection is integrally related to reflection of the Trinity.

76. As Frei writes: "[S]ince the world truly rendered by combining biblical narratives into one was indeed the one and only real world, it must in principle embrace the experience of any present age and reader. Not only was it possible for him, it was also his duty to fit himself into that world in which he was in any case a member, and he too did so in part by figural interpretation and in part of course by his mode of life. He was to see his disposition, his actions and passions, the shape of his own life as well as that of the era's events as figures of that storied world" (3).

77. Joseph Frank observes that in the narrator, Dostoevsky "creat[ed] a figure that evokes a 'modernized' version of the tone and attitude typical of the pious narrators of the hagiographical lives of Russian saints," "an up-to-date version of the pious, reverent, hesitant, hagiographical style of the Russian religious tradition" (*Prophet* 573). Victor Terras points out, "The narrator's manner is that of a 'conversation with the reader,' and his vocabulary and syntax tend to be those of an oral narrative: sentences and paragraphs are not well-constructed and well-balanced . . ." (*Companion*

87). Robin Feuer Miller describes the narrator-chronicler as "chatty, often digressive" (*Worlds* 16).

78. Auerbach goes on to describe what might be called an "Augustinian" aesthetic: "The lowly or humble style is the only medium in which such sublime mysteries can be brought within the reach of men. It constitutes a parallel to the Incarnation, which was also a *humilitas* in the same sense, for men could not have endured the splendor of Christ's divinity. But the Incarnation, as it actually happened on earth, could only be narrated in a lowly and humble style. The birth of Christ in a manger in Bethlehem, his life among fishermen, publicans, and other common men, the Passion with its realistic and scandalous episodes—none of this could have been treated appropriately in the lofty oratorical, tragic, or epic style. According to the Augustan esthetic, such matters were worthy, at best, of the lower literary genres. But the lowly style of Scripture encompasses the sublime. Simple, vulgar, and crassly realistic words are employed, the syntax is often collo-quial and inelegant; but the sublimity of the subject matter shines through the lowliness, and there is hidden meaning at every turn. . . . The common denominator of this style is its humility" (*"Sermo Humilis"* 51–52).

79. "[Y]ou're like a little child, . . . that's how we look on you . . . ," says Andrey, the coach driver to Dmitri on his frantic, prayerful ride to Mokroe (389), where he will become "a new man."

80. Even before Bakhtin had been translated into English, Gibson noted the link between polyphony and *kenosis* and rightly observed that "any novelist of any quality allows his creatures room to grow in" (70). In this light, he makes an interesting comparison between Dostoevsky and Doro-thy Sayers (68–69).

81. Of course, silence can itself be passive-aggressive power ploy; some may read Christ's silence in Ivan's poem in this way. I read it as non-coercive love. "Christ's essential identity lies in being *pro nobis* and *pro me*; Christ is he who exists for my and our sake. If Christ for a moment sought to coerce my response, that would mean that he ceased to be 'for me' in this radical sense; he would be seeking to implement his will as a rival to mine, and this is precisely what he has forgone in becoming human" (Williams, *Christ* 190).

82. Robin Miller cites Dutch scholar J. M. Meijer who, in 1958, first noted "situation rhyme" in *The Brothers Karamazov*.

Chapter 2: Beauty and Re-formation

83. In *Either/Or* Volume II, even Kierkegaard makes clear that the ethical can include the aesthetic; that "'the flesh' is not sensuousness, it is selfishness" and that "the joy and the fullness which is found in the sensuous when it is innocent can well be admitted to Christianity.... [L]et us not be too spiritual" (50).

84. Aidan Nichols cites this line from "Revelation" as well as the one previously cited in his chapter on "Form" in *A Key to Balthasar*. I have found Nichols' numerous works on von Balthasar to be very helpful.

85. Here is a more complete excerpt from this important letter, the first Dostoevsky wrote upon his release from prison, to the woman who gave him the copy of the New Testament that he read during his years of confinement: "And not because you are religious, but because I myself have experienced and felt it, I shall tell you that at such a time one thirsts for faith as 'the withered grass' thirsts for water, and one actually finds it, because in misfortune the truth shines through. I can tell you about myself that I am a child of this century, a child of doubt and disbelief, I have always been and shall ever be (that I know), until they close the lid of my coffin. What terrible torment this thirst to believe has cost me and is still costing me, and the stronger it becomes in my soul, the stronger are the arguments against it. And, despite all this, God sends me moments of great tranquility, moments during which I love and find I am loved by others; and it was during such a moment that I formed within myself a symbol of faith in which all is clear and sacred for me. This symbol is very simple, and here is what it is: to believe that there is nothing more beautiful, and more perfect than Christ; and there not only isn't, but I tell myself with a jealous love, there cannot be. More than that—if someone succeeded in proving to me that Christ was outside the truth, and if, *indeed*, the truth was outside Christ, I would sooner remain with Christ than with the truth" (*Selected Letters* 68). A. Boyce Gibson notes that in this letter to Fonvizina, Dostoevsky uses the Russian word *istina*, "a word technically specified to denote theoretical truth," whereas by the time of *The Brothers Karamazov* he had moved to a conception of truth as *"pravda-spravedlivost'*, truth as righteousness" (23). Sammon makes a comparable point: "In choosing Christ over the truth, Dostoevsky exhibits a similarity with a Kierkegaardian account of faith that is willing to pass beyond, even die to, truth as analytic clarity of concepts and categories, a truth that has been reduced to a mere expression of human thought, and instead inhabit the truth of a God who inhabits

life and death" (126). Ksana Blank's illuminating discussion of *istina* and
pravda shows how each Russian word for truth has dialectically conflicting
meanings, and concludes: "[Dostoevsky's] works advocate the wholeness
of truth, viewing their counterparts not in their negation of each other but
in their constant dynamic interplay" (98). I agree with Steven Cassedy and
find Dostoevsky's "religious nationalism" to be the "least interesting" part
of his religious vision (181). Ecumenically minded Soloviev tried to address this issue with Dostoevsky.

86.   Forms of the word "truth" appear 148 times in Garnett's English
translation of novel. W. J. Leatherbarrow notes that for Dostoevsky "lying
is a demonic condition, [and] is taken up again in various modulations
throughout the novel" (141).

87.   Robert Louis Jackson's integrative summary of Dostoevsky's various
jottings is very helpful: "At the center of Dostoevsky's Christian aesthetic—
as it becomes more explicit in his notebooks and *belles lettres* in the last
decade of his life—is the image of Christ. . . . 'The moral ideal is Christ.'
Yet again, 'not Christ's morality, not his teaching will save the world, but
precisely faith that the Word became flesh. This faith is not alone intellectual recognition of his teaching, but direct attraction. One must believe
precisely that this is the final ideal of man, the whole embodied Word, God
embodied.' . . . Christ came so that mankind might know that the human
spirit can be in heavenly glory 'in fact and in flesh, and not only in the
dream and in the ideal.' 'Beauty will save the world,' Dostoevsky observed
in his notebooks to *The Idiot*. 'The world will become the beauty of Christ,'
we read in the notebooks to *The Devils*" (*Form* 56). See David Lyle Jeffrey
on the relative paucity of the Greek word for beauty in the New Testament,
but the frequent use of the word *kalon*, which integrates both good and
beautiful (32–35). Dostoevsky knew the ways that people dis-figure their
beauty and that of others by denying their creatural identity as *imago Dei*.
Throughout his *Writer's Diary*, begun before and continued contempora-
neously with the composition of his final novel, he points to child abuse,
exploitation of the poor, sloth, alcoholism, pride, suicide, and despair—
and he rails against these grotesque de-formations. But he also depicted
the human capacity to be re-formed, to become *beautiful* and *truthful* and
good. In the ancient Greek conception of *kalon*, the good, true, and beautiful, work as an integral whole in their erotic pull. Similarly, Dostoevsky
claimed "Only that is moral which coincides with your feeling of beauty
and with the ideal in which you embody it" (cited by Scanlan 151, n.37). In
one *Diary of a Writer* entry, he addresses dancers at an imaginary ball, and

declares that the potential for "a golden age" of transfigured humanity is within their grasp: "[Y]our trouble is that you yourselves don't know how beautiful you are! Do you know that each of you, if you only wanted, could at once make everyone in this room happy and fascinate them all? And this power exists in every one of you, but it is so deeply hidden that you have long ceased to believe in it" (308). For Dostoevsky, being good proves difficult when we refuse to see our own and others' beauty.

88. See Sammon, 49–68.

89. On icons, see Rowan Williams (especially 189–226) and Sophie Ol-livier, "Icons in Dostoevsky's Works."

90. Leonid Ouspensky's full explanation is helpful: "The image of God is ineffaceable in man. Baptism only reestablishes and purifies it. The like-ness to God, however, can increase or decrease. Being free, man can assert himself in God or against God" (159). In sin, people besmirch the likeness; in grace, with penance, they recover it. This is the human call to sanctifica-tion, integral to the process that culminates in deification: "[A] saint is more fully man than a sinner is. He is free from sin, which is essentially foreign to the human nature; he realizes the primordial meaning of his existence; he puts on the incorruptible beauty of the Kingdom of God, in the construction of which he participates in his own life. . . . [T]rue beauty is the radiance of the Holy Spirit, the holiness of and the participation in the life of the world to come" (Ouspensky 160–61). Of the human vocation to holiness, von Balthasar, citing the theologian Matthias Scheeben, writes: "The more profound concept of sanctity rests on the fact that the proper life of the will in its innermost power and fullness of energy does not sim-ply consist of orienting and directing the will to that which is objectively good and beautiful. . . . Rather the proper life of the will consists in its '. . . *transformation into* the objectively good and beautiful, a transformation which, in the case of our will, appears to be partly the root and source . . . of its striving, but partly also the goal and perfection of this . . . striving'" (*Glory I, Seeing the Form*, 111–12; emphasis added). In his *Writer's Diary*, Dostoevsky insists that such striving is an imperative: "man, too. . . needs to humanize and 'image himself'. . . ." (325). Or, as he wrote in 1864 in his anguished reflection upon his first wife Masha's death, "man strives to transform himself into the *I* of Christ" (*Unpublished Dostoevsky* 41). The full human realization of the transformative process in which one fully recovers one's identity as *imago Dei* is that of deification, the attainment of Godmanhood. Dostoevsky's understanding of the image of Christ

as salvific is grounded in his faith in Christ's incarnation, the humble embrace of our human condition by the divine Logos. As St. Athanasius writes: "He . . . assumed humanity that we might become God" (86).

91. See Dostoevsky's 1861 essay, 'Mr. — bov and the Question of Art" in which he attempts to persuade the utilitarian critic that "art will be true to man only if its freedom of development is not hampered. . . . The more freely it develops, the more normal the development of its true and *useful* path will be and the more quickly it will find it" (135, emphasis in original).

92. On the recent and (from my vantage point) ill-advised change in the words of the Catholic Eucharistic prayer from "for all" to "for many" see Gerald O'Collins with John Wilkins, *Lost in Translation* (71–72).

93. See also Julian Connolly's "Confession in *The Brothers Karamazov*," Robert Belknap's "The Unrepentant Confession," and Russell Hillier's "Confessional Moment." Diane Oenning Thompson observes, 'In Dostoevsky's fiction, salvation always begins with confession'" (*Memory* 110).

94. As Julian Connolly notes, Dostoevsky's good confessors never finalize the person whom they are counseling: "they speak not as a judge or from a position of superiority, but from awareness that he or she is also a sinner" ("Confession" 15). Mikhail Bakhtin saw confession to be "the object of Dostoevsky's vision and depiction" and, congruent with my claims regarding Dostoevsky's incarnational realism, claimed that "the image of the ideal human being or the image of Christ represents for him the resolution of ideological quests" (*Problems* 97).

95. In her *Oxford Handbook* essay on Bakhtin, Caryl Emerson writes, "What cannot be finalized cannot be wholly known. The unknowability of persons is the most God-like thing about us. . . . Just as God is unknowable and unfinalizable, so is every person." She cites Randall Poole's essay, "The Apophatic Bakhtin."

96. Caryl Emerson's phrase is apt: Myshkin's chief attribute is his "stubborn, reductive benevolence" ("Problems" 515). Myshkin refuses to see anything *but* the possibility of good in the other. His propensity for reductiveness and refusal to choose has destructive effects, as Rowan Williams discusses (*Dostoevsky* 46–55).

97. See Alina Wyman's excellent, extended analysis of Alyosha. As she writes, Alyosha is "a more effective Christlike hero, whose empathy toward

others closely resembles *vzhivanie* [active empathy]. The secret of Alyosha's success is the rare balance he shows as both an exemplary giver and an exemplary recipient of love" (176). My study of Alyosha is very much consonant with Alina's.

98. The key theme of the Hindu spiritual classic *Bhaghavad-Gita*.

99. Bakhtin's phrase; see "the problem of great time" (*Speech Genres* 170).

100. For example, in "Author and Hero" he articulates a both/and desideratum: "The demand is: live in such a way that every given moment of your life would be both the consummating, final moment and, at the same time, the initial moment of a new life" (122).

101. Alina Wyman's work on active empathy deeply engages the affinities between Scheler and Bakhtin.

102. Timothy Verdon offers a related insight into "visibility": "The image of pilgrims going from one church to another in highlights an important connection: that between *prayer* and *visibility*. Every journey undertaken in a spirit of prayer leads in fact to something visible. . . . Like the first disciples, pilgrims set out in response to the One who says, 'Come and see' (John 1:39a), and in Veronica's Veil or some other relic—as in the architecture and art they find on reaching their destination—they contemplate his face and behold his abode under the form of images. . . . 'He is the image of the unseen God' (Col 1:15). Our point is that visibility itself is a 'space of prayer' for those who believe in the incarnate Word" (92–93).

103. In her essay in the *Oxford Handbook*, Caryl Emerson draws upon Marilyn Louise Gray's 2011 dissertation, and "approaches Bakhtin as a non-canonical Christian personalist. His thought presumes a human being who is outward-reaching but not acquisitive, answerable for deeds but not autonomous, and although at any given moment a conscious working unity, never, until death, a unified or graspable whole" ("Bakhtin").

104. As Thomas Pfau writes: "Arguably the most conspicuous causality associated with the rise of a secular and voluntarist model of agency is that of 'personhood'. . . . That is, the idea of the individual as centered on a rich, unique, and dynamic spectrum of intellectual and affective dispositions and states—and their experience as both generative and transformative of the very idea of self *as a person*—has all but vanished." (*Minding the Modern* 199–200).

105. Ivan rejects the harmony forgiveness may make possible and insists, "I would rather remain with my unavenged suffering and unquenched indignation, *even if I am wrong*" (212, emphasis in text). He thus corrodes his capacity to keep his promise that he will protect his father, and ushers in "hell" in "heart" and "head" (228).

106. Bakhtin regretted that he couldn't say all he wished due to Soviet censorship. In 1993, Bocharov recalled a conversation he had with Bakhtin in 1970, in which the latter claimed his book on Dostoevsky was "morally flawed" because it "misrepresented the church" and could not talk of "the main thing, what Dostoevsky agonized about all his life—the existence of God" (Bocharov 1994, 1012, cited by Emerson, "Bakhtin" 2020). Bakhtin also saw in Christ the ideal of such integral personhood. "In Christ we find a synthesis . . . infinite severity toward himself" (the closure of responsibility) and "boundless kindness toward the other" (the openness of grace) (*Author* 56). Bakhtin's "sense of faith" helped him understand Dostoevsky's "integral attitude . . . oriented toward a higher and ultimate value . . . which makes demands on the whole man" ("Reworking" 294). It fostered Bakhtin's later concepts: the "higher super-addressee" (*Speech Genres* 126), who understands us even when our current interlocutor may not; and "great time" which attends to quotidian *chronos* even as it anticipates a *kairos* when "every meaning will have its homecoming festival" (*Speech Genres* 170). See essays in *Bakhtin and Religion: A Feeling for Faith.*

107. In a June 13, 1874 letter Vladimir Soloviev—who had yet to befriend Dostoevsky—chided his cousin and then-fiancé E. V. Selvina: "I don't know why *Crime and Punishment* troubled you. Read it to the end, and it would also be useful to read all of Dostoevsky: *he is one of a few writers who have still preserved the Divine image and likeness in our time*" (*Karamazov Correspondence* 13; emphasis added).

108. As Merton writes, monastic asceticism aims at "the recovery of our true self . . . created for union with God. It is the purification, and liberation of the divine image in man, hidden under layers of 'unlikeness' . . . The work of recovery of this lost likeness is effected by stripping away all that is alien and foreign to our true selves . . ." (*Silent Life* 22). Note too Merton's discussion of Zosima and (implicitly) Alyosha, contrasting them to Ferapont, at the beginning of *Contemplative Prayer*. See also, in the Appendix, his appreciation of Zosima's dictum in letters to Milosz.

109. Here follows a long but necessary discursive note on "self" and "person": Yuri Corrigan's discussion in "Defining Terms: Self, Personality,

Spirit, Mind, Consciousness, Soul" (11–13) is indispensable in understanding the Russian conceptions of "person" and "self." He writes : "I use
the term 'self' throughout this book as roughly equivalent to the concept
of personality or *lichnost'*, with the caveat that 'self' is generally narrower
than 'personality.' This imperfect comparison reflects Dostoevsky's own
ambiguity regarding the problem of *lichnost'*, since he used that term
sometimes as an antonym for the 'I.' When he opposed the two terms, the
'I' or 'self' (*ia*) denotes the site of consciousness, while 'personality' (*lichnost'*) includes the more expansive terrain that underlies and transcends
the activity of being aware. When he uses the terms as synonyms, *lichnost'*
tends to take on the more negative quality of a self-enclosed individual
consciousness. More determinate for Dostoevsky is the opposition of
bezlichnost' (facelessness, impersonality) to *samootverzhenie* (selflessness):
the first is an intensely negative and detrimental state of being and the
other a desirable Christian ideal. For Dostoevsky, it is a bad thing to lose
one's personality, but a good thing to lose one's self" (12). So too in the
Catholic tradition, the light of which I bring to my analysis of Dostoevsky.
For example: "[Jacques] Maritain's distinction between the individual and
the person is strikingly present in Merton's discussions of the false and
true selves. Maritain's theory of the person is straightforward and clear. He
holds that Pascal's idea that 'the ego is hateful' is the correlative contrast
to St. Thomas's statement that 'the person is that which is noblest in the
whole of nature.' Maritain writes that the selfish ego is hateful, the creative
self is that which is noblest and most generous of all" (Carr 27–28, citing
Maritain's *Scholasticism and Politics*).

Also illuminating is my September 29, 2019 email correspondence
with Peter Winsky, currently a doctoral candidate at UCLA, working on a
dissertation on Dostoevsky. I queried Peter on his recently posted review
of the Bulgarian Dostoevsky Society's International Symposium "The Anthropology of Dostoevsky." Peter's review can be found here: https://slavic.
ucla.edu/news/to-uncover-the-secret-of-the-person-while-preserving-the-
secret-as-a-secret-a-review-of-the-bulgarian-dostoevsky-societys-inter-
national-symposium-the-ant/. Peter begins his review by quoting from a
youthful Dostoevsky: "In his letter of August 16, 1839, Fyodor Mikhailovich
wrote to his brother Mikhail Mikhailovich that 'the person is a mystery . . .
I am studying that mystery because I want to become a person.'" I observed
that whereas Peter translated the word from this letter as "person," Joseph
Frank, in *Selected Letters*, had used the words "man" and "human being."
Given its personalist valence, I wished to use Peter's translation, and asked
whether Dostoevsky had used the same word when—about forty years
after the letter to his brother—he wrote private notes stating his authorial

intentions: "with full realism, to find the man [or the human] in the man.
. . . They call me a psychologist: not true: I am only a realist in a higher
sense, i.e., I depict all the depths of the human soul" (from notes cited by
Fanger, 215). I asked Peter: "In Dostoevsky's original Russian, can 'man' be
read as 'person'? And is this the word from which *lichnost'* derives? I too am
deeply interested in the way personalism animates Dostoevsky's last novel,
and in the roots of 'person' in patristic deliberations on the Incarnation and
Trinity." To my query, Peter responded with clarity and generosity: "As far
as I know I am one of the first people to consistently translate Dostoevsky's
use of человек (*chelovek*) to the English *person* for philosophical reasons.
The decision was made for numerous reasons. The primary two being that
person conveys with more force my interest in the effect of Dostoevsky's
anthropological perspectives as conditioned by his Orthodox understanding of Christ, and for the more practical reason of attempting to move away
from using *man* as a term to represent a unique human being. *Human,*
therefore, is also less effective insofar as it strips the understanding of Dostoevsky's discourse against the strong materialistic and humanist ideologies
of the late 19th century. Although личность (*lichnost'*) may be translated
to *person*, it is more often than not rendered as *personality* (a prime example of this is Bakhtin's use of лисность -> *personality* by Caryl Emerson
in her translation of *The Problems of Dostoevsky's Poetics).* The influence of
Christian theology renders this term more closely to the Greek *prosopon,*
which is also grounded in the anatomical description of the face, but comes
close to a metaphysical quality of relational being. Человек (*chelovek*) on
the other hand, which Dostoevsky uses in the quotes you have provided
([which] comes from unpublished writings of his between 1880-81 on topics for his *Writer's Diary* . . .) is from the old Slavic for "those who cultivate."
However, in by the 19th century its meaning had come much closer to the
Greek. In Vladimir Dahl's foundational *Tolkovyi slovar' zhivaro velikoruskago iazyka* (*Explanatory Dictionary of the Living Great Russian Language*)
we find that *chelovek* entails "every one of a group of people; the highest of
earthly creatures, having been given wisdom, free will, and verbal speech . . .
fleshy and mortal... worthy of that title 'being.'" (Vladimir Dahl, *Tolkovyi
slovar' zhivaro velikoruskago iazyka, Second Edition, vol. II,* (St. Petersburg:
Izdanie knigoprodavtsa-tipografa M.O. Vol'fa, 1882), 258-9). *Chelovek* is
also used consistently by the Orthodox Church (see the Slavonic form of the
Niceno-Constantinopolitan Creed) and conforms to the Orthodox idea that
human contemplation of God works from the primacy of the relationship
within the Trihypostatic Godhead and then subsequently between humans
and the Incarnation. In this way being precedes essence, or perhaps it is better to say the mode of being-in-relation defines the essence of something.

In light of these facts, and in short: you could very easily use *person* instead of *man* here, as far as I am concerned. Dostoevsky is using the term to describe the unique human being but in the contemporary vernacular."

A coda: In previously published work, influenced especially by Gary Saul Morson and Caryl Emerson's 1990 study of Bakhtin, I had used the term "*prosaic* sense of self." Upon first encountering their groundbreaking study, I discerned a kinship between Bakhtin's conception of the self (in all its complexity), and Bakhtin's analysis of Dostoevsky's conception of "the deepest I," and to Thomas Merton's emphasis upon the "true self" as the *ordinary*, everyday self, which Merton observes in the desert fathers, the monastic tradition, and which—especially in his dialogue with Buddhism—he emphasized in his later work. Anne Carr's analysis is illuminating: "Created in the image of God, one has lost the likeness by becoming centered on the self and separated from God as the source of reality. One is still the image of God, but the loss of charity—participation in the life of God—means that one is a caricature of one's *true self.* . . . [T]he obscure image of God remains in human freedom as the power of spiritual self-determination. But in its distorted form it appears as a kind of relative omnipotence in which one's own will is supreme" (38; emphasis added). Carr also observes that in "Merton's later reflections," the "true self" is "ultimately the ordinary and familiar self who recovers . . . the original affirmation given in one's limited, relational, created being and is thus open to the transformation offered, in Christian terms, in the economy of grace, sacrament, and prayer" (126).

Dostoevsky depicts the extreme, voluntarist assertion of the false and "supreme" will in characters like Kirillov in *Demons* who exemplifies that the *telos* of the presumptive man-god is, finally, suicide. But Dostoevsky also depicts the possibility, especially through confessional dialogue, of recovering "the true self," "the deepest I," and "the economy of grace" in his portrayal of Zosima, Alyosha, and others.

110. David Ford notes that in Dante's *Divine Comedy* "a long journey of face to face encounters culminates in a vision of God. At the heart of that vision is the face of Christ. It is the ultimate transformation, as imagination is overwhelmed and desire and will are moved by 'the Love that moves the sun and other stars'" (25).

111. David Ford makes a related insight, pointing to that most Dostoevskian of French novelists, Georges Bernanos. Near the end of *Diary of a Country Priest*, the main character writes in his final entry: "How easy it is to hate oneself! True grace is to forget. Yet if pride could die in us, the supreme grace would be to love oneself in all simplicity—as one would

love any of those who themselves have suffered and loved in Christ" (*Diary* 296). These words lent the title to Paul Ricœur's *Oneself as Another*. Ricœur's work itself suggests the helpful "theme of a self-esteem in which . . . self does not simply mean *myself* but embraces myself and that of others" (Ford 90). This is the "good taste of self" of which Lynch writes, and to which I often allude in this study.

112. Joseph Conrad, for one, thought *The Brothers Karamazov* "sound[ed] like some fierce mouthings from prehistoric ages" (Letter to Edward Garnett, May 27, 1912).

113. "Two-edged sword" (or "doubled edged weapon") is a scriptural image (Heb 4:12) employed a number of times in the novel to describe things that "cut both ways." Practices typically seen as good in themselves—self-sacrifice, confession, human psychology—can "cut both ways" and take a "two-edged" form. Robin Feuer Miller illuminates: the "literal translation from the Russian is 'a stick with two ends' (37) and observes recurring instances (*Worlds* 21, 37, 47, 110, 130).

114. "Intercreatural" is Graham Pechey's coinage, which recognizes "the third" presence, the "superaddressee" in interpersonal relations. Bakhtin writes of "a third party in the dialogue," "a higher *superaddressee* (third), whose absolutely just responsive understanding is presumed, either in some metaphysical distance or in distant historical time . . ." ("Text" 126).

115. In *Just Mercy: A Story of Justice and Redemption*, Bryan Stevenson describes his work with prisoners on death-row. As he writes: "I would remind them that each of us is more than the worst thing we have ever done" (290). In a subsequent note, I relate Bryan's story of an inmate to whom he had given a copy of *The Brothers Karamazov*.

116. See Deborah A Martinsen's incisive analysis of Fyodor buffoonish exhibition at the monastery (2–10). As she astutely observes: "By uncovering shame, Dostoevsky implicates us in the painful experience of exposure and self-consciousness that can lead to individual and social redemption" (*Surprised* 18).

117. This raises the question of whether a person can ever become permanently vicious and incapable of performing virtuous actions. But grace is always available, and all things are possible with God.

118. See J. L. Austin on performative utterance in *How to Do Things with Words*.

119. See Thomas Werge's astute analysis, "Word as Deed in Dostoevsky's *Crime and Punishment*."

120. Bakhtin writes: "there is always something essential in me that I can set over against that world, namely my inner self-activity, my subjectivity. . . . I always have a loophole . . . through which I can save myself from being no more than a natural given" (*Author and Hero* 40).

    The theological implications of the benevolent loophole are suggested near the end of the film *Dead Man Walking* in the conversation between Sister Helen Prejean and Matthew Poncelet, the man on death row to whom she is ministering:

Sister: Do you ever read the Bible?

Matthew: I ain't much of a Bible reader, but I pick it up from time to time.

Sister: Like W. C. Fields read his Bible. —

Matthew: Who?

Sister: W. C. Fields. He used to play this drunken character in the movies. He's dying and a friend comes and sees him reading the Bible. The friend says, "W. C., you don't believe in God. Why are you reading the Bible?" And Fields says, "I'm looking for a loophole."

Matthew: I ain't looking for no loophole.

http://ethicsupdates.net/applied/punishment/death_penalty/Script%20 of%20Dead%20Man%20Walking—highlighted.pdf

121. Discussing *Notes*, John Sykes, Jr. rightly observes that "Dostoevsky points to Christ-like kenotic self-sacrifice as the antidote to the cycle of humiliation/domination created by the will to power" (87).

122. Steven Cassedy helpfully complicates our understanding of Russian kenoticism by noting its Western influences, especially "German Protestant theology" (11). Cassedy claims that "the man who introduced kenosis into Russian Religious discourse in 1892 was an Orthodox theologian by the name of Mikhail Mikhailovich Tareev," who was himself "inspired, at least in part, by Dostoevsky" (11). He concludes, "whether or not there was a kenotic tradition in Russia like the one Fedotov described, there is no doubt that Dostoevsky was interested in the two topics of suffering and humility" (153).

123. I use the NRSV translation here, and elsewhere the New American Bible, except where noted.

124. Fedotov writes: "Theodosius draws his main religious inspiration from the contemplation of the human nature of Christ[,]. . . of His descent to earth. . . . In the light of this Christology, one is fully entitled to term the spirituality of Theodosius as 'kenotic', using the Pauline word of 'kenosis' or emptying of Christ. . . . Theodosius himself quotes the Epistle to the Philippians. His word to his mother about Christ who 'became poor for our sake' is also Pauline (II Corinthians 8:9). . . . The kenotic idea has its practical expression with Theodosius in three Christian virtues: poverty, humility, and love, in their complete unity as one inseparable whole" (127–28). See also Stanton on the tradition of elders in Russian Orthodoxy.

125. Note too the link between the virtues of humility and prudence: the Greek word for "mind" (here translated as "attitude") is *phrēn* (plural, *phrēnes*), the root of *phronesis*—practical wisdom or prudence. Christ exemplifies both self-emptying active love and prudence. My thanks to Brian Armstrong and Robin Parry for pointing out to me the Greek word for "mind."

126. Caryl Emerson emphasizes the ephemeral effect of the penetrated word: "It can only enter at a specific time and place to work a temporary realization. . . . The penetrated word makes authority real, but only for the moment; it remains personal, historical, conditional. ("Tolstoy" 157). But while the penetrated word is always spoken prudently, carefully attentive to the particularities of this person, place, and time—its effects may *accrue*. The word is like a seed that takes root in memory, and over time, can bear fruit. But its capacity to accrue authority depends on the person who utters it. As Bakhtin points out (and Emerson, too, observes), "never, in the case of Myshkin" is the penetrated word spoken "in a decisive voice" (*Problems* 242).

Chapter 3: The Elder Zosima

127. There are a number of historical sources for Zosima. Nel Grillaert points out that "Dostoevsky integrated many of the scenes and people he had witnessed in Optina, such as [Elder] Amvrosy addressing crowds of pilgrims and speaking words of consolation and moral support into the novel" ("Orthodox Spirituality" 189). Cassedy notes that "Dostoevsky read extensively in a five-volume edition of Tikhon of Zadonsk's works" (60);

see Nadejda Gorodetzky's *Saint Tikhon of Zadonsk: Inspirer of Dostoevsky* for an illuminating discussion of Tikhon's life and its Dostoevskian resonances.

128. T. S. Eliot, "East Coker," *Four Quartets*.

129. Leontiev critiques what he calls Zosima's "rosy Christianity" (Lantz, *Encyclopedia* 232). Sergei Hackel's critique of the nationalism that creeps into Zosima's rhetoric (in the "So Be It" chapter) is fair, but his claims that Zosima ignores the sacramental life of the church is belied by Zosima's request for the sacraments as he prepares for his death. Nor can Zosima's sacramental view of nature be reduced to "nature mysticism."

130. The story that Zosima tells of the saint, who gave the bear bread and a blessing is drawn from the Life of St. Sergius of Radonezh (c. 1314–92), and recalls St. Francis's taming of the wolf from Gubbio. St. Sergius is also a saint in the Roman Catholic Church. (Terras, *Handbook* 248).

131. https://en.wikiquote.org/wiki/Catherine_of_Siena.

132. Pope Benedict XVI, for example, writes: "[C. H.] Dodd was basically right. Yes, Jesus' Sermon on the Mount is 'eschatological,' if you will, but eschatological in the sense that the Kingdom of God is 'realized' in his coming. It is thus perfectly possible to speak of an 'eschatology in process of realization'" (*Jesus of Nazareth* 188). For a comparable Orthodox perspective see "Already But Not Yet" by Father John Breck: https://oca.org/reflections/fr.-john-breck/already-but-not-yet.

133. References given in *Catechism*: St. John Chrysostom, *De virg.* 10, 1:PG 48, 540; Cf. John Paul II, FC *[Familiaris consortio]* 16.

134. A similar sensibility imbues Robert Bresson's film *Au Hasard Balthazar* with its loving attentiveness to the face of the donkey.

135. "On purpose" is the recurring phrase in the novel that invariably suggests willfulness.

136. See also Ronald Hingley who points to the victimizing mockery in Dostoevsky's novels and R. L. Busch who emphasizes—via Bakhtin—the parodic and satiric. Jan Van Der Eng, "A Note on Comic Relief in *The Brothers Karamazov*," highlights the role of Madame Khokhlakova.

137. One thinks here of Heidegger's discussion of *Gelassenheit*, "releasement toward things and openness to the mystery . . ." (*Discourse on*

Thinking 55), although, as is characteristic of his later writings, Heidegger speaks here of a "letting be" toward things, not people. Long before Heidegger, however, Meister Eckhart uses the word to describe one's proper relationship to God: "detachment *[Gelassenheit]* is receptive to nothing at all except God" (286). I am grateful to David Morgan for pointing the Eckhart passage out to me many years ago. The counterpart of *Gelassenheit* in Chinese philosophy is *wu wei*, an attitude of receptive non-action that one can integrate into one's most arduous acts—including active love. Relevant is Steven Connor's insistence "that the arts of inhibition are not in fact the opposite of action, but rather the modulation of action and, therefore, the action of modulation" (208).

138. See Alina Wyman's surpassing study of "active empathy."

139. "For Thomas a principal means of tracing the way back to what we really want"—and thus vital to "practical wisdom"—"is prayer, *oratio*" (Turner 180).

140. Anthony Ugolnik observes: "In Orthodox cultures the encounter with God and the flash of insight that conveys religious meaning occur not so often in private reflection as in encounter with another. That encounter is sometimes expressed in dialogue with a spiritual elder or holy individual who has 'absorbed' the Word and can now reflect it. But often the encounter is silent, like the icon itself. It emerges through the act of embrace. To embrace another, even a sinner, is to encounter directly the image of Christ." Ugolnik points the example of Sonia in *Crime and Punishment* who, "even in her sin, becomes an icon of the Christ whose selflessness she reflects," and to Christ with the Inquisitor (51).

141. For recent discussion of ways in which institutional authority of the Roman Catholic Church might take a more kenotic form, see Carroll et al.

142. Ruth Coates highlights "the Fall motif" in Bakhtin's *Philosophy of the Act*, and writes: "In Bakhtin's universe, one cannot name oneself, and all autonomy is falsely conceived. . . . [T]o claim autonomy is both self-destructive and destructive of the world" (32).

143. Tatyana Buzina comments on the expression "the devil knows," which also appears in *The Brothers Karamazov*: "In mistakenly accusing Dmitri [of murdering his father], Rakitin prefigures the erroneous verdict of the human trial. What is more, the allusion to the devil in the phrase 'the devil knows what!' (*chert znaet chto!*) carries us forward to the devil in

Ivan's nightmare. The devil certainly *knows*, that is, he openly voices everything that Ivan tries so hard to suppress" ("Two Fates" 70).

144. In *I and Thou*, Buber uses the image of the gaze to describe authentic dialogue and mutuality: ". . . *I* and *thou* take their stand not merely in relation, but also in the solid give-and-take of talk. The moments of relation are here, and only here, bound together by means of the element of the speech in which they are immersed. Here what confronts us has blossomed into the full reality of the *Thou*. Here alone, then, as reality that cannot be lost, are gazing and being gazed upon, knowing and being known, loving and being loved" (103). Bakhtin was familiar with Buber's work. For a brief comparative study of the two thinkers, see Nina Perlina, "Bakhtin and Buber: Problems of Dialogic Imagination."

145. Of Christ's silence with and kiss of the Inquisitor, George Steiner writes: "Christ's refusal to engage in the duel yields a dramatic motif of great majesty and tact" (*Tolstoy or Dostoevsky*, 342). Steiner's emphasis upon tact toward the other is evident in his later *Real Presences*. The other he writes of here is a work of art, but the analogy he uses to describe such an approach to art is that of "our encounter with the freedom of presence in another human being, or attempts to communicate with that freedom, [which] will always entail approximation" (175): "Where there is *cortesia* between freedoms, a vital distance is kept. A certain reserve persists. Understanding is patiently won and, at all time, provisional. There are questions we do not ask our 'caller' . . ." (176). Zosima reveals such *cortesia*.

146. https://www3.nd.edu/~afreddos/summa-translation/Part%202-2/ st2-2-ques49.pdf. Freddoso translation of *Summa*, in process, on line.

147. As Caryl Emerson points out, "theologically inflected poetics" is Graham Pechey felicitous description of Bakhtin's early work. See Pechey's *Mikhail Bakhtin: The Word in the World* (153).

148. While affirming his main point, I would qualify Lynch's phrase "the absolute wish of man." Given the reality of human fallenness, the modifier "absolute" seems excessive.

149. Hart's thesis is that complete knowledge would *necessitate* the choice of God (*Universal*).

150. In *The Freedom of Morality* (St. Vladimir's Press, 1984.) This passage is also cited by Caryl Emerson, ("Problems" 523).

151. Father Sergei Hackel claims that Zosima does not receive the last rites, and asserts that "the death of Zosima, 'unhousel'd . . . unanel'd', is yet one more expression of his separateness from sacred structures and prescriptions of his Church" (150). Hackel's description of Zosima is far more applicable to Father Ferapont, who "was seldom seen at church" and who did not keep "to the rules binding all the rest" and "the common regulations" (288).

152. Indeed, "lover of humankind" is itself a phrase that cuts both ways. It is applied to Alyosha and Ivan's Christ, and has a source in Isaac the Syrian's notion of "luminous love of humanity" (Alfayev 73).

153. Some years ago, in conversation, Caryl Emerson pointed out that the stress on the particular is quite clear in the original Russian. She stressed, though, that in Russian the word is closer to "guilty" than responsible. But "guilt" makes the dictum harder to comprehend: how can we be guilty for everything? Her analysis is helpful: "Just as I cannot know what actions caused me, so I cannot know what my action might cause" and, further, "our light could have shone forth and did not, and who can now calculate the effect of that missed good?" ("Mysterious" 172). Rowan Williams's commentary also illuminates the maxim: "To take responsibility is so to act and speak that the options of others are clarified, not controlled. And this can happen only when there is an imaginative penetration into what is other: I become responsible when I can indeed 'answer' for what is not myself, when I can voice the needs or hopes of someone other without collapsing them into my own" (*Dostoevsky* 171).

154. This is the recurring thesis of De Lubac's *Catholicism:* "Catholicism is essentially social . . .in the deepest sense of the word, . . . first and foremost in the heart of its mystery, in the essence of its dogma. . . . prayer is essentially the prayer of all, for all" (15–16).

155. See Martin Buber, "Guilt and Guilt Feeling," in which he discusses Dostoevsky as an example. See also: Katchadourian's *Guilt*, a wide-ranging discussion and a helpful outline of the differences between healthy and unhealthy guilt, and Maurice S. Friedman's discussion of "existential guilt" as being a necessary corrective to the psychoanalytic emphasis on neurotic guilt feelings (218).

156. Quoted by Kathleen Norris in *Dakota* 174.

157. I first heard the distinction between "true guilt" v. "guilt feeling" in a formative class taught by Edward Weisband in Fall, 1976. More recently, in *The Macabresque*, Weisband has written a magisterial analysis of the ways guilt-feeling and shame feed into a the mass-*nadryv* of hideous "carnivelesque" (15) violence: *"Performative transgressions punish victims as objects; but such punishments are also aimed at perpetrators themselves as their own self victimizers. . . .* This is very character of the psychodynamics of reification, to attribute substantiality to the identities of others on the basis of closed categories but, in so doing, to relate to oneself as a 'thing,' and thus, in effect, to 'thingify' one's freedom. This prompts an effort to will the unwillable. How psychic structures and economies develop, how shame and anxiety become intertwined within human personality, points toward a congenital tug of war between anxiety and sadism, guilt and shame" (183). Weisband analyzes a number of genocidal regimes from the previous century: Nazi, Stalinist, Maoist, Turkish, Cambodian, Rwandan, and Bosnian. His analysis can be applied to the Grand Inquisitor, Dostoevsky's prophetic portrayal of tyrannical *nadryv, auto-da-fé,* and mass violence. It can also be linked also to Averintsev's trenchant critique of Bakhtin's celebration of carnival "'There is no violence lurking behind laughter'—how odd that Bakhtin could make so categorical a statement! All of history, literally, cries out in protest against it. There are many contrary examples that one feels almost helpless about choosing the most striking ones" (85). Weisband's analysis attends to many such examples.

158. The title of a classic work by the eighteenth-century French Jesuit Jean Pierre de Caussade.

159. Measure and prudence are integral: "Saint Thomas undeniably understood the term *'measure'* in the same sense in regard to the dependence of willing and working upon the command of prudence and in regard to the formation of knowledge by reality. He expressly compares, under the aspect of 'measure', the relation of reality and knowledge, and the relation of the practical reason to concrete moral action." (Pieper, *Truth* 164).

160. See Maxwell Parlin's splendid paper, "Luke, Acts, and Active Love: The Validity of Terrestrial Time in *The Brothers Karamazov.*" Unpublished. Presented at the Association for Slavic, East European, and Eurasian Studies Convention, San Francisco, CA, Thursday, November 26, 2019.

161. Bakhtin contributes to the assessment of Dostoevsky as "apocalyptic" when he suggests that "the peaks," the "culminating points" of the novelist's "crucial" confessional dialogues "rise above the plot in the

abstract sphere of pure relationship, one person to another" (*Problems* 265). "Above," "abstract sphere," "pure"—the terms suggest the end-time, atemporality, eternity ushered in by apocalypse, not the prosaic realities of the earthbound here and now. The confessional dialogues are powerful in that the confessor often reaches the "deepest I," "the pure deep I from within" ("Reworking" 294) of the other. But this "pure I" never escapes the exigencies of its situation, its time and place. Indeed, confessors like Zosima and Alyosha must often "bring down to earth" the person with whom they speak through careful attention to the person's particular stage of development. Never static, the authoritative word they utter is born out of a kenotic attention to this person, in this situation, at this time. The prosaic confessor helps the other to accept and act within the limits of the present moment, "full of event potential" (*sobytiina*) as it is. "Full of event potential" is Bakhtin's phrase (*Problems* 81). Morson and Emerson comment that it "might also be rendered as 'eventnessful'; what Bakhtin has in mind is a conception of truth that allows every moment of existence to be rich in potential. This alternate, prosaic conception of truth would not be 'placed above existence,' but would arise from the experience of the 'open present' in each moment. Here Bakhtin's three global concepts—prosaics, unfinalizability, and dialogue—combine" (*Prosaics* 236). If we understand Dostoevsky's process of creation as polyphonic—that is, that he respects his characters as existing others with whom he is on an equal plane—then we might understand Dostoevsky's conception of "plot" as consonant with his conception of "existence." Thus, if Zosima and Alyosha, in confessional dialogues, assist others in embracing and acting within their particular situations, they do so within, not above, the plot, the "open present" of each moment in the novel's time.

162. Typically respectful of Fyodor's unfinalizability, the narrator adds, "It was difficult even now to decide: was he joking or was he really moved?" (43).

163. "Ruptured grief" is Victor Terras's translation (*Companion* 147).

164. As Roger Cox states: "for the Inquisitor there is no miracle, no mystery, and no authority—only 'magic,' 'mystification,' and 'tyranny'" (210).

165. This is the story that Pope Francis finds so moving and so exemplary of the human capacity for mercy (see note below). As Susan McReynolds observes in her edition of the novel, "Zosima [here] paraphrases words of Isaac the Syrian (died 700 A.D.) who said 'there is no unforgivable sin except the sin of the unrepentant'" (50, n.4). Julian Connolly's analysis

of this scene ("Confession" 17–18) is excellent. Anna Schur contrasts the younger Zosima's response to Mikhail—counseling him to make a public confession, with all the juridical consequences—and the Elder's response to this woman in what she sees as "roughly, at least, . . . comparable moral situations" (112). In my reading, the two cases are quite different, and the woman was likely responding in self-defense. In both cases, Zosima exercises prudent casuistry.

166. See Alina Wyman's emphasis upon the capacity to receive gifts. See also Richard Peace on "the two poles of Zosima's teachings: 'active love'— the *caritas* of giving; and humility—the virtue of accepting" (291).

167. A similarly comical and contemporary rendering of the human demand for gratitude can be found at the beginning of an episode of Seinfeld aptly titled "The Good Samaritan":
(Jerry is driving alone talking on his car phone to Elaine at home in her bed)
    Elaine: You know it's bad enough you have a car phone, you have to use the speaker?
    Jerry: It's safer! Plus it's more annoying to the other person.
(Driver cuts in front of Jerry)
    Jerry: Oh look at this guy.
    Elaine: What's goin' on?
    Jerry: Oh there's a guy trying to get in front of me, he has to ask permission. Yes. Go ahead. Get in, get in.
    Elaine: Did you get a thank you wave?
    Jerry: No, nothing. How could you not give a thank you wave? Hey buddy! Where's my thank you wave?
(Jerry sticks his head out the window)
    Jerry: Give me that wave!
https://www.seinfeldscripts.com/TheGoodSamaritan.html

168. At the start of the next chapter, "So Be It! So Be It!" the narrator notes that "the elder's absence from his cell had lasted for about twenty-five minutes" (56). Terras notes "a compression of clock time" here (151), but considering Zosima's consciousness of time in these scenes (he asks Madame Khokhlakova's forgiveness for not being able to stay longer [56]), I see no reason not to take the narrator at his word. Dostoevsky, through his narrator, is careful to attend to the hours and days going by, and this contributes significantly to the novel's emphasis on the quotidian.

169. Of unstable irony Wayne Booth writes: "no stable reconstruction can be made out of the ruins revealed through the irony. . . . No statement can really 'mean what it says'" (*Irony* 240–41).

170. In *Author and Hero* Bakhtin points to this New Testament confessional moment as an example of "confessional self-accounting," in faith, before God (144–45). Ivan lacks the full faith and trust to make such an accounting, but he approaches such an act in this scene of blessing.

171. Mochulsky suggests that readers remember this scene as the novel concludes with Ivan still struggling through his illness: "The just man blesses the sinner's 'incessant striving' and predicts that he will fall and rise up. The author of *The Legend of the Grand Inquisitor* will not perish like Stavrogin, whose heart was frozen" (783).

172. Dmitri protests against human "broadness" in his "Confession of an Ardent Heart" with Alyosha. He decries the way a person can hold the ideal of Sodom and the Madonna at the same time: "Yes man is broad, too broad, indeed. I'd have him narrower" (98). Robert Louis Jackson points to the echo of the Grand Inquisitor here (*Art* 339).

173. Edward Wasiolek insightfully contrasts Zosima's bow before Dmitri with that of Katya: "Zosima's bow stays the hand of the murderer; Katerina's raises it" (*Fiction* 159).

174. His sense of humor steady and gentle as ever, Zosima chides her as a "naughty girl" (56), listens to her "serious" explanation, and blesses her "tenderly" (56). When she catches Alyosha's eye, Lise's "triumphant" smile seems innocent enough. After reading the "Little Demon" chapter, the scene takes on a darker cast of willfulness.

175. "In describing Father Zosima, Dostoevsky is here describing Wittgenstein's ideal of psychological insight. When, after being persuaded by Wittgenstein to read *The Brothers Karamazov*, Drury [his friend] reported that he had found the figure of Zossima very impressive, Wittgenstein replied, 'Yes, there really have been people like that, who could see directly into the souls of other people and advise them'" (Monk 549).

Chapter 4: Alyosha's First Three Days

176. As Valentina Vetlovskaya has observed, Alyosha is the novel's "hagiographic hero," whose life is patterned upon an "organic" integration of

two kinds of saint's lives: that of Theodosius, "who senses, almost from infancy, his lofty calling, and subsequently follows it without swerving," and Ephraim the Syrian, "who turns to God and gives himself up to the same asceticism *after many trials, mistakes, and errors*" (156; emphasis added).

177. David Cunningham refers to William W. Rowe "for a much more extensive list of triads" (154, n.23).

178. In his final counsel, Zosima particularly commends the Gospel of Luke, a gospel that is unique in its emphasis upon the quotidian, its repetitions of phrases like "daily" and "each day."

179. Preceding these, Fyodor utters words that comprise something like a travesty of Zosima's later words of commission to Alyosha: "You will burn and you will burn out, you will be healed and come back again. And I will wait for you" (27). The adumbration suggests that *both* men are Alyosha's fathers.

180. Dostoevsky's term for what he saw as a disturbing trend: children from broken families, finding temporary shelter and sustenance with an unstable set of successive benefactors, "accidental families."

181. Vetlovskaya also points to these youthful, not yet prosaic, attributes of Alyosha at the start of the novel (154–55). See also Michael Holquist's chapter "How Sons Become Fathers: *The Brothers Karamazov*" and Donna Orwin, who observes, "Alyosha is more, not less, convincing as a character because he is not all wise" (138).

182. Gabriel Marcel emphasized availability (*disponibilité*) to the other person as vital to intersubjective relations. See *Cain* 147.

183. The next day, Ivan tells Alyosha that he respects him for the way that he "stands firm" (198).

184. See Suzanne Fusso's discussion of this scene (74).

185. Robert L. Belknap elucidates the similarities and differences between buffoonery and *nadryv* (*Structure* 33–39).

186. René Girard's famous concept. In her biography of René Girard, Cynthia Haven relates a touching personal anecdote: "After the death of the eminent Dostoevsky scholar Joseph Frank [on February 27, 2013], another late-life friend, I spent an evening with his widow, the French mathematician Marguerite Frank, sorting through mountains of his papers

on the coffee table and the floor. From one pile, she plucked out and passed to me a little known article by Girard, "Dostoevsky's Demons." She had disregarded it . . . but Joe Frank had saved it for a reason, so I read it later on that evening. Girard's article ends with the death of Dostoevsky: 'He died on January 8, 1881 in St. Petersburg, not long after the publication of *The Brothers Karamazov*. It's there that we find—in the passage in which Ivan Karamazov tells the legend of Jesus Christ's returning to the world, only to encounter the Grand Inquisitor—Dostoevsky's most famous analysis of modern culture's repudiation of its religious inheritance in favor of Enlightenment philosophy's narcissistic individualism. And it's there in *The Brothers Karamazov* as well that we find—in the unconditional love the dying Zosima wills—Dostoevsky's answer'" (275).

René Girard died on November 4, 2015, and Cynthia Haven closes her biography with a description of Girard's requiem Mass, which she attended "at Palo Alto's St. Thomas Aquinas Church. . . . On the cover of the program, I read the final lines from *The Brothers Karamazov*, continuing the thoughts I had recently written for this postscript. Let these be the last words, then, for me as well as for René Girard: 'Certainly we shall all rise again, certainly we shall see each other and tell each other with joy and gladness all that has happened'" (*Haven* 279).

187. I'm grateful to Saul Morson's articulation of this shared insight regarding the gift during a discussion during the July 2019 Symposium of International Dostoevsky Studies in Boston. See also Pedrag Cicovacki: "[Dostoevsky's] understanding of life as a gift is opposed" to misconceptions of life as property or promise. "Dostoevsky is firmly convinced that life is not something one *has* but something one *is*" (*Affirmation of Life* 210–11).

188. See the Orthodox *Lenten Triodion*, Holy Friday "Royal Hours": "Thus says the Lord to the Jews: 'O My people, what have I done unto thee?'" (Mic 6:3) (606). Recent Orthodox scholarship has reflected upon the anti-Semitic accents in the liturgy.

189. See Alina Wyman's splendid close analysis of this scene, 187–99.

190. Quoted by Bate in his biography of Keats (249).

191. "Revel" is Madame Khokhlakova's perspicacious assessment when she greets Alyosha upon his arrival (159).

192. For an incisive study of the violent dynamics of forced speech, and a far less beneficent view of human dialogue than Bakhtin's, see Aaron Fogel's *Coercion to Speak.*

193. In his dissertation, including his chapter on *The Brothers Karamazov,* Leslie Wright Smith observes that confessors like Zosima and Alyosha "actually talk very little, but do more listening as confessors" (125), and that those who confess find peace in silence, ultimately, not in language (25). An article by Peter Meyers on the life of a south side of Chicago priest, "Father Marty" offers a similar insight: "'Sometimes it's a matter of knowing when to shut up,' he says of his life's work" (48) as a parish priest and confessor.

194. See Timothy Snyder's *Bloodlands.* Snyder estimates that 14 million noncombatants were slaughtered by the willfulness of Hitler and Stalin between 1933–45.

195. Bakhtin's writes: "The most important aspect of this surplus is love . . . and then confession, forgiveness . . . finally, simply an active (not a duplicating) understanding, a willingness to listen. This surplus is never used as an ambush, as a chance to sneak up from behind. This is an open and honest surplus . . ." ("Reworking" 299).

196. Pieper, *Living the Truth* 165

197. Pope Francis also employs the image of the sick in hospitals: "[I]t is necessary to go out: to go out from the church and the parishes, to go outside and look for people where they live, where they suffer, and where they hope. I like to use the image of a field hospital to describe this 'Church that goes forth'" (*Mercy* 52).

198. Terras also points to Ivan's use of "bitter irony" (223), as does Joseph Frank (*Mantle* 604–7). Fittingly, Ivan's devil uses the word "charming" in his viciously ironic stabs at Ivan's writing (546).

199. Denis Zhernokleyev notes a parallel between this scene and Raskolnikov's attack on Sonia in *Crime and Punishment:* "[Raskolnikov's] vicious attack culminates in the same way as Ivan's feuilletonistic blitzkrieg against Alyosha, with a theodicean provocation: 'And what does God do for you?' he asked, probing her further (*CP* 257)." Unpublished manuscript, quoted with permission of the author.

200. See Chapter 2 of Susan McReynolds's provocative study.

201. Friesenhahn's analysis illuminates Dostoevsky's christological and trinitarian understanding of human suffering, albeit in the novel's "oblique, artistic form": "Balthasar's theology of the Trinity depicts the essence of God as kenotic (self-giving) love and . . . this understanding of God's nature serves as the basis for the Christian answer to the problem of evil. The Cross of Jesus Christ is the ultimate historical expression of God's Triune nature, such that by uniting our sufferings to the Cross, we also thereby participate in the inner life of God. The Cross connects human suffering to God's Trinitarian essence of self-giving love in a fashion that redeems all human suffering and renders it of salvific value, both to the sufferer and to others. Suffering by the grace of salvation offered to humanity by Jesus Christ, the Incarnate Son, becomes a participation in the Trinity and is thus ultimately transformed by the Triune God into joy" (*Trinity* 2). Other helpful attempts to heal this "radical disjunction" between the discourse of theodicy and pastoral counsel include Eleanor Stump's *Wandering in Darkness* and Daniel Castelo's *Theological Theodicy*.

202. The moment recalls that in *Crime and Punishment* in which Svidrigailov has trapped and threatened Dounia. When she suddenly casts off the revolver with which she had the power to kill him and make her escape, he senses his "deliverance" from a dark, bitter feeling and, in a very different voice, asks if she could ever love him. "Never!" she responds. "There followed a moment of terrible, dumb struggle in the heart of Svidrigailov. . . . 'Here's the key.' He took it out of the left pocket of his coat and laid it on the table behind him, without turning or looking at Dounia. 'Take it! Make haste!' . . . [T]here seemed a terrible significance in the tone of that 'make haste'" (446). Dounia's impulsive renunciation of violent power over another opens up in Svidrigailov, for a moment, the capacity to release another he himself was about to impose violence upon. But his "make haste" is, like the Inquisitor's "Go," divided: moments later, a "smile of despair" "contort[s] his face" (447), a foreshadowing of his suicide the next day. See Carol Apollonio's sensitive analysis which illuminates as it goes "against the grain": "[Svidrigailov] lets Dunia go. His suicide . . . resolves the tensions of the novel and clears the way for equilibrium. . . . Unappreciated both inside and outside the bounds of the novel's world, Svidrigailov plays a sacrificial, purifying role" (*Secrets* 86).

203. Gibson astutely observes: after Alyosha's christological response (213) "one would expect the 'Legend' to illustrate the difficulties of universal forgiveness. And from the prologue, featuring 'The Wanderings of Our Lady through Hell,' one would still expect it. But . . . Ivan perplexes us

by moving to different issues altogether," most prominently Christ's gift of freedom (182).

204. As Ralph Matlaw explains, Dostoevsky planned a reply to K. D. Kavelin who "had attacked Dostoevsky's view in an 'Open Letter' in *The Russian Herald*, November, 1880." Matlaw translates Dostoevsky's notes: "throughout Europe there *has not been* and does not exist so powerful an *expression* [of these ideas] from the atheistic point of view as mine. It is clear that I do not believe in Christ as a child, but my *hosannah* has passed through a great *furnace of doubt*, as my devil says in the book" ("From Dostoevsky's Notebooks" 667; emphasis in original).

205. See *Problems* 258–60, for Bakhtin's analysis of Ivan's "bifurcated," "internal dialogue" as revealed in his dialogues with Smerdyakov.

206. In Yiddish: "Man plans, God laughs." Catholic writer Tobias Wolff taught *The Brothers Karamazov* at Stanford University, and one of his favorite moments in the novel is Fyodor's response to Ivan's denial of God's existence: "Who is it laughing at man?" (120). See Contino, "This Writer's Life": https://www.commonwealmagazine.org/writers-life.

207. The recapitulation of all things in Christ is a key idea in the second-century church father St. Irenaeus of Lyon. See von Balthasar's volume, *Scandal of the Incarnation*, "Incarnation as Recapitulation" (53–93).

208. As with Snegiryov and Ivan, another example of the cry for divine justice to manifest itself.

209. Relatedly, Joseph Frank observes the way in which Dostoevsky's experience of love for his wife Anna infused his rendering of Mitya's love for Grushenka: "When creating the intensity of Dmitry Karamazov's sensual intoxication with Grushenka, he did not have to *invent* such feelings at all; and now, for the first time in his work, he portrays the mutation of such tempestuous sensuality into the complex union of genuine love and self-sacrificial devotion that he celebrates in the happiness of his own marriage" (*Mantle* 450). Paul Friedrich aptly observes: "[Grushenka] is an extreme beauty, a *ras-krasavita*, but the physical passion she arouses passes over and blends with a religious love—thus symbolizing the fusion between the sexual and the religious that *The Brothers Karamazov* is, to a large degree, about" (51). For a profound reading of Sonya Marmeladova's hospitality to Raskolnikov, see Valentina Izmirlieva, "Hosting the Divine Logos."

210. Kant points to persistent "dear self" at the start of the second section of *Grounding* (407, Ellington translation).

211. In *The Symposium*, Diotima describes human flesh as "perishable rubbish" (212c, Hamilton translation).

212. See Sammon, *Called to Attraction* 49–68.

213. In the context of Matthew and Luke's descriptions of Christ's birth, Sammon writes: "the arrival of Jesus, which is also the arrival of beauty into the world, happens against all expectations. In this sense, Jesus bears the Greek sense of beauty as *paraprosdokian*: that which surprises, or arrives against expectations, compelling those who witness it to reinterpret their original view of the event (as well as the whole of reality itself!)" (33).

214. Later, torn by his decision of whether or not to escape, Dmitri declares to Alyosha "It's your decision that will decide it" (502).

215. Contrast the way Alyosha stands up, above Katerina, the day before: "He was standing at the table and did not sit down" (167). On becoming proximate to others, see Bryan Stevenson: https://www.carnegiefoundation.org/blog/empathy-and-social-justice-the-power-of-proximity-in-improvement-science/.

216. Rakitin refuses to open himself to the unexpected encounter that has just taken place before him. "He had expected something quite different by bringing Grushenka and Alyosha together" (308), but remains willfully, maliciously ironic. Leaving Alyosha with a curse, he goes off to his own back alley.

217. I draw the phrase "interior affinity" from Pope Benedict XVI, who comments on progress in ecumenical relations between the Western and Eastern Churches (*Light of the World* 167)

218. For this quote, I use Pevear and Volokhonsky's translation.

219. As I presented at the International Dostoevsky Symposium in Granada in June, 2016, I find the incarnational theology of Maximus the Confessor to be illuminative of the "Cana" chapter. In my remarks, I observed that Joseph Frank had noted "one of the few nonpartisan studies of Dostoevsky's Christology": Ryszard Przybylski's *Dostoevsky and the 'Cursed Problems,'* published in Warsaw in 1964. Przybylski "links [Dostoevsky's] ideas with that of the seventh-century theologian Maximus

[the] Confessor, who exercised an important influence on . . . Russian Orthodox theology," (*Liberation*, 386 n.6) including Dostoevsky's younger friend Soloviev. Maximus completed the task of the fifth-century Council of Chalcedon: he reaffirmed that Christ is both God and human, "without separation or confusion." But in contrast to the monothelites, he clarified that Chalcedonian doctrine by insisting that Jesus had two wills, divine and human. Maximus termed Christ's human will as his *"natural will"*—in full conformity to the divine will. In his earthly life, Jesus knew temptation but remained sinless, even in Gethsemane when he prayed, "Father, if you are willing, remove this cup from me; yet, not my will, but yours be done" (Luke 22:42). Christ accepts his vocation, and thus his will is natural. Indeed, for Maximus the natural will of every person, his or her deepest wish, is to accept our own vocation as *imago Dei*, our calling to deification, to conformity with the divine will, and thus to perfect freedom. Weakened by original sin, however, our will is "gnomic," prone to agonizing deliberation and eventual choice, but often of paths we don't truly wish to take. By grace, we can recover our "natural will," which comports with what Bakhtin calls "the deepest I," the "I" that can say with St. Paul, "it is no longer I who live but Christ who lives in me" (Gal 2:20). (See also Berthold's translation of Maximus, 298). In contrast, the Grand Inquisitor recognizes *only* the unredeemed gnomic will when he claims that "nothing is more seductive for man than his freedom of conscience and nothing is a greater cause of suffering" (221). Dostoevsky's characters are, indeed, often agonized in their deliberations: "Decide for me!" they plead. Often, they contort their wills in the lacerating de-formation of *nadryv*: they will perversely, infernally *against* both self and other. But some, like Alyosha, reveal the redemptive alternative. Maximus insists that true freedom follows from true vision; acetic self-denial clarifies our vision, our true desire. Similarly, Father Zosima teaches: "Obedience, fasting, and prayer are laughed at, yet only through them lies the way to real, true freedom. I cut off my superfluous and unnecessary desires, I subdue my proud and wanton will and chastise it with obedience, and with God's help I attain freedom of spirit and with it spiritual joy" (271). Saying no to occasional pleasures can strengthen one's capacity to say "yes" to what one most truly wishes: to say "yes" to the Person who offers abundant life (John 10:10). But such a "yes" entails taking up "the cross, not the gallows" (549), to borrow the dichotomy posed by Ivan. Maximus writes, "[W]hen you see that your mind is giving itself over to sins in thought, and you do not resist, know that your body too will not be long in falling with those sins" (68). On the eve of the trial Ivan sees that his thoughts *had* affected his vision: He had promised Alyosha that he would protect their father, but reserves

"full latitude" in his murderous wishes (129). The next day, his body follows his mind to Moscow (242), and his wish becomes reality. Alyosha's mystical moment in solitude is situated in the communal context of the church's liturgy. The scene thus suggests the "cosmic liturgy," so vital to Maximus's vision, as does the final scene of the novel, Alyosha's "speech at the stone" with the boys. In "Cana of Galilee" Alyosha recovers his natural will. He apprehends and receptively responds to the real. To draw on the language of Maximus, as explicated by Ian McFarland, Alyosha does not choose in the modern sense of "free choice." Rather, he willingly receives the divine gift of vocation (See "The Theology of the Will").

"[S]teadfast for the rest of his life," remembering always that "someone visited my soul at that hour," he leaves the monastery and begins his work as a monk in the world—patiently, prudently guiding others toward the exercise of their own "natural" wills. Dostoevsky saw "Cana" as "perhaps the most significant [chapter] in the whole novel" ("Letter to N. A. Lyubimov," Norton Critical Edition, 663). Here he invites his reader to perceive the way the event of the incarnation has forever linked the earthly with the infinite, and made possible the transformation of our wills. A Maximal Chalcedonian vision unites what seems irreconcilable. As has been noted, Bakhtin himself highlighted the "structural affinities or parallels between the Dostoevskian word and the Chalcedonian one. . . . Dostoevsky's language is bifurcated but not binary . . ." (Mihailovic, 130).

In my analysis of the "Cana" chapter here, I use the Pevear/Volokhonsky translation. For the sake of coherence, I'll dispense with page references to this brief chapter which comprises pp. 359–63 of that translation. Other page references refer to Norton Critical edition.

220. The novel rings with countless such "rhymes." In this chapter, Alyosha falls asleep on his knees, as does, in a very different key, Ferapont (288); Zosima "raise[s] Alyosha a little with his hands" as, in the previous chapter, Alyosha bends down to Grushenka, and "gently [takes] her hands" (P/V 357).

221. Dostoevsky's attitude toward the Jesuits may be more complex than usually acknowledged, as we will see later in discussing the casuistry that Alyosha and Mitya employ.

222. The repetitions here—"uncouth, uncouth"—and elsewhere recall Book 6, the life of Zosima written by Alyosha in the form of a *zhitie*, or saint's life, the style of which is "rhythmic, sounds and words are repeated,

especially *umilenie* (tender emotion) as noun, verb, adjective, and adverb"
(Rosen, 729).

223. See Carol Apollonio's chapter "The Mothers Karamazov," in *Dostoevsky's Secrets* and Liza Knapp's "Mothers and Sons: The Ladies of
Skotoprigonevsk."

224. See von Balthasar on Irenaeus: "[T]he reconciliation of the world and
God, of nature and grace [. . .] has its foundation in the one Incarnation.
This indestructible interweaving of things is the true touchstone of what
is Catholic" (*Scandal* 53). James Matthew Wilson observes that Catholic
aesthetics "concerns itself . . . *with form as a whole and, finally, the whole
of reality, created and uncreated*" ("Confessional Reading" in *Cambridge
Companion*; emphasis added, 48).

225. Henri de Lubac writes: "Catholic spirituality has not to choose . . .
between an 'interior' and a 'social' tendency, but all their extended forms,
in their extensive variety, will share in both." See *Catholicism* 343.

226. *"Tout est grace,"* words attributed to St. Therese of Lisieux, and are
quoted at the conclusion of Bernanos's *Diary of a Country Priest.*

227. See "Selections from Dostoevsky's Letters," 663.

228. See Morson, "Introductory Study" to Dostoevsky's *Writer's Diary:*
"'The man-god encountered the God-man, Apollo Belvedere encountered
Christ' (8/80, 3.30)" (34).

229. Hopkins, "for Christ plays in ten thousand places / Lovely in eyes,
and lovely in limbs not his" "As Kingfishers Catch Fire." https://www.poetryfoundation.org/poems/44389/as-kingfishers-catch-fire.

Chapter 5: Mitya

230. Kate Holland observes the narrative tension here between openness
and closure, "The ellipses that represent the murder of Fyodor Karamazov
signify the turn from tragic inevitability to novelistic potentiality" (180).

231. Kate Holland's discussion of this scene bears affinities to my own. She
notes that the flight to Mokroe takes place at the same time as Alyosha's
Cana experience, "thus suggesting the possibility of Mitya's rebirth" (181),
and that Andrey's "folk legend" of Christ's forgiveness of those in hell

"provides the model for Mitya's subsequent moral and spiritual development in the novel" (182).

232. In "An Onion," Dostoevsky describes Grushenka as "a plump, rosy
beauty of the Russian type" (296) but when Alyosha sees her in November,
after a five-week illness, he finds that "her face was even more attractive
than before, and he liked to meet her eyes when he went in to see her. A
look of firmness and intelligent purpose had developed in her face. There
were signs of spiritual transformation in her . . ." (475).

233. Amy Ronner astutely analyzes the ways in which Dostoevsky represents the legal institutions of his time and place, and the way his insights
continue to bear relevance to our own justice system. Recent articles
suggest growing skepticism that police interrogation, especially as guided
by the "Reid technique," can lead to the truth. See Eli Hager, "The Seismic
Change in Police Interrogations," The Marshall Project, March 7, 2017:
https://www.themarshallproject.org/2017/03/07/the-seismic-change-in-
police-interrogations. See also "Do Police Interrogation Techniques Produce False Confessions?" *The New Yorker*, December 9, 2013, 42, 44 (also
cited by Ronner, 137).

234. Girard too links Dostoevsky and Weil (*Resurrection* 62).

235. Weil's thought here might be linked with that of Zosima in the "So
Be It, So Be It" chapter. For Weil, "However the code may be reformed,
punishment cannot be humane unless it passes through Christ. . . . It is important that the law should be recognized as having a divine character . . ."
(155). Zosima looks to the "complete transformation from a society almost
heathen in character into a single universal and all-powerful Church" (62),
which "would succeed in restoring the excluded, in restraining those who
plan evil, and in regenerating the fallen" (62). As pointed out earlier, Zosima's utopian vision here is hardly "prosaic". Although Weil's ideas bear a
kinship to Zosima's, hers *can* be understood as more realistic to the degree
that they are embodied in *particular* interactions between representatives
of the law and suspect or criminal.

236. Bryan Stevenson, attorney and prisoner advocate, writes eloquently
of his work with prisoners in *Just Mercy*. On March 18, 2016, he presented
a lecture at Pepperdine University. I attended with great anticipation,
especially since I had led a faculty-staff discussion of his book and had
asked my students to attend and listen for connections to Dostoevsky's
The Brothers Karamazov, which we were then studying. Toward the end

of his lecture, Mr. Stevenson told a story, rendered here as I remember it: "It was midnight. The phone rang. It was one of my clients in the prison. I was irate: 'Why are you calling me? You know you're not supposed to be using the phone at this time of night!' 'I know, I know,' the man said, 'but I just had to call you.' 'What's the emergency?' 'It's that book you gave me, I just finished it. I had to talk to you about it.'" That book was *The Brothers Karamazov*.

237. See Eric Naiman's "Kalganov."

238. A performative utterance is a word that, in the saying, comprises a deed, makes something happen. See J. L. Austin, *How to Do Things with Words*.

239. In *Sources of the Self*, Charles Taylor observes a "grace-dispensing" "apostolic succession" in *The Brothers Karamazov*: "from Markel to Zosima to Alyosha to Grushenka" (452). The grace-filled utterances of Grushenka are especially portrayed in these scenes at the end of Book 9.

240. See Harriet Murav on the descent/ascent pattern in Mitya's torments.

241. Léon Bloy's words were made famous by Graham Greene, who used them as the epigraph to his novel *The End of the Affair*. They are drawn from a letter Bloy wrote to Georges Landry on April 25, 1873. See *Lettres de Jeunesse (1870–1893)* (Paris: Edouard-Joseph, Editeur á Paris, 1920.) My thanks to David Bentley Hart for readily providing me with this reference.

242. Pope John Paul II's *"Salvifici Doloris"—On the Redemptive Meaning of Suffering* takes this passage from St. Paul as its point of departure.

243. Many contemporary writers have critiqued such positivist reduction of personhood. For two relevant examples see Rowan Williams, reflecting (with the help of philosopher Raymond Tallis) on the contemporary materialist "passion to reduce what we can say about a conscious mind, let alone the freedom of the will" (*Human* 20) and Marilynne Robinson's reminder that "the strangeness of reality consistently exceeds the expectations of science" (*Absence* 124).

244. Fulop-Miller, quoted by Dirscherl, S.J., 121

245. Victor Terras also observes this.

246. Not everything Fetukovich says is, to borrow Gary Saul Morson's phrase, "verbal pollution." But like so much in this novel, which rejoices in reversals of the expected and the irreducible unfinalizability of persons, Fetyukovich—like Ivan's devil—cuts both ways. His analysis of Smerdyakov, for example, in which he observes that "despair and penitence are two very different things" (619), is cogent and accurate.

247. "*The Brothers Karamazov* is a joyful book": the first line of Pevear and Volokhonsky's "Introduction" to their translation—with which I agree!

248. Indeed, the marriage itself promises its own crosses: when Dmitri learns that Grushenka had offered a bit of charity to the impecunious Poles, the "new man" gets jealous "on purpose" (478). Grushenka then reacts by sending them "a dozen pies" and "three rubles," and insists that Alyosha report to Dmitri that she's done so. Alyosha—no longer shy around such erotic fireworks—responds perfectly: "'I wouldn't tell him for anything,' he said smiling" (478). For a stunning imagining of the descendants of Mitya and Grusha, hear Robert Hass read his poem "Hello, I'll be your waiter tonight, and my name is Dmitri." https://www.youtube.com/watch?v=DYFoPvNGogU.

249. See Robin Feuer Miller's essay on the parabolic dimension in Dostoevsky in "The Gospel According to Dostoevsky: Paradox, Plot, and Parable" in *Dostoevsky's Unfinished Journey*.

Chapter 6: Ivan Fyodorovich Karamazov

250. Smerdyakov is, of course, the fourth, though unacknowledged brother. On Smerdyakov's nightstand sits a copy of "The Sayings of the Holy Father Isaac the Syrian." (The "big yellow book" [525] hides the money, but has Smerdyakov left it unread?) One of seventh-century Isaac's sayings has a remarkably Augustinian ring: "Dive away from sin into yourself and there you will find the steps by which to ascend" (34).

251. In *City of God*, Augustine writes of Cain: "The first founder of the earthly city was . . . a fratricide, overcome by envy, he slew his own brother, a citizen of the Eternal City, on pilgrimage in this world" (15.5).

252. See Yuri Corrigan on childhood trauma in Dostoevsky.

253. On this passage, Rowan Williams writes: "[T]he refusal to accept a world in which atrocities happen is also a refusal to accept the actuality

of healing or forgiveness. And while this is in many ways an appropriate aspect of the human response to atrocity—as in the memorial inscription at Auschwitz, 'O earth, cover not their blood'—the shadow side of it is the denial of any future freedom to alter relations or transform memories. Does the protest end up paralyzing freedom itself?" (*Dostoevsky* 39).

254. For an excellent discussion of Dostoevsky's "Ethics of Altruism" that links his "mystical sense of responsibility" with its "correspondence with the ideal image of Christ, who in the atonement took upon himself the sins of all humanity (109), see James P. Scanlan's *Dostoevsky the Thinker*.

255. Mitya's version appears in his "Hymn": "we are all responsible for all" (499). In my reading, the echo of "all for all" implies that in our "intercreatural" relations (Graham Pechey's Augustinian coinage), we cooperatively share in the salvific work of Christ when we take up our responsibility and serve in humble, active love. The notion of the cooperative "fellow-worker" is an important one in Orthodox thought. As Timothy (Kallistos) Ware writes: "To describe the relation between the grace of God and human freedom, Orthodoxy uses the term co-operation or synergy (*synergeia*); in Paul's words: 'We are fellow-workers (*synergoi*) with God' (1 Corinthians 3.9)" (221). The *Catechism of the Catholic Church* understands this relation very similarly, and draws on Augustine in its articulation: "God brings to completion in us what he has begun, 'since he who completes his work by cooperating with our will began by working so that we might will it': 'Indeed we also work, but we are only collaborating with God who works, for his mercy has gone before us. It has gone before us so that we may be healed, and follows us so that once healed, we may be given life; it goes before us so that we may be called, and follows us so that we may be glorified; it goes before us so that we may live devoutly, and follows us so that we may always live with God: for without him we can do nothing.' God's free initiative demands *man's free response*, for God has created man in his own image by conferring on him, along with freedom, the power to know him and love him" (2001–2). The first imbedded quotation here is from Augustine's *De gratia et libero arbitrio*, 17: PL 44, 901; the second is from Augustine's *De natura et gratia*, 31: PL 44, 264.

256. We see this twice: atop the stairs, Ivan hovers with malevolent, finalizing omniscience—unlike the narrator!—and listens to his father "stirring down below." He calls it "the basest action of his life" (239); when he arrives in Moscow after making his getaway from domestic entanglements, and he calls himself a "scoundrel" (242).

257. Bakhtin points to this scene as an instance of the penetrated word (*Problems* 255–56).

258. The Grand Inquisitor goes on to gloat "The most painful secrets of their conscience, all, all they will bring to us, and we shall have an answer for all. And they will be glad to believe our answer, for it will save them from the great anxiety and terrible agony they endure at present in making a free decision for themselves" (225).

259. Sergei Averintsev "invit[ed] Orthodoxy to approach the line of Aristotle and Thomas Aquinas, which accepts the middle way and presents a keen religious explanation of the natural world instead of jumping to condemn and reshape it . . ." (Epstein, *Spirituality* 28).

260. "Consciousness of sin gives us the feeling that we are evil, and a kind of pride sometimes finds a place in it. When we force ourselves to fix the gaze, not only of our eyes but of our souls, upon a school exercise in which we have failed through sheer stupidity, a sense of our mediocrity is borne in upon us with irresistible evidence No knowledge is more to be desired" (Weil 109).

261. Morson and Emerson also link Zosima's teaching on personal responsibility with Bakhtin's early ethical philosophy (*Rethinking* 20)

262. The devil, of course, is presented by Dostoevsky not only as a brain-fever-induced "double" of Ivan, but also as very possibly real. The devil knows things that Ivan could not know on his own, particularly that it is Alyosha knocking at the window, "with the most interesting and surprising news" (547). Indeed, the devil plays on the possibility that he *is* real just to keep Ivan in the torturous state between belief and disbelief, the tortured state toward which Zosima articulates and attends early in the novel (66). The reader, too, faces an interpretive dilemma.

263. Smerdyakov and the devil share what I would call—to revise Caryl Emerson's earlier-cited phrase concerning Myshkin—a reductively *malevolent* view of Ivan.

264. In the novel, the bow in fact emerges as a means of "signature": Zosima's conversion to and embrace of a life of responsibility to others begins with his bow to Afanasy.

265. Terras glosses the scene: "Van'ka' is a hypocoristic of 'Ivan'; hence Ivan must, subconsciously at least, recognize himself in the peasant's song . . ." (*Companion* 381).

266. Much like the anonymous suicide in the first chapter cast herself as Shakespeare's Ophelia.

267. Licharda was a "[s]ervant used as a tool in the murder of his master in the *Tale of Bova*, a seventeenth-century Russian adaptation of *Bevis of Hampton*" (Norton, first edition, Ralph Matlaw, ed. 249).

268. As with Mitya and Kolya (as we will see in the next chapter) encounter with a humble peasant proves especially crucial.

269. Another resonance of Luke's Gospel's special emphasis on "each day," "daily." See, for example, Luke 9:23.

270. Regarding this moment, Bakhtin aptly cites an 1877 letter of Dostoevsky to G. A. Kovner: "it is still better if I justify you rather than you justify yourself" (*Problems* 257). In his 1961 notes "Toward A Reworking of the Dostoevsky Book," Bakhtin writes, "Justification cannot be self-justification, recognition cannot be self-recognition. I receive my name from others . . ." (288). Justification, be it granted horizontally or vertically, must be received as a gift from the other or Other.

271. Deborah Martinsen continues: "Whereas Christ suffers mockery and humiliation, Ivan's devil suffers the air's iciness. Whereas Christ is put to death, Ivan's devil catches cold and suffers from rheumatism. These comic contrasts emphasize Christ's transcendence and the devil's worldliness, thereby reflecting the struggle in Ivan's soul between ethical action and earthly desire" (*Surprised* 210). In a later essay, Deborah notes Ivan's obsession with incarnation, and provocatively interprets Ivan's devil as "a mental construct" ("Incarnate" 53) in which "Ivan's Romantic imagination battles with his Realist view of self and the world" (66) and "helps Ivan to accept and even embrace brotherhood" (71). Perhaps so. But given that the devil knows things Ivan couldn't know—for example, that his brother Alyosha is at the door (547)—I think that Dostoevsky leaves it up to the reader to decide. If Ivan's devil is real, I'm inclined to agree with Gibson's claim that he seeks to intensify Ivan's self-division and "to keep him in perpetual confusion" (203, n.49). Alyosha arrives and mediates grace, through his loving, prayerful presence.

272. Such claims can point, for example, to two moments in the novel: Dmitri's claim to Alyosha that, "God and the devil are fighting [and] the battlefield is the heart of man" (97), and the devil's claim to Ivan that if he were to "bawl hosannah, . . . the indispensable minus would disappear at once. . . . And that would mean, of course, the end of everything . . ." (545). Robin Feuer Miller cites the words of Mikhail, Zosima's mysterious visitor, "The Lord vanquished the devil in my heart" (*BK* [269]) and claims that the words "recall Mitya's and Dostoevsky's own attraction to the Manichean heresy" (78). If, however, Dostoevsky understands the devil as creature, created by a superior, loving Creator, who has fallen through perverse choices (among them, lying), the charge of Manichaeism cannot stick. In such a view, God's grace must always be stronger than any power of the devil, seductive as his temptations may be. A person's will may be divided into warring halves, but that doesn't mean it is composed of two antithetical natures or substances, as the Manichaens claimed. See *Confessions*, 8.9.21–8.10.24.

273. Ivan knows this, as seen in the words he gives the Grand Inquisitor, who refers to the devil as "the spirit of self-destruction and nonexistence" (219).

274. Book 6 concludes with Zosima's discourse on hell, where like "the Starets Leonid, in effect the founder of eldership (*starchestvo*) at Optina Pustyn" (Hackel, 156), he prays for those who commit suicide, and reflects upon those who "remain proud and fierce even in hell," who "yearn for death and annihilation. But they will not attain to death" (279). Evil itself is an absence, but the creature can never annihilate what God has created. In Zosima's unorthodox and provocatively loving view, God continues to love and call the souls in hell (302). Given the image of this divine, loving calling, I cannot agree with Sergei Hackel when he argues that "some references to God towards the very end of [Zosima's discourse on hell] hardly compensate for [God's] absence hitherto" (155). For an appreciation of Zosima's words (and Grushenka's apposite legend of "the onion"), see Chapter Three of von Balthasar's *Dare We Hope "That All Men Be Saved"?* Balthasar concludes the chapter with a discussion of Book 21 of *City of God*, which presents Augustine's very different, closed image of hell, but implicitly suggests a bridge between Zosima and Augustine by arguing the "foolish[ness]" of tying "the so incomprehensibly rich and many-sided theology of Augustine down to this single point. If his uncountable thought-provoking ideas do not permit being unified into a consistent system, they are, nevertheless, linked to one another in a living way and point together

toward a center that is none other than the heart aflame with love that the saint is repeatedly depicted as holding in his hand. If that is true—and the great Tradition has always seen the great 'Father of the Western world' in this way—then we are not entitled to regard his hard eschatological statements, which grew still harder in his old age, simply as a turning away from his innermost concern" (71).

275. See Nietzsche's *Genealogy of Morals*, and his apostrophe on the man-god, "Zarathustra the Godless" (II.25).

276. "Gave It a Name" is a song about guilt by Bruce Springsteen that begins with a verse about the murder of Abel by Cain, the biblical figure linked to Ivan. "Give it a name" is, I think, a therapeutic phrase, and certainly useful for any pastoral counselor trying to get another person to identify, articulate, and act upon a problem.

277. Victor Terras glosses Ivan's words: "An allusion to the wedding ritual of the Russian peasants, where the bride would go through a routine of wavering between joining her betrothed and refusing to do so" (*Companion* 409).

278. In his analysis of the failed confessional discourse of Dostoevsky's Underground Man, Bakhtin observes that his "word about himself is not only a word with a sideward glance; it is also . . . a word with a loophole" (*Problems* 232–33).

279. Augustine comments on this line in *On Christian Doctrine*: "Unless, perhaps, because a cup of cold water is a small and most insignificant thing, we should also regard as small and most insignificant the promise of the Lord that he who gives such a cup to one of his disciples 'shall not lose his reward'" (145). Hanging upon the cross, Jesus says, "I am thirsty" (John 19:27), which suggests another link between Ivan and Christ. My thanks to Maire Mullins for reminding me of this scriptural passage.

280. He "overdid" it and some wouldn't shake his hand as they thought he was reactionary (542). The moment chimes with two previous hand-shake refusals: Zosima clings too hard to his newfound humility and refuses his "rival's" offer to shake hands (259). After the interrogation, Nikolay Parfenovich "hide[s] his hands behind his back" (430) when Mitya offers his.

281. I read Ivan's confession with more hope than, for example, Julian Connolly, who primarily hears Ivan's accusation and "scorn for those present at the scene": "While the urge Ivan feels to lay bare his responsibility

and to seek relief from his torment has positive underpinnings, he has not yet overcome his pride and therefore not achieved a state of the repentance and willingness to accept suffering" ("Confession" 25–26). Peter Brooks compares the court's failure to comprehend both Ivan's confession and Mitya's and concludes that "where confession is concerned . . . the law needs to recognize that its conceptions of human motivation and volition are particularly flawed" (64).

282. Mitya's words resonate even more fully when we extend Terras's ear for Lukan echoes and Zosima's affirmation of Lukan parable: Ivan's trajectory can be seen in the light of that "Gospel of Mercy," with its emphasis on second chances. One notable image: whereas in Mark 11 and Matthew 21, Jesus curses the barren fig tree, Luke's Jesus speaks a parable that suggests that even seemingly barren trees are "unfinalizable":

> And he told them this parable: "There once was a person who had a fig tree planted in his orchard, and when he came in search of fruit on it but found none, he said to the gardener, 'For three years now I have come in search of fruit on this fig tree but have found none. [So] cut it down. Why should it exhaust the soil?' He said to him in reply, 'Sir, leave it for this year also, and I shall cultivate the ground around it and fertilize it; it may bear fruit in the future. If not you can cut it down.'" (Luke 13:6–9)

As Walter Reed observes, "within the parable there is a voice that asks for mercy as well as one that demands judgment" (*Word* 109).

283. Cited by Emerson in "Zosima" 171.

Chapter 7: Alyosha's Three Days in November

284. Anna describe her husband's loving relationship with his children "I was positively astounded at my husband's ability to soothe a child" (*Reminiscences* 283). Joseph Frank notes his defense of young people as "seeking the truth" and on their "first step in their eventual acceptance of a supernatural Christ; and he saw his mission as that of supplying the leadership in this direction that was so woefully lacking" (*Mantle* 380).

285. For a listing of Erikson's Eight Stages of Psychosocial Development and brief discussion see: https://www.simplypsychology.org/Erik-Erikson.html.

286. Andrew E. Arterbury summarizes the many commentators who see a betrothal scene in John 4, but argues that it is, in fact, "a literary depiction of ancient hospitality" (63). For an excellent analysis on the role of hospitality in the New Testament, Eastern Orthodoxy, and Dostoevsky, see Valentina Izmirlieva, "Hosting the Divine Logos."

287. See Dan McAdams for an excellent discussion of generativity as a virtue: *Self Transcendence and Virtue.*

288. Orthodoxy does not require celibacy for priests, only for monks and bishops.

289. Caryl Emerson crystallizes this idea: "Anyone who bestows form on us in this way—whether kindly or unkindly—increases our repertory of choices and responses and is thus a benefactor, an author, a participant in aesthetic activity" (*Hundred Years* 214). For a study of internality, trauma, and the way a "personality relinquishes itself to the will of the other as a form of 'exit' from its own unbearable anguish," see Yuri Corrigan. "As in the earlier works, where Dostoevsky's conception of the collective self was grounded in the inwardly debilitating effects of childhood trauma, the four brothers of his final novel are all conceived of as wounded and unstable personalities who fear introspection and who cling to another personality as a means of stabilization and nourishment" (*Riddle* 122).

290. Obsessing on a theoretical wish can lead to acting upon it. Gary Saul Morson's analysis of Raskolnikov (which draws upon Tolstoy's) sheds light on Ivan's situation: "We typically assume that to act one must first choose to act, but that is psychologically naive. Raskolnikov lives in a state of mind in which nothing is quite real and everything is hypothetical. Completely abstracted from his surroundings, he has long been 'so completely absorbed in himself' that he has fallen into extreme slovenliness. He spends his time dreaming of theories and what it would be like to commit a crime based on them. Strictly speaking, it is not crime that fascinates him, but the possibility of it. The possible is what is most real to him. . . . The crime emerged not from a specific decision but from a state of mind, resulting from his neglect of prosaic duties and kindnesses, and from his cherishing 'bookish dreams.' Because he let himself sink into and persist in dreams where murder is a possibility, he is, without having chosen murder, still morally responsible for it. Every moment in which he fostered the theoretical state of mind, in which abstract considerations displaced common decency, made the crime more possible" ("*Crime and Punishment* at 150" 8–9). Regarding Ivan, Morson writes, "Dostoevsky offers a sort of realistic

proof of Christ's doctrine by showing that evil derives primarily not from actions but from wishes, for wishes shape the field of possibility. Crimes happen because our wishes create those possibilities, one of which is bound to be realized. . . . As Zosima explains, everyone contributes to evil, and so all bear responsibility" (*Narrative* 141).

291. Victor Terras: "The opening words of a fable by Ivan Dmitryev (1760–1837). "The Rooster, the Cat, and the Little Mouse" (1802). Susan McReynolds' note, *Brothers Karamazov*, 442, n.7.

292. Is Zosima being "pragmatic" here? I prefer to say "prudent." In an unpublished manuscript, "Dostoevsky as Apologist," Steven Horst argues that throughout his corpus, Dostoevsky's Christian vision rejects ideologies in the name of a "pragmatic test of truth." But while Christ *did* say "by their fruits you will know them" (Mt. 7:16), this does not make him a consequentialist, for he also claimed to be "the way, the truth, and the life" (Jn 14:6). While incarnational realism is practical, it seeks to discern the truth of matters, beyond what immediately "works."

293. As Joseph Frank observes, Dostoevsky's notes to Book 10 "sketch out other serious and even abhorrent possibilities" of children's torture and even suicide. "Happily, none of these suggestions are followed because they would have clashed too sharply with the tonality of childlike innocuousness that Dostoevsky wished to retain" (*Prophet* 490). And yet, the chimes that recall Ivan suggest Kolya's diabolical potential, as Alyosha will observe ("the devil has taken the form of that vanity and entered into a whole generation" [470]).

294. The phrase "on purpose" is repeated almost sixty times in the novel, and invariably suggests willfulness.

295. Here is sociologist Christian Smith's helpful definition of "person": "[A] conscious, reflexive, embodied, self-transcending center of subjective experience, durable identity, moral commitment, and social communication who—as the efficient cause of his or her own responsible actions and interactions—exercises complex capacities for agency and intersubjectivity in order to sustain his or her incommunicable self in loving relationships with other personal selves and with the nonpersonal world" (*Person* 103).

296. The words recall the wise peasant Makar Evanovich Dolgoruky in *The Adolescent* who counsels Arkady to see "the mystery in every tree, in every blade of grass" (354), to say his evening and morning prayers

(357–58), and, (like Zosima) to pray for those who commit suicide (383). They also call to mind "The Peasant Marey" whose "maternal smile" (154) and comfort Dostoevsky remembers in the February 1876 *Writer's Diary*.

297. As noted by Susan McReynolds in her edition of the novel (83, n.3).

298. Echoed near the end of Bernanos's *Diary of a Country Priest*. Bernanos once expressed his desire as to redo Dostoevsky's work through the lens of Catholicism (Sonnenfeld, *Crossroads* 71–72).

299. The Grand Inquisitor claims to "love" but reduces persons to "sheep" (223).

300. Pieper, citing Paul Claudel (*Cardinal Virtues* 22).

301. A pedagogical note: This is one of those scenes—and there are many in the novel—that lend themselves to a dramatic reading in class. Students love to take on roles and voices.

302. As Simone Weil notes, contempt is the opposite of loving attention. Forms of the word "contempt" appear over a hundred times in the novel.

303. See also Alyosha's chastising of his father for baiting Ivan—"leave off attacking him" (122), and his forceful words to Katerina in the Epilogue (633). Each time, Alyosha speaks "emphatically."

304. See the experience of Alyosha at the end of "Cana of Galilee": "Someone visited my soul in that hour" (312) and at the start of "the speech at the stone": "something seemed to shake in [Alyosha's] heart" (644).

305. See Edward Weisband's *The Macabresque* on theatrical, willfully imposed cruelty directed at an audience (49).

306. T. A. Kasatkina's observations on the connection between Zhuchka/Perezvon and the terrible dogs who kill the child in Ivan's "Rebellion" are perceptive and moving.

307. See Carla Arnell (92–94)

308. See Linda Ivanitis, *Dostoevsky and the Russian People*.

309. Here I use Pevear and Volokhonsky's translation as "cannon fodder" (132) more powerfully suggests Ivan's contempt for Smerdyakov, and the reduction of his personhood as a means to a revolutionary end.

310. Joseph Frank points out that in 1880, late in his composition of the novel, Dostoevsky had a conversation with Aleksey Suvorin as to whether he would turn over people plotting a possible assassination of the Tsar: "at the conclusion of this dialogue, and under its stimulation, . . . he outlined for his listener one of the possible continuations envisaged for his second volume (several others are mentioned in various memoirs). In this version, Alyosha Karamazov prepared himself 'to pass through the monastery and become a revolutionary. He would commit a political crime. He would be executed. He would have searched for truth, and in these searches, naturally, he would have become a revolutionary.' While such words can only remain hypothetical, they surely indicate the close affinity between his morally positive hero Alyosha and the radicals" (*Prophet* 484). I agree with Frank's assessment—certainly Alyosha would share some of the radicals' concerns for social justice—but have never been able to imagine Alyosha becoming a violent revolutionary.

311. See Joseph Frank's extensive discussion of young Dostoevsky's friendship with Belinsky (*Revolt* 172–98).

312. In the Penguin edition version of the chapter "Elders" David McDuff translates both "immediate action" and "swift achievement" (28) as "quick deed." I'm grateful to my student Raquel Grove for pointing this phrase out to me in her own excellent essay on *The Brothers Karamazov*.

313. As Leslie Farber has observed of willfulness: "the consequences of willing what cannot be willed is that we fall into the distress we call anxiety" (79). In the wake of Nietzsche and Dostoevsky's Kirillov, Farber sees ours as "the age of disordered will" in which "with the disappearance of the divine Will from our lives, we have come to hunger not for His Will . . . but for our own sovereign will, which is our modern way, this side the omnipotence of suicide or madness. And all exhortations notwithstanding, this we cannot will" (112).

314. As Walter Ong never tired of emphasizing *catholicos* means "through the whole." As he wrote to Anthony Low upon being awarded the 1996 Conference on Christianity and Literature Lifetime Achievement Award: "Today Christianity is discernibly 'through-the-whole'—a better definition of "Catholic" than "universal" is. https://www.christianityandliterature. com/Walter-Ong. The vital Russian word *sobernost* refers to "the wholeness of the community."

315. See Tikhon's response to Stavrogin's plan to publish his confession: "even in the form [and the substance] of this great penance there is something ridiculous" (*Devils* 702).

316. See the way this phrase is repeated by Ivan at the trial: "Have you any water? Give me a drink for Christ's sake!" (577). Victor Terras notes: "The commentators of PSS [the Russian edition of Dostoevsky's works] suggest that 'water' here is a symbol of 'living water' of faith. . . . Ivan, who has used the devil's name often throughout the novel, here for the first time invokes Christ" (*Companion* 410).

317. In Balthasar's theology, both Father and Holy Spirit share in the kenosis of Christ. See his *Mysterium Paschale*.

318. Reformed philosopher Alvin Plantinga has called John Paul II's *Salvifici Doloris* "surely one of the finest documents (outside the Bible) ever written on this topic, and surely required reading for anyone interested in the so-called problem of evil, or the problems that suffering can pose for the Christian spiritual life or, more generally, the place of suffering in the life of the Christian." "Faith and Reason: Alvin Plantinga." *Books and Culture*, July/August 1999. https://www.booksandculture.com/articles/1999/julaug/9b4032.html.

319. See Pope Francis on the practice of holiness in everyday life, "Gaudete et exsultate." http://w2.vatican.va/content/francesco/en/apost_exhortations/documents/papa-francesco_esortazione-ap_20180319_gaudete-et-exsultate.html.

320. Regarding ephemeral epiphanies, the words of Czech theologian Tomáš Halík come to mind. Halík is describing the breakthrough experience of Eckhart's *"gellasenheit"* ("letting go") and observes: "that breakthrough is glimpsed and briefly experienced, but sometime such moments are immediately followed by a beneficially humbling relapse of 'dependence' of the outward man on old and new 'somethings.' (How often have I naively thought that such experiences of God's touch were the final, definitive 'epiphany.' It took subsequent confrontation with my own weakness and doubts on the 'downward journey from Mount Tabor' to remind me of the angel's words to Elijah: 'Get up and eat, otherwise the journey will be too much for you'") (43).

321. Kolya now *wants* to understand Psalm 137. But the conclusion of this unforgettable psalm has brought many up short, especially its final address

to the "daughters of Babylon": "Blessed the one who seizes your children, and smashes them against the rock" (Ps 137:9). Responding to an earlier version of my analysis of this scene, Robin Feuer Miller asked me "How do these lines integrate themselves into the psalm as a whole? The psalm itself seems to embody the same light and darkness as Dostoevsky's works" (Response to "Dostoevsky and Internality Panel," AATSEEL Conference, February 3, 2018). Saints Augustine and Benedict read these troubling lines allegorically such that the "babes" are read as evil desires or thoughts. For recent studies see Stowe and McCaulley.

322. See Scanlan, 209–12. See also the work of David I. Goldstein and Maxim D. Shrayer. Both Susan McReynolds (199, n.1) and Amy Ronner (41, n.160) present the sad record of Dostoevsky's anti-Semitism.

323. As Ulrich Schmid observes, "Dostoevsky was the only non-German writer who attracted Heidegger's attention" and he kept the Russian novelist's portrait on his desk: "The comparative analysis of both author's stances towards their nation-states . . . help[s] explain Heidegger's allegiance to Hitler and Dostoevsky's worship of the Tsar" (38).

324. See Gabriel Marcel's concept of "availability," which bears affinities with Bakhtin's ideas of self and other relations: "This availability is not passive; rather, the exigent self actively seeks out relationships with others, just as she is actively engaged in the concern for others. Whereas a subject's passivity can result in fear, hesitancy, and powerlessness, the action of the exigent self can allow her to positively change a situation for another person. The force of the exigent life comes through the experience of being that is only found in sharing with others in being. The most significant end achievable for an individual is to be immersed in the beings of others, for only with others does the self experience wholeness of being. (This isn't to say, of course, that the self *will* experience wholeness just in virtue of her being available to others. Availability is a risk one takes, since it is only through availability that the potential for fullness emerges as possible.)" From the *Internet Encyclopedia of Philosophy*: https://www.iep.utm.edu/marcel/

325. Characters use the phrase "despise me" at least seventeen times in the novel.

326. Relatedly, C. S. Lewis writes, "I willingly believe that the damned are, in one sense, successful, rebels to the end; that the gates of hell are locked on the inside" (*The Problem of Pain* 127). In *The Great Divorce*, he writes:

"There are only two kinds of people in the end: those who say to God, 'Thy will be done' and those to whom God says, in the end, 'THY will be done.' All that are in Hell choose it. Without that self-choice, there could be no Hell. No soul that seriously and constantly desires joy will ever miss it. Those who seek, find. To those who knock, it is opened" (72–73).

327. An image of such communal conforming from Dante's *Purgatorio:* on the terrace of the gluttonous Dante meets his friend, Forese Donati, who explains that the purgatorial hunger and thirst experienced by him and his fellow penitents is freely *joined to* and *participates in* Christ's pain on the cross: "I speak of pain but I should speak of solace, / for we are guided to those trees by that / same longing that had guided Christ when He / had come to free us through the blood He shed / and, in His joyousness, called out: '*Eli*'" (Mandelbaum trans. 23.71–75).

328. A line from Bruce Springsteen's song "Better Days."

329. See Charles Taylor, drawing from Earl Wasserman, on the "subtler languages" of literature in *A Secular Age* (357).

330. Recall, too, Mikhail's attempt at solitary self-purgation (264).

331. Note the "anxiety" he feels when talking with Madame Khokhlakova (487).

332. After her initial "vindictive, venomous" words, Grushenka keeps herself from saying more: "She stopped speaking, as though suppressing something" (639).

333. The chapter is both symphonic in its recapitulations and liturgical. I think both of Mahler's 9th symphony and the a cappella chant of the Divine Liturgy. The "subtler language" of Dostoevsky's final novel validates the gifts of both pre-modernity and modernity.

334. Some find it sentimental, in Czeslaw Milosz's words, "a bit too sweet and kitschy" (*ABC's* 101). Ksana Blank, for example, echoes Robert Louis Jackson in finding it "Schilleresque," and critiques the "ecstatic" tone of Alyosha's speech as "out of place" "with the sobriety of the orthodox burial rite" (63).

335. After his resurrection, Jesus breaks bread (Luke 24:30–31), and eats fish (Luke 24:42–43) with his disciples.

336. Relatedly, Emmanuel Levinas writes, "responsibility does not give one time, a present for recollection or coming back to oneself; it makes one always late" ("God and Philosophy"143).

337. See too Anne Hruska, 489.

338. The birds also recall young Markel, Zosima's brother, who asks their forgiveness—and are, I hope, called to mind in the cover image of this book.

339. Smurov clear-sightedly sees Ilyusha's stone. I hear here a possible echo of Scripture: Abraham's names the place atop Mount Moriah, where Isaac does *not* die "YHWH-yireh" (Gen 22:14). Here is Robert Alters' commentary: "The place-name means 'the LORD sees.' The phrase at the end means literally 'he sees' or 'he will be seen. . . . It is. . . not clear whether it is God or the person who comes to the Mount who sees/is seen" (*Genesis* 106). I see Smurov's clear-sightedness, an integral part of prudence, as analogous to Abraham's, whose willingness to sacrifice his son Isaac becomes, in the Christian patristic imagination, a *figura* for trinitarian love. See Greta Maztner-Gore for further insightful discussion of Smurov, Smerdyakov, and other minor characters in the novel.

340. Walter Ong writes: "For much evil, there is no human answer at all, but for the Christian, if there is not a simple answer, there is a response, in God's own response. The response is that we must counter evil with good. In the incarnation of the Son, in Jesus Christ, the infinite God responds to evil by entering into the human condition, with its suffering and its subjection to evil, to overcome suffering and evil by good, culminating in the obedience that Jesus expressed on the cross" ("Realizing" 40).

341. Prudence draws on the past through the memory of experience: "our interior senses are perfected by memory and experience so as readily to judge particular situations as they arise . . ." (*Summa*, McDermott trans. 376–77).

342. As Susan McReynolds notes, "these final passages invoke the liturgical language of the Orthodox funeral service, in which the prayer 'Eternal Memory' is sung" (Norton ed., 646, n.6).

343. Or "fount and apex." See *Lumen Gentium*, 11. http://www.vatican.va /archive/hist_councils/ii_vatican_council/documents/vat-ii_const _19641121_lumen-gentium_en.html.

344. The Memorial Acclamation of the Eucharistic prayer avows Christ's death, resurrection, and restorative return: "Christ has died. Christ is risen. Christ will come again." As Josef Ratzinger notes, "The words of institution alone are not sufficient; the death alone is not sufficient; and even both together are not sufficient but have to be complemented by the Resurrection, in which God accepts this death and makes it the door into a new life. From out of this whole matrix—that he transforms his death, that irrational event, into an affirmation, into an act of love and of adoration—emerges his acceptance by God and the possibility of his being able to share himself in this way" (*God is Near Us* 39).

345. See St. Thomas, *Summa*, McDermott trans., 380.

346. Charles Taylor distinguishes transcendence from simple flourishing. See "Introduction" to *A Secular Age*.

347. Dante finished *Paradiso* just before he died. Dostoevsky completed *The Brothers Karamazov* just before he died. See Mark Taylor, *Last Works* for further reflections on artists' last works. Kroeker and Ward observe that the reader completes the novel in his or her real life. Alyosha's final words resonate with the reader, "And thus it might become possible to take up the second novel, the drama of our own lives, in a manner that shapes the future of the present moment by remembering the end" (28).

348. Pope Benedict XVI, *Sacrament of Charity* (par. 51).

Appendix: Testimony from an Array of Catholic Readers of *The Brothers Karamazov*

349. https://onbeing.org/programs/martin-sheen-spirituality-of-imagination/

350. See Zwick, 222.

351. See Faggen, 55. Note Merton's affirmative use of the word "romantic," which in this study I have used negatively, in contrast to "realist." A brief recognition of the both/and reality is in order: As Donald Fanger long ago observed, Dostoevsky is *both* romantic *and* realist. Walter Reed's discussion of the personalist and romantic dimension of Bakhtin's early ethical thought is relevant: "Bakhtin's own distinctive version of the literary person interpersonally articulated remains central. Once we understand its interpersonal as well as intrapersonal character, its focus

on an individuality which is also a sociality . . . the modes of personhood elaborated in ["Author and Hero"] can provide a compelling scheme for the interpretation of literary texts of all kinds, especially the literary texts of Romanticism. For the creative individual, however problematic he or she may be, is the central (though by no means the exclusive) concern of Romanticism" (*Romantic* 6).

352. See Desmond, 117.

353. See Küng, 142–43.

354. See Muggeridge, "Forward" 3.

355. Guardini opens his 1933 study *Religious Figures in Dostoevsky's Work* (1977, 17) with these words, translated here by George Pattison ("Dostoevsky"). A few years ago, Pope Francis cited Guardini's book on Dostoevsky: "The wisdom and love of [Zosima, counseling the woman who has murdered her abusive husband] is just as obvious and so, too, is the meaning of holiness, 'that is, an existence lived in faith and able to see that God is close to human beings; he holds their lives in his hands.' The pope said Father Guardini taught that when people accept that their existence is in God's hands, their personal will becomes doing God's will.

For Father Guardini, doing God's will is something that must have a concrete reflection in the way one lives with and treats other people, the pope said. The philosopher makes a distinction between being part of 'a people'—what Christians are called to be—and simply being a collection of individuals." https://www.catholicnews.com/services/englishnews/2015/recognize-gods-closeness-extend-it-to-others-pope-says.cfm

356. See de Lubac, *Drama* 244–46.

Bibliography

Adams, Marilyn. *Horrendous Evils and the Goodness of God*. Ithaca, NY: Cornell University Press, 1999.

Alfeyev, Hilarion. *The Spiritual World of Isaac the Syrian*. Collegeville, MN: Liturgical, 2008.

Alter, Robert. *Genesis: Translation and Commentary*. New York: Norton, 1996.

Anderson, Roger B. *Dostoevsky: Myths of Duality*. Gainesville, FL: University of Florida Press, 1986.

Apollonio, Carol. "Dostoevsky's Religion: Words, Images, and the Seeds of Charity." In *Dostoevsky Studies* 13. Special issue on "Dostoevsky and Christianity." (2009) 23–36.

————. *Dostoevsky's Secrets: Readings against the Grain*. Evanston, IL. Northwestern University Press, 2009.

————, ed. *The New Russian Dostoevsky: Readings for the Twenty-First Century*. Bloomington, IN: Slavica, 2010.

Aquinas, St. Thomas. *Summa Theologica*. Translated by Fathers of the English Dominican Province. Notre Dame, IN: Christian Classics, Ave Maria, 1981.

————. *Summa Theologica*. Translated by Alfred Freddoso. Online: https://www3.nd.edu/~afreddos/summa-translation/Part%202-2/st2-2-ques49.pdf.

————. *Summa Theologiae*. A Concise translation by Timothy McDermott. Westminster, MD: Christian Classics, 1997.

Aristotle. *Nicomachean Ethics*. Translated by Terence Irwin. Indianapolis, IN: Hackett, 1999.

Arnell, Carla A. "'Love beyond Logic': On Cannons, Castles, and Healing Tomfoolery in Dickens *Great Expectations* and Dostoevsky's *Brothers Karamazov*." *Renascence* 69.2 (2017) 81–97.

Arterbury, Andrew E. "Breaking the Betrothal Bonds: Hospitality in John 4." *Catholic Biblical Quarterly* 72.1 (2010) 63–83.

Athanasius, St. *On the Incarnation*. Translated by Sister Penelope Lawson, C.S.M.V. New York: Macmillan, 1946.

Auerbach, Erich. "*Figura*." (1959) In *Scenes from the Drama of European Literature*, translated by Ralph Manheim, 11–76. Minneapolis, MN: University of Minnesota Press, 1984.

————. *Mimesis: The Representation of Reality in Western Literature*. Translated by Willard R. Trask. Princeton, NJ: Princeton University Press, 1953.

————. "*Sermo Humilis.*" In *Literary Language and Its Public in Late Antiquity and in the Middle Ages*, translated by Ralph Manheim, 25–82. Princeton, NJ: Princeton University Press, 1965.

Augustine, St., *City of God.* Translated by Henry Bettenson. New York: Penguin, 1984.

————. *Confessions.* Translated by Henry Chadwick. Oxford: Oxford University Press, 1991.

————. *Enchiridion on Faith, Hope, and Love.* Translated by J. B. Shaw. Washington, DC: Regenery, 1996.

————. *On Christian Doctrine.* Translated by D. W. Robertson, Jr. Indianapolis, IN: Bobbs-Merrill, 1981.

————. *Sermons to the People.* Translated and edited by William Griffin. New York: Image, 2002.

Austin, J. L. *How to Do Things with Words.* Edited by J. O. Urmson and Marina Sbisa. Oxford: Clarendon, 1975.

Averintsev, Sergei. "Bakhtin, Laughter, and Christian Culture." In *Bakhtin and Religion: A Feeling for Faith*, edited by Susan M. Felch and Paul J. Contino, 79–96. Evanston, IL: Northwestern University Press. 2001.

Bakhtin, Mikhail. "Author and Hero in Aesthetic Activity." In *Art and Answerability*, edited by Michael Holquist and Vadim Liapunov, 4–256. Austin, TX: University of Texas Press, 1990.

————. "Discourse in the Novel." In *The Dialogic Imagination*, edited by Michael Holquist, translated by Caryl Emerson and Michael Holquist, 259–422. Austin, TX: University of Texas Press, 1981.

————. "From Notes Made in 1970–71." In *Speech Genres and Other Late Essays*, edited by Caryl Emerson and Michael Holquist, translated by Vern W. McGee, 132–58. Austin, TX: University of Texas Press, 1986.

————. "Response to a Question from the *Novy Mir* Editorial Staff." In *Speech Genres and Other Late Essays*, edited by Caryl Emerson and Michael Holquist, translated by Vern W. McGee, 1–9. Austin, TX: University of Texas Press, 1986.

————. *Problems of Dostoevsky's Poetics.* 1963. Edited by and Translated by Caryl Emerson. Minneapolis: University of Minnesota Press, 1984.

————. "The Problem of the Text in Linguistics, Philology, and the Human Sciences: An Experiment in Philosophical Analysis." In *Speech Genres and Other Late Essays*, edited by Caryl Emerson and Michael Holquist, translated by Vern W. McGee, 103–31. Austin, TX: University of Texas Press, 1986.

————. *Toward a Philosophy of the Act.* Translation and notes by Vadim Liapunov, edited by Vadim Liapunov and Michael Holquist. Austin: University of Texas Press, 1993.

————. "Toward a Methodology for the Human Sciences." In *Speech Genres and Other Late Essays*, edited by Caryl Emerson and Michael Holquist, translated by Vern W. McGee, 159–72. Austin, TX: University of Texas Press, 1986.

————. "Toward a Reworking of the Dostoevsky Book (1961)." In *Problems of Dostoevsky's Poetics*, edited and translated by Caryl Emerson, 283–302. Minneapolis, MN: University of Minnesota Press, 1984.

Balthasar, Hans Urs von. *Cosmic Liturgy: The Universe According to Maximus the Confessor.* Translated by Brian E. Daley, S.J. San Francisco, CA: Ignatius, 2003.

————. *Dare We Hope "That All Men Be Saved."* Translated by Dr. David Kipp and Rev. Lothar Krauth. San Francisco: Ignatius, 1988.

———. *Epilogue*. Translated by Edward T. Oakes, SJ. San Francisco: Ignatius, 2004.

———. *The Glory of the Lord: A Theological Aesthetics. Volume I: Seeing the Form*. Translated by Erasmo Leiva-Merikakis. Edited by Joseph Fessio S.J. and John Riches. San Francisco: Ignatius, 1982.

———. *The Glory of the Lord: A Theological Aesthetics. Volume III: Lay Styles*. Edited by John Riches; translated by Andrew Louth, John Saward, Martin Simon, and Rowan Williams. San Francisco: Ignatius, 1986.

———. "Revelation and the Beautiful." In *Explorations in Theology. I. The World Made Flesh*. Translated by A.V. Littledale with Alexander Dru. (1964),. 95-126 San Francisco: Ignatius, 1989.

———. *The Scandal of the Incarnation: Irenaeus Against the Heresies*. Translated by John Saward. San Francisco: Ignatius, 1990.

———. *Theodrama: Theological Dramatic Theory II: Dramatis Personae: Man in God*. Translated by Graham Harrison. San Francisco: Ignatius, 1990.

Banerjee, Maria Němcová. *Dostoevsky: The Scandal of Reason*. Great Barrington, MA: Lindisfarne, 2006.

Barron, Robert. *The Priority of Christ*. Grand Rapids: Baker Academic, 1997.

Bate, William Jackson. *John Keats*. Cambridge: Harvard University Press, 1963.

Belknap, Robert. *The Genesis of "The Brothers Karamazov."* Evanston, IL: Northwestern University Press, 1990.

———. *The Structure of "The Brothers Karamazov."* Evanston, IL: Northwestern University Press, 1989.

———. "The Unrepentant Confession." In *Russianness: Studies on a Nation's Identity. In Honor of Rufus Matthewson*, 113–23. Ann Arbor, MI: Ardis, 1990.

Benedict XVI (Pope). *Deus Caritas Est [God is Love]*. 2005 http://www.vatican.va/holy_father/benedict_xvi/encyclicals/documents/hf_ben-xvi_enc_20051225_deus-caritas-est_en.html

———. *God is Near Us*. San Francisco: Ignatius. 2012.

———. *Jesus of Nazareth*. San Francisco: Ignatius, 2007.

———. *The Light of the World: The Pope, the Church, and the Signs of the Times: A Conversation with Peter Seewald*. Translated by Michael J. Miller and Adrian J. Walker. San Francisco: Ignatius, 2010.

———. Meeting with the Clergy of the Diocese of Bolzano-Bressanone, August 6, 2008, http://www.vatican.va/holy_father/benedict_xvi/speeches/2008/august/documents/hf_ben-xvi_spe_20080806_clero-bressanone_en.html.

———. *Sacramentum Caritatis [Sacrament of Charity]*. http://www.vatican.va/content/benedict-xvi/en/apost_exhortations/documents/hf_ben-xvi_exh_20070222_sacramentum-caritatis.html.

———. *Spe Salvi [In Hope We Are Saved]*. http://www.vatican.va/holy_father/benedict_xvi/encyclicals/documents/hf_ben-xvi_enc_20071130_spe-salvi_en.html.

Berdyaev, Nicholas. *Dostoevsky*. New York: Meridian, 1957.

Bergamino, Federica. "Introduction." *Church Communication, and Culture*. Special Issue, "Dostoevsky" 2.3 (2017) 203-05.

Berlin, Isaiah. *Russian Thinkers*. Harmondsworth, UK: Penguin, 1978.

Bernanos, Georges. *The Diary of a Country Priest*. Translated by Pamela Morris. New York: Carroll and Graff, 2002.

Berman, Anna. "Lateral Plots: Brothers and the Nineteenth-Century Russian Novel." *Slavic and East European Journal* 61.1 (2017) 2-28.

———. "Siblings in *The Brothers Karamazov*." *The Russian Review* 68 (April 2009) 263–82.

Bettenson, Henry. *Documents of the Christian Church*. 4th ed. Oxford: Oxford University Press, 2011.

Bird, Robert. *Fyodor Dostoevsky*. Chicago: Reaktion Books, University of Chicago Press, 2012.

———. "Refiguring the Russian Type: Dostoevsky and the Limits of Realism." In *A New Word on The Brothers Karamazov*, edited by Robert Louis Jackson, 17–30. New Haven, CT: Yale University Press, 2004.

Blake, Elizabeth A. *Dostoevsky and the Catholic Underground*. Evanston,IL: Northwestern University Press, 2014.

Blank, Ksana. *Dostoevsky's Dialectics and the Problem of Sin*. Evanston, IL: Northwestern University Press, 2010.

Booth, Wayne. *The Company We Keep: An Ethics of Fiction*. Berkeley: University of California Press, 1990.

———. *The Rhetoric of Irony*. Chicago: University of Chicago Press, 1974.

Bouchard, Larry D. *Theater and Integrity: Emptying Selves in Drama, Ethics, and Religion*. Evanston, IL: Northwestern University Press, 2007.

Bowers, Katherine, Connor Doak, and Kate Holland, eds. *A Dostoevskii Companion: Texts and Contexts*. Boston: Academic Studies Press, 2018.

Boyle, Nicholas. *Sacred and Secular Scriptures: A Catholic Approach to Literature*. South Bend, IN: University of Notre Dame Press, 2005.

Brague, Rémi. *Curing Mad Truths: Medieval Truths for the Modern Age*. South Bend, IN: University of Notre Dame Press, 2019.

Brazier, P. H. *Dostoevsky: A Theological Engagement*. Eugene, OR: Pickwick, 2016.

Brooks, Peter. *Troubling Confessions: Speaking Guilt in Law and Literature*. Chicago: University of Chicago Press, 1990.

Buber, Martin. "Guilt and Guilt Feeling." In *Cross Currents: Exploring the Implications of Christianity for Our Time: An Anthology of the Best of Cross Currents 1950–1990*, edited by William Birmingham, 63–92. New York: Crossroad, 1989.

Burgos, Juan Manuel Burgos. *An Introduction to Personalism*. Translated by R. T. Allen. Washington, DC: Catholic University Press of America, 2018.

———. *I and Thou*. Translated by Ronald Gregor Smith. New York: Scribner's, 1958.

Busch, R. L. *Humor in the Major Novels of Dostoevsky*. Bloomington, IN: Indiana University Slavica Publishers, 1987.

Buzina, Tatyana. "Two Fates" In *A New Word on The Brothers Karamazov*, edited by Robert Louis Jackson, 68–73. New Haven, CT: Yale University Press, 2004

Cain, Seymour. *Gabriel Marcel's Theory of Religious Experience*. Berne: Lang, 1995.

Carr, Anne. *A Search for Wisdom and Spirit: Thomas Merton's Theology of the Self*. South Bend, IN: University of Notre Dame Press, 1988.

Carroll, Anthony J., and Marthe Kerkwijk, Michael Kirwan, James Sweeney, eds. *Towards a Kenotic Vision of Authority in the Catholic Church* (Ser. IV, Vol. 8; Ser. VIII, Vol. 8). Washington, DC: Council for Research in Values & Philosophy, 2015.

Cassedy, Steven. *Dostoevsky's Religion*. Palo Alto, CA: Stanford University Press, 2005.

———. "P. A. Florensky and the Celebration of Matter." In *Russian Religious Thought*, edited by Judith Deutsch Kornblatt and Richard F. Gustafson, 95–111. Madison, WI: University of Wisconsin Press, 1996.

————. "Who Says Miracles Can't Be the Basis for Faith? More Reasons Why Dostoevsky's Religion Isn't Christianity." *Dostoevsky Studies*. Special Issue: *Dostoevsky and Christianity*. Guest Editor Susan McReynolds. 13 (2009) 37–46.

Castelo, Daniel. *Theological Theodicy*. Eugene, OR: Cascade, 2012.

Catechism of the Catholic Church. http://www.vatican.va/archive/ENG0015/_INDEX. HTM.

Cicovacki, Pedrag, and Maria Granik, eds. *"The Brothers Karamazov": Art, Creativity, and Spirituality*. Heidelberg: Universitätsverlag C. Winter, 2010.

Cicovacki, Pedrag. *Dostoevsky and the Affirmation of Life*. New Brunswick, NJ: Transaction, 2012.

————. "The Role of Goethe's *Faust* in Dostoevsky's Opus." *Dostoevsky Studies*. 14 (2010), 153–63.

Clark, Katerina, and Michael Holquist. *Mikhail Bakhtin*. Cambridge: Harvard University Press, 1984.

Coates, Ruth. *Christianity in Bakhtin: God and the Exiled Author*. Cambridge: Cambridge University Press, 1999.

Connor, Steven. *Giving Way: Thoughts on Unappreciated Dispositions*. Palo Alto, CA: Stanford University Press, 2019.

Coetzee, J. M. "Confession and Double Thoughts: Tolstoy, Rousseau, Dostoevsky." *Comparative Literature* 37.3 (1985) 193–232.

Connelly, Julian W. "Confession in *The Brothers Karamazov*." *The Brothers Karamazov: Art, Creativity, and Spirituality*, edited by Pedrag Cicovacki and Maria Granik, 13–28. Heidelberg: Universitätsverlag C. Winter, 2010.

————. *Dostoevsky's "The Brothers Karamazov."* New York: Bloomsbury, 2013.

Contino, Paul J. "William F. Lynch" *Religion and Literature* 41.2 (2009) 237–44.

————. "Zhuangzu." In *Finding Wisdom in East Asian Classics*, edited by William Theodore de Bary, 80–92. New York: Columbia University Press, 2011.

Corrigan, Yuri. *Dostoevsky and the Riddle of the Self*. Evanston, IL: Northwestern University Press, 2017.

————. "Dostoevskii on Evil as Safe Haven and Anesthetic." *Slavic and East European Journal* 63.2. (2019) 226–43.

Cox, Roger L. *Between Earth and Heaven: Shakespeare, Dostoevsky, and the Meaning of Christian Tragedy*. New York: Holt, Rinehart, Winston, 1969.

Crossan, Frederick J. "Structure and Meaning in St. Augustine's *Confessions*." In *The Augustinian Tradition*, edited by Gareth B. Matthews, 27–38. Berkeley: University of California Press, 1999.

Cunningham, David. "*The Brothers Karamazov* as Trinitarian Theology." In *Dostoevsky and the Christian Tradition*, edited by George Pattison and Diane Oenning Thompson, 135–55. Cambridge: Cambridge University Press, 2001.

Cunningham, Lawrence S., ed. *Thomas Merton: Spiritual Master*. Mahwah, NJ: Paulist, 1992.

Dante Alighieri. *The Divine Comedy*. Translated by Allen Mandelbaum. New York: Everyman's Library, 1995.

————. Trans. Burton Raffel. Evanston, IL: Northwestern University Press 2010.

D'Arcy, Martin. *The Mind and Heart of Love*. New York: Meridian, 1956.

De Lubac, Henri, S.J. *Catholicism: Christ and the Common Destiny of Man*. Translated by Lancelot Shepherd and Sister Elizabeth Englund, OCD. San Francisco: Ignatius, 1988.

————. *The Drama of Atheist Humanism*. Translated by Edith M. Riley. New York: Meridian, 1967.

Desmond, John F. *Fyodor Dostoevsky, Walker Percy, and the Age of Suicide*. Washington, DC: Catholic University Press, 2019.

Dirscherl, Denis, S.J. *Dostoevsky and the Catholic Church*. Chicago: Loyola University Press, 1986.

Dolbilov, Mikhail. "Roman Catholicism." In *Dostoevsky in Context*, edited by Deborah A. Martinsen and Olga Mairova, 202–8. Cambridge: Cambridge University Press, 2015.

Dostoevsky, Anna. *Reminiscences*. Translated by Beatrice Stillman. New York: Liveright, 1975.

Dostoevsky, Fyodor. *The Adolescent*. Translated by Andrew MacAndrew. New York: Norton, 1971.

————. *The Brothers Karamazov*. Edited by Susan McReynolds Oddo. Second Norton Critical Edition. New York: Norton, 2011.

————. *The Brothers Karamazov*. Richard Pevear and Larissa Volokhonsky. New York: Vintage, 1990.

————. "From Dostoevsky's *Notebooks*." In *The Brothers Karamazov*, edited by Susan McReynolds Oddo, 666–67. Second Norton Critical Edition. New York: Norton, 2011.

————. "Selections from Dostoevsky's Letters." In *The Brothers Karamazov*, edited by Susan McReynolds Oddo, 653–66. New York: Norton, 2011.

————. *Crime and Punishment*. Translated by Constance Garnett. New York: Random House, Modern Library, 1950.

————. *The Devils*. Translated by David Magarshack. Harmondsworth, UK: Penguin, 1953.

————. *The Idiot*. Translated by David Magarshack. Harmondsworth, UK: Penguin, 1955.

————. *Memoirs from the House of the Dead*. Translated by Jessie Coulson. Worlds Classics. Oxford: Oxford University Press, 1983.

————. "Mr. ___bov and the Question of Art." In *Dostoevsky's Occasional Writings*, translated by David Magarshack, 86–137. Evanston, IL: Northwestern University Press, 1997.

————. *Notes from Underground*. Translated by Mirra Ginsburg. Toronto: Bantam, 1974.

————. *Selected Letters of Fyodor Dostoyevsky*. Edited by Joseph Frank and David I. Goldstein, translated by Andrew R. MacAndrew. New Brunswick, NJ: Rutgers University Press, 1987.

————. *The Unpublished Dostoevsky*. Volume 1. Edited by C. R. Proffer. Ann Arbor, MI: Ardis, 1973.

————. *A Writer's Diary*. Translated and annotated by Kenneth Lantz. Vols. I and II. Evanston, IL: Northwestern University Press, 1994.

Dreyfuss, Hubert, and Charles Taylor. *Retrieving Realism*. Cambridge: Harvard University Press, 2015.

Dupré, Louis. *Passage to Modernity*. New Haven, CT: Yale University Press, 1993.

————. *Transcendent Selfhood: The Loss and Rediscovery of the Inner Life*. New York: Seabury Press, 1976.

Eckhart, Meister. *The Essential Sermons, Commentaries, Treatises, and Defense.* Translated by Edmund Colledge, O.S.A. and Bernard McGinn. Mahwah, NJ: Paulist, 1981.

Elie, Paul. *The Life You Save May Be Your Own: An American Pilgrimage.* New York: Farrar, Straus, Giroux, 2003.

Eliot, George. *Middlemarch.* Harmondsworth, UK: Penguin, 1965.

Eliot, T. S. *Four Quartets.* New York: Houghton, Mifflin, Harcourt, 1971.

Emerson, Caryl. "Afterword." In *Bakhtin and Religion: A Feeling for Faith,* edited by Susan M. Felch and Paul J. Contino, 177–92. Evanston, IL: Northwestern University Press. 2001.

———. *The Cambridge Introduction to Russian Literature.* Cambridge: Cambridge University Press, 2008.

———. *The First Hundred Years of Mikhail Bakhtin.* Princeton, NJ: Princeton University Press, 2008.

———. "Mikhail Bakhtin." In *The Oxford Handbook of Russian Religious Thought,* edited by George Pattison, Randall A. Poole, Caryl Emerson. Oxford: Oxford University Press, forthcoming 2020.

———. "Problems in Bakhtin's Poetics." *Slavic and East European Journal* 32:4 (1988) 503–25.

———. "Tolstoy and Dostoevsky: Seductions of the Old Criticism." In *Reading George Steiner,* edited by Nathan A. Scott, Jr. and Ronald A. Sharp, 74–98. Baltimore, MD: Johns Hopkins University Press, 1994.

———. "The Tolstoy Connection in Bakhtin." In *Rethinking Bakhtin: Extensions and Challenges,* edited by Gary Saul Morson and Caryl Emerson, 149–72. Evanston, IL: Northwestern University Press, 1989.

———. "Word and Image in Dostoevsky's Worlds: Robert Louis Jackson on Reading that Bakhtin Could Not Do." In *Freedom and Responsibility in Russian Literature: Essays in Honor of Robert Louis Jackson,* edited by Elizabeth Cheresh Allen and Gary Saul Morson, 245–66. Evanston, IL: Northwestern University Press, 1995.

———. "Zosima's 'Mysterious Visitor': Again Bakhtin on Dostoevsky, and Dostoevsky on Heaven and Hell." In *"A New Word" on The Brothers Karamazov,* edited by Robert Louis Jackson, 155–79. Evanston, IL: Northwestern University Press, 2004.

Eng, Jan van der, and Jan M. Meijer. *The Brothers Karamazov by F. M. Dostoevskij.* 1971. Reprint, Berlin: De Gruyter, 2011.

Epstein, Mikhail. *Russian Spirituality and the Secularization of Culture.* Translated by Maria Barabtarlo. USA: Lulu.com, 2011.

———. "The Teachings of Yakov Abramov as Interpreted by his Disciples." Compiled, commented, and edited by Mikhail Epstein. *Symposion: A Journal of Russian Thought* 3 (1998) 29–66.

———. *The Transformative Humanities: A Manifesto.* Translated and edited by Igor Klyukanov. New York: Bloomsbury, 2012.

Faggen, Robert. *Striving Towards Being: The Letters of Thomas Merton and Czeslaw Milosz.* New York: Farrar, Straus and Giroux: 1996.

Fanger, Donald. *Dostoevsky and Romantic Realism.* Cambridge: Harvard University Press, 1965.

Farber, Leslie H. *The Ways of the Will: Selected Essays.* New York, Basic, 2000

Fedotov, George P. *The Russian Religious Mind (I).* Cambridge: Harvard University Press, 1946.

Felch, Susan M., and Paul J. Contino, eds. *Bakhtin and Religion: A Feeling for Faith.* Evanston, IL: Northwestern University Press. 2001.

———. "Words and Things: The Hope of Perspectival Realism." *Faithful Imagination in the Academy: Explorations of Belief and Scholarship,* edited by Janel M. Curry and Ronald A. Wells, 13–30. Lanham, MD: Lexington, 2008.

Felski, Rita. *The Limits of Critique.* Chicago: University of Chicago Press, 2015.

Flath, Carol A. "The Passion of Dmitri Karamazov." *Slavic Review* 58.3 (1999) 584–99.

Fogel, Aaron. *Coercion to Speak: Conrad's Poetics of Dialogue.* Cambridge: Harvard University Press, 1985.

Ford, David. *Self and Salvation: Being Transformed.* Cambridge: Cambridge University Press, 1999.

Francis I (Pope). *The Name of God Is Mercy: A Conversation with Andrea Tornielli.* Translated by Oonagh Stransky. New York: Random House, 2016.

Frank, Joseph. *Dostoevsky: A Writer in His Time.* Princeton, NJ: Princeton University Press, 2012.

———. *Dostoevsky: The Seeds of Revolt. 1821–1849.* Princeton, NJ: Princeton University Press, 1976.

———. *Dostoevsky: The Years of Ordeal, 1850–1859.* Princeton, NJ: Princeton University Press, 1983.

———. *Dostoevsky: The Stir of Liberation, 1860–1865.* Princeton, NJ: Princeton University Press, 1986.

———. *Dostoevsky: The Miraculous Years, 1865–1871.* Princeton, NJ: Princeton University Press, 1995.

———. *Dostoevsky: The Mantle the Prophet, 1871–1881.* Princeton, NJ: Princeton University Press, 2002.

———. *Selected Letters of Fyodor Dostoevsky.* Edited by with David I. Goldstein. Translated by Andrew R. MacAndrew. New Brunswick: Rutgers, 1987.

Freccero, John. *Dante: the Poetics of Conversion.* Edited by Rachel Jacoff. Cambridge, MA: Harvard University Press, 1986.

Frei, Hans W. *The Eclipse of Biblical Narrative: A Study in Eighteenth and Nineteenth Century Hermeneutics.* New Haven, CT: Yale University Press, 1974.

Friederich, Paul. "Grushenka." *Dostoevsky Studies* 11 (2007) 38–55.

Friedman, Maurice S. *Martin Buber's Life and Work* Detroit, MI: Wayne State Press, 1988.

Friesen, Leonard G. *Transcendent Love: Dostoevsky and the Search for a Global Ethic.* South Bend, IN: University of Notre Dame Press, 2016.

Friesenhahn, Jacob H. *The Trinity and Theology: The Trinitarian Theology of von Balthasar and the Problem of Evil.* London: Routledge, 2016.

Fusso, Susanne. *Discovering Sexuality in Dostoevsky.* Evanston, IL: Northwestern University Press, 2006.

Gatrall, Jefferson J. A. *The Real and the Sacred: Picturing Jesus in Nineteenth-Century Fiction.* Ann Arbor, MI: University of Michigan Press, 2014.

Gibson, Boyce. *The Religion of Dostoevsky.* Philadelphia: Westminster, 1973.

Gillespie, Michael Allen. *The Theological Origins of Modernity.* Chicago: University of Chicago Press, 2008.

Gilson, Étienne. *Thomist Realism and the Critique of Knowledge.* Translated by Mark A. Wauck. San Francisco, CA: Ignatius, 1986.

Girard, René. *Deceit, Desire, and the Novel: Self and Other in Literary Structure.* Translated by Yvonne Freccerro. Baltimore, MD: Johns Hopkins University Press, 1965.

———. *Resurrection from Underground: Feodor Dostoevsky.* Edited by and Translated by James G. Wilson. East Lansing, MI: Michigan State University, 2012.

Givens, John. *The Image of Christ in Russian Literature: Dostoevsky, Bulgakov, Pasternak.* DeKalb, IL: Northern Illinois University Press, 2018

Goldstein, David I. *Dostoevsky and the Jews.* 1976. Reprint, Austin, TX: University of Texas Press, 1981.

Golstein, Vladimir. "Accidental Families and Surrogate Fathers: Richard, Grigory, and Smerdyakov." In *"A New Word" on The Brothers Karamazov*, edited by Robert Louis Jackson, 90–106. Evanston, IL: Northwestern University Press, 2004.

Gorodetzky, Nadejda. *Saint Tikhon of Zadonsk: Inspirer of Dostoevsky.* Crestwood, NY: St. Vladimir's Seminary Press, 1976.

Gray, Marilyn Louise. "Russian Theological Anthropology and Bakhtin: The Aesthetics of the Divine Image." PhD diss., University of California, Los Angeles, 2011.

Gregory, Brad A. *The Unintended Reformation: How a Religious Revolution Secularized Society.* Cambridge: Harvard University Press, 2012.

Grillaert, Nel. "The Final Word Cannot Be Said: Apophatic Consciousness in Dostoevsky's *The Brothers Karamazov.*" In *Dostoevsky Monographs VI*, edited by Jordi Morillas, 22–48. St. Petersburg: Dmitry Bulanin, 2015.

———. "Orthodox Spirituality." In *Dostoevsky in Context*, edited by Deborah A. Martinsen and Olga Mairova, 187–93. Cambridge: Cambridge University Press, 2015.

———. "Raise the People in Silence: Traces of Hesychasm in Dostoevskij's Fictional Saint Zosima." *Dostoevsky Studies* 15 (2011) 47–88.

Guardini, Romano. *Religiöse Gestallen in Dostojewskis Werk*, München: Kösel Verlag: 1951.

Guroian, Vigen. *Incarnate Love: Essays in Orthodox Ethics.* South Bend, IN: University of Notre Dame Press, 1999.

Hackel, Sergei. "The Religious Dimension: Vision or Evasion? Zosima's Discourse in *The Brothers Karamazov.*" In *New Essays on Dostoevsky*, edited by Malcolm V. Jones and Garth M. Terry, 139–68. Cambridge: Cambridge University Press, 1983.

Halík, Tomáš. *I Want You to Be: On the God of Love.* Translated by Gerald Turner. South Bend, IN: University of Notre Dame Press, 2016.

Hart, David Bentley. *The Beauty of the Infinite: The Aesthetics of Christian Truth.* Grand Rapids: Eerdmans, 2003

———. *The Doors to the Sea: Where Was God in the Tsunami?* Grand Rapids: Eerdmans, 2005.

———. *The Experience of God: Being, Consciousness, Bliss.* New Haven, CT: Yale University Press, 2017.

———. *That All Shall Be Saved: Heaven, Hell, and Universal Salvation.* New Haven, CT: Yale University Press, 2019.

Haven, Cynthia. *Evolution of Desire: A Life of René Girard.* East Lansing, MI: Michigan State University Press, 2018.

Heidegger, Martin. *Discourse on Thinking.* Translated by John M. Anderson and E. Hans Freund. New York: Harper and Row, 1966.

Hick, John. *Evil and the God of Love*. 1966. Reprint, New York: Palgrave Macmillan, 2010.

Highfield, Ron. *The Faithful Creator: Affirming Creation and Providence in an Age of Anxiety*. Downers Grove, Illinois: Intervarsity Press, 2015.

Hillier, Russell. "Bearing and Sharing All: A Study of the Confessional Moment in Dostoevsky's Life and Fiction." *Literature and Theology* 18.4 (2004) 442–63.

Hingley, Ronald. *The Undiscovered Dostoevsky*. London: Hamish Hamilton, 1962.

Holland, Kate. *The Novel in the Age of Disintegration: Dostoevsky and the Problem of Genre in the 1870s*. Evanston, IL: Northwestern University Press, 2013.

Holquist, Michael. *Dostoevsky and the Novel*. Princeton, NJ: Princeton University Press, 1977.

Hruska, Anne. "The Sins of the Children in *The Brothers Karamazov*: Serfdom, Hierarchy, and Transcendence." *Christianity and Literature* 54.4 (2005) 471–95.

Hüttar, Reinhold. *Bound for Beatitude: A Thomistic Study in Eschatology and Ethics*. Washington, DC: Catholic University Press, 2019.

Imbelli, Robert. *Rekindling the Christic Imagination: Theological Meditations for the New Evangelization*. Collegeville, MN: Liturgical, 2014.

Isaac the Syrian. *On Ascetical Life*. Translated by Mary Hansbury. Crestwood, NY: St. Vladimir's Seminary Press, 1989.

Ivanov, Vyacheslav. *Freedom and the Tragic Life: A Study in Dostoevsky*. Translated by Norman Cameron. New York: Noonday, 1959.

Ivanitis, Linda. *Dostoevsky and the Russian People*. Cambridge: Cambridge University Press, 2011.

Izmirlieva, Valentina. "Hosting the Divine Logos: Radical Hospitality in Dostoevsky's Crime and Punishment." In *The Routledge Companion to Literature and Religion*, edited by Mark Knight, 277–88. London: Routledge, 2016.

Jacobs, Alan. *A Theology of Reading: The Hermeneutics of Love*. Boulder, CO: Westview, 2001.

Jackson, Robert Louis. *The Art of Dostoevsky: Deliriums and Nocturnes*. Princeton, NJ: Princeton University Press, 1981.

———. *Dialogues with Dostoevsky: The Overwhelming Questions*. Palo Alto, CA: Stanford University Press, 1993.

———. *Dostoevsky's Quest for Form: A Study of His Philosophy of Art*. 2nd ed. Bloomington, IN: Physsardt, 1978.

Jeffrey, David Lyle. *In the Beauty of Holiness: Art and the Bible in Western Culture*. Grand Rapids: Eerdmans, 2017.

John Chrysostom. *Divine Liturgy*. South Canaan, PA: St. Tikhon's Seminary Press, 1977.

John of Damascus. *On the Divine Images*. Crestwood, NY: St. Vladimir's Seminary Press, 2003.

John Paul II (Pope). *Fides et Ratio [Faith and Reason]*. http://www.vatican.va/holy_father/john_paul_ii/encyclicals/documents/hf_jp-ii_enc_15101998_fides-et-ratio_en.html.

———. "Letter to Artists" (April 4, 1999). http://www.vatican.va/holy_father/john_paul_ii/letters/documents/hf_jp-ii_let_23041999_artists_en.html.

———. On the Salvific Meaning of Suffering." http://w2.vatican.va/content/john-paul-ii/en/apost_letters/1984/documents/hf_jp-ii_apl_11021984_salvifici-doloris.html.

Johnson, Junius. *Christ and Analogy: The Christocentric Metaphysics of Hans Urs von Balthasar*. Minneapolis, MN: Fortress Press, 2013.

Johnson, Luke Timothy. *Living Jesus: Learning the Heart of the Gospel*. San Francisco: Harper San Francisco, 2000.

Johnson, Lee D. "Struggle for Theosis: Smerdyakov as Would-Be Saint." In *"A New Word" on The Brothers Karamazov*, edited by Robert Louis Jackson, 74–89. Evanston, IL: Northwestern University Press, 2004.

Jones, Malcolm. *Dostoevsky and the Dynamics of Religious Experience*. London: Anthem, 2005.

———. *Dostoevsky After Bakhtin: Readings in Dostoevsky's Fantastic Realism*. Cambridge: Cambridge University Press, 1990.

Jones, Malcolm V., and Garth M. Terry, eds. *New Essays on Dostoevsky*. Cambridge: Cambridge University Press, 1983.

Jonsen, Albert R., and Stephen Toulmin. *The Case for Casuistry: A History of Moral Reasoning*. Berkeley, CA: University of California Press, 1989.

Just, Felix, S.J. "The Essential Key to Catholic Theology: Both/And Not Either/Or." http://catholic-resources.org/Both-And.htm.

Kant, Immanuel. *Grounding for the Metaphysics of Morals*. Translated by James Ellington. Indianapolis, IN: Hackett.

Kantor, Vladimir. "Pavel Smerdyakov and Ivan Karamazov: The Problem of Temptation." In *Dostoevsky and the Christian Tradition*, edited by George Pattison and Diane Oenning Thompson, 189–225. Cambridge: Cambridge University Press, 2001.

Kaplan, Grant, and Holly Coolman. "The Development of Doctrine: The Tübingen School and John Henry Newman." In *The Oxford Handbook of Catholic Theology*, edited by Lewis Ayers and Medi Ann Volpe, 612–29. Oxford: Oxford University Press, 2018.

Kasatkina, Tatiana Alexandrovna. "Commentary on a Commentary: The Medelianka and the Return of Zhuchka." In *The New Russian Dostoevsky: Readings for the Twenty-First Century*, edited by Carol Apollonio, 267–69. Bloomington, IN: Slavica, 2010.

Katchadourian, Herant. *Guilt: The Bite of Conscience*. Palo Alto, CA: Stanford University Press, 2010.

Kierkegaard, Søren. *Either/Or Volume II*. Translated by Walter Lowrie. Princeton, NJ: Princeton University Press. 1971.

———. *Fear and Trembling*. Translated by Alastair Hannay. New York: Penguin. 1986.

Kjetsaa, Geir. *Dostoevsky and His New Testament*. Oslo: Solum Forlag, 1984.

———. *Fyodor Dostoevsky: A Writer's Life*. Translated by Siri Hustvedt and David McDuff. New York: Fawcett Columbine, 1987.

Knapp, Liza. *The Annihilation of Inertia: Dostoevsky and Metaphysics*. Evanston, IL: Northwestern University Press, 1996.

———. "Mothers and Sons in *The Brothers Karamazov*: Our Ladies of Skotoprigonevsk." In *"A New Word" on The Brothers Karamazov*, edited by Robert Louis Jackson, 31–52. Evanston, IL: Northwestern University Press, 2004.

Kostalevsky, Marina. *Dostoevsky and Soloviev*. New Haven, CT: Yale University Press, 1997.

Kroeker, P. Travis, and Bruce K. Ward. *Remembering the End: Dostoevsky as Prophet to Modernity*. Boulder, CO: Westview, 2001.

Kurrick, Maire Jaanus. "The Self's Negativity." 1979. In *Modern Critical Interpretations: The Brothers Karamazov*, edited by Harold Bloom, 97–118. New York: Chelsea House, 1988.

Küng, Hans. *On Being a Christian*. Translated by Edward Quinn. New York: Image, 1984.

Lantz, Kenneth. *The Dostoevsky Encyclopedia*. Westport, CT: Greenwood, 2004.

Lawrence, D. H. *Introductions and Reviews*. Edited by N. H. Reeve and John Worthen. Cambridge: Cambridge University Press, 2005.

Leatherbarrow, W. J. *A Devil's Vaudeville: The Demonic in Dostoevsky's Major Fiction*. Evanston, IL: Northwestern University Press, 2005.

———. *Fyodor Dostoevsky: The Brothers Karamazov*. Cambridge: Cambridge University Press, 1992.

Leclercq, Jean. *The Love of Learning and the Desire for God*. New York: Fordham University Press, 1982.

The Lenten Triodion. Translated by Mother Mary and Archimandrite Kallistos Ware. South Canaan, PA: St. Tikhon's Seminary Press, 2002.

Lewis, C. S. *The Great Divorce*. New York: HarperCollins, 2001.

———. *The Problem of Pain*. New York: HarperCollins, 2001.

Levinas, Emmanuel. "God and Philosophy." *Basic Philosophical Writings*, edited by Adriaan T. Peperzak, Simon Critchley, and Robert Bernasconi, 129–48. Bloomington, IN: Indiana University Press, 1996.

Linner, Sven. *Dostoevskij on Realism*. Stockholm: Almqvist and Wiksell, 1967.

———. *Starets Zosima "The Brothers Karamazov": A Study in the Mimesis of Virtue*. Stockholm: Almqvist and Wiksell. 1975.

Lonergan, Bernard. *Insight*. Edited by Frederic Crowe, SJ and Robert Doran, SJ. University of Toronto Press, 1992.

Lossky, Vladimir. *The Mystical Theology of the Eastern Church*. Crestwood, NY: St. Vladimir's Seminary Press, 1976.

Louth, Andrew. *Maximus the Confessor*. London: Routledge, 1996.

Love, Jeff, and Jeffrey Metzger, eds. *Nietzsche and Dostoevsky*. Evanston, IL: Northwestern University Press, 2016.

Lynch, S. J. William F. *Christ and Apollo. The Dimensions of Literary Imagination*. 1960. Reprint, Wilmington, DE: ISI, 2004.

———. *Images of Faith: An Exploration of the Ironic Imagination*. South Bend, IN: University of Notre Dame Press, 1973.

———. *Images of Hope: Imagination as Healer of the Hopeless*. South Bend, IN: University of Notre Dame Press, 1965.

MacDonald, Gregory, ed. *All Shall Be Well: Essays in Universal Salvation and Christian Theology*. Eugene, OR: Cascade, 2011.

MacIntyre, Alasdair. *After Virtue*. 2nd ed. South Bend, IN: University of Notre Dame Press, 1984.

Maritain, Jacques. *The Peasant of the Garonne*. Translated by Michael Cuddihy and Elizabeth Hughes. New York: Holt, Rinehart, and Winston, 1968.

———. *The Person and the Common Good*. South Bend, IN: University of Notre Dame Press, 1985.

Martin, Jennifer Newsome. *Hans Urs von Balthasar and the Critical Appropriation of Russian Religious Thought*. South Bend, IN: University of Notre Dame Press, 2015.

Martin, Michael. *The Submerged Reality: Sophiology and the Turn to a Poetic Metaphysics.* Kettering, OH: Angelico, 2015.

Martinsen, Deborah A. "Dostoevsky's Struggle for Faith." *Christianity and Literature* 60.2 (2011) 309–21.

———. "The Devil Incarnate." In *"The Brothers Karamazov": Art, Creativity, and Spirituality,* edited by Cicovacki and Granik, 45–71. Heidelberg: Universitätsverlag C. Winter, 2010.

———. *Surprised by Shame: Dostoevsky's Liars and Narrative Exposure.* Columbus, OH: Ohio State University Press, 2003.

Martinsen, Deborah A. and Olga Mairova, eds. *Dostoevsky in Context.* Cambridge: Cambridge University Press, 2015.

Matthiesen, Michon M. *Sacrifice as Gift: Eucharist, Grace, and Contemplative Prayer in Maurice de Taille.* Washington, DC: Catholic University of America Press, 2013.

Matzner-Gore, Greta. *Dostoevsky and the Ethics of Narrative Form: Suspense, Closure, Minor Characters.* Evanston, IL: Northwestern University Press, 2020.

Maximus the Confessor. *Maximus the Confessor, Selected Writings.* Translated by George C. Berthold. Mahwah, NJ: Paulist, 1985.

McAdams, Dan. "'I Am What Survives Me' Generativity and the Self." In *Self-Transcendence and Virtue: Perspectives from Philosophy, Psychology, and Theology,* edited by Jennifer Frey and Candace Vogler, 251–73. London: Routledge, 2018.

McCauley, Esau. *Reading While Black: African American Biblical Interpretation as an Exercise in Hope.* Downers Grove, IL: IVP Academic, 2020.

McFarland, Ian. "The Theology of the Will." In *The Oxford Handbook of Maximus the Confessor,* edited by Pauline Allen and Bronwen Neil, 516–32. Oxford: Oxford University Press, 2015.

McReynolds, Susan. "Introduction." *Dostoevsky Studies* Special issue, "Dostoevsky and Christianity" 13 (2009) 5–22.

———. *Redemption and the Merchant God: Dostoevsky's Economy of Salvation and Anti-Semitism.* Evanston, IL: Northwestern University Press, 2008.

Meijer, J. M. "Situation Rhyme in a Novel of Dostoevskij." In *Dutch Contributions to the Fourth International Congress of Slavicists,* 115–28. The Hague: Mouton, 1958.

Merton, Thomas. *Contemplative Prayer.* New York: Image, 1996.

———. *The Hidden Ground of Love.* Edited by William Shannon. New York: Farrar, Straus, and Giroux, 1985.

———. *New Seeds of Contemplation.* New York: New Directions, 1972.

———. *The Silent Life.* New York: Farrar, Straus, and Giroux. 1999.

Meyers, Peter. "Father Marty." *Life,* August, 1991, 48–56.

Mihailovic, Alexandar. *Corporeal Worlds: Mikhail Bakhtin's Theology of Discourse.* Evanston, IL: Northwestern University Press, 1997.

Milbank, John. *Theology and Social Theory: Beyond Secular Reason.* Oxford: Blackwell, 1990.

Miller, Robin Feuer. *The Brothers Karamazov: Worlds of the Novel.* 1992. Reprint, New Haven, CT: Yale University Press, 2008.

———. "*The Brothers Karamazov* Today." In *"A New Word" on The Brothers Karamazov,* edited by Robert Louis Jackson, 3–16. Evanston, IL: Northwestern University Press, 2004.

———. *Dostoevsky's Unfinished Journey.* New Haven, CT: Yale University Press, 2007.

———. "Dostoevsky and Rousseau: The Morality of Confession Reconsidered." 1979. In *Dostoevsky: New Perspectives*, edited by Robert Louis Jackson, 82–98. Englewood Cliffs, NJ: Prentice Hall, 1984.

Milosz, Czeslaw. *Milosz's ABC's*. Translated by Madeline Levine. New York: Farrar, Straus and Giroux, 2001.

———. *To Begin Where I Am: Selected Essays*. Edited by Bogdana Carpenter and Madeline G. Levine. New York: Farrar, Straus, Giroux, 2001.

Mochulsky, Konstantin. *Dostoevsky: His Life and Work*. Translated by Michael A. Minihan. Princeton, NJ: Princeton University Press, 1967.

Monk, Ray. *Ludwig Wittgenstein: The Duty of Genius*. New York: Penguin, 1991.

Montemaggi, Vittorio. *Reading Dante's Commedia as Theology: Divinity Realized as Human Encounter*. Oxford: Oxford University Press, 2016.

Moore, Andrew. *Realism and Christian Faith: God, Grammar, and Meaning*. Cambridge: Cambridge University Press, 2003.

Moran, John P. "'This Star Will Shine Forth from the East: The Politics of Humility." In *Dostoevsky's Political Thought*, edited by Richard Avramenko and Lee Trepanier, 51–72. Lanham, MD: Lexington, 2013.

Morson, Gary Saul. "Contingency and Freedom, Prosaics and Process." *New Literary History* 29.4 (1998) 673–86.

———. "The Disease of Theory: *Crime and Punishment* at 150." *The New Criterion*. 34.9. (2016) 4–10.

———. "The God of Onions: *The Brothers Karamazov* and the Mythic Prosaic." In *"A New Word" on The Brothers Karamazov*, edited by Robert Louis Jackson, 107–24. Evanston, IL: Northwestern University Press, 2004.

———. "Introductory Study." In *A Writer's Diary*, Vol. I, translated and annotated by Kenneth Lantz, 1–117. Evanston, IL: Northwestern University Press, 1994.

———. *Narrative and Freedom: The Shadows of Time*. New Haven, CT: Yale University Press, 1994.

———. *On Prosaics and Other Provocations: Empathy, Open Time, and the Novel*. Boston: Ars Rossica, 2013.

———. "Verbal Pollution in *The Brothers Karamazov*." *Poetics and Theory of Literature* 3 (1978) 223–33.

Morson, Gary Saul, and Caryl Emerson. "Introduction." In *Rethinking Bakhtin: Extensions and Challenges*, 1–60. Evanston, IL: Northwestern University Press, 1989.

———. *Mikhail Bakhtin: Creation of a Prosaics*. Palo Alto, CA: Stanford University Press, 1990.

Muggeridge, Malcolm. "Foreword." In *The Gospel in Dostoevsky: Selection from His Works*. Rifton, NY: Plough, Hutterian Bretheren, 1988.

Murav, Harriet. *Holy Foolishness: Dostoevsky's Novels and the Poetics of Cultural Critique*. Palo Alto, CA: Stanford University Press, 1992.

Murphy, Francesca Aran. *Christ the Form of Beauty: A Study in Theology and Literature*. Edinburgh: T&T Clark, 1995.

———. *God is Not a Story: Realism Revisited*. Oxford: Oxford University Press, 2007.

Murphy, Michael. *A Theology of Criticism: Balthasar, Postmodernism, and the Catholic Imagination*. Oxford University Press, 2008.

The New American Bible. http://www.usccb.org/bible/books-of-the-bible/index.cfm.

Naiman, Eric. "Kalganov." *The Slavic and East European Journal* 58. 3 (2014) 394–418.

Nichols, Aidan. *A Key to Balthasar*. Grand Rapids, MI: Baker Academic, 2011.

Nietzsche, Friedrich. *A Genealogy of Morals*. Translated by Walter Kaufman. New York: Vintage, 1989.

Noll, Mark A. *Jesus Christ and the Life of the Mind*. Grand Rapids: Eerdmans, 2011.

Norris, Kathleen. *Dakota: A Spiritual Geography*. Boston: Houghton Mifflin, 1993.

Oakes, Edward T., S.J. *Infinity Dwindled to Infancy: A Catholic and Evangelical Christology*. Grand Rapids: Eerdmans 2011.

————. *Pattern of Redemption: The Theology of Hans Urs von Balthasar*. London: Bloomsbury, 1997.

O'Collins, SJ, Gerald and John Wilkins. *Lost in Translation: The English Language and the Catholic Mass*. Collegeville, MN: Liturgical Press Academic, 2017.

Okey, Stephen. *A Theology of Conversation: An Introduction to David Tracy*. Collegeville, MN: Liturgical, 2018.

Ollivier, Sophie. "Icons in Dostoevsky's Works." In *Dostoevsky and the Christian Tradition*, edited by George Pattison and Diane Oenning Thompson, 51–68. Cambridge: Cambridge University Press, 2001.

O'Malley S.J., John W. *The First Jesuits*. Cambridge: Harvard University Press, 1993.

————. *Vatican I: The Council and the Making of the Ultramontane Church*. Cambridge: Harvard University Press, 2018.

Ong, S.J., Walter J. "Realizing Catholicism: Faith, Learning and the Future." *Faith and the Intellectual Life*, edited by James Heft, 31–42. South Bend, IN: University of Notre Dame Press, 1996.

————. "Yeast." *America*, April 7, 1990.

Orwin, Donna Tussing. *Consequences of Consciousness: Turgenev, Dostoevsky Tolstoy*. Palo Alto, CA: Stanford University Press, 2007.

Ossorgin VIII, Michael M. "Holbein's Visually Polyphonic Dead Christ Reveals Contrasting Perspectives in Dostoevsky's *The Idiot*." *Dostoevsky Studies* 21 (2017) 51–68.

Ouspensky, Leonid. *Theology of the Icon*. 2 vols. 1978. Translated by Anthony Gythiel. Crestwood, NY: St. Vladimir's Seminary Press, 1992.

Panichas, George A. *Dostoevsky's Art: The Burden of Vision*. 1985. Reprint, New Brunswick, NJ: Transaction, 2009.

Papanikolaou, Aristotle, and George E. Demacopoulos, eds. *Orthodox Readings of Augustine*. Crestwood, NY: St. Vladimir's Seminary Press, 2008.

Parry, Robin A., with Ilaria L. E. Ramelli. *A Larger Hope: Universal Salvation from the Reformation to the Nineteenth Century*. Eugene, OR: Cascade, 2019.

Pattison, George, and Diane Oenning Thompson, eds. *Dostoevsky and the Christian Tradition*. Cambridge: Cambridge University Press, 2001.

Pattison, George. "Dostoevsky." In *The Oxford Handbook of Russian Religious Thought*, edited by George Pattison, Randall A. Poole, Caryl Emerson. Oxford: Oxford University Press, 2020.

————. *God and Being: An Enquiry*. Oxford: Oxford University Press, 2011.

Pechey, Graham. "Eternity and Modernity: Bakhtin and the Epistemological Sublime." In *Critical Essays on Mikhail Bakhtin*, edited by Caryl Emerson, 355–77. Boston: G. K. Hall, 1999.

————. "Intercultural, Intercreatural: Bakhtin and the Uniqueness of 'Literary Seeing.'" In *Bakhtin and His Intellectual Ambience*, edited by Boguslaw Zylko, 276–91. Gdansk: Wydawnictwo Uniwersytetu Gdanskiego, 2002.

——. *Mikhail Bakhtin: The Word in the World*. London: Routledge, 2007.

Pelikan, Jaroslav. "Introduction." In *Maximus the Confessor: Selected Writings*, translated by George C. Berthold, 1–13. Mahwah, NJ: Paulist, 1985.

——. *Jesus through the Centuries: His Place in the History of Culture*. New Haven, CT: Yale University Press, 1985.

Peace, Richard. "One Little Onion and a Pound of Nuts: The Theme of Giving and Accepting in *The Brothers Karamazov*." In *Aspects of Dostoevskii: Art, Ethics and Faith*, edited by Robert Reid and Joe Andrew, 283–92. Amsterdam: Rodopi, 2012.

Perlina, Nina. "Bakhtin and Buber: Problems of Dialogic Imagination." *Studies in Twentieth Century Literature* (Fall 1984) 13–28.

——. *Varieties of Poetic Utterance: Quotation in "The Brothers Karamazov."* Lanham, MD: University Press of America, 1985.

Pfau, Thomas. *Minding the Modern*. South Bend, IN: University of Notre Dame Press, 2015.

Pieper, Josef. *The Four Cardinal Virtues*. South Bend, IN: University of Notre Dame Press, 1966.

——. *Living the Truth*. "The Truth of All Things." Translated by Lothar Krauth. "Reality and the Good." Translated by Stella Lange. San Francisco: Ignatius, 1989

Pinckaers, Servais, OP. *The Pinckaers Reader: Renewing Thomistic Moral Theology*. Edited by John Berkman and Craig Steven Titus. Washington, DC: Catholic University Press, 2005.

Plato. *Symposium*. Translated by Walter Hamilton. New York: Penguin, 1952.

Poole, Randall A. "The Apophatic Bakhtin." In *Bakhtin and Religion: A Feeling for Faith*, edited by Susan M. Felch and Paul J. Contino, 151–76. Evanston, IL: Northwestern University Press, 2001.

Przywara, Erich. *Analogia Entis: Metaphysics: Original Structure and Universal Rhythm*. Translated by John R. Betz and David Bentley Hart. Grand Rapids: Eerdmans, 2016.

Pyman, Avril. "Dostoevsky and the Prism of the Orthodox Semiosphere." In *Dostoevsky and the Christian Tradition*, edited by George Pattison and Diane Oenning Thompson, 103–15. Cambridge: Cambridge University Press, 2001.

Quenot, Michael. *The Icon: Window on the Kingdom*. Crestwood, NY: St. Vladimir Seminary Press, 1992.

Rausch, Thomas, S.J. "Catholic Anthropology." In *Teaching the Tradition: Catholic Themes in Academic Disciplines*, edited by John J. Piderit, S.J. and Melanie M. Morey, 31–46. Oxford: Oxford University Press, 2012.

Reed. Walter L. *Dialogues of the Word: The Bible as Literature according to Bakhtin*. Oxford: Oxford University Press, 1993.

——. *Romantic Literature in the Light of Bakhtin*. New York: Bloomsbury, 2014.

Reid, Robert, and Joe Andrew. *Aspects of Dostoevskii: Art, Ethics and Faith*. Amsterdam: Rodopi, 2012.

Rice, James L. *Dostoevsky and the Healing Art: An Essay in Literary and Medical History*. Ann Arbor, MI: Ardis, 1985.

Robinson, Marilynne. *Absence of Mind: The Dispelling of Inwardness from the Modern Myth of the Self*. New Haven, CT: Yale University Press, 2010.

Rolnick, Philip A. *Person, Grace, and God*. Grand Rapids: Eerdmans, 2007.

Ronner, Amy D. *Dostoevsky and the Law*. Durham, NC: Carolina Academic Press, 2015.

Rose, Fr. Seraphim. *The Place of Blessed Augustine in the Orthodox Church.* 1983. Reprint, Platina, CA: St Herman of Alaska Brotherhood, 2007.

Rosen, Nathan. "Style and Structure in *The Brothers Karamazov.*" In *The Brothers Karamazov,* Norton Critical Second Edition, edited by Susan McReynolds Oddo, 724–32. New York: Norton, 2011.

Rosenshield, Gary. "Mystery and Commandment in *The Brothers Karamazov: Leo Baeck and Fedor Dostoevsky.*" *Journal of the American Academy of Religion* 62.2 (1994) 483–508.

———. *Western Law, Russian Justice: Dostoevsky, The Jury Trial, and the Law.* Madison, WI: University of Wisconsin Press, 2005.

———. "The Realization of the Collective Self: The Rebirth of Religious Autobiography in Dostoevsky's *Notes from the Hours of the Dead.*" *Slavic Review* 50.2 (1991) 317–27.

Rowe, William W. "*Crime and Punishment* and *The Brothers Karamazov,* Some Comparative Observations." *Russian Literature Triquarterly* 10 (1975) 331–42.

Scanlan, James P. "Dostoevsky's Arguments for Immortality." *Russian Review* 59 (2000) 1–20.

———. *Dostoevsky the Thinker.* Ithaca, NY: Cornell University Press, 2002.

Schiller, Friedrich. *On the Aesthetic Education of Man.* Translation by Keith Tribe. New York: Penguin, 2016.

Schmemann, Alexander. *For the Life of the World.* Crestwood, NY: St. Vladimir's Press, 1997.

Schmid, Ulrich. "Heidegger and Dostoevsky: Philosophy and Politics." *Dostoevsky Studies* 15 (2011) 37–45.

Schur, Anna. *Wages of Evil: Dostoevsky and Punishment.* Evanston, IL: Northwestern University Press, 2012.

Schuman, Sharon. *Freedom and Dialogue in a Polarized World.* Newark, DE: University of Delaware Press, 2014.

Shankman, Steven. *Turned Inside Out: Reading the Russian Novel in Prison.* Evanston, IL: Northwestern University Press, 2017.

Sheehan, Donald. *The Grace of Incorruption.* Edited by By Xenia Sheehan. Brewster, MA: Paraclete, 2015.

Shrayer, Maxim D. "Dostoevskii, the Jewish Question, and *The Brothers Karamazov.*" *Slavic Review* 61.2 (2002) 272–91

Shukman, Anne. "Bakhtin's Tolstoy Prefaces." In *Rethinking Bakhtin: Extensions and Challenges,* edited by Gary Saul Morson and Caryl Emerson, 137–48. Evanston, IL: Northwestern University Press, 1989.

Smith, Christian. *What Is a Person?* Chicago: University of Chicago Press, 2011.

Smith, Leslie Wright. "The Elusive Confessant: A Study of Author and Character in Dostoevsky, Mauriac, and O'Connor." PhD diss., University of Texas, Austin, 1986.

Snyder, Timothy. *Bloodlands: Europe between Hitler and Stalin.* New York: Basic, 2010.

Soloviev, Vladimir S. *The Karamazov Correspondence: Letters of Vladimir S. Soloviev.* Edited and Translated by Vladimir Wozniuk. Boston: Academic Studies Press, 2019.

———. *Lectures on Divine Humanity.* Translated by Peter Zouboff. Revised and edited by Boris Jakim. Hudson, NY: Lindisfarne, 1995.

———. "Seven Paschal Letters: XI. Christ is Risen!" In *Politics, Law, and Morality: Essays by V. S. Soloviev*, edited by and translated by Vladimir Wozniuk, 91–110. New Haven, CT: Yale University Press, 2000.

Sonnenfeld, Albert. *Crossroads: Essays on the Catholic Novelists.* York, SC: French Language, 1982

Spaemann, Robert. *Persons: The Difference between "Someone" and "Something."* Translated by Oliver O' Donovan. 1996. Reprint, Oxford: Oxford University Press, 2017.

Spohn, Wiliam C. *Go and Do Likewise: Jesus and Ethics.* New York: Continuum, 1983.

Stanton, Leonard J. "*Zeder gol'm's Life of Elder Leonid of Opitina* as a Source of Dostoevsky's *The Brothers Karamazov.*" *The Russian Review* 49.4 (1990) 443–55.

Steiner, George. "To Civilize Our Gentlemen." *Language and Silence: Essays on Language, Literature and the Inhuman*, 55–67. 1967. Reprint, New York: Atheneum, 1986.

———. *Real Presences.* Chicago: University of Chicago Press, 1989.

———. *Tolstoy of Dostoevsky: An Essay in the Old Criticism.* 1959. Reprint, Chicago: University of Chicago Press, 1985.

Stepenberg, Maia. *Against Nihilism: Nietzsche Meets Dostoevsky.* Montreal: Black Rose, 2019.

Stevenson, Bryan. *Just Mercy: A Story of Justice and Redemption.* New York: Spiegel and Grau, 2015.

Stowe, David W. *Song of Exile: The Enduring Mystery of Psalm 137.* Oxford: Oxford University Press, 2016.

Stump, Eleonore. "Augustine on Free Will." In *The Cambridge Companion to Augustine*, edited by Eleonore Stump and Norman Kretzmann, 124–47. Cambridge: Cambridge University Press, 2001.

———. *Wandering in Darkness: Narrative and the Problem of Suffering.* Oxford: Oxford University Press, 2010.

Supino, Valentina. *I Soggiorni di Dostoevskij in Europa e la Loro Influenza Sulla sua Opera.* Firenze: LoGisma editore, 2017.

Sutherland, Stewart D. *Atheism and the Rejection of God.* Oxford: Blackwell, 1977.

Sykes, John D. *God and Self in the Confessional Novel.* London: Palgrave Macmillan 2018.

Tambling, Jeremy. *Confession: Sexuality, Sin, the Subject.* Manchester: Manchester University Press, 1990.

Taylor, Charles. "The Concept of a Person." In *Human Agency and Language: Philosophical Papers*, 97–114. Cambridge: Cambridge University Press, 1985.

———. *A Secular Age.* Cambridge: Harvard University Press, 2007.

———. *Sources of the Self: The Making of Modern Identity.* Cambridge: Harvard University Press, 1989.

Taylor, Mark. *Last Works: Lessons in Leaving.* New Haven, CT: Yale University Press, 2018.

Terras, Victor. *A Karamazov Companion.* Madison, WI: University of Wisconsin Press, 2002.

———. *Reading Dostoevsky.* Madison, WI: University of Wisconsin Press, 1998.

Thiselton, Anthony C. *The Hermeneutics of Doctrine.* Grand Rapids: Eerdmans, 2007.

Thompson, Diane Oenning. *The Brothers Karamazov and the Poetics of Memory.* Cambridge: Cambridge University Press, 1991.

———. "Problems of the Biblical Word in Dostoevsky's Poetics." In *Dostoevsky and the Christian Tradition*, edited by George Pattison and Diane Oenning Thompson, 69–99. Cambridge: Cambridge University Press, 2001.

Tilley, Terrence W. *Evils of Theodicy*. Eugene: OR: Wipf and Stock, 2000.

———. *Inventing Catholic Tradition*. Maryknoll, NY: Orbis, 2000.

Todd III, William Mills. "*The Brothers Karamazov* and the Poetics of Serial Publication." In *The Brothers Karamazov*, edited by Susan McReynolds Oddo, 689–96. New York: Norton, 2011.

Trace, Arthur. *Furnace of Doubt: Dostoevsky and "The Brothers Karamazov*. Peru, IL: Sherwood Sugden, 1988.

Tracy, David. *The Analogical Imagination: Christian Theology and the Culture of Pluralism*. New York: Crossroad, 1991.

———. *Filaments, Theological Profiles: Selected Essays, Volume 2*. University of Chicago Press, 2020.

———. *Fragments, The Existential Situation of our Time: Selected Essays: Volume 1*. University of Chicago Press, 2020.

Trepanier, Lee. "The Politics and Experience of Active Love in *The Brothers Karamazov*." In *Dostoevsky's Political Thought*, edited by Richard Avramenko and Lee Trepanier, 31–50. Lanham, MD: Lexington, 2013.

Turner, Denys. *Thomas Aquinas: A Portrait*. New Haven, CT: Yale University Press, 2013.

Twombly, Charles C. *Perichoresis and Personhood: God, Christ, and Salvation in John of Damascus*. Eugene, OR: Pickwick, 2015.

Ugolnik, Anthony. *The Illuminating Icon*. Grand Rapids: Eerdmans, 1989.

Van Den Bercken, Wil. *Christian Fiction and Religious Realism in the Novels of Dostoevsky*. London: Anthem, 2011.

Van Der Eng, Jan. "A Note on Comic Relief in *The Brothers Karamazov*." 1958. In *The Brothers Karamazov by FM Dostoevskij*, edited by Jan Van Der Eng and Jan M. Meijer, 149–63. The Hague: Mouton, 1971.

Verdon, Timothy. *Art and Prayer: The Beauty of Turning to God*. Brewster, MA: Paraclete, 2014.

Vetlovskaya, Svetlana. "Alyosha Karamazov and the Hagiographic Hero." In *Modern Critical Interpretations: The Brothers Karamazov*, edited by Harold Bloom, 151–68. New York: Chelsea House, 1988.

Walsh, David. "Dostoevsky's Discovery of the Christian Foundation of Politics." In *Dostoevsky's Political Thought*, edited by Richard Avramenko and Lee Trepanier, 9–30. Lanham, MD: Lexington. 2013.

Ward, Bruce K. *Redeeming the Enlightenment: Christianity and the Liberal Virtues*. Grand Rapids: Eerdmans, 2010.

———. "Transcendence and Immanence in a Subtler Language: The Presence of Dostoevsky in Charles Taylor's Account of Secularity." In *Aspiring to Fullness in a Secular Age: Essays on Religion and Theology in the Work of Charles Taylor*, edited by Carlos D. Colorado and Justin D. Klassen, 262–90. South Bend, IN: University of Notre Dame Press, 2014.

Ware, Timothy. *The Orthodox Church. An Introduction to Eastern Christianity*. London: Penguin, 2015.

Wasiolek, Edward. *Dostoevsky: The Major Fiction*. Cambridge: MIT Press, 1964.

Weil, Simone. *Waiting for God*. Translated by Emma Crawford. New York: Harper, 1973.

Weisband, Edward. *The Macabresque: Human Violation and Hate in Genocide, Mass Atrocity, and Enemy-Making*. New York: Oxford University Press, 2018.

Werge, Thomas. "The Word as Deed in *Crime and Punishment*." *Renascence* 27 (1975) 207–19.

Williams, Rowan. "Balthasar and Difference." In *Wrestling with Angels: Conversations in Modern Theology*, edited by Mike Higton, 77–85. Grand Rapids: Eerdmans, 2007.

———. *Being Human: Bodies, Minds, Persons*. Grand Rapids: Eerdmans, 2018.

———. *Christ the Heart of Creation*. London: Bloomsbury, 2018.

———. *Dostoevsky: Language, Faith and Fiction*. Waco, TX: Baylor University Press, 2008.

———. "'Religious Realism': On Not Quite Agreeing with Don Cupitt." In *Wrestling with Angels: Conversations in Modern Theology*, edited by Mike Higton, 228–54. Grand Rapids: Eerdmans, 2007.

Wilson, Jessica Hooten. *Giving the Devil His Due: Demonic Authority in the Fiction of Flannery O'Connor and Fyodor Dostoevsky*. Eugene, OR: Cascade, 2017.

———. *Walker Percy, Fyodor Dostoevsky, and the Search for Influence*. Columbus, OH: Ohio State University Press, 2017.

Wilson, James Matthew. "Confessional Reading." In *Cambridge Companion to Literature and Religion*, edited by Susan M. Felch, 35–50. Cambridge: Cambridge University Press, 2016.

Wood, Ralph C. "Dostoevsky on Evil as a Perversion of Personhood: A Reading of Ivan Karamazov and the Grand Inquisitor." *Perspectives in Religious Studies* 26.3 (1999) 331–48.

Wood, James. *The Broken Estate: Essays on Literature and Belief*. New York: Random House, 1999.

Wright, N. T. *The New Testament and the People of God*. Minneapolis, MN: Fortress, 1992.

Wyman, Alina. *The Gift of Active Empathy: Scheler, Bakhtin, and Dostoevsky*. Evanston, IL: Northwestern University Press, 2016.

Yannaras, Christos. *The Freedom of Christian Morality*. Crestwood: NY: St. Vladimir's Press. 1984.

Young, Sarah. "Introduction: Dostoevsky Today." In *Dostoevsky on the Threshold of Other Worlds: Essays in Honour of Malcolm Jones*, edited by Sarah Young and Lesley Milne, xiii–xx. Ilkeston, UK: Bramcote, 2006.

Zakharov, Vladimir. "The Dostoevsky Syndrome." In *The New Russian Dostoevsky*, edited by Carol Apollonio. Bloomington, IN: Slavica, 2010.

Zhernokleyev, Denis. "The Empty Tomb: Apophasis in *Crime and Punishment* and *The Brothers Karamazov*." In *Dostoevsky's Apophatic Novel* (in manuscript, used by permission).

———. "Mimetic Desire in Dostoevsky's *The Idiot* with Continual Reference to René Girard." *The Dostoevsky Journal* 20 (2019) 77–95.

Ziolkowski, Margaret. "Dostoevsky and the Kenotic Tradition." In *Dostoevsky and the Christian Tradition*, edited by George Pattison and Diane Oenning Thompson, 31–40. Cambridge: Cambridge University Press, 2001.

Zizioulas, John D. *Being as Communion: Studies in Personhood and the Church*. 1985. Reprint, Crestwood, NY: St. Vladimir's Seminary Press, 1993.

Zwick, Mark, and Louise Zwick. *The Catholic Worker Movement: Intellectual and Spiritual Origins.* Mahwah, NJ: Paulist, 2005.

Index of Subjects

Index of Names

Index of Scripture References